AUSTRI...
RUSSIANS
POLES
COSSACKS
KURDS
SIBERIANS
KALMUKS
JAPANESE
ANNAMITES
TONKINESE
AUSTRALIANS
RUMANIANS
MAORIS
MADAGASCANS
SEPOYS
BULGARS
TURKS
GHURKAS
PATHANS
ARABS
SIKHS

...T INTO CONFLICT. THIS CHART HAS BEEN PREPARED TO SHOW THE MANY VARIED TYPES IN THE ARMIES ENGAGED
...E IN WHICH THEY LIVE.

THE
WORLD'S
WAR

'This is a ground-breaking and important book that will surely reframe our understanding of the Great War. In graphic and meticulous detail Olusoga brings to life the untold story of how black and brown men perished on the Western Front and in the multiple theatres of war across the globe. He charts a First World War that was global not just because it dominated the lives of the sons and daughters of Europe, but because it engulfed the sons and daughters of empire as well, and for that reason it can be described as the world's first global war.'

The Rt Hon. David Lammy MP

'In a great rarity for this centenary year, David Olusoga has written an unusual and original book – and written it beautifully, too. His vivid, readable and carefully researched account is a reminder that the war of 1914–1918 was not just one of French *poilus* and British soldier-poets, but truly a world war, involving millions of men from Africa, Asia, the Caribbean, and leaving behind a seldom-explored legacy of death and memory that stretched around the globe.'

Adam Hochschild, author of *King Leopold's Ghost* and
To End All Wars: How the First World War Divided Britain

DAVID OLUSOGA presented the BBC's two-part series *The World's War*, screened in August 2014. A historian and BBC producer, he is a specialist on the themes of colonialism, slavery and racism. David is the co-author of the much-praised *The Kaiser's Holocaust* (2010).

THE WORLD'S WAR

DAVID OLUSOGA

HEAD
of ZEUS

For Mrs Marion Olusoga, to whom I owe everything

CONTENTS

LIST OF ILLUSTRATIONS

Plate Section 1

1. 'The Empire Needs Men' poster (1915) by Arthur Wardle / Library of Congress
2. The *First World War Deeds of Corporal Mike Mountain Horse* / Collection of the Esplanade Museum, Medicine Hat, Alberta, Canada
3. Encampment of the 3rd (Lahore) Division on Marseilles race-course (1914), photographed by Horace Grant / Mirrorpix
4. Indian soldier cooking / Bain Collection (Library of Congress)
5. Lieutenant General Sir James Willcocks / Bain Collection (Library of Congress)
6. Mir Dast on the terrace of Brighton's Royal Pavilion Hospital (1915) / Royal Pavilion & Museums, Brighton and Hove
7. Patients and staff beneath the dome of the Royal Pavilion Hospital, Brighton / Royal Pavilion & Museums, Brighton and Hove
8. Gurkhas and Jats, all ranks, of the Indian Corps (23 July 1915) / Wikimedia (Government of India, 1915)
9. Indian Corps troops in late 1915 / By kind permission of Dominique Faivre
10. Alhaji Grunshi (1918) / Wikimedia Commons
11. Colonial troops in Ebolowa, German Cameroon / Bain Collection (Library of Congress)
12. Indian dead after the Battle of Tanga (1914) / Deutsches Bundesarchiv
13. General J.C. Smuts / Bain Collection (Library of Congress)
14. Carriers serving the *Schutztruppe* of German East Africa / Deutsches Bundesarchiv
15. German colonial war funds poster depicting von Lettow-Vorbeck (1918) / Library of Congress

Plate Section 3

Plate Section 4

PREFACE

IN THE MIDDLE of the 1960s my parents, only recently married, journeyed to my father's homeland of Nigeria on a ship called the MS *General Mangin*. Built at St Nazaire in 1953, the liner ran a service from Marseilles's ancient harbour to Point-Noire on the coast of the former French Congo (now the Republic of Congo, or Congo-Brazzaville). By the 1960s, the passengers who filled her cabins were French, British and African, many of them the citizens of now-independent African nations. They were officials, expats, businessmen, students and entrepreneurs. To my mother, and indeed to most of the non-French passengers on board, the ship's name meant nothing; but to the French passengers, veterans of the baccalaureate, the name of Charles Mangin was a familiar one. It was Mangin, the firebrand general, who had earned himself the nickname 'the Butcher' for his actions on the Western Front during the First World War; and it was Mangin who had, in the years leading up to 1914, convinced himself – and soon millions of his countrymen – that Africa was a vast reservoir of men, the human raw material from which France might forge new legions to help overcome the military might of Germany.

When the *General Mangin* landed in Lagos in 1966 to deposit my parents, there were still millions of men and women on the African continent who remembered the First World War, people who had seen the French recruiting parties scour the villages of West Africa for men to serve, turning Mangin's theories into reality. In the port town of Dakar, in Senegal, where the *General Mangin* had earlier called, lived the last of the *Tirailleurs Sénégalais*, Mangin's army of West African soldiers, who could count among their honours the titanic battles at Verdun, Ypres and the Chemin des Dames. Other Africans, in East and Central Africa, could recall the suffering and hunger that befell their communities when the war against the German colonial forces swept through their fields, towns and villages. In Nigeria there were still veterans of the West African Frontier Force, men who had fought against other Africans recruited by the Germans to defend the Second Reich's colonies of Cameroon and German East Africa.

In the same years that my parents set up their home in Africa, historians in Europe – pioneers in the burgeoning field of oral history – were embarking on the great task of recording the voices and experiences of veterans of the First World War. Yet, in this great trawl of the collective memory of the war generation, the veterans of Africa were largely ignored. Just half a century after the conflict had come to an end, their service and the suffering wrought by the war upon the continent of my birth had already been marginalized and forgotten.

As a resident of Lagos in the late 1960s, my mother, by then the parent of mixed-race children, was astonished one day to come across a war memorial which at that time stood on Lagos Island, in the heart of what was still the capital of recently independent Nigeria. It had been erected between the wars and was dedicated to the thousands of Nigerians who had fought and laboured in the First World War. My mother was well read, multilingual and a product of a fine British grammar school; but her education had taught her nothing of the participation of non-white, non-European peoples in that war.

Twenty years later, and living in the North-East of England, I learnt of the 'Great War', in part through the story of my local regiment – back when young boys in England had 'local' regiments with which to associate. Visits to the little museum of the Durham Light Infantry inspired a fascination with the First World War that has endured for a third of a century. The most powerful moment for me, in a lifetime of reading about the 1914–18 conflict, was when I came across a trench map of a section of the Western Front that had been manned by 'my' regiment. Men who, seventy years earlier, had sat in the same classrooms of the same Victorian red-brick schools that I was attending had, during the war, named their stretches of the line after the streets of our shared home-town of Gateshead – 'Bensham Bank' and 'Coatsworth Road', streets that I, an immigrant child from Africa, now played in. For many of the soldiers of the Durham Light Infantry, their first encounter with people like me, people from Africa, would have been in the zones behind the Western Front into which were drawn millions of men – the soldiers and labourers from the colonial worlds of the early twentieth century.

This book is an attempt, although an inevitably incomplete one, to explore that moment of encounter and to describe the experiences of the often forgotten armies who came from beyond the borders of Europe to fight and labour in the First World War. It aims also to examine some of the forces – political, ideological, religious, economic and demographic – that drew these disparate multiracial cohorts into the world's first truly global conflict. Limits of time and space have resulted in painful omissions. There was no space for an exploration of the multi-ethnic struggle fought on the Gallipoli peninsula, nor the far greater conflagration that swept across the deserts of Mesopotamia, a 'side show' of the First World War that now seems more important than ever, as the lines drawn in the sands of Arabia in 1919 begin to disintegrate. Likewise, the contributions of the Maoris of New Zealand, the Aboriginal peoples of Australia, and the soldiers and labourers who came from North Africa and French Indochina are mentioned only in passing.

No book can ever hope to cover everything, but I hope that this book will, like the television series that it accompanies, play a small part in the slow process of historical rediscovery, the engine of which has been the pioneering efforts of the many scholars whose work I refer to and cite throughout.

David Olusoga

CHAPTER 1

'WELTKRIEG'

A new concept – the world's war

———— • ————

THE ENVIRONS OF YPRES, FLANDERS, 22 APRIL 1915. It is, in the words of the British Official History of the First World War, 'a glorious spring day' on the West Flanders Plain. Reports coming in from reconnaissance planes flying missions over the great arc of trenches to the east of Ypres describe considerable 'liveliness behind the German lines' but nothing that is particularly out of the ordinary.[1]

At about 4pm, German artillery begins shelling British and French lines, but then at 5pm exactly, a sudden and ferocious bombardment opens up against the small villages in front of Ypres, which up until now have largely escaped the attentions of the enemy guns. At that same moment, all along a four-mile stretch of the German front line, thousands of hands scrabble to open thousands of taps that are attached to rows of metal canisters. Each canister weighs 90 pounds, and 6,000 of them have recently been hauled into place behind the German parapets. Their collective contents weigh 160 tons. The artillery bombardment stops abruptly at 5.10pm, and it is around now that troops from the French 45th and 78th divisions – Algerians and Moroccans, including both white colonialists and North Africans – notice two strange clouds moving inexorably towards their trenches. Some men also report hearing a 'hissing' noise coming from the German lines. The clouds will later be described as being 'green', 'yellowish-green' or 'grey green'. British observers, who are watching from their own lines to the south, report that from a distance they resemble a 'bluish white mist, such as is seen over water meadows on a frosty night'. The *Daily Mail*, in a dispatch published four days later, will tell its readers that the clouds looked 'like a yellow low wall', which advanced slowly across no man's land, pushed by the prevailing winds.[2]

Even as the clouds approach, the French and African soldiers remain in their positions. Interpreting the clouds as smoke to cover an impending German assault, the troops peer through mist, looking for the silhouettes of attackers. They do not realize that the vapour itself is their most deadly enemy. As the miasma reaches the French lines, being heavier than air it slides down the sides of their trenches and snakes around the boots of the now panicking soldiers. There is an acrid smell in the air. Men notice a metallic taste at the back of their throats. Then the gargled screams and desperate splutters begin.

On this day, many of the 6,000 French casualties of this, the first poison gas attack on the Western Front, simply collapse, slipping beneath the sea of green at the bottom of their trenches. Others cough up a burning yellow fluid – as one Canadian captain observes, they 'literally cough their lungs out'.[3] The membranes of their eyes are similarly damaged, resulting in temporary blindness. The weapon they have been attacked with is chlorine gas. On contact with the moisture of the lungs, it forms hydrochloric acid and hypochlorous acid, which burn the soft membranes and tissue. What is left of the victims' lungs rapidly fills with fluid. Frothing at the mouth, the afflicted men begin to drown, literally, in their own bodily fluids.

The French and North African troops who leave their trenches to escape this new weapon are struck down by old ones – machine guns and rifles. The Germans have carefully halted their own artillery fire to avoid blast waves from the explosions disrupting the westward progress of the gas clouds, and they now pour bullets into the stumbling panicked men, many of them already rendered sightless and choking. There is, by now, a great flight of men rushing backwards through the gas and the hail of bullets. Ian Sinclair, a Canadian lieutenant colonel whose lines are behind those subsumed by the gas clouds, later reports that Algerian troops 'started to pour into our trench coughing and bleeding and dying all over the place, and then we realised what it was'.[4] The British, still watching from their positions to the south of the French lines, suddenly see French North African troops fleeing into the areas behind their lines. Those who have been hit the hardest are in terrible distress. Desperate and insensible, they struggle to communicate in broken French and in their own languages. They are without officers, and many are without weapons. In uncharacteristically vivid terms, the British Official History later describes how:

It was impossible to understand what the Africans said, but from the way they coughed and pointed to their throats, it was evident, if not suffering from the effects of gas, they were thoroughly scared. Teams and wagons of the French field artillery next appeared retiring, and the throng of fugitives soon became thicker and more disordered, some individuals running.[5]

An anonymous eyewitness account from the British lines leaves little to the imagination:

Utterly unprepared for what was to come, the [French] divisions gazed for a short while spellbound at the strange phenomenon they saw coming slowly toward them. Like some liquid the heavy-coloured vapour poured relentlessly into the trenches, filled them, and passed on. For a few seconds nothing happened; the sweet-smelling stuff merely tickled their nostrils; they failed to realize the danger. Then, with inconceivable rapidity, the gas worked, and blind panic spread. Hundreds, after a dreadful fight for air, became unconscious and died where they lay – a death of hideous torture, with the frothing bubbles gurgling in their throats and the foul liquid welling up in their lungs. With blackened faces and twisted limbs one by one they drowned – only that which drowned them came from inside and not from out. Others, staggering, falling, lurching on, and of their ignorance keeping pace with the gas, went back. A hail of rifle

fire and shrapnel mowed them down, and the line was broken.
There was nothing on the British left – their flank was up in the air.
The northeast corner of the salient around Ypres had been pierced.
From in front of St. Julien away up north toward Boesinghe there
was no one in front of the Germans.[6]

As the effects of the gas spread, birds literally fall from the skies.
The fresh green shoots of early spring that have erupted on the
still-standing trees of the Ypres Salient turn brown and wither.
Even the rats that swarm and multiply in the fetid trenches
succumb to the poison, dying in their thousands.

——— · ———

In the trenches next to the French, on 22 April 1915, was the 3rd
Canadian Brigade, which now rushed men into position to cover
the gap in the front lines caused by the shock of this new German
offensive – the Second Battle of Ypres. To their right were units
of *Tirailleurs* (Riflemen) from French Algeria, who had so far
escaped the gas and held their positions. Together, they faced
the inevitable German attack through the breach in the lines. On
this day, in this war that many were still calling the 'Great
European War', few among the desperate defenders on the
Allied side were men whose homes were now in Europe.
    Canada was, in 1914, a nation of both immigrants and indig-
enous peoples. Two-thirds of the Canadian Expeditionary Force
may have been born in Britain, but there were also Japanese
Canadians, French-speakers from Quebec, and Canadian
Flemings whose forebears were from Belgium and who, in effect,
were fighting for their ancestral homeland in the trenches of
Flanders; some were now within miles of their parental homes.
Among the Canadian ranks were also Native Canadians. It is
likely that the first man from the indigenous peoples of the
American continent to die in the First World War was killed on
22 April 1915. Angus Laforce had come from his home in
Kahnawake, Quebec, to fight on the Western Front. A man from

the Mowhawk people, he was reported missing on the night of 22 April. His remains were never found. Another Native Canadian, Lieutenant Cameron D. Brant of the Six Nations people from the Grand River, died in one of the counter-attacks at Ypres.[7] For him, fighting for Britain was in effect a family tradition. Lieutenant Brant's great-grandfather had fought against the French in the Seven Years War and taken up arms for the British during the American Revolution one-and-a-half centuries earlier, and now the same warrior tradition had led Brant to the trenches of Ypres. Among those who survived the attacks of 22 April was Albert Mountain Horse, from the Blood Indian reserve in Alberta. One of three brothers, Albert wrote to his brother Mike just after these events:

> As I am writing this letter the shrapnel is bursting over our heads. I was in the thick of the fighting at Ypres and we had to get out of it. The Germans were using the poisonous gas on our men – oh it was awful – it is worse than anything I know of. I don't mind rifle fire and the shells bursting around us, but this gas is the limit.[8]

Despite the prompt actions of the Algerians and Canadians, the Germans forced their way through the four-mile-wide gap opened up by the gas attack. They overran the abandoned French trenches and advanced two miles, capturing a considerable portion of the Ypres Salient, including the shattered village of Langemarck and territory near the village of St Julien. French artillery had been seized and for the first time since November 1914, before the Western Front had solidified, the Allied forces faced the prospect of Ypres itself being overrun and the British driven back towards the coast. Yet the Germans, having severely underestimated the power of their new terror weapon, failed to amass enough troops to fully take advantage of the situation, and their first attacks were halted by nightfall and by the effects of British artillery. Allied counter-attacks were launched on 23 April, in which the Canadians were again heavily involved, and there was a second gas attack by the Germans on 24 April.

Among the divisions now rushed to the Ypres sector was the
Lahore Division of the Indian Corps. Between 24 and 25 April,
the Indians endured a gruelling march north from their recently
won positions around the French village of Neuve Chapelle.
They marched with heavy loads, sometimes over a hundred
pounds in weight, over muddy, shattered roads; some suffered
from the effects of 'trench foot' after so long in the front lines;
others had been hobbled by frostbite. They had little food and
almost no rest *en route*. On the next day, 26 April 1915, at 2.05pm
a combined Allied force was assembled to attack. It included
Englishmen from the hills of Northumbria and the ancient cities
of Durham and York; Irishmen of the Connaught Rangers;
Indian sepoys from the Punjab, Afghanistan and Nepal; men
from across France; and 'Turcos' of the French Colonial Army
– Algerians and Moroccans. Together, this unlikely multiracial
force, still without gas masks, attacked a dug-in enemy of whose
exact positions they were unsure and whom they knew to be
equipped with chemical weapons. After enduring heavy losses
from well-targeted artillery, which was directed from above by
German spotter planes, and facing concentrated rifle and
machine-gun fire, their attack was halted. No units of this highly
variegated Allied army reached the German front lines; they
became mixed up in the chaos – men from four continents
trapped a maelstrom of incoming fire. The 47th Sikhs, who were
in the first wave, lost 348 men out of an attacking strength of 444.
In all, there were 2,000 men killed, wounded or listed as missing
from the Indian regiments alone.

Twenty minutes into the attack, at around 2.30pm, with the
assault having effectively stalled and the troops struggling to
secure any viable defensive positions, a series of nozzles was
raised above the parapets of the German trenches, and again the
green clouds of chlorine gas poured forth. Carried by the wind,
the mist moved silently towards the attackers. They had been
instructed to tie to their faces handkerchiefs or the ends of their
turbans, dipped in chloride of lime or, more distastefully, urine:
the ammonia in urine went some way to neutralizing the effects

of the gas, which had now been identified by a Canadian chemist as a form of chlorine. This improvised measure offered some protection; but it was no guarantee:

> *The most they [Indian troops] could do was to cover their noses and mouths with wet handkerchiefs or pagris [turbans], and, in default of such a poor resource, to keep their faces pressed against their scanty parapet. It was of little avail, for in a few minutes the ground was strewn with the bodies of men writhing in unspeakable torture, while the enemy seized the opportunity to pour in a redoubled fire.*[9]

The casualty rate – those killed, wounded or 'missing' – among the Indian regiments at the Second Battle of Ypres reached over 30 per cent, slightly higher than the rate for the British soldiers fighting with them.[10]

Among the Indians struggling for breath within the clouds of gas was Mir Dast, then a *jemadar* (officer) assigned to the 57th Rifles of the Ferozepore Brigade. An Afridi Pathan, from the Maidan Valley in Tirah, on the North-West Frontier of the British Raj, he was a decorated career soldier of long experience. After all other officers in his vicinity had been killed, Mir Dast attempted to hold his position against German counter-attacks. Gathered around him were the survivors of the gas attack, many of whom were severely weakened by the effects of the chlorine. They managed to hold their trenches until nightfall, when they were able to retreat under the cover of darkness. Withdrawing across the body-strewn battlefield, Mir Dast encountered small groups of survivors who, sick and terrified, were huddled in abandoned sections of trench or cowering in shell holes. He and his unit gathered up these unfortunates and led them to safety. Although himself wounded and weakened by gas inhalation, Mir Dast then repeatedly left the British lines and ventured back out into no man's land to bring back a further eight injured officers, both British and Indian. For this act of extraordinary bravery, Mir Dast received yet another wound from German gun fire – and a recommendation for the Victoria Cross.

★

It was on the afternoon of 22 April 1915 that Europe – so it is said
– entered a new age of barbarism. Gas was the weapon that more
starkly than any other stripped solders of their ancient position of
warrior and reduced them to mere victims. It was not a weapon
that was wielded in any finely targeted way but merely 'released'
or 'deployed'. Death was carried by the wind, and although there
was skill in its use, it was the skill of the chemist and the meteo-
rologist rather than the craft of the soldier. No weapon made men
feel more vulnerable, and no weapon was more of an equalizer.
Debilitated, blinded and haggard, its victims were literally forced
to hold onto one another, irrespective and unaware of rank, race
or nationality. That moment of history is one that we think we
know well, yet our image of it – and so many others – has been
shaped and influenced by historiographical traditions that have
tended to marginalize the role of, and even overlook the presence of, colonial and non-European soldiers. Although most of
the men who fought and died in defence of the Ypres Salient in
April and May 1915 were white Europeans, many thousands were
drawn from distant lands, the colonial subjects of two empires.

Speaking to the House of Lords five days after 22 April, Lord
Kitchener, Britain's Secretary of State for War, reported that:

> *The Germans have, in the last week, introduced a method of plac-*
> *ing their opponents hors de combat by the use of asphyxiating and*
> *deleterious gases, and they employ these poisonous methods to pre-*
> *vail when their attack, according to the rules of war, might have*
> *otherwise failed. On this subject I would remind your Lordships*
> *that Germany was a signatory to the following Article in The Hague*
> *Convention – 'The Contracting Powers agree to abstain from the*
> *use of projectiles the object of which is the diffusion of asphyxiating*
> *or deleterious gases.'*[11]

The Dutch city of The Hague, where the Convention of 1907 had
been held, is only about 100 miles to the north of Ypres. Both

The Hague and Ypres are ancient cities steeped in the highest traditions of European culture. The chlorine gas used in the attack had been produced in the factories of the great German chemical firms of the IG cartel, clustered around the Ruhr, less than 200 miles away from Ypres. The development of chlorine as a weapon had been masterminded by a German Nobel Prize-winning chemist, Fritz Haber, who worked in the Kaiser Wilhelm Institute set in Dahlem, a leafy suburb of Berlin. Haber was one of the academic stars of one of the most cultured nations in Europe. In the weeks that followed the attack, the French would turn to their own Nobel Prize-winner, Victor Grignard, to help them develop their own terror weapons. Everything about the gas attack on 22 April 1915, other than the range of races and ethnicities among the victims, was firmly European.[12] Yet when searching for a precedent, or an act of comparable 'frightfulness' against which Germany's newest crimes could be compared, Kitchener felt compelled to look beyond Europe to Africa, where he had spent much of his military career. In the same speech, the old colonial soldier suggested that in using chemical weapons Germany 'has stooped to acts which will surely stain indelibly her military history, and which would vie with the barbarous savagery of the dervishes of Sudan.'[13]

It was, in truth, artillery that most profoundly de-skilled the profession of soldiering in the First World War. It was the guns, not gas nor even the machine gun, that killed the most men. But while the calibre of the guns that appeared on the Western Front was new and the explosive yield of their shells vastly increased, the weapon itself was seemingly familiar. Poison gas was suitably novel to be shocking in a way that artillery was not. And despite Kitchener's condemnations, gas would not stay an exclusively German affair for long. The British, within months, had synthesized their own gas weapons and used them against the Germans at the Battle of Loos in September 1915 – another attack in which thousands of men from India were to fight and die.

At Loos, those Indian troops at least had primitive gas masks to defend them. This piece of personal protection evolved at an

incredible pace over the course of the conflict, soon taking on its
modern configuration. In doing so, it became the emblem of
total war, other-worldly and hyper-modern, the face of Europe's
home-produced barbarism. The gas mask became, ultimately,
the European equivalent of the ceremonial war masks of tribal
societies, which so fascinated early twentieth-century European
ethnographers, who regarded them as symbols of the supposed
backwardness and savagery of the peoples ruled over by the
imperial powers. The innovation and use of poison gas on the
Western Front made a nonsense of the supposed superiority of
white, European civilization over the subjects of empire.

★

In the storage vaults of the Esplanade Museum in Medicine Hat,
Canada is a century-old, decorated calfskin. It was once the property of Corporal Mike Mountain Horse, younger brother of
Albert who was gassed at Ypres. After being exposed to the effects
of chlorine gas on two further occasions, Albert was invalided
home, but he died one day after reaching Quebec in November
1915, succumbing to tuberculosis. Generations earlier, Albert
Mountain Horse's people, the Bloods, had been encouraged to
denounce their warrior culture by the Canadian authorities.
Albert had been drawn into the army and then into the First
World War through the influence of Samuel Henry Middleton, a
local missionary who had encouraged him to leave his reserve
and go to war. After receiving the news of her son's death, Albert's
mother took a knife and attempted to kill Middleton. She was
dragged away by her remaining sons. At Albert's funeral, the
Blood men followed the procession on horseback, and the older
men voiced the ancient war chants as the coffin approached
them.[14] Mike Mountain Horse, who later wrote an autobiography, described how the effect of his brother's death on him was
to awaken long-suppressed warrior traditions:

> *Reared in the environment of my forefathers, the spirit of revenge for*
> *my brother's death manifested itself strongly in me as I gazed down*

on Albert lying in his coffin that cold wintery day in November 1915. Soon after the funeral I obtained leave from my work as an interpreter and scout for the Royal North-West Police at Macleod, and with my brother Joe Mountain Horse and a number of Indian boys from neighbouring reserves, I enlisted in the 191st Battalion for service overseas.[15]

As he followed in his brother's footsteps and prepared to depart for France, Mike Mountain Horse went through the traditional ceremonies given in honour to a warrior leaving to go to war – as his ancestors had enacted for generations. Arriving in France in 1917, he fought at Vimy Ridge, in a battle that – according to war-time legend – was the event that made Canada into 'a true nation' rather than a mere dominion of the British Empire. His description of the battlefield is as powerful, literary and evocative as any passage in one of the great European war memoirs:

Lying on top of Vimy Ridge one night along with a number of the other Indian boys, the scene before our eyes might best be described as that of a huge stage with lighting effects – Verey lights from the Hun lines, and flames from bursting shells in the city of Lens. The red glare thrown back appeared like a great fire in the sky all the time. The trenches ran through almost to the heart of the French coal mining city. Here a brigade of the Germans had entrenched themselves so well that incessant bombardment by artillery and bombing from the air did not aid the boys from the Dominion to any great extent ... Along the miles of trenches one could see planes dropping bombs on German lines, followed by geysers of smoke and dirt shooting skywards like volcanoes in eruption. One could witness houses bursting suddenly into flame as projectiles from heavy artillery of the enemy struck them. One could walk past Canadian howitzer batteries about a mile from the trenches and hear the 57 inch shells from these guns screaming overhead on their errands of death and destruction.[16]

After surviving the great fiery cauldron of Vimy Ridge, Mike Mountain Horse fought again at the Battle of Cambrai in

November 1917, the first massed tank attack in history, and was buried under the ruins of a shelter for four days after it was covered by rubble thrown up by explosions. Before one offensive, he and his fellow Bloods gathered in a small clearing in the shattered woods behind the front lines to pray together. Under the trees, beyond the easy reach of artillery, they made their offerings. 'Some made supplication for the successes of the allies while others prayed for a happy return to their fathers and mothers or to their families.'[17] One of the Bloods, the unforgettably named George Strangling Wolf, took a knife and cut off a strip of his own flesh from around his knee. Holding up the bloody offering towards the sun, he prayed aloud: 'Help me, Sun, to survive this terrible war, that I may meet my relatives again. With this request, I offer you my body as food.'[18] He then buried his flesh in the mud of northern France. Strangling Wolf, whose official army records list his religion as 'Church of England', survived the war under the gaze of the Sun Spirit of his ancestors.

Mike Mountain Horse also survived, and in 1919 he returned to the Blood Reserve with the Distinguished Conduct Medal on his chest. Years later he dictated his *Great War Deeds* to his friend the artist Ambrose Two Chiefs, which the latter painted onto calfskin in the traditions of the Indians of the Great Plains.* Between them, the two men created an object that seems out of time, not of the early twentieth century or the modern, industrial age. The *War Deeds* is an attempt at a realistic depiction of war, yet it also contains traditional symbols. The black, stick-like figures painted onto the skin fight with rifles; they are shown in what are clearly the trenches and the dugouts of the Western Front. Lines of artillery are shown, high-explosive shells detonating over the heads of the simple figures. The Germans wear their pointed *Pickelhaube* helmets. Each of the twelve panels is a representation of a real event, ordered not chronologically but ranked in order of importance to Mike Mountain Horse. One panel records

* The *Great War Deeds of Mike Mountain Horse* was probably painted sometime in the 1930s.

those four days in 1917 that he spent buried in a collapsed bomb shelter at Cambrai; another depicts an attack on a German position, where the Canadians captured the artillery. The figures fire at one another, the bullets marked as black dots. There are panels that tell of trench raids in 1917 and some that relate to the Battle of Amiens in August 1918. *The Great War Deeds of Mike Mountain Horse* is a work of art in the tradition of those painted by his forefathers, whose war deeds recorded mounted skirmishes between men armed with bows and arrows or the trade muskets of the nineteenth century. They celebrated the taking of horses and the capture of knives and European guns, recording the events through which men could lay claim to status and chieftaincies. But Mike Mountain Horse took that tradition into a kind of war his ancestors could never have imagined.

There are other objects that have a similar capacity to challenge our impressions of the First World War and the men who fought in it. In Belgium and France a handful of specialist collectors and eagle-eyed experts have unearthed brass shell-casings that were engraved with dragons and ancient poetry by the Chinese men who came to Europe to work as labourers on the Western Front. Far removed from these collectors' pieces is a simple concrete dug-out, which is slowly subsiding under its own weight in the corner of a cow-field in Belgian Flanders. Inside is an Arabic arch, on which an inscription from the Koran has been carefully engraved: 'There is no greater God than Allah. If you believe in Allah you will be Victorious like the Victory of Tadmor and Namar.' Behind the walls of the bunker, Muslim soldiers once sheltered from the thunderous guns that were the masters of the Western Front. We know almost nothing about these men – who they were or where they came from. They might have been subjects of the British Raj or just as plausibly North Africans from the French colonies, or even Muslim troops from French Senegal. All we know is that they were here, and that they found a way to leave behind the mark of their faith. On the outskirts of the Côte d'Azur town of Fréjus is a mosque built in the Malian style, from red, ferrous mud. It was constructed for West African soldiers who served in the French Army and were stationed here during the winter months of the war. It now stands closed and padlocked to protect it from vandals, a mute victim of the swirling ethnic tensions of twenty-first-century France. That this place of worship was built for men who fought and died for France a century ago seems to little deter today's 'culture warriors', who see it as the unwelcome intrusion of an alien culture; in March 2014, Fréjus became one of only two French towns to vote in a mayor from Marine Le Pen's *Front National* party.

In 2005 the historian Santanu Das came across another treasure of the war in the National Archives in Delhi. In an envelope marked 'His Majesty's Office', which had not been opened since it was deposited with the archivists long ago, Das discovered the trench notebook of Jemadar Mir Mast, the brother of the heroic Mir Dast. Mir Mast's notebook was the tool of a resourceful man, an experienced soldier who had, in just a matter of weeks, been transported from a world he knew and understood in India and thrust into a war on another continent – a war that was incomprehensible to him, as it was to much of the rest of the world. Caught between empires, cultures and languages, as well as between life and death, Mir Mast clearly struggled to make sense of the Western Front. Alongside maps and sketches on one page of the notebook is a long list of Urdu words with their English equivalents – the words Mir Mast felt were worth remembering. Many are clearly practical: 'haversack', blanket', 'hungry', or 'please'. Others like 'testacles' [*sic*], 'breasts', 'nephew' and 'honeymoon' have no obvious relevance to the battlefield. As Santanu Das has pointed out, the trench notebook raises more questions than it answers. Why *those* words? An Indian Urdu-speaking soldier, whose units had been thrown into battle alongside English soldiers, was he adjusting to the rough argot of the English Tommies he fought alongside? How much contact did he and other Indian soldiers have with French and Belgium civilians, and with women? Mir Mast left behind him a paper trail matched by few other colonial soldiers, and he is to re-surface repeatedly in the story that follows, in the most unexpected ways.

And yet, despite leaving so large an archival footprint, we know little about who he was or what the war meant to him, and in that respect he is like most of the men who came from distant lands to fight in the World's War.

★

There had been other, so-called 'world wars'. Both the Seven Years War (1754–63) and the French Revolutionary and Napoleonic Wars were – as many historians have pointed out – global conflicts, fought out in Europe, the Caribbean and the Americas. Likewise, England's earlier confrontation with Hapsburg Spain took place on the shipping lanes of the English Channel, on the fields of the Netherlands, off the jagged coast of Ireland and in the harbours and on the islands of the New World. However, while they ranged over vast areas, none of these earlier conflicts were 'world wars' in the sense that emerged in the early twentieth century. In these previous struggles, great powers and empires had fought one another across distant continents and over open oceans, but they had involved the indigenous peoples of those territories only marginally. In a purely geographic sense, they were world wars. But in the demographic sense they were better understood as European quarrels writ large across the globe.

The Great War of 1914–18 was the first true world war in that it was the first in which peoples and nations from across the globe fought and laboured alongside one another, rarely in equality other than equality of suffering. Yet, even in the years and months leading up to the conflict, few in Europe were capable of envisaging that the coming war would bring black and brown peoples from the European empires, and the citizens and subjects of independent non-white nations, into Europe itself. Even those who took it upon themselves to speculate as to the shape of future conflicts got it wrong. Military planners, in Britain, Germany and to a lesser extent France, largely failed to foresee this, just as they failed to grasp that profound changes in military technology had silently made wars of sweeping movements and great cavalry manoeuvres almost obsolete. To most, the idea that armies of black Africans, and Asians from the Indian subcontinent and beyond, would march *en masse* to war in France and Belgium was just as unimaginable as the tank or poisoned gas.

Writers of fiction fared little better. However, the term 'world war' first emerged not in the reports of the pre-war military but as the title of a rather trashy German novel. Written in 1904, *Der Weltkrieg: Deutsche Träume* ('The World War: German Dreams') was the dubious work of August Wilhelm Otto Niemann, a German nationalist. Niemann's novel accurately predicted how, a decade later, the alliance system would drive Europe into two armed camps, and that when war broke out the conflict would range across the world. While he envisaged rebellions of Indian soldiers in the British Indian Army, he failed to make the imaginative leap that Britain, in the event of war with Germany, would transport 850,000 men from that army to France, Africa and the Middle East to fight against Germany and its allies.

What was inconceivable in 1904 became almost instantly necessary in 1914. Within forty-eight hours of Britain's declaration of war on 4 August 1914, the War Cabinet made the decision to dispatch two divisions of Indian troops first to the Middle East, but with an eye to deploying them in Europe. By November 1914, Indian soldiers were aiming their brand new Mark III Lee-Enfield rifles at the grey enemy figures in *Pickelhauben* who emerged through the late-summer fields around the small Belgian city of Ypres. Alongside them were thirty-seven battalions of French troops from Senegal, Algeria and Morocco, who had taken up their positions in the emerging front. By the time the manoeuvrings of 1914 had fizzled out and the Western Front had stabilized, the fantasy of a 'white man's war' had, like all the other assurances about the war (that it would be short and decisive, decided by rapid advances, and 'all over by Christmas'), been exposed as naive.

From the comfortable viewpoint of a century later it seems obvious that it was always going to be a global conflict, and also one inevitably fought for imperial gain. Four decades before 1914, during the final stages of the Franco-Prussian War in

February 1871, British Prime Minister Benjamin Disraeli prophesied in the House of Commons as to what the emergence of a
unified Germany would mean for Europe. The Franco-Prussian
conflict, he warned:

> ... *represents the German revolution, a greater political event than*
> *the French revolution of last century ... Not a single principle in the*
> *management of our foreign affairs, accepted by all statesmen for*
> *guidance up to six months ago, any longer exists. There is not a*
> *diplomatic tradition which has not been swept away. You have a*
> *new world, new influences at work, new and unknown objects and*
> *dangers with which to cope ... The balance of power has been*
> *entirely destroyed, and the country which suffers most, and feels the*
> *effects of this great change most, is England.*[19]

In 1907, the nature of that great change was frankly summarized
by Viscount Esher, then a member of the British Committee of
Imperial Defence. He too reached for the metaphor of revolutionary France, warning that:

> *The German prestige, steadily rising on the continent of Europe, is*
> *more formidable to us than Napoleon at his apogee. Germany is*
> *going to contest with us the Command of the Sea, and our commer-*
> *cial position. She wants sea-power and the carrying trade of the*
> *world. Her geographical grievance has got to be redressed. She must*
> *obtain control of ports at the mouths of the great rivers which tap the*
> *middle of Europe. She must get a coastline from which she can draw*
> *sailors to her fleets, naval and mercantile. She must have an outlet*
> *for her teeming population, and vast acres where Germans can live*
> *and remain Germans. These acres only exist within the confines of*
> *our Empire. Therefore, l'Ennemi c'est l'Allemagne.*[20]

The colonies, and particularly those in Africa, were in the late
nineteenth century regarded by the more optimistic observers as
Europe's safety-valve, an arena in which international tensions
might be defused, thereby avoiding the risk of military

confrontations breaking out between the great powers in Europe itself. The colonial world was a great repository of territories, coaling-stations, spheres of influence, trade concessions and treaty-ports, which Europeans diplomats could use to sweeten any deal or appease any disgruntled nation. More cautious voices, however, had long understood that the age of empire could easily end in war, and probably would once the available stock of unclaimed colonial real estate has been exhausted. The nations who had done poorly in the scramble for territory would seek to redraft the map of the world, while those who had done well – most notably Britain – would seek to preserve their empires and maintain the status quo.[21] In 1914 the British Empire – the greatest of them all – ruled over 400 million subjects and covered a quarter of the land surface of the Earth. The French Empire had over 200 million subjects. Germany, the colonial late-comer, had an empire that although territorially vast was, in economic and strategic terms, in no way commensurate with the country's growing military and economic power. The enormous extent of colonial possessions held in Africa by tiny Belgium and by chaotic, near bankrupt Portugal, were regarded by some in Berlin as almost a standing insult to German prestige and power.

Despite all these tensions it was not in the end colonial rivalries that took Europe to war in 1914 but rather the continent's own internal divisions, both ancient and modern. Amplified by the alliance system, as well as by accident and miscommunication, a Balkans crisis mutated into a global war in a way, and at a velocity, that even a century later remains hardly credible. However, the Balkan conflict that began with Austria-Hungary's declaration of war on Serbia, on 28 July 1914, became a world war not on 3 August when Germany marched into Belgium, but on 4 August when Britain entered the fray. If there had ever been realistic hopes that the world outside Europe might have been largely spared involvement, they were dashed by London's declaration of war. At that moment, farmers in Bengal and the Punjab, Pashtuns from the North-West Frontier, Hausas and Yoruba from the villages of Nigeria, along with the Ashanti and Fante of the Gold

Coast, the Boers, Zulus, San and Shona of southern Africa, and the peoples of New Zealand, Canada and Australia (ancient Aboriginals to the newest arrivals) – all became subjects of an empire at war: 'My empire ... united calm and resolute, and trusting in God', as King George V proclaimed it to be in early August 1914.[22]

In one sense the German High Command was alert to the likelihood that Britain's entry would globalize the conflict – perhaps more aware than many in London. In the early hours of 31 July 1914, which was Germany's own deadline for either mobilizing or standing down its army, Chief of the General Staff Helmuth von Moltke – a man perhaps already on the brink of some sort of nervous breakdown – was awoken by his adjutant Hans von Haeften. Appraised of the situation and of new rumours of full Russian mobilization, Moltke, standing on the precipice of a fateful decision, warned with remarkable prescience and insight: 'This war will turn into a world war in which England will also intervene. Few can have an idea of the extent, the duration and the end of this war. Nobody today can have a notion of how it will end.'[23] The British saw the threat of a 'world war' rather differently. Their empire was still, memorably, a vast swathe of intercontinental pink on most maps – a substitute for British scarlet, against which the names of cities, rivers and mountains might become illegible – all held to the motherland by thick black shipping lines. Indeed, the British Empire appeared, in some respects, all the greater for the geographical distortions produced by the favoured Mercator Projection used by cartographers. In what the historian Linda Colley has described as this 'single, insufficiently examined image', whole territories in Africa, appearing as solid blocks of pink, concealed the reality that on the ground British influence gradually faded away with each mile travelled from the coast or away from the British centres of colonial power. This map, which was famously hung in every school classroom in Britain, disguised the 'territorial fragility' of the whole complex, unlikely structure. It exaggerated both the real extent and the global reach of British power, distortions and vulnerabilities to which Britain's ruling elite was fully awake when war came.

The two armed blocks of Europe in 1914 both sought a globalization of the war, but in diametrically opposite ways. France went
to war for its territories lost to Germany in 1871, for revenge, and
for national security; Britain fought now in order to avoid having
to confront a victorious, expanded Germany at some later date.
But when it came to empires, both were fighting to maintain the
status quo. Neither went to war in order to expand their colonies
at the expense of Germany. However, both the British and the
French did seek to draw men, money and resources from the 600
million peoples of their combined empires. France more energetically and enthusiastically than Britain aimed to deploy colonial
manpower in Europe – men who were to serve as both soldiers
and labourers. Both allies set out to exploit the wealth and natural
resources of the colonies in the war effort. But they had no ambitions to see the war spread to the theatres outside Europe, beyond
the necessary campaigns to capture the German colonial hold-
ings in Asia and Africa and to neutralize the German navy.
Germany's leaders sought the exact opposite: genuinely and vis-
cerally resenting the deployment of colonial soldiers of
'non-European stock' on the Western Front, they expended huge
sums of money and vast amounts of energy attempting to spread
the war into the lands from which those combatants had been
drawn. Germany sought to turn the British Empire into the British
Achilles heel, forcing Britain to deploy men and resources to
maintain its colonial grip around the world, and to this end
Germany drafted strategic plans to globalize the war. The German
alliance with Ottoman Turkey was intended, in large part, to
achieve exactly that. This was part of a wider global strategy of
using revolution and religious discord as weapons to change the
balance of power in a post-war world.

These divergences of perspective and strategy were summed
up in the war's nomenclature. While the British and French
called the war of 1914 the 'Great War' and '*La Grande Guerre*'
respectively, the Germans almost from the start called it by the
name echoed in the country's Official History of the conflict: the
Weltkrieg.[24]

★

While the British did not go to war in order to seize German colonial territories, they were quite happy to do so when the opportunity arose. The far bigger concern was the defence of the pre-war empire in the face of the German and Ottoman efforts to stoke the fires of nationalism, anti-British sentiment and religious unity. Yet, the outbreak of war was met with a genuine and hugely appreciated wave of pro-British, pro-imperial sentiment. The empire of the 'white dominions' and India was perhaps never so united as in August and September 1914. Indian nationalists, including Gandhi (who was then in London), passionately advocated support for the British war effort, partly in the hope that loyalty in the moment of crisis would lead to the granting of greater autonomy once the danger had passed. The South African Native National Congress – precursor of the African National Congress – made the same calculation. However, local tensions between Boer and Briton in South Africa led to a muted reaction among the white population there. Africans in the dependencies had no power and therefore no choice as to whether to support the war or not, while white British settler communities tended to support the war with great impromptu demonstrations of nationalism and support for the ideals of empire as they perceived them.

British propagandists built on this moment by painting a picture of the empire as a great family of peoples, paternally led by Britain and joined together in some supposedly moral mission for civilization. Wartime propaganda used the image of the Indian and African soldier, fighting in a war against Germany, as firm evidence of the superiority of the British Empire. The hierarchies of race that underpinned and informed imperial rule were encoded into wartime propaganda posters. Thus, white troops from the dominions of Australia, Canada and New Zealand were given centre stage, alongside the British, with Indians behind them, and black Africans positioned usually in the background – an imperial, but not an equal, community.

While a few wartime writers repeated the old mantras of the nineteenth century, which claimed the British to be a race of born
rulers ('God's chosen people' echoed the words of one 1916
writer), others followed the official line that presented the
empire as a brotherhood of humanity, one that was being brought
closer together by the shared experience of war.[25] In his religious
tract *Brothers All: The War and the Race Question*, Edwyn Bevan, the
Christian philosopher and classicist, began his opening chapter
'The Meeting of the Races' with a simple statement:

> *The war which we are witnessing marks an epoch, not only in the
> history of England or of Europe, but in the history of mankind. If
> there were any spectator who, through the unnumbered ages, had
> followed the course of the creature called Man upon this planet, he
> would … never have seen a war which engaged so large a part of
> the men upon earth, which affected, directly or indirectly, the whole
> world, as this war does.*[26]

For a pamphlet written so early in the war, before America had
entered the fray, Bevan's work was insightful. With the Indian
Corps fighting in France alongside French troops from North
Africa and West Africa, with British forces fighting side-by-side
with the army of Japan in China, and with black British soldiers
on the march against the Germans in Africa itself, Bevan reflected
on the meaning of this new phenomenon:

> *… we find brown men and yellow men and black men joined with
> ourselves in one colossal struggle, pumping out their treasure, pour-
> ing out their blood, for the common cause — Japanese and English
> and Russians carrying on war as allies on the shores of the Pacific,
> Hindus and Mohammedans from India coming to fight in
> European armies on the old historic battlefields of Europe, side by
> side with Mohammedans from Algiers and black men from Senegal.
> We had often spoken of the wonderful drawing together of the world
> in our days, but we never knew that it was to be represented in such
> strange and splendid and terrible bodily guise.*[27]

While there was nothing particularly controversial in this, Bevan also attempted to explain why so many men, from so many nations and races, had taken up arms or grasped the labourers' spade in the war effort. He genuinely believed that:

> *What gives the moment its significance is that the presence of these Indian troops does not represent solely the purpose of England. It represents in some degree the will of India ... We may speak truly of co-operation in the case of India, as in the case of Japan. It is the promptitude, the eagerness and the unanimity of this voluntary adherence which has seemed to England almost too good to be true.*[28]

... which of course it was. For Japan was fighting to build up its leverage in East Asia and to establish its place among the ranks of the great powers. The men of the Indian Corps fought because they were highly professional soldiers who obeyed orders. Their attitude was lauded by an Indian middle-class and an aristocratic elite, both of whom hoped that the loyalty and the blood of the sepoys would buy influence and gratitude later on.

In truth, the deployment of Asians and Africans to the battlefields of Europe in 1914, and their mobilization and recruitment for service elsewhere, was loaded with problems. It was a phenomenon that challenged the central tenets of colonial theory and went against powerful taboos of the late nineteenth and early twentieth centuries. In the war in Europe, black and brown men were ordered to fight and kill white men. All the colonial powers worried that once armed and once shown that the myth of white supremacy was just that, soldiers from Africa and Asia would prove the greatest threat to the long-term futures of their empires. There were those in Britain who were appalled by the sight of Indian troops in British uniforms, fighting in a European war against a European enemy. Lord Stamfordham and Sir Valentine Chirol, the celebrated pro-imperial journalists of *The Times,* were both concerned by the equal treatment of Indian troops, and they feared what one writer to the newspaper called 'the passionate love of battle which is now stirring in the hearts of the warlike races of Hindustan'.[29]

The challenge facing the British and French in deploying their imperial manpower was that in doing so they might find they had won the war but, in the process, rendered their empires ungovernable in the future. How might they put the genie back in the bottle? Both countries were to prove extremely adept at doing just that, though they started the war unsure of how far India and the African colonies could be pushed – both in terms of recruitment and wartime taxation – before serious opposition emerged. The French showed themselves willing to push their African colonies into open rebellion if it gave them more men with which to fight the Germans. Colonial uprisings could be dealt with later if they could not be avoided completely. The image of the First World War as the graveyard of empires is only half the story. Defeat, bankruptcy and revolution destroyed the German Empire, the Austro-Hungarian Empire, the Russian Empire and the ancient Ottoman Empire. But the victorious imperial powers – despite localized rebellions and the rise of nationalist sentiment in some colonies – ended the war with their empires intact and the subject peoples maintained in positions of inequality and subordination. Not only this, the British and French empires in 1919 became *larger* than they had ever been. Both were bloated, having feasted upon the carcass of the Ottoman Empire, and engorged, after having absorbed Germany's former colonies in Africa. Although some of their new colonies were disguised as League of Nations 'mandates', this was little more than a ruse to keep the Americans happy. No 'wind of change' blew across Africa (or Asia) in 1919. The peoples of the British Empire did not become 'Brothers All', as Bevan had quaintly dreamed.

Nevertheless, more than any preceding event the First World War did expose the complexities and hypocrisies that surrounded race and colonialism in the early twentieth century. There were huge differences in the behaviour of the Allied nations towards non-white peoples, and war itself changed those attitudes further. Different races were treated differently, at different times, and in different theatres of war. The French put Algerian, Moroccan and West African troops into the trenches from 1914 onwards, whereas the British recruited thousands of Africans but never permitted them to fight in Europe. Black British troops from the West Indies were sent to the Western Front, but only allowed to labour behind the lines. (Yet a handful of black men, from Britain's own small black community – among them Northampton Town FC's star forward Walter Tull – slipped through the military colour bar and fought with distinction.) The British organized the Maoris of New Zealand into a Pioneer Corps, who fought in the Middle East, while Aboriginal men from Australia were reduced to labourers. White South Africans fought in the front line, while black South Africans could only hold the status of labourers. The Americans only allowed a handful of their black regiments to enter combat, and half of them were placed under the command of French officers rather than white Americans. This led the US Army to issue a secret order that asked French officers to treat the African-American soldier as 'an inferior being' to avoid offending white American sensibilities. The French quietly refused for fear of offending their African troops. In the war in Mesopotamia (Iraq) and Palestine, Muslim Indians were allowed to fight the Turks, while Muslim Egyptians were tasked with digging trenches and driving camel trains. The official reasoning behind this overall jumble of illogic and prejudice was complicated in the extreme, and shaped by local concerns, colonial practice and the vagaries of war.

*

To an enormous number of people, the First World War arrived suddenly, out of a clear summer sky and following a crisis seemingly too small and insignificant to have generated such epic consequences. The war euphoria that erupted across Europe during the first days of August 1914 was so convulsive as to have almost obscured the briefer moment of shock that preceded it. Since Prussia's defeat of France in 1871, most of Europe had been free of war. The British had to look back to Waterloo in 1815 to their previous entanglement on the continent (unless one counts

Crimea in the 1850s). However, throughout that near half-century of peace on the continent, Europe's armies had been involved in another kind of warfare – the series of wars, invasions, expeditions and punitive raids in their colonies. Those colonies – pre-industrial societies in Africa and Asia – had provided the testing grounds for new weapons and new tactics. Indeed, some of the new weapons had become virtually *synonymous* with colonial wars. It seems difficult to understand why the lessons of these 'small wars' were not applied to military thinking and planning in 1914; but they were not to any meaningful extent.

Advances in artillery had been enormous, but such heavy and cumbersome weapons had not been suitable, or necessary, in the small wars of empire, so their fearsome evolution had remained largely concealed from the great mass of the population. But it was the Maxim heavy machine gun, more than any other weapon, that had transformed warfare in ways whose lessons were not absorbed.[30] There were soldiers in the British Expeditionary Force of 1914 who took the Maxim gun with them to war, and who had themselves used the devastating weapon against tribal peoples in the colonies. They at least knew the potential of the Maxims and their variants, yet their commanders seemed unable to comprehend that the 'Devil's Paintbrush' – the ultimate tool of colonial domination – now ruled the battlefields of their *own* continent.

If there was one group for whom both the power of modern weapons, and the experience of multiracial armies, should have been apparent, it was the British and French generals, a high proportion of whom had built their careers fighting for empire. General, later Field Marshal, Sir Douglas Haig had fought against the Mahdists in Sudan, the Boers in South Africa and had campaigned in India. Earl Kitchener (of Khartoum) had commanded British forces in Sudan and also served in India. The career of Sir John French, who led the British Expeditionary Force of 1914, had taken him to Sudan, Abyssinia (Ethiopia), Eritrea and South Africa. Horace Smith-Dorrien, who led British Imperial forces in the Second Battle of Ypres, had fought in the Anglo-Zulu War, under Kitchener against the Mahdists in Sudan, in the Second Anglo-Boer War, and in the campaign to tighten British control of the Tirah Valley on India's North-West Frontier. On the French side, Joseph Joffre had fought in China and Tonkin (Vietnam), while Robert Nivelle had made his name in Tunisia, Algeria and China, during the suppression of the Boxer Rebellion. Philippe Pétain had served in Morocco, while Charles Mangin – the army's great colonial expert – had served in Sudan, Mali, Senegal and across French North Africa.

While most of these men had had considerable experience of the power of industrial weapons, particularly fast-firing rifles and the variants of the Maxim machine gun, they struggled in 1914 to understand the extent to which such weapons had trans-formed warfare. At the Battle of Omdurman (1898), British rifles, field artillery and the mile-long range of the Maxim gun meant that none of the enemy – Sudanese Dervishes under the Mahdi's successor – got within 800 yards of the British lines.[31] It was for his role in this one-sided contest that Kitchener had been elevated to the peerage. Yet the centrality of machine guns to his triumph in Sudan was not something Kitchener was ever able to fully acknowledge. Nor was he capable of fully grasping that the devastation the Maxim gun had wrought upon Africans would befall *all* attackers, of whatever race or nationality, who attempted an assault over open ground against similarly equipped defenders. Omdurman did not lead Kitchener to use his new status as peer of the realm and hero of empire to call for radical rethinking of what the British still called 'musketry' in the years before 1914.

The Germans – often claimed to be ahead in this respect – were, at first, almost as prone as the British to see the machine gun as a colonial weapon that was of little relevance to a 'real' war in Europe. But in Germany lessons were sinking in. In 1908, a deputy in the Reichstag was pleased to report a noticeable change in attitudes. 'A year ago,' he informed the chamber, 'people in military circles were not so conscious of the value of machine guns as they are today. Then there were many people, even in the German Army, who still regarded the machine guns as a weapon for use against Herero and "Hottentots".'[32]*

The small wars of empire made sense to Edwardian Britain, Third Republic France and Wilhelmine Germany – they seemed to represent the proper order of things. The modern weapons were in white hands, the enemies were black- and brown-skinned men of 'lower races', and the wars themselves were fought in the enemy's homelands, all of them reassuringly distant from Europe's shores. European casualties were generally light, the costs of campaigning modest (especially in the case of the parsimonious British), and the emerging narratives easy to convert into heroic adventure stories. These wars were in reality, as the historian Correlli Barnett has pointed out with reference to the British Army, not a picture of warfare as it really was but merely vivid examples of a very 'specialized form' of warfare, utterly divorced from that which would be fought 'between great industrial powers'.[33] Yet it was all the British public knew. Despite all the interconnectedness of the pre-1914 world, what took place in the imperial realm was widely regarded as being of marginal significance to any war in Europe. Europe was, conceptually speaking, not only a separate continent but a separate realm, its borders regarded by many as the frontier between the civilized world and the rest of humanity. It was believed – both consciously and subconsciously – that European conflicts belonged to another, distinct tradition, one with its own history that stretched back to Agincourt and Waterloo, for which wars against 'savages' could offer few lessons.

In a similar manner, before 1914 the manpower of the empires was deemed of only marginal importance by most. Armies raised in the colonies – or armies that might yet be raised there – were of little interest to most pre-war military planners, though there were some notable exceptions. In the British case, the War Office

* A reference to Germany's genocidal campaign against the Herero and Nama people of its South West Africa colony (modern Namibia), which was just concluding in 1908.

in London had only limited interactions with the Colonial Office, and the interests of the government in Delhi and the government in London were divergent when it came to the training, recruitment and equipping of Indian soldiers. The views of the few men among the French and the British ranks who foresaw a role for Indian and colonial troops in a European war were sidelined.

The First World War represented the breakdown of all these barriers. Weapons once dismissed, or falsely categorized, as tools of colonial conquest were demonstrated to have silently and universally transformed the balance of power between defender and attacker, favouring the former. The awesome capacity of the machine gun to kill thousands of men in hours, or even minutes, had been concealed by geographic distance and the racial difference of its first victims. But the fields of dead who lay scattered in 1914 were largely white men, Europe's own, and no longer the 'lesser' peoples of Africa and Asia. Preconceptions that had sealed Europe off from the realities of its own destructiveness and latent barbarism suddenly gave way in the summer and autumn of 1914. For the French, British and Germans, the myth of the transformative power of the individual hero, along with notions of 'spirit', *élan* and 'pluck', collapsed under the weight of the 400 rounds that spewed from the heavy machine guns every minute, or were demolished by the effects of shells filled with shrapnel and high-explosive TNT and Melanite. That Africans, Indians and others were present in Europe in 1914 to witness the belated homecoming of the weapons and fallacies of the age of empire seems apposite – as well as tragic.

Yet even as it was happening, the generals still struggled to comprehend the sudden interconnectedness of these phenomena that had long been conceptualized as being separate. Despite Moltke's premonitions of the war's dimensions, the Germans were slow in 1914 to fully realize the potential significance of the manpower of the British and French empires, even when the first of those soldiers were on the battlefield facing German troops. All the armies were slow to accept that the fully automatic machine gun and barbed wire had rendered obsolete great swathes of military doctrine, especially the existing doctrine of the attack. While the French, for many reasons, had enormous difficulties coming to terms with the futility of frontal assaults, the British were particular resistant to increasing the number of machine guns per battalion. As late as the summer of 1915, Lord Kitchener, Secretary of State for War by 1914, was confronted by Sir Eric Geddes of the Ministry for Munitions over why so few orders had been placed for new machine guns. Despite constant reports from front-line officers calling for additional heavy machine guns, Kitchener remained adamant that the British Army would not require more than two per battalion and that the absolute maximum should be four per battalion; any more he regarded as 'a luxury' – to the disgust of the energetic Minister of Munitions, David Lloyd George.* The minister went on to order over 100,000 new machine guns for 1916. Yet it was Kitchener and not Lloyd George or Geddes who had seen thousands of men killed before his eyes by Maxim guns. Kitchener's inability to recast the weapon, in his mind, as being central to the war in Europe was, under the circumstances, astonishing.

One who understood, clearly and early, the new age and the links between the current war and the bloody history of colonial conquest was not a soldier but a writer. H.G. Wells was a man as schooled in recent history as he was astute at projecting possible futures. In 1916 he published one of his best, most important, and most forgotten novels, *Mr. Britling Sees It Through*. In this quasi-autobiographical work, the eponymous hero is, like Wells himself, a celebrated writer. Cultivated, cosmopolitan and well-informed, Mr Britling watches as society around him is forced to confront 'Prussian Militarism'. His international friendships are

---

* Geddes, who was then deputy to Lloyd George, was so shocked by this assessment that he asked Kitchener to sign a memorandum stating his views. Geddes then presented this to a suitably horrified Lloyd George, who almost ripped the document in two. As C.J Chivers notes in *The Gun* (2011), p.130, Lloyd George's response was: 'Take Kitchener's maximum, square it, multiply that result by two; and when you are in sight of that, double it again for good luck.'

put under intolerable strain, and his little part of England changes under the effects of war. Surveying the first few months of the conflict, Mr Britling acknowledges that the horrors that have befallen the people of Britain, France and Belgium are little different to those inflicted upon colonial peoples in Africa and Asia, by those same imperial powers.

> *The Germans in Belgium were shooting women frequently, not simply for grave spying but for trivial offences … Then came the battleship raid on Whitby and Scarborough, and the killing among other victims of a number of children on their way to school. This shocked Mr. Britling absurdly, much more than the Belgian crimes had done. They were English children. At home! … The drowning of a great number of people on a torpedoed ship full of refugees from Flanders filled his mind with pitiful imaginings for days. The Zeppelin raids, with their slow crescendo of blood-stained futility, began before the end of 1914 … It was small consolation for Mr. Britling to reflect that English homes and women and children were, after all, undergoing only the same kind of experience that our ships have inflicted scores of times in the past upon innocent people in the villages of Africa and Polynesia …*[34]

In *The War of the Worlds,* published sixteen years earlier, Wells had compared the rout of humanity at the hands of the Martians to the near extermination of the Tasmanian Aboriginals by British settlers and soldiers in the early nineteenth century. He clearly understood that as well as bringing to Europe the peoples of their empires, Britain and France and Germany were importing the barbarism that had been used to conquer their imperial subjects' homelands and subjugate their forefathers.

★

The machine gun proved to be one way in which technology interacted with empire to help make the conflict a world war. Sometimes the technologies of the war have been overlooked in their impact, as in the case of Marconi's radio, which played a part in spreading the war to the colonies.[35] It was the existence of German radio transmitters that made it necessary for the British and French to so-rapidly attack remote German colonial possessions in Africa – territories that might otherwise have been merely blockaded or pounded into submission from the sea at some later, more convenient, date. However, the bulk of the new technologies in the war had a much heavier, distinctly *industrial* imprint. The machine gun was exactly what it described, the literal fusion of the 'machine' and the 'gun', which translated into the mechanization of killing and the reduction of the craft of its soldier-operator to the repetitive labour of the factory worker.[36] The heavy artillery that obliterated the forts of Belgium and the 'Paris Gun' that crashed shells down on the French capital in 1918 were the products of the great industries of the Ruhr. The name of Krupp, the renowned German armaments company, is as essential to any telling of the story of the First World War as the name of any general.

The war was industrial in another sense, too. The weapons might have been high-tech, but many required vast amounts of manual labour. To move the guns, and feed them with shells, was a giant logistical and labour-intensive operation. Their emplacements had to be dug by hand and the dedicated railways that delivered their shells had to be built, maintained, operated and repeatedly moved and re-established elsewhere. The German artillery men who built the platforms using quick drying cement, from which the guns were to be fired, were as essential to their successful operation as the men who fired the shells. Each offensive launched on the Western and Eastern fronts required huge numbers of men to prepare the war materials needed if the attack were to have a chance of success. The lessons both sides took from their failed offensives of 1915 were that the attacks of 1916 would have to be bigger and better supplied than those attempted so far.

Equally labour-intensive was the defensive war. At the heart of the First World War on both the Western and other fronts was the low-tech phenomenon of the trench, one of the emblems of the conflict. The machine gun and the rifle forced armies into siege warfare on a continental scale. General Haig in 1915 advised his government and his fellow commanders to think of the Western Front as 'a fortress' that could not easily be breached. The creation, extension, reinforcement and maintenance of such fortifications, and the construction of new lines and reserve trenches behind the front lines, required the skills of the engineer and the muscle of vast armies of soldiers and labourers. The unglamorous history of labour and labour migration is an essential, if often unwritten, aspect of the First World War, and here again those powers that could drew on the resources of their empires – and those of nations beyond.

Perhaps the most useful precedents for understanding how the search for this labour necessarily globalized the war are not earlier conflicts – pre-industrial, semi-industrial or localized as they were – but the great engineering projects of the late nineteenth and early twentieth centuries. The French attempt to build an inter-oceanic canal across the Isthmus of Panama in the last years of the nineteenth century, and the successful American project to do the same in the first years of the twentieth, along with the construction of the Union Pacific Railway and various British railway projects in East Africa – all had required huge pools of cheap, non-white, migrant labour, which drew on the great reservoirs of poor men in the European empires and in states such as China and Japan, where there were large numbers of impoverished rural people. These were the men who answered the call for labour, seeing such projects as a chance to make some money and advance in life. The enthusiasm in the Caribbean, for example, at the outbreak of war in 1914 was inspired not only by a genuine sense of being part of the British Empire, but also by the rapid appreciation that the war offered men of the Caribbean, as soldiers or labourers, a route out of the stifling, atrophying unemployment that had blighted islands like Jamaica and Barbados ever since the completion of the Panama Canal, which drew heavily on Caribbean labour, had severed that life-line of employment and remittances. Put simply, the First World War now represented the greatest employment opportunity on earth.

The Western Front itself was an epic engineering feat, greater
than an inter-oceanic canal or a trans-continental railway. It
required the movement of more earth, the laying of more railways, the building of more camps and depots, and the felling of
more trees than any project known to date. Men from the colonies and beyond worked not just behind the lines, but in the
factories and the ports too, in the enormous enterprise of manufacture and distribution that the war necessitated. And like all
great labour-intensive projects of the age, the workforce was
made up of poor men from everywhere and anywhere. The two
fronts together, the Western and Eastern, were among the largest
structures human beings have ever made, their temporary nature
perhaps having obscured that fact.* The mobilization of colonial
labour, alongside the mobilization of the women of Europe on
the home fronts in munitions factories and much else, was the
only viable means to keep such a war machine primed.

 If the movement of labour for the war effort was a wartime
imperative, and for thousands of people an economic opportunity, it was also a vestigial, ironic, reflection of the global economic
interconnectedness of the pre-1914 world, of the kind that had
convinced many that a general war on a global scale was an
impossibility. That optimistic assumption was, in retrospect, fanciful. Perhaps we can see that today better than contemporaries
could. The pre-war world of 1914 was the age of world fairs,
expositions and trade-missions – and those extravaganzas were
merely the most exciting manifestations of an economic reality
that we in the twenty-first century have largely forgotten. The
pre-1914 world was one built upon a system of integrated global
trade. Raw materials and finished goods pulsed around the world
on arterial shipping lanes, through which sailed vast merchant
fleets, armadas that dwarfed the world's navies, even at the height
of the Anglo-German arms race to build the largest number of
the most powerful dreadnought-type battleships. Global trade

---

* Although generally a more fluid and mobile war, the conflict on the
Eastern Front did see the construction of hundreds of miles of trenches.

brought about a global integration of capital, raw materials and industrial goods, and also of labour. The First World War was therefore not simply a human tragedy; it was also a catastrophic rupture, which ripped apart this interwoven global economy. So great was that rupture, and so deep the divisions that it left behind, that it was not until the 1970s that the world returned to the levels of international trade and economic integration that it had known in 1914.[37] Today we fret about the positive or deleterious consequences of globalization, a seemingly recent phenomenon. But our modern age is best understood as the *second* age of globalization, the first beginning sometime in the 1870s and coming to an abrupt and shuddering halt in the autumn and winter of 1914, as world trade turned to world war.

★

The replacement of economic globalization with an unprecedentedly global war forced Europeans into closer contact with peoples of other races, and in new types of relationships; it forced them to confront and question what it was they meant by 'race' – a term which, as in the designation 'British race', seemed capable of loose applicability to almost any people who shared a culture, background, kinship or colour. Nationalism and its close cousin, ethnic nationalism – the idea that it was natural for every distinct people to occupy its own nation state – seeped into the bloodstream of Europe.

Inherent within the process of defining or demonizing the enemy as some kind of alien 'other' was a process of defining one's own national characteristics, and it was here that the fluid border between cultural characteristics and racial traits became even more vague, allowing it to be crossed on a daily basis by propagandists and writers of all hues. In Britain, the Germans were depicted in numerous propaganda campaigns as a people whose cultural progress had atrophied, leaving them culturally stuck somewhere in the fifth century when – or so British writers claimed – their Hunnic ancestors under Attila had brought down the Roman Empire. So the Germans were the 'Huns' (or even more dehumanized, in the

singular 'Hun'), a people whose debased *Kultur* had given the
world not Goethe or Beethoven but rather militarism, or
'Prussianism' as some writers preferred to pointedly call it. Germans
were by nature rude and crass, lacking in discretion and liable to
behave in ways that were dishonourable. They transgressed every
rule and had no truck with fair play or sportsmanship. They were
also guttural of language and coarse of habit. In the boys' adventure story *With Haig on the Somme*, written in 1917 by D.H. Parry, a
German agent is uncovered when his deplorable table manners
and gluttony are witnessed during a communal meal.[38] In another
wartime epic, the heroes come across an exquisite French château
in which Germans have been billeted:

> *Empty wine bottles lay beside a priceless marquetry table, whose top
> had been burned with cigar ends; and as the men scattered rapidly
> through the adjoining rooms, they found everywhere traces of
> German 'kultur' which the vandals had left behind them. Upstairs
> it was the same thing; hangings torn and slashed for the mere lust
> of destruction, smashed china, objectionable caricatures scrawled
> upon the walls, and upon the open grand piano in the salon a copy
> of the Hymn of Hate, with a half-smoked cigarette beside it. 'The
> beasts!' exclaimed young Wetherby, hot with indignation.[39]*

But if German-ness was innate, congenital, ordained by race,
could the 'Hun' be reformed? Was the problem German *Kultur*
or the German 'race' itself? The more forward-thinking propagandists of the Second World War could draw a distinction
between the ideology of National Socialism and the culture of
the German people.* In the First World War the racialization of

---

* In the Second World War, the theme music to the BBC's European
Service, broadcast into occupied Europe, was the opening bars of Beethov-
en's *Fifth Symphony* – a phonic emblem of the 'real Germany' that had been
temporarily overcome by the bacillus of Nazism. It was appropriate, for
Beethoven himself had been a romantic champion of personal freedom
and a critic of his former hero Napoleon, the last European tyrant against
whom Britain had been forced to fight on the continent.

the Germans had no equivalent counterbalance, and so the Kaiser and the Prussian military elite were not seen as a junta who were holding captive a cultured European people, but rather as an accurate reflection of the characters and inner drives of 67 million Germans. It was the 'Huns' who had sacked Rome and, so it was said, plunged the world into darkness, and now their supposed descendants were ready to repeat the same crime one-and-a-half millennia later. Britain, France and their allies were now all that stood between Europe and a second Dark Ages.

Anti-German sentiment became ever more racialized, influencing the wartime attacks on the homes and property of Germans or suspected Germans living in Britain. But it did not stop there. There were occasions on which this flood of ethnic nationalism spilled over into attacks on any foreigners, and not specifically enemy nationals. As non-Europeans were few and conspicuous in a Britain with only a tiny black population, they were a clear and easy target. There was a chaotic feel to Britain's wartime riots and attacks on foreigners, motivated as they were by ignorance, opportunism and a frenzy of rage. The country, especially the capital, became palpably more anti-Semitic, and any minority suspected of not doing its bit was treated with mistrust and even hostility. But there were contradictions aplenty. While black Britons, the Chinese, and the Russian Jewish communities all faced attacks by mobs, pride in the empire, and pride and relief that the non-white men of the empire were at arms in defence of the motherland, became to some extent a balancing force. While black Londoners could be attacked, black and brown soldiers from the colonies felt their treatment in Britain was warm and hospitable. This was not always the case, but it was often enough to be commented on in letters and memoirs.

The propensity among the British to racialize the Germans and distrust racial foreigners went hand in hand with an increasingly racialized understanding of themselves. The war took place not just at the zenith of empire but near the high water mark of the race idea. It erupted at a moment when Social Darwinism exerted a powerful grip on high ideas and the popular imagination, from the lecture hall to the beer hall. Ideas of the degeneracy of races, their contamination by the polluting blood of other, lower races, were gaining ground. Social Darwinists in Britain worried that indolence, sloth and decadence had shaken off the harsh hand of nature and allowed the British to fall into the stupor of the lotus eater. The classically educated ruling classes feared that Berlin was Sparta to London's Athens, the home of a people who were better fed, better disciplined and hardened by the constant preparation for war. Were the British working classes puny weaklings compared to the men of the Ruhr and the Rhine? Was Britain faced not just with an economic and military rival but by a fitter and more virile race? And might defeat not just roll back the frontiers of the British Empire but cast the British race into decline, as the stronger Teutons spread into new territories and multiplied? And what might that mean for the world and the 'lower races' if the paternal hand and wise council of the British race, supposedly a race of natural rulers and born colonists, were forced off the world stage? All of these neuroses spiralled around the Edwardian imagination. As the boundaries between race and nation became all the more fluid under the colossal pressures of the new phenomenon of 'total war', these potent fears and preoccupations became the nightmares of Britain's ruling elite and their colleagues in the white dominions.

In the end, the political and military leaderships of Britain and France – if they were to mobilize the human resources of their empires – had to reach an accommodation between assumptions and ideas about race on the one hand, and the imperatives of war on the other. One response was the complex paraphernalia of ethnic distinctions that informed colonial recruitment – in the British case the 'martial races' theory, and in the French case the concept of *les races guerrières*. But in their actions they exacerbated the Germans' own Darwinian fears. The German government and press feared that their enemies, by infusing their armies with the life strength of primitive but virile peoples, had loaded the Darwinian dice against Germany. German wartime propaganda tended to present the country as the victim of a racial betrayal by

the Entente powers and stressed the imagined racial homogene-
ity of the German and Austrian armies against the racial and
cultural diversity of their enemies. Sven Hedin, a pro-German
Swedish explorer who wrote a propagandistic account of life
behind the German lines in 1914, described a dying German
soldier in a field hospital:

> *Here is a reservist. What a tremendous figure of a man. What can
> Latins, Slavs, Celts, Japs, Negroes, Hindoos, Ghurkas, Turcos, and
> whatever they are called, do against such strapping giants of the
> true Germanic type? His features are superbly noble, and he seems
> pleased with his day's work. He does not regret that he has offered
> his life for Germany's just cause.*[40]

Such inflation of the racial prowess of the 'Germanic type' hints
at a deep and early sense of insecurity and victimhood that many
Germans felt, at their racial as well as their national isolation.
The issue of race became, increasingly, an area of contestation
and one of the conflict's defining characteristics, as the Great
War evolved inexorably into the World's War.

★

Empire, colonialism, race and multiple theatres of war were
defining features of this war. Yet, bizarrely, the First World War
has a unique characteristic that has – among other consequences
– come to *submerge* the war's multinational, multi-ethnic, multiracial dimensions. The historical war has been overwhelmed by
what the historian David Reynolds has called the 'literary war', a
popular memory of the conflict formed from the collected fragments of prose and war poetry, which, over the course of the
twentieth century, coalesced into a dominant but narrow image
of the conflict.[41] This process, by which history has been overshadowed by literature, has had many distorting effects, among
which is that it has rendered invisible those aspects of the war
that were inherently unappealing to the poets and prose-writers
of the time. Features of the conflict to which they were little

exposed, or in which they found no inspiration, along with elements that did not subsequently fit into the narrative that was built around their powerful words, were discarded or consigned to footnotes. The literary war focuses on lost generations, the follies of a callous establishment and the sheer pity of it all. It is a powerful and important condemnation of a conflict that cost millions of lives, but it is hardly a comprehensive exploration of the greatest war the world had ever known. Seventy million men were mobilized during the First World War. From that mass levy, there emerged only about 1,000 published memoirs, most of which are long out of print and forgotten beyond the world of academic history. Only a handful – Jünger, Blunden, Remarque, Graves – have become classics, textbooks known to students and casual readers and works through which the war has for a century been understood.[42] The list of war poets whose words are remembered a hundred years later is similarly circumscribed.

One facet long obscured by the victory of literature over history, and by the narrowness in terms of both class and race among the authors of that literature, is the global nature of the conflict. No great memoir or work of poetry emerged from the war in Africa, the war at sea, or the battles in Asia and the Pacific. In English, only T.E. Lawrence's turgid and self-mythologizing *Seven Pillars of Wisdom* came out of the war in the Middle East. What has been lost sight of is not only the true geographic scope of the war but its fundamental demographics. More words have been written over the past century about the few dozen middle-class officers who wrote their war memoirs and penned their war poetry than about the 4 million non-white, non-European soldiers who fought for Britain, France and their allies, let alone the millions of civilians who laboured at war work or who suffered hardships and loss when the war swept through their communities.[43] Any reconception of the First World War as the *World's War* is, at one level, about recovering those stories and those perspectives, or – to put it another way – about restoring the names of Mike Mountain Horse, Mir Dast and Mir Mast to the collective memory alongside those of Siegfried Sassoon, Robert Graves and Wilfred Owen.

CHAPTER 2

'ACROSS THE BLACK WATERS'

India in Europe – the 'martial races'

—————

MARSEILLES, THE MORNING OF 26 SEPTEMBER 1914. The *Castilia* and the *Mongara*, two ships of the British India Company, steam into the broad waters of Marseilles' old port. On deck and below in the holds are the units of the Lahore Division of the British Indian Corps, with their horses and mules and as much of their equipment as they have been able to gather together and load. On this first transport from British India comes a battery of the Royal Horse Artillery, a signal company, a field ambulance and a section of the Mule Corps too. At 9 o'clock the next morning, two more ships dock at Marseilles, carrying between them the men and horses of the 15th Lancers. One by one, ship by ship, units are landed, the various composite pieces of an Indian army that was disassembled and chaotically loaded in Bombay and Karachi seven weeks earlier. Now, at Marseilles, the whole complex, international, multiracial jigsaw puzzle is to be reassembled and rapidly prepared for war. These first 'bizarre and incongruous' days at Marseilles are later described by Lieutenant Colonel J.W.B. Merewether of the Indian Corps:

> *Working parties of the Indian troops in their sombre but business-like khaki were mixed with assistants in the shape of French seamen, French labourers, stevedores, and our own Army Service Corps men. Nobody understood anyone else's language; parties of Indians could be seen gesticulating and illustrating their wants by vigorous pantomime to sympathetic but puzzled Frenchmen. However, all*

was good humour and an intense desire to help, so matters soon
arranged themselves.[1]

The Lahore Division are not only the first Indian soldiers to land
in France this year; they are the first Indians ever to take part in a
war in Europe. As each new regiment, or part of a regiment, lands,
they march through the long boulevards that stretch up the gentle
hills of Marseilles away from the waters of the old port. Crowds
gather under the dappled shade of the early autumn trees to cheer
them on: '*Vive Angleterre!*', '*Vivent les Hindous!*'[2]

——— · ———

The arrival of Indian troops in France was an event. In the words
of *The Times* (2 October 1914), 'They had an enthusiastic welcome
and were the centre of a triumphal procession. The physique of
the Indian troops impressed the spectators.'[3] Another article
described 'stirring scenes', noting how:

> *Women presented the troops with cigarettes and fruit and girls*
> *strewed flowers on the road and pinned them to tunics and tur-*
> *bans. The enthusiasm reached fever heat when the Ghurkhas struck*
> *up the 'Marseillaise' on their weird instruments. Many of the*
> *younger natives leapt three feet in the air waiving the Union Jack*
> *and Tricolour.*[4]

The Special Correspondent of *The Times* found himself in expansive, lyrical mood when contemplating the significance and
spectacle of the Indian Corps:

> *Today it has been my great good fortune to assist at the making of*
> *history. I have seen the troops of one of the world's most ancient*
> *civilizations set foot for the first time on the shores of Europe. I have*
> *seen proud Princes of India ride at the head of thousands of soldiers*
> *... fired with the ardour of the East, determined to help win their*
> *Emperor's battles or die ... I have seen welded before my eyes, what*

may well prove to be the strongest link in that wonderful chain
which we call the British Empire ....[5]

These were exotic sights, enthralling for the local French popu-
lace, who were, he continued, 'bent on having a glimpse ... so that
every second-storey window and every roof within a like area was a
coveted vantage seat'. There were not only Indians in this 'remarkable medley of soldiers', but also an influx of men from France's
empire in the shape of 'picturesque Zouaves and Turcos from
Algeria, white-turbaned swarthy Moors from Morocco, coal-black
negroes from Senegal'. Merewether was likewise astonished by the
pageant of peoples and races he encountered, as Marseilles was
shaken from its peacetime slumber to become a great garrison city
in which the tribes of empire were gathered for war, so different to
the city's pre-war image as the place of 'acrobats or lace-sellers on
the quays' or 'itinerant musicians with their eternal *"Funiculi,*
Funicula"'. As he observed, now 'everything was given over to war'.[6]
   One of the Indian regiments marched up from the port
behind its own band. Even cosmopolitan Marseilles had never
witnessed an army of turbaned Indians, wearing British uniforms
marching behind a band of Indian musicians playing the Scottish
bagpipes. A photograph of Sikh soldiers parading along one of
Marseilles's leafy boulevards was made into a postcard; its caption
(in English and French) read 'Gentlemen of India marching to
chasten German Hooligans'. This ancient city and its port –
where once the great battle fleet of the Ottoman Sultan Suleiman
the Magnificent had ranged in the mid-16th century – was once
again the temporary home of warriors from the East and from
Africa, its parks and open spaces transformed into military
encampments. The Indian troops of the Meerut Division were
allotted a site at La Valentine, to the west of the city, while the
Lahore Division did rather better, being billeted at the Marseilles
racecourse and the adjoining Parc Borély, one of the city's most
elegant destinations. As they pitched their tents and stockpiled
their equipment, *The Times* carried a message addressed to the
Indian Corps from 'King-Emperor' George V:

I know with what readiness my brave and loyal Indian soldiers are prepared to fulfil their sacred trust on the field of battle, shoulder to shoulder with comrades from all parts of my Empire. I bid you go forward and add fresh lustre to the glorious achievements, the noble traditions, the courage and chivalry of my Indian Army, whose honour and fame is in your hands.[7]

Most of the 24,000 soldiers of the Lahore and Meerut divisions were long-service veterans. A century later it is perhaps impossible to conceive how strange and disorientating they must have found their arrival in the south of France. These soldiers – most of them illiterate and from rural backgrounds, who had been born on the borders of poverty and were now summoned by their regiments within days of the outbreak of a war thousands of miles away – had crossed the 'Black Waters' of the deep oceans. These were men who had never left their homelands before and who, for the most part, knew very little about the outside world. Marseilles was to be their base port for the next fourteen months; it was to here that many of the wounded would return, and it was here where reinforcements would arrive.

Although in theory a sealed military area, the Indian encampment at the racecourse and Parc Borély became an unofficial tourist attraction. In the last days of September, Massia Bibikoff, a young Russian amateur artist in Marseilles, was given permission to enter Parc Borély in order to make a series of sketches.[8] She felt:

… as if I had been transported by a wave of a magician's wand into a world utterly detached from the present. Good Heavens, what variety everywhere and in everything! I arrived in the midst of the turmoil of pitching camp. All over the great race-course there was nothing but soldiers, carts, empty wagons, a few tents already pitched; and all this chaos with an accompaniment of shouts and orders and braying mules made up a scene so unexpected, so out of the common in our days, that for a moment I stopped involuntarily in breathless astonishment, feasting my eyes on the truly incomparable vista.

There was something of a mutual fascination between her and the Sikh soldiers she observed:

Seldom, save for the Cossacks, have I seen such fine men. There was not one less than some five feet eleven in height, slender, beautifully proportioned, while many are of real beauty. Their expression is gentle and remarkably sympathetic, especially when, as so often happens, a kindly smile lights up their bronze faces. But what can it be round their chins? I look closer and see their beards carefully twisted up and held in place by a thin string of black silk which they fasten behind their ears ... I asked a French interpreter about this, and he told me that no Sikh has the right to cut off a single one of his hairs from the day he is born. 'You will also notice, Mademoiselle, the iron ring which they have on their turban. It is the distinctive mark of their caste, which is forged from a dreadful weapon of old times, and is given them by the Guru or High Priest ... This is the special warrior caste ... If I looked at them with natural curiosity they repaid me in kind. From the moment of my appearance in their camp a great many of them stopped their work and crowded round.

Bibikoff's war diary is so strikingly honest and open that it is difficult to believe it was ever intended for publication. In it, she admits with girlish candour: 'The fact is I have lost my heart to these proud and gallant bronze-skinned soldiers.' She seems to have been completely carried along by the great outburst of excitement, nationalism, romanticism and orientalism that consumed Marseilles in the autumn of 1914; yet her diary is completely lacking in racial judgement; rather, there is a heartfelt fascination with, and sympathy for, the Indian soldiers.

Another visitor of note to the camp was Horace Grant, one of the famous Grant Brothers who became star staff photographers for the *Daily Mirror*. From the dates of his photographs, Grant seems to have arrived at the Marseilles racecourse on 30 September 1914. He took a whole collection of photographs that show the Lahore Division preparing itself for war. Using an old-fashioned panoramic camera, probably sited on the high vantage point of the nearby Château Borély, Grant produced a stunning overview of the scene that solidifies everything Bibikoff described and sketched. The panorama shows the racecourse as a sea of canvas, with long terraces of tents arranged like a series of New York city blocks. Overhead hangs a hazy layer of smoke from cooking fires. The racetrack itself has been transformed into an oval parade ground, around which the men of the Indian Corps can be seen training and marching. By the white rails of the track have been stacked rows of huge, tapped barrels that contain drinking water, and neatly arranged not far from them are the mountain-guns of the artillery batteries. On the fringes of the panorama are the mules shipped across the world to haul those guns into battle. Here and there are clusters of men engaged in rifle drill, while others sit on the grass, cross-legged, fitting car-tridges to the canvas belts of the machine guns. With the skyline of Marseilles beyond the edge frame, and only the mountains and the waters of the Mediterranean as a distant backdrop, it is a scene that could as easily be in Bombay or Calcutta.

Grant's panorama is also a picture of an army that is essentially Victorian, in both equipment and organization. Although the men of the Indian Corps were seasoned veterans, unlike most of the continental conscripts already at the front, there is still some-thing innocent about the scenes – the little clusters of figures, the dated artillery pieces, the mules and marching drills. The same innocence is palpable in images taken just weeks earlier of the Kaiser's army, marching off to an industrial war wearing their leather *Pickelhaube* helmets, and the legions of France in their blue tunics and red trousers. The Indian Corps had perhaps more excuse than most to be under-prepared, being an army created for frontier wars against rebellious tribes and now sud-denly hurried across oceans.

★

Seven weeks earlier, a meeting of the War Council was held at 10 Downing Street. In attendance alongside the Cabinet were General Douglas Haig, then commander of I Corps of the British

Expeditionary Force, and Lord Kitchener as the newly appointed Secretary of State for War. Both men had long predicted that Britain would, in the end, be forced to fight a war against Germany. Both had prophesied that when that war came, it would be long and protracted; in 1909 Kitchener had estimated that any war with Germany would last at least three years.[9] At Downing Street on 6 August, as plans for the deployment of the British Expeditionary Force (BEF) took shape, Kitchener called for the mobilization of the Indian Army. Orders were to be issued for the call up of the 3rd Indian Division (renamed the Lahore Division) and the 7th Division (which became the Meerut Division). The minutes taken confirm that Prime Minister Herbert Asquith believed his 'cabinet were averse to sending native troops too far West, and he felt very strongly that it was undesirable'.[10] However, the situation in France was so grave and the warnings of a long war had such an impact that the plan agreed was for the two Indian divisions to be dispatched, in the first instance to Egypt, and there readied for potential use in France. The next day King George V issued a formal pardon to all men of the Indian Army currently absent without leave or in a state of desertion, giving them until October to hand them-selves in. It was on 8 August that the newly named Indian divisions received orders for mobilization and the chaotic scramble to assemble men, arms and equipment began.

The scenes in the two ports of embarkation, Bombay and Karachi, were as frenetic as those at the various regimental head-quarters, military cantonments and railway stations. Units were forced to depart only partially formed, others could not get all their officers to the ports of embarkation before their transports had to depart, and some British officers were on leave in Britain or in transit when the call came. Likewise, Indian officers and men who were on leave in their remote home villages could not easily be contacted. Despite the best work of the army and the Indian railways, many regiments left only partially equipped, in the hope that the mess could be sorted out at their destination – and where that would be was still uncertain too. As the transports were loaded in Bombay, the enterprising management of the Taj Mahal Hotel offered white officers a preferential rate to bring in custom.[11] Sepoys – the ordinary Indian privates – and Indian officers were not similarly welcomed; they stayed in camps or in the warehouses by the docks. On 24 August the first ships of the Lahore Division sailed from Karachi. As the troops had not been informed where they were heading, there were constant rumours: that they were being sent to Egypt to guard the Suez Canal, then that they were to be stationed in Malta to free up white British soldiers for deployment in Europe. There was also a pervasive fear within the army, and among India's ruling elite, that if the Indians were intended to fight in Europe the war might be over before they could make their presence felt on the battlefield.

The departure of this great armada of transport ships and escorts represented a profound break with British imperial tradition. The Indian Army had fought beyond the borders of the Raj before, but never in Europe. Its soldiers had recently, and controversially, been denied the opportunity to prove their valour during the Second Anglo-Boer War in South Africa (1899–1902). But now, within two days of Britain's declaration of war, the decision had been made to prepare them for a role on the European continent, in a conflict in which Britain itself was imperilled and in which they would face a white enemy. While the architects of the modern Indian Army had never had any difficulty envisaging Indian troops doing battle with Russian soldiers in the valleys of Afghanistan, they had rarely imagined them at war in the heart of Europe against a Western European foe.

The decision was down to simple arithmetic. In total numbers of fighting men, the Triple Entente powers – Britain, France, and Russia – had the advantage over Germany and Austria-Hungary; but the British Expeditionary Force dispatched to Rouen and Boulogne on 12 August was, by the standards of the great conscript armies of the continental powers, minuscule. Whereas the German Army was 1.9 million strong and the forces of Austria-Hungary 450,000, the British Expeditionary Force fielded just 70,000 men, albeit superbly trained and experienced ones. The

British Indian Army, though, was the largest volunteer army in the world, with 150,000 of its 240,000 men ready for immediate service.

That the Indian Corps was ultimately deployed in Europe, rather than sent to garrison the Middle East or the Mediterranean, was decided by the flow of events during their transit. The war in the West rapidly descended into a series of almost daily crises and reversals for the French, British and Belgians. The German war plan – the famous Schlieffen Plan – appeared to be unstoppable and the Kaiser's army nearly invincible. Fortresses designed to halt armies – some of them recently re-designed, re-armed and reinforced – were either bypassed or crushed (in some cases literally) by guns of unheard-of calibre and destructive power. What mattered now were not fortifications but men and their rapid deployment. At the Battle of Mons, on 23 August, the BEF had crashed headlong into a German force that was overwhelmingly superior in size and firepower. Despite the legendary marksmanship of the British troops, they were forced back into a desperate retreat. What Britain needed from its Indian Army in 1914 were simply men – to hold lines, plug gaps and halt German assaults with rifle fire and bayonets.

Germany had been far better prepared for war than any of its enemies; however, that preparedness relied on a short war in the West. Germany's chief enemy appeared to be time: the more of it that elapsed, the more Britain and France would have the opportunity to draw men and materials from their empires, and the more prospect there was that Russia would be able to fully mobilize its vast army and place its semi-feudal economy on something approaching a war footing. The long continental war that Kitchener and Haig had prophesied was exactly the war that Germany desperately sought to avoid, for in such a conflict Britain would adapt its industries to war production, strangle German trade and imports with the iron tentacles of the Royal Navy, and recruit an army large enough to play a full role alongside France and in concert with Russia (in the east).

By mid-September, the French counter-thrust on the Marne ended any hopes of success for the Schlieffen plan. Germany's generals and armies responded by adapting and improvising with a series of frantic assaults, beginning a pattern of failed out-flanking movements followed by desperate entrenchments to secure ground taken. Mile by mile during this 'race to the sea', the trenches of the Western Front were born. But while there was still hope of outflanking the British and French, the Germans kept attacking. It was into the eye of this tempest that Britain flung its Indian troops. By the time they reached the Suez Canal, all talk of their spending the war standing guard over that water-way, or garrisoning islands in the Mediterranean, had evaporated, as the British Army confronted arguably the most desperate situ-ation in its history – just over the Channel.

★

As the flotilla of ships carried the Indian divisions to France, the decision to deploy the Indians was transformed – organically, as well as by propaganda officers – into a dramatic demonstration of all that was right and moral about the British Empire. A degree of war euphoria, imagining the future heroic service of the Indian troops, took hold in both India and Britain. The dispatch of the Indians was taken by journalists and politicians in both London and Delhi as proof that the ties that bound the British Empire were stronger than ever, and were set to be further strengthened by the shared experience of the war. It was believed that this great imperial adventure, in which Indians and Britons would fight side-by-side, presumably in equality, would usher in a new age of cooperation and mutual respect. On 31 August 1914 *The Times* painted a vivid picture of India's 'Eagerness to Serve in Europe':

> *India has thrown herself energetically into preparation for war, and a wave of ardent loyalty is sweeping over the country. The presence of British Indian troops in the fighting line, accompanied by their own Princes was the one thing necessary to seal India's passionate devo-tion to the empire in the noble and heroic struggle now going on.*[12]

A similarly effusive editorial by the *Calcutta Bengali* read:

> *We desire to say that behind the ranks of one of the finest armies in the world there are the multitudinous people of India, ready to co-operate with the Government in the defence of the Empire which, for them means, in its ultimate evolution, the complete recognition of their rights as Citizens of the finest State in the world … in the presence of a common enemy, be it German or any other power, we sink our difference, we forget our little quarrels and close our ranks and offer all that we possess in defence of the great Empire to which we are all so proud to belong, and with which the future prosperity and advancement of our people are bound up. India has always been loyal in the hour of danger.*[13]

In his short but perfectly timed tract *India and the War*, Sir Ernest Trevelyan, a Calcutta high-court judge, claimed that in the India of 1914 all 'Distinctions of race and creed have disappeared at the first suggestion of danger to the empire. Hindus, Mohammedans, Parsees and Buddhists are all uniting.'[14] And the Viceroy of India informed the Secretary of State for India on 8 September 1914 that 'There is a wave of loyalty, instinctive and emotional loyalty, which has swept over the people of India.' He added that even among 'the Indian educated classes' there was 'a loyalty based on reason and the recognition of facts … It is sensible of the undeniable benefits conferred by British rule.'[15]

The British press was fascinated, too, by the fact that the fighting men of India had marched to war with the blessings and the financial assistance of the so-called 'Native Princes', through whom one-third of India was indirectly ruled via a patchwork of treaties and agreements. In August 1914, George V sent a message to the 'Princes and People of My Indian Empire' appealing to both for assistance and loyalty. The response was immediate and unequivocal.[16] The princes fell firmly behind the war effort, and they raised vast amounts of money to equip and supply the Indian Corps. Some princes personally volunteered for service. The viceroy happily informed London that:

The Rulers of the Native States in India, who number nearly seven hundred in all, have with one accord rallied to the defense of the Empire and offered their personal services and the resources of their States for the War. From among the many Princes and Nobles who have volunteered for active service, the Viceroy has selected the Chiefs of Jodhpur, Bikaner, Kishangarh, Rutlam, Sachin, Patiala, Sir Pertab Singh, Regent of Jodhpur, the Heir Apparent of Bhopal and a brother of the Maharaja of Cooch Behar, together with other cadets of noble families. The veteran Sir Pertab would not be denied his right to serve the King-Emperor in spite of his seventy years, and his nephew, the Maharaja, who is but sixteen years old, goes with him.

When the viceroy's telegram was read in the House of Commons the following day, Andrew Bonar Law, Conservative Party leader,[17] asked if the government was 'taking every possible step to have the message circulated throughout the whole Empire?' The backbench MP William Thorne even called for a copy of the telegram to be sent immediately to the Kaiser.[18]

As war euphoria took a firm hold in both Delhi and London, the rallying cries of the newspapers and the politicians were reinforced by a chorus of voices emanating from penny pamphlets that were rushed into print. The Christian philosopher Edwyn Bevan, perhaps the most eloquent of the pamphleteers of 1914, published his impassioned tract *Brothers All: The War and the Race Question*, arguing that the deployment of Indian troops to Europe represented not simply the rejection of an outdated racial taboo but was also the mutual will of the peoples of both Britain and India. Railing against the attempts of German propagandists to portray it otherwise, he wrote:

To our enemies the disregard of the 'colour bar' in the combination against them is a matter for reproach. We know already that they charge us with disloyalty to the cause of European culture, and we must be prepared to hear the charge flung against us with still greater passion when the war is over, and echoed in German books for generations to come ... As a matter of fact, there is nothing very new or strange in the employment by a civilized Power of alien troops, as a weapon … If we were merely using Indian troops in the same way, without any will of their own, there would be nothing so very remarkable in it … What gives the moment its significance is that the presence of these Indian troops does not represent solely the purpose of England. It represents in some degree the will of India. However the complex of feelings which we describe as 'loyalty' in India is to be analysed … behind the Indian troops there is the general voluntary adherence of the leading classes in India, the fighting chiefs and the educated community, to the cause for which England stands.[19]

India's 'leading classes', its growing professional and political elites, hoped the war would lead to change of some sort. M.K. Gandhi, at that time in London, was among the many who believed that Indian participation in the war would be rewarded with some form of self-government, and he and others threw their efforts behind the troops. The moderate Indian National Congress was fully supportive of the imperial war effort and deployment of Indian soldiers to the Western Front, and the viceroy's telegram of September 1914 duly expressed British thanks for the loyalty and assistance of a long list of Indian political, religious and civic organizations.

★

The Indian Army that was encamped at Marseilles in autumn 1914 had been designed, carefully and over time, to fight and win small colonial wars in India, or in other flashpoints of empire. From the 1860s onwards, it had acted as the 'fire brigade' of the British Empire, dampening down revolt and discord wherever needed.[20] It was not equipped – as General Haig knew all too well – for a war in Europe, despite the strong pre-war urging of more far-sighted generals cognizant of the danger posed by Germany.

It was also a hybrid, multi-ethnic, multi-faith, multi-racial, multi-faceted entity, the product of several cultures. The Raj (or Crown Colony of India, sometimes called the Empire of India) encompassed modern Burma, Pakistan and Bangladesh too, while the kingdoms of Bhutan and Nepal, home to the Gurkhas, were also under Raj domination. A large proportion of the Indian soldiers who landed in Marseilles in 1914 were therefore from villages and cities that are today no longer in India itself. But this is not to say that it was a cross-section of the Raj's 300 million people. To understand its make-up in 1914, it is necessary to understand the impact of events almost sixty years before.

The Indian Army was a force shaped, above all, by the history of the Indian Mutiny of 1857, a crisis that grew into a war of independence against British rule in India, which in those pre-Raj days was still in the hands of the East India Company.* It was led by regiments of the Bengal Army of Northern India, and was sparked by an array of relatively minor grievances, some of them long-standing, many of them caused or exacerbated by a sloppy lack of concern for the religious sensitivities of both Hindu and Muslim soldiers; but it spread and mutated, becoming a civil and military uprising, and it came close to breaking Britain's hold on the subcontinent before it was suppressed in 1858. Much of the army remained loyal to the British, and both Muslim and Hindu regiments fought alongside British forces against the rebels.

The consequences of the rebellion – other than the brutal suppression and punishment of the defeated and captured rebels – were not only the end of East India Company rule and the creation of the Raj in its place, but far-reaching army reforms. A Royal Commission, led by the Secretary of State for War, recommended the disbandment of the regiments that had mutinied, a reduction in the size of the Indian Army overall and a full reorganization of recruitment policy. The British came out of the Mutiny with a changed mindset, one that came to see the ethnic and religious diversity of India as the key to imperial security. Race and ethnicity, whether real or confected, were to become regarded as the guarantee of military loyalty. As the mutinous regiments were disbanded, often leaving the loyal soldiers literally weeping,

* The Indian Mutiny is referred to in modern India as the Indian Rebellion or the First War of Indian Independence.

recruitment was expanded among those peoples who had remained loyal, most notably the hill tribes of the Punjab.

These policies were reinforced in the later decades of the nineteenth century by the emergence of ethnography as an accepted science. Building on accepted 'scientific' assumptions and India's existing ethnic and caste differences, ethnographers (most of them amateurs) concluded that only *some* of the peoples of India were 'martial races' – and here they used words like 'race', 'clan', 'tribe', 'people' and 'class' almost interchangeably. Whole swathes of the Indian population, they concluded, should be rejected for military service not just because they were deemed untrustworthy, but also because they were innately 'passive' or effeminate. Ethnography reinforced empirical theories emerging from 1857, and so groups like the Punjabis – both Muslims and Sikhs – that had proved their worth by remaining largely loyal in the Mutiny were now awarded the stamp of approval as 'martial races'.

Ethnography in India was underwritten by what is today called 'geographic determinism', the belief that the climate and topography of a region shape and meld the characters and cultures of its peoples. In this view, the millions of Indians from the broad, warm plains of southern India as well as those from Bengal and the Deccan Plateau had, over generations, been rendered passive and effeminate by their soporific climate.* (Indeed, in 1881,

---

* The natural corollary of the British belief that some tribes or races were naturally noble, war-like and dependable was that others were considered to lack those qualities. There were those peoples who, while not simply being written off as potential recruits, represented such a confluence of negative qualities as defined by British ethnography that they needed to be specially categorized and closely monitored – and, if necessary, suppressed. The Criminal Tribes Act of 1871 stands alongside the martial-races theory in the history of applied ethnography. This Act built upon previous legislation to define a handful of India's minorities as innately criminal. They were, in this conception, literally born criminals. Among the tribes targeted by this legislation were some of India's nomadic, itinerant peoples, notably the Gypsies, whose lives of constant movement and palpable independence jarred with the ambitions of imperial order and control. They were not alone; British legislation also defined the Badhaks, Dakoo and Kuzzak peoples as criminal tribes.

Lord Roberts, one of the early architects of the recruitment of 'martial races' and commander-in-chief of the Madras Army, concluded that in courage and physique 'the sepoys of lower India are wanting. No amount of instruction will make up for these shortcomings.'[21]) Conversely, the men of the hills of the north, where the winters were cold and the land only marginally productive, were regarded as being toughened by their environment and rendered war-like by geography, isolation and competition for scarce land and resources.[22] The Gurkhas of mountainous Nepal were cited as the perfect example of a warrior race, a people who had been tempered by the harshness of their environment. Yet, to enable these distinctions to work, facts on the ground that appeared to contradict the theory were expunged. Ethnic groups that had little in common were amalgamated into larger, simpler categories, and some groups were even invented to help the theory along. The Gurkhas were never one people but rather a group of Nepalese clans; the reasons why some other Nepalese clans were *not* considered martial was not always clear or rational – especially when inter-marriage and migration blurred the boundaries. Likewise, the term 'Dogras', used by the British right up to the First World War to describe men from hill tribes in eastern Punjab, was a British invention.[23]

The application of simple categories from the martial-races theory provided a means for young British officers, arriving in India for the first time, to make sense of the complex mass of peoples, faiths, cultures and languages of the subcontinent; indeed, it had already been conveniently codified in a series of recruiting handbooks written by officers. Among the first was Eden Vansittart's 1890 *Notes on Goorkhas,* which was designed to assist recruiting officers in distinguishing genuine Gurkhas from the (presumed to be) lesser tribes of the Nepalese hills. Nine years later came P.D. Bonarjee's *Handbook of the Fighting Races of India,* which was followed in 1911 by the classic work on the subject, Major George MacMunn's *The Armies of India.* MacMunn, whose work was still in print in the 1930s, was not a man to mince his words. 'It is one of the essential differences between the East and the West,' he pronounced,' that in the East, with certain exceptions, only certain clans and classes can bear arms; the others have not the physical courage necessary for the warrior.' [24] He explained that:

> ... to understand what is meant by the martial races of India is to understand from the inside the real story of India. We do not speak of the martial races of Britain as distinct from the non-martial, nor of Germany, nor of France. But in India we speak of the martial races as a thing apart and because the mass of the people have neither martial aptitude nor physical courage ... the courage that we should talk of colloquially as 'guts'.[25]

In MacMunn's analysis, it was not a matter of class and status; rather, India's history as well as its climate and topography had made some races martial and others effeminate. India's ruling peoples he tended to discard as the 'effeminate intelligentsia'. 'It is extraordinary,' he lamented:

> ... that the well-born race of the upper classes in Bengal should be hopeless poltroons, while it is absurd that the great, merry, powerful Kashmiri should have not an ounce of physical courage in his constitution, but it is so. Nor are appearances of any use as a criterion. Some of the most manly-looking people in India are in this respect the most despicable.[26]

'The existence of this condition,' he complained, 'much complicates the whole question of enlistment in India.'

By 1914, the army's faith in the idea of the martial races had, if anything, become even more deeply ingrained. The commander of the Indian Corps, Lieutenant General Sir James Willcocks, and J.W.B. Merewether, whose account of their time in France and Belgium was the most comprehensive, were adherents. Willcocks was an extremely senior soldier, experienced in Britain's colonial campaigns; he was well respected and highly motivated. He was also a great believer in his Indian troops. Merewether was likewise a champion of the Indian soldier. In an appendix to his 1918 *The Indian Corps in France* he offered his readers a glossary of each of the martial races, beginning with an explanation that the great bulk of India's people were 'without physical courage and unfit for any military service'. He went on to sketch out the various 'types' within the Indian Corps of 1914, being particularly impressed with the Sikh from the Punjab: 'generally a fine tall man of strong physique and stately bearing, with the manly virtues inculcated by his religion strongly developed ... The chief traits of the Sikhs are a love of military adventure and a desire to make money.' The Jats – a Hindu people – he described as 'tall, large-limbed, and handsome, and remarkable for their toughness and capacity for enduring the greatest fatigue and privation', in addition to which during the Indian Mutiny 'they distinguished themselves greatly against the rebels'. The Pathans – from what is now Pakistan and Afghanistan – were 'tall handsome men', identifiable by an 'easy but swaggering gait – that speaks of an active life among the mountains'. However, while the individual Pathan was 'an ideal raider or skirmisher, full of dash', Pathan units in the army were 'often wanting in cohesion and power of steady resistance, unless led by British officers'. Afridi soldiers (also from the modern Afghan–Pakistan border area) Merewether believed were 'ruthless, treacherous and avaricious'. But, he reassured his readers, 'If you can overcome this mistrust, and be kind in words to him, he will repay you by great devotion, and he will put up with any punishment you like to give him – except abuse.' For Merewether, it was the Gurkhas who represented the highest perfection of the martial races of India. While he complained that they all looked the same, he was adamant that there was 'much about the Ghurkha which especially appeals to the British soldier; his friendliness, cheeriness, and adaptability make him easier to get on with than other classes'. Finally there were the Muslim soldiers from the Punjab, whom Merewether saw as 'all-round soldiers with an attachment to their officers which is proverbial. They may, on the whole, be said to be steady and reliable – rather than brilliant in any particular respect.'[27]

The army that sat preparing its weapons and unloading its stores in Marseilles in 1914 was a direct product of this complex history and system of classification. It was made up only of men from the martial races and dominated by soldiers from the clans and hill tribes of the Punjab – Sikhs and Muslims – and Gurkhas from semi-autonomous Nepal. There were also Pashtuns, warriors from the lawless and infamously ungovernable tribal regions that still span the border of Pakistan and Afghanistan, whose fathers and grandfathers had once determinedly fought the British.

*

While the martial-races theory explains the ethnic composition of the Indian Corps, the culture that existed within the army was a product of other lessons learnt since 1857. Eventually the British did examine the Mutiny and its causes with a degree of self-criticism and self-awareness. Perhaps as powerful as the urge to disarm and marginalize the 'disloyal' ethnic groups within the Indian Army was a determination never to repeat the shoddy cultural insensitivity and bureaucratic carelessness that had underlain the Mutiny.

The Indian Expeditionary Force that came to France was thus to be a unique cultural institution. It was a force in which every British officer was a career soldier, who lived in India on a semi-permanent basis. Each British officer was expected to learn the languages of the men under his command and to do so to a high level. Respect for the religions of India was now central to innumerable aspects of the force, and the army accommodated prayers and holy festivals of men from all the major religious groups of India. Even amid the extreme conditions that prevailed on the Western Front, Willcocks ensured that his Muslim troops were able to observe Ramadan, while his Sikhs received 3,000 sets of bracelets and religious daggers, specially made for them in Sheffield.[28] The sensitivities around diet were also meticulously adhered to. Horace Grant's photographs of the Marseilles encampments show men newly arrived cooking chapatti bread on the racecourse, as well as sacks of flour and giant brass storage pots which held *dhal* (lentils) and *ghee* (butter). To provide the men with meat, British Army quartermasters set out to buy thousands of goats – an animal whose meat offended neither Hindu nor Muslim. When it was calculated that to feed the Indian Corps on goat meat for just a few months would require the slaughter of most of the goats of southern France, a British mission was dispatched to neutral Spain and to Corsica, to buy up thousands of goats. The French government agreed to waive import duties. A grateful soldier of the Indian Corps wrote that 'animals intended for the food of Sikhs are slaughtered by a Sikh by a stroke of a sword on the back of the neck, and those intended for Muslims, by a Muslim in the lawful way, by cutting the throat. Our [employers have] made the most satisfactory arrangements.'[29]

Culturally, this was an army in which there was a degree of mutual respect and cooperation between the races, and between white officers, Indian officers and men. It had a powerful *esprit de corps*, and the British sense of nationalism and loyalty sat relatively comfortably along the Indian notion of *Izzat* – an Urdu word meaning honour and reputation, of both soldier and family. The status of families in their home villages and towns could be built on the service records of their sons. The martial-races theory had, to some extent, been internalized by the favoured tribes, who came to identify themselves as warrior peoples too, for whom military prowess and martial honour were essential expressions of their ethnic identity. Indian soldiers who served in the First World War expressed repeatedly in their letters the desire to prove their loyalty and demonstrate their military skill. Many (but not all) regarded courageous war service as their manifest duty. As men who had 'tasted the king's salt' – enjoyed the wages and the comforts of military service – they were now expected to pay with their service and their blood. The army reforms after 1857 coupled the concept of *Izzat* with the idea of empire and the 'king-emperor'. Indian soldiers in their letters repeatedly referred to 'our government' and the need to show loyalty to it. Others mentioned the awe and reverence they had felt in the physical presence of the king-emperor during his visit to their camps in December 1914. Recalling the effect of George V's visit to India for the Grand (Delhi) Durbar of 1911 – the lavish ceremony to mark the king-emperor's recent coronation and to witness confirmations of India's loyalty – Willcocks felt that:

> *Men who had never dreamed of seeing their Emperor in person, saw him with their own eyes, knew him to be a living entity, and went away feeling themselves sharers in an unequalled Empire. It is not too much to say that the King's visit did more to bind to the Throne in loyal bonds the Indian Army than any triumphs won by the greatest of India's former Emperors. Only those who know India and its people, and know them well, can understand the magnitude of the event.*[30]

Bound together by these shared memories, sentiments and traditions, the Indian Corps of 1914 was a well-ordered, cohesive and self-confident institution; what it was not, though, was an army materially prepared for industrial war.

The immediate military effectiveness of the Indian Corps as it arrived in Marseilles was undermined by a scarcity of equipment, in part a consequence of the speed of its deployment. September and October 1914 were, thankfully, unusually warm, and the fact that the Indians were still wearing their thin tropical uniforms was not an immediate problem. Attempts to equip them with warmer winter kit at Marseilles were incomplete. The Gurkhas were issued with woollen vests, but other units left Marseilles with little in the way of new clothing. There were other, potentially more serious, problems with equipment, and here the Indian Corps was the victim of history. Ever since 1857 the British had ensured that the Indian Army was always one generation behind in weaponry. However, on arrival at Marseilles the Indian troops were ordered to hand in the older rifles with which they had fought the whole of their careers – the Mark II Lee-Enfield – and were re-equipped with the latest Mark III models, weapons of the same pattern as the rest of the British Army. The new rifles had a more sophisticated sighting system and were more powerful. These were small differences, which the highly skilled marksmen of the Indian Corps could master; but adjusting to them would require a little time and practice. The plan was to give the Indians several weeks to train with their new weapons, and Horace Grant's panoramas show clusters of men undergoing rifle drill. His more intimate portraits show Sikh troops sitting on the grass, examining their new Lee-Enfields and surrounded by neat stacks of the rifles. However the growing emergency at the front meant that some units of the Indian Corps were to be thrown into battle with weapons of which they had almost no experience; some fired them for the first time at living German targets.

———————

ORLÉANS STATION, OCTOBER 1914. The platforms of Orléans Station are crowded with tall stacks of ammunition cases, watched over by Sikh guards. Mules, horses and artillery pieces are unloaded from long trains, as Indian and British soldiers work together to transfer war materials from railway wagons to mule carts and army trucks. Until this month, only the inhabitants of Marseilles have witnessed the Indian Corps at first hand. But now the scale and complexity of their deployment can be witnessed by the engine drivers, conductors, and platform workers of the French national railways. By day and night, in tiny provincial stations, smoky marshalling yards, echoing platforms and goods depots, the railwaymen of France peer into steamy carriages, catching sight of exotic uniforms and unfamiliar faces. They catch snatches of foreign languages and the smells of unknown foods.[31] Since the outbreak of war in August they have grown accustomed to the armies of their own empire – the men from Morocco, Tunisia and Algeria, Berbers and Tuaregs, in short red tunics and voluminous blue trousers, others wearing white headdresses. They have met the 'Black Guard Dogs of Empire', the French

West African *Tirailleurs Sénégalais*, tall and thin men wearing red fezzes. But *Les Hindous* of the Lahore Division, wearing British uniforms and now heading north from Marseilles to Orléans in their thousands, are an even more exotic and unfamiliar sight. Between the railhead and their new, temporary, camps the Indians receive another rapturous welcome, as the people of Orléans line the main boulevards in crowds three- and four-deep.

Accompanying them until mid-October is photographer Horace Grant, who creates a photographic record of their march to war – photos that have an immediacy, informality and poignant detachment of a later era: an Indian officer, with an open face and a self-conscious smile, holds a bouquet of flowers given him by one of the townswomen; the same officer, bouquet still in hand, passes a group of schoolgirls who have been excused from their lessons, the little girls in white frilled dresses, the younger girls held aloft by the older ones, huddled together and waving energetically, their expressions a mixture of excitement and wide-eyed curiosity; women in long Edwardian dresses standing in doorways, wicker baskets on their arms, offer fruit to the passing Indians; a line of Indian troops march past a throng of French soldiers – older, portly men in uniform, most probably reservists – who eagerly shake the hands of the tall thin Sikhs, all smiling warmly and laughing at the strangeness of their sudden proximity. One of the last photographs shows two columns of Sikh troops marching away from camera, up a wide French country avenue.

On 18 October, the Lahore Division will board trains from Orléans to be rushed north to their assembly points at Arques and Blendecques, in Nord Pas-de-Calais.

———— • ————

On 19 October 1914, as the Indian Corps were moving north, the fighting that was to coalesce into the First Battle of Ypres had already begun. British forces, badly depleted and having suffered heavy casualties, were outnumbered by the Germans two-to-one:

fourteen German divisions to seven British.* The British sector consisted of a series of trenches, outposts and *ad hoc* defensive positions in a bulge around the Belgian town, which was just a few miles behind the fluid front line. To the north were the desperate remnants of the Belgian Army, about 60,000 men. To the south were the French.

On 22 October, four days shy of a month since the *Castilia* and the *Mongara* had docked at Marseilles, the first Indian units arrived at the front, driven there by a fleet of red London buses, still emblazoned with advertisements for 'Buchanans Black and White Whisky' and 'Carters' Liver Pills'. Later that day, they entered the line between the villages of Messines and Wijtschate (Wytschaete), to the south of Ypres.[32] 'Asia had dropped into Europe,' wrote General Willcocks later, adding:

> ... *the descendants of Timour, of Guru Govind, of the ancient Hindus, had come to fight the Huns on the historic plains of Flanders. Seventy miles in a direct line from us lay the immortal field of Waterloo; seventy-five miles away were the cliffs of Dover. The man must have been carved out of wood who would not have rejoiced at his good fortune; the heart atrophied that did not beat the faster at the thought that he was given a chance, however humble, of taking his share in the greatest conflict of all times.*

To the frustration of Willcocks, the Indian soldiers were not deployed as a unified force to defend a sector of their own, but rather thrown into battle piecemeal wherever they were needed. The first to see action were the 57th Wilde's Rifles, who were sent to hold the lines developing around Wijtschate, on one of the low ridges to the east of Ypres upon which the defence of the whole sector rested. Although only about 150 feet above sea level at their highest, these innocuous features in an otherwise drab and monotonous landscape were critical to British hopes of halting

---

* The British were also able to call on three divisions of dismounted cavalry – horses were of little use in the muddy morass of Flanders.

the German advance. If the ridges were captured, then Ypres itself could not be effectively defended, and if Ypres were to fall the Channel ports were at risk – a prospect that would spell disaster.

The fighting around Ypres in October and November 1914 was, however, not *yet* trench warfare. The lines consisted of isolated strongpoints, machine-gun emplacements and improvised slit trenches, hastily scratched into the wet Flanders mud. There were dangerous gaps between the strongpoints or beyond the sweep of the defending machine guns. The potential for the enemy to outflank or slip between positions was ever present. At times, German attacks came across whole sectors of the front and threatened to simply overwhelm the defenders; at others, the Germans launched targeted offensives aimed at specific objectives, on a narrow front. The whole area was within the range of the German guns, and hour by hour the ancient town of Ypres, with its Cloth Hall and ramparts, was being pounded into rubble.

A platoon of the 57th Wilde's Rifles was photographed on the edge of Wijtschate on 22 October – dug in, along an avenue still lined with undamaged trees, the buildings behind intact with even their windows unbroken. Civilians can be seen loitering outside the 'Nieuw Staenyzer' Inn, a landmark that still 'exists' today; like the rest of the village the present version is a simulacrum of the original, for Wijtschate was obliterated by the war. Captured and recaptured, it was shelled to dust and mud over the course of four years. The men of the 57th Rifles were among the last troops to see Wijtschate as an intact and pristine settlement. By the standards of later defences, their improvised position hardly qualified as a trench; they were lined up in what is little more than a narrow ditch, the earth from their meagre excavations piled up to form a forward parapet, on which they rested their rifles. The photographs show smiling faces and clean uniforms. A British officer wears a turban held on his head by a non-regulation chin-strap: while the white officers were expected to learn native languages and immerse themselves in the cultures of their men, clearly they were not required to master the near-miraculous art of wrapping a turban. With trees still in leaf, the

Indians' thin khaki drill uniforms do not yet seem out of place, despite the coming winter.

It was on 22 October, too, that the first Indian soldier to fall in the First War World was killed, in the Ypres sector. The name of Naik Laturia from the Punjab is one of the 54,896 etched on the walls of the Menin Gate in Ypres, the memorial for those whom, as the dedication reads, 'the fortune of war denied the known and honoured burial given to their comrades in death'.[33] Eight days later, the 57th Rifles with the 129th Baluchis (who had entered the line on 23 October) were subject to an intense German bombardment, followed by a determined assault on their positions. One company of the Rifles was decimated by German machine guns; in another company there was only one survivor, Jemadar Ram Singh, who was badly wounded. The 129th Baluchis suffered comparable losses. The ground into which they dug their positions was so heavily waterlogged that their fox-holes filled up with water. Only by adding parapets were they able to find anything approaching proper protection from enemy fire; but there was, as yet, no barbed wire to prevent the positions being rushed by determined attackers.

The German forces confronting the Indian Corps had both artillery support and hand-grenades; the Baluchis had little of the former and none of the latter. The Indian Corps learned how to resort to improvised grenades made out of jam tins filled with dynamite. General Willcocks was well aware of the disadvantages under which his troops were fighting:

> ... our men had to face mortars, hand-grenades, high explosive shell, and a hundred other engines or contrivances of war, with which they themselves were not provided. Here were these gallant fellows just arrived and exposed to every form of terror, and they could reply only with their valour and the rifles and two machine-guns per battalion with which they were armed, and yet they did it.[34]

The list of medals and commendations presented to the Indian Corps by the end of 1914, alongside the equally long list of

casualties, speaks of the intensity of the fighting. Outnumbered
at every turn, they desperately held onto their allocated positions. In one engagement, Havildar (Sergeant) Ganga Singh of
the 57th Rifles killed five German soldiers (some accounts say
six) with his bayonet, until it finally broke in two; he then fought
on with a sword until he collapsed, wounded. Incredibly, he was
later found alive when the trenches he had so ferociously
defended were re-taken by the 5th Dragoon Guards. On 31
October the 129th Baluchis were in the line near the village of
Hollebeke, another of the tiny settlements that blocked the road
to Ypres. Two isolated Indian machine-gun crews faced down a
German attack. After one gun was put out of action by artillery
fire and the crew killed, Sepoy Khudadad Khan kept the last gun
firing, until his position was overrun and all his comrades killed.
Khan was severely wounded and only survived by hiding under a
pile of bodies and crawling back to his regiment after nightfall.
He was evacuated to England for treatment and awarded the
Victoria Cross, the first Indian soldier to receive the highest
military honour. It is today on display in Khan's home village,
Dab (Chakwal), in Pakistan.

Towards the end of November, the rumble of artillery bombardment faded and the sounds that echoed across the flooded
fields of Flanders were those of digging and hammering as hundreds of thousands of men shored up, extended, deepened and
reinforced trenches. The end of the First Battle of Ypres was
bought about by the onset of winter as well as by the physical and
material exhaustion of the armies. The British lines had held, and
German efforts to break through had been thwarted – but at a
terrible cost. The Indian Corps were now holding ten miles of the
twenty-five-mile British sector. With no flank left to turn there was
– literally – no room for manoeuvre. Willcocks concluded that the
Indians had suffered a 'toll as heavy as the British units had to pay,
and yet comparatively it was heavier, because it was taken from
men who had had no opportunity of realising what it was all
about'.[35] In Parliament, the Under Secretary of State for India,
Charles Roberts, acknowledged the Indian contribution to both

the stabilization of the front in Europe and the war elsewhere, telling the House: 'we have warmly to recognise the substantial help which is being afforded to the Empire by the appearance of Indian troops at a great number of points in a battle line which extends from Tsingtau [*sic*] to La Bassée across the breadth of three Continents.'[36]

★

At the end of 1914, General Haig declared himself convinced that the Indian line on the Western Front was 'now very strong'.[37] Nevertheless, the Indian Corps, like the British Expeditionary Force beside which they had fought, was a shadow its former self. Around a quarter of the men who had landed at Marseilles in September and October had received wounds of some sort. Under the acute stress of combat, some had inflicted wounds on themselves in a desperate bid to find a way out of a hellish and seemingly hopeless situation – and a few of those found guilty of this breach of military law were executed. In all, 2,000 Indians had been killed.[38]

The winter that set in following the crisis of autumn 1914 was one of the coldest ever recorded in northern France and Belgium. It was then that the Western Front truly became the troglodyte world of legend. Men stood for days in freezing mud, were driven to despair by lice and beset at night by rats that ate the flesh of the dead. It was the winter of 1914–15 that brought into common usage the terms 'trench foot', 'trench coat' and 'shell shock'.[39] In photographs of the Indian Corps from that time, men sit wrapped in blankets, huddled in trenches that are filled with mud and topped by snow. They appear more like vagrants or desperate refugees than soldiers. One wrote home that 'The trench is 260 miles long, it rains without ceasing every day and many men have been killed by the cold.'[40]

There is a palpable defensiveness in the memoirs of Willcocks, and to a lesser extent Merewether, about the performance of the Indians in the freezing temperatures they were forced to endure. In the months and years that followed their withdrawal from France and Belgium a mythology grew up that Indian troops were incapacitated by the cold conditions. One proponent of this idea was the author Arthur Conan Doyle, who wrote in 1916 that the Indians had been 'fighting at an enormous disadvantage'. In his view:

> *There are inexorable axioms of Nature which no valour nor constancy can change. The bravest of the brave, our Indian troops were none the less the children of the sun, dependent on warmth for their vitality and numbed by the cold wet life of the trenches ... To stand day after day up to his knees in ice-cold water is no light ordeal for a European, but it is difficult to imagine all that it must have been to a Southern Asiatic.*[41]

That men who had never set foot on the subcontinent should believe that the brown-skinned soldiers of India were incapable of tolerating a winter in northern Europe was understandable. Less comprehensible is that British officers, who knew India and had personal experience of its enormous range of temperatures and altitudes, could remain convinced that men from the snowy Kathmandu Valley or the hills of the Punjab would find the temperatures of a Flanders winter intolerable. The martial-races theory postulated that those same tribes had been toughened and hardened by their lives in the mountains, yet somewhere on the sea passage from Bombay and Karachi that element of the theory seems to have been thrown overboard. All soldiers, of all races, on all sides, suffered in the winter of 1914–15; none of the armies was properly equipped or effectively prepared to face the conditions of modern war combined with that harsh winter's effects. If the men of the Indian Corps suffered more than most on the Western Front – and there is some reason to believe they did – it was because they were the most poorly outfitted for the conditions, still in their utterly unsuitable drill uniforms. Yet they were still infantilized as 'children of the sun'.

As well as being forced to endure the cold, every soldier on the Western Front in those first months of the war suffered from a profound sense of dislocation; but again perhaps none more so than the Indians. First, there was the matter of geography: many of the Indian soldiers, men from illiterate or semi-literate village societies, had little grasp of it. They understood that their deployment was beyond India, 'across the Black Waters', to what was dimly understood as *vilayati* – a Hindi word which in vague terms meant variously 'abroad', 'Europe' or 'Britain' (and from which the army slang 'Blighty' evolved, meaning Britain). The Indian troops were well aware of how long their journey to Marseilles had taken. They had passed through the Red Sea, the Suez Canal and had seen Egypt, before steaming across the Mediterranean, all the time their understanding of the world growing. Yet so much of this experience was novel that it was difficult for them (as it would be for any first-time international traveller of the period) to gather a proper understanding of the distances over which they had moved. Sir Walter Lawrence, a brilliant civil servant who became Kitchener's eyes and ears on all matters relating to the Indian Corps in Europe, wrote to the War Secretary in December 1915 explaining that Indian troops on the front were prone to confuse Austria for Australia and mixed up Paris and Persia.[42]

The factor that was most disorientating for the men of the Indian Corps was, though, neither the cold nor the confusions of geography; it was the nature of their deployment. In the chaos and crisis of October and November 1914 they had been thrust into battle according to the flow of the fighting. As units headed up from Marseilles and became available, they were used to patch holes in the line or block German advances. They were consequently not given the opportunity to fight as a cohesive unit. This went against the powerful sense of community – something akin to village or even family life – that underpinned the complex culture of the Indian Corps. It was diluted and undermined when they were thrown into combat in small groups, among other units of which they knew nothing. While it may have been an unavoidable necessity, the practice had an impact on the morale of the men. As Willcocks explained:

They had been trained to the understanding that when they entered into the battle it would, at any rate at first, be alongside the British comrades with whom they had served in Brigades in India; these at least they knew and understood; and even if this could not be, they had every reason to believe they would at least fight as battalions under their own Commanding Officers; but here none of these things happened. They were split up in fragments, and that they stood the strain as well as they did is the best possible testimony to their discipline and efficiency. As an Indian officer said to me on the return of the two battalions to re-join their Headquarters, talking about the separation from their own Brigades, 'Sahib, they do not understand anything about us'.[43]

A related issue was the impact of losing a high proportion of the corps' white officers. The once almost unquestioned view, pervasive at the time, was that Indian units became passive and directionless without a British voice to give orders. In February 1915 the Office of the Censor of Indian Mails referred to men 'feeling their own helplessness without their British officers'.[44] And Willcocks was adamant that 'even the best Indian troops in European warfare need the leading of British officers'.[45]

More recently, historians have overturned that view. There is much battlefield evidence and many contemporary accounts that contradict or refine that assessment. The loss of officers impacted on all armies. What can be said of the Indian Corps, given their environment of the Western Front, is that the loss of white officers dramatically increased a sense of isolation. The bonds between officers and men were unusually close within the Indian Army, and the loss of each white officer had the effect of reducing the number of men in the combat zone who spoke the languages of the sepoys and who were thus able to translate and explain to the men something of what was going on around them. Simple cultural questions as much as life-and-death matters on the battlefield could be answered and addressed only by these bilingual officers. To envisage oneself in the sensory chaos of the Western Front, amid the thunder of guns and the clatter of rifle fire, accompanied by the babble of incomprehensible European languages, with critical orders shouted in foreign tongues, is to understand a little of what the Indian Corps experienced, as the officers, among whom they had lived and fought for years, fell around them. Such officers were literally irreplaceable.

As casualties mounted, the Indian Corps struggled to replace losses of all ranks, not just white or Indian officers. Through its supply lines, which stretched back to its base port of Marseilles, the corps did have access to reinforcements sent from India. However, many of the fresh troops who arrived on the transports were men over the age of forty, who had not been dispatched in August 1914 as they were not deemed fit enough for active service. Some were even thought unfit for service in India itself. Willcocks, quoting a damning official report, was distinctly unimpressed:

> One lot of reservists was classed as 'utterly valueless'. Of nineteen men of one regiment 'three are fit for service'. Another small draft was classed together as 'particularly poor', of another out of thirty-five men sent 'ten are plague convalescents who have not even yet recovered their full vigour'. One boy was referred to as fourteen years of age, and another as a 'mere child'. Of a draft of sixty-seven reservists nine were of 'indifferent physique' and fifty-eight 'unfit'. India appeared anxious to fill up sorely-needed shipping with trash of this sort.[46]

This lack of adequate reserves was, ironically, in large part a consequence of the martial-races theory, which concentrated recruitment within a restricted pool of communities and ethnic groups. An Army Commission, headed by Marshal Lord Nicholson, had concluded before the war that the recruitment structure of the army was too restrictive to satisfy the demands of 'serious war'. By 1915 the Commission had been proved correct.[47] The result was that the sway of the martial-races theory partially gave way, as the British were forced to widen the pool of recruits.

★

In one important respect, the men of the Indian Corps differed from other non-European imperial subjects who fought in the First World War. Most of the latter left little individual trace. Men recruited from pre-literate societies fought their wars in literary silence, leaving no written accounts for historians to weave into the broader history of the conflict; often the only voices to be preserved are those of their European commanders or the occasional journalist who took an interest in men from far-off nations. There are just a handful of full war memoirs written by colonial and non-European troops. The men of the Indian Corps are, though, the great exception. Thousands of their letters were intercepted, censored and analysed by a special army office, the Censor of Indian Mails, which was established in late September 1914 and headquartered soon afterwards in Boulogne. It was run by a British captain, E.B. Howell, formerly of the Political Department of the Indian Civil Service. While most of the original letters are lost, the transcriptions of the thousands that were typed up, translated into English, and subjected to the Censor's comments did survive the war. They remain, carefully preserved, in a series of huge ledgers in the British Library.

Although, as scholars like Santanu Das have pointed out, these intercepts should be read with care, and deciphered and understood within a wider cultural and military context, they offer a large window onto the inner lives and experiences of the Indians who fought for Britain. The letters are composed by men in the trenches, or in camps behind the lines, or men lying wounded in hospitals in France and Britain. Written to family and friends, they carry the men's views of the war, their perception of the scale of the fighting, their cultural observations of the British and the French, their reactions to enemy propaganda and their often distorted understanding of the geopolitics behind the war. As many of the sepoys in the Indian Corps were not literate, they dictated the letters to literate comrades or army scribes, who at times added their own literary flourishes. Although there were attempts to keep the activities of the censors secret, the soldiers did understand that their letters were being read by higher authorities, and by men who were not their trusted officers. Initially the Office of the Censor of Indian Mails was created to monitor letters arriving from relatives in India; but quickly it began to intercept and censor outgoing mail, and by March 1915 was processing 20,000 outgoing letters each week. There were only four officers to do this work, and unsurprisingly they complained of sore eyes and lack of sleep; as Howell explained in one of his reports, 'the mere deciphering of any one letter may be as much as two hours work'.

The most powerful of the letters tend to be those that attempt to convey the shock of modern warfare. In January 1915 one soldier wrote: 'It is very hard to endure the bombs, father. The bullets and the cannon balls come down like snow. The mud is up to a man's middle. The distance between us and the enemy is 50 paces.'[48] The same month a sepoy serving at the front described the ferocity of industrial firepower in terms that his family in rural India would understand: 'The enemy's guns roasted our regiments even as the grain is parched. Corpses lay on every side and the blood ran in little rivers.' A letter rejected by the Censor for its honesty as much as its tone of desperation read:

In this sinful country it rains very much and also snows and many men have been frostbitten. Some of their hands and feet cannot be stretched out and those who stand cannot sit down again. Some have died like this and some have been killed by bullets. In a few days you will hear that in our country only women will be left. All the men will be finished here. Thousands and hundreds of thousands of soldiers have been killed. If you go onto the battlefield you will see corpses piled upon corpses so that there is no place to put hand or foot. Men have died from the stench. No-one has any hope of survival. The whole world is being brought to destruction. I cannot describe the war because 30,000 men have been destroyed and 20,000 more will be destroyed.[49]

Again and again, Indian soldiers attempting to describe the scale of the slaughter fell back on metaphors and similes taken from the rural life they knew – grain being tossed on to the fire, or walnuts falling from trees. One described the dead as being the 'chaff upon the threshing floor'; a Muslim sepoy felt he and his comrades were 'like goats tied to the butcher's stake. We have no idea when he will come, and there is no one who will release us. We have given up all hope of life.'[50] More graphically still, one letter reads: 'Men are dying like Maggots. No one can count them, not in thousands but in hundreds of thousands.'[51] The more religiously focused of the men compared the battles in France and Belgium to the legends of their faiths or the gargantuan struggles of the Hindu epics – 'the name of Germany is breathed throughout the world like the name of Harankash' (a devil), or in the description of German aircraft as being 'like the great bird of Vishnu'.[52] 'Having seen this war, all that has been written in Mahabharat and in the Ramayan is altogether true,' reported one sepoy to his family.[53]

The intercepted letters of the Indian Corps became what Howell called a 'trench telescope', a mechanism by which the army authorities were to spy on the Indian troops, understand their concerns, seek out signs of disloyalty or sedition, and watch for any falls in morale. Critically, the army aimed to determine how far the Indian Corps could be pushed before the men gave up hope and morale collapsed. Howell was always looking for signs that some critical breaking-point was being approached. At the start of January 1915 he began to note that while many soldiers were still determined to remain dutiful to 'our government', they also showed 'a tendency to break into poetry which I am inclined to regard as a rather ominous sign of mental disquietude. The number of letters written by men who have obviously given way to despair has also increased both absolutely and relatively.'[54] An Indian civil servant of some standing and a man proud of his linguistic abilities, Howell went to pains to translate the Urdu poetry – perhaps as an intellectual exercise as much as in the hope that it contained anything of real intelligence value. In the same report Howell noted that:

A number of letters from men with their units at the front have been examined. They betray undeniable evidence of depression ... The tendency during the month has been for these letters to increase in numbers and in length. At the same time there has been a marked change in tone. Grumbling is still almost entirely absent and there is never a hint of resentment or anti-British feeling ... but adverse signs are growing more conspicuous ... What is more significant still is the proportion of letters which, though they show no sign of giving way to despair or of any faltering in devotion to duty, yet give a melancholy impression of fatalistic resignation to a fate that is regarded as speedy and inevitable. This feeling too appears to be spreading.[55]

In the minds of Howell and the army authorities, the information gleaned from the Indian letters also allowed them to use the Western Front as a grim testing ground for the martial-races theory. Howell commented on how each of the various 'races' were behaving under the appalling pressure of combat, and whether they were coping in accordance with the general theory. In one report, of the weekend of 27 March 1915, he noted:

It is instructive to note the different behaviour of men of different races under the pressure of despair. The Sikh either grows sulky or tries to malinger. Vide extract No. 55 of the last collection. The Muhammadan of the Punjab wails and prays. The Pathan also believes in the efficacy of prayer, but being a man of quicker wit than either of the others in some cases seems definitely to have taken means to help himself.[56]

The spread of negative stories from the front, through soldiers' letters, into the high-recruitment areas of the subcontinent such as the Punjab and the Kathmandu Valley was a cause of concern. Many men were from military families, and some attempted to warn their brothers not to join up, or if they were already in the army to do all in their power to be avoid being sent to France. An Afridi wrote to his brother, who was attached to another regiment: 'If we can find a way, I will save myself ... If you can, do not remain fit for duty Become "sick" & do not go to the battle again.' Other messages attempted to convey the same meaning while avoiding the attention of the Censor. Howell was at times apparently impressed when such warnings were hidden or coded behind metaphor. In his report of 13 February 1915 he wrote:

> *Orientals excel in the art of conveying information without saying anything definite. When they have a meaning to convey in this way, they are apt to use the phrase 'Think this over till you understand it', or some equivalent, as an indication that they are doing so to the reader. This phrase is becoming increasingly common in letters from all sources.*

A powerful and recurring theme in the censored letters is a deep sense of grievance against one particular British policy, which exposed a cultural gulf between the British and Indian soldiers. By the traditions absorbed in the Indian Army, when a man had fought bravely and been wounded in battle he had fulfilled his obligations as a warrior: it was inconceivable that a man who had suffered wounds and acquired *Izzat* should be nursed back to health only to be sent, once again, to face mortal danger. To the British, however, convalescence and recovery of a soldier naturally led to his return to active duty. The British Army seems to have struggled to fully grasp the extent to which Indian soldiers felt differently about this. As early as December 1914 Howell was warning his superiors how deeply this grievance was felt. One Garhwali soldier, recovering from his wounds, had asked: 'How can a man be saved? There is no chance of it. Even he who has been wounded and recovers has to go again and fight?'[57] A week earlier, a Sikh soldier had written to his brother, telling him: 'Since the 10th February I have returned to the trenches. For the wounded who recover to some extent are sent back there. My heart is very sorrowful.'[58] This point of deep cultural difference was one that the post-1857 Indian Army had never been able to smooth over, and it was thrown into stark relief by the devastating casualty rates experienced on the Western Front.

★

By the spring of 1915 British and Indian forces had managed to hold the line and helped halt all German attacks on the Ypres sector. They had, however, never been on the offensive, other than small-scale, localized counter-attacks. In December 1914, Russian attacks on the Eastern Front had drawn German troops away from France, thereby increasing the potential impact of any Allied attacks in the West. Determined to show that the British Army was a full partner, and unwilling to wait for the arrival of Kitchener's volunteer armies then in training, the commander of the BEF, Sir John French, began preparations for the first British offensive. It was to be launched against Neuve Chapelle, a small and insignificant village about twenty miles from the town of Ypres, which had found itself sandwiched between the two sides in the autumn of 1914.

Today, Neuve Chapelle, with its terraces of small houses and simple brick church, has been rebuilt. The fields in which so many men fought and died are once again used to grow cabbages. Other than the war memorial in front of the church and the brass cartridge cases brought to the surface each year by the plough, there is little to indicate that a battle was ever fought here. Yet even before the offensive of 1915, blood had already seeped into the soil around Neuve Chapelle. The Indian Corps themselves had taken the village in October 1914, in the period when possession of it passed back and forth between opposing armies. In spring 1915, though, Neuve Chapelle was firmly in German hands, at the centre of a salient – a protrusion of the German lines into British-held territory, a great looping bulge on the map that almost invited attack. Even more enticingly, beyond Neuve Chapelle was the valuable high ground of Aubers Ridge, and beyond that the strategic town of Lille, a major German transport hub. Neuve Chapelle stood opposite the heart of the sector of the British line that was defended by Indians, who would inevitably become part of the offensive. When the attack did come, almost half of the attacking troops would be Indians.

The Battle of Neuve Chapelle is what passed for a success on the Western Front of 1915 – a success with a cost. The plan was for the 7th and 8th British divisions and the Indian Corps to take the village and then push on into the open country and, if possible, seize Aubers Ridge. Preparations were extensive and professionally handled, with many of the lessons learnt in the eight months of war effectively applied. There was a great concentration of firepower and stockpiling of shells. The Royal Flying Corps won, and then maintained air supremacy, and used that advantage to take good aerial photographs of the enemy positions, which, along with the clear and plentiful maps that were made available to the attackers, helped the British to plan and execute the assault. Yet, despite all the careful preparation, the battle itself followed the same basic plot as almost every battle fought in France and Belgium until 1918, with short-term success being squandered, allowing the enemy to regroup and prevent a 'breakthrough'.

Following a bombardment by 500 guns of various calibre – the biggest British operation of the war to date – the assaulting forces, both British and Indian, attacked together at 8:05 on the morning of 10 March. The artillery had done its job, the enemy barbed-wire entanglements were mainly broken, and some of the front-line trenches had been pulverized. The Germans were outnumbered by about seven to one, by an attacking force that was 60,000 strong. German troops who had endured the worst of the bombardment were in a state of shock, dazed by the unexpected onslaught, and the British and Indians took their trenches within the first hour of fighting. After a scheduled pause to allow for a second artillery bombardment, the British troops, along with men from both the Lahore and Meerut divisions, attacked the village itself. Fighting house-to-house, they forced out the Germans, who retreated to rear positions. In a story that was soon being told and retold in the British newspapers and illustrated magazines, Rifleman Gane Gurung of the 2nd Gurkhas launched a one-man assault on one house from which German troops had been firing. Moments after bursting through the front door, Gane, all five feet and two inches of him, was seen marching out of the house with his rifle trained on eight German soldiers whom he had taken prisoner, each of them far larger than himself. Gane was later awarded the Order of Merit for his actions.

After the Germans had been driven from the village, they were pushed into a nearby wood, the Bois de Biez. When the British and Indian forces reached the wood it was dusk, and although the area appeared to be empty, suggesting the German forces had fallen back, the situation was highly dangerous and uncertain. The flank was exposed, and with no confirmation that the Germans had fled it was decided not to enter into the woods but rather to hold positions along the Layes Brook, a ditch that offered the only cover in the cabbage fields between the village and the Bois de Biez. There, they dug in for the night. Under the cover of darkness, however, the Germans brought up significant reinforcements and constructed their own new line of defences both in the woods and in front of them. At dawn, the men of the Garhwal Brigade saw the newly excavated German trenches, complete with barbed wire and machine guns. The assaults that followed against the improvised German defences resulted in heavy Indian losses. A German counter-attack on the third day was similarly calamitous, resulting in considerable losses among the Germans.

The day after the battle, a Sikh officer of the 47th Sikhs, a regiment of the Lahore Division, wrote to his father in the Punjab describing his experience:

> … since the 10th we have been engaged in a great battle. At first the enemy were in some places two hundred yards from us, in others three hundred, & in others one hundred yards & over against them were we. We killed them & they killed us. Now we have begun to advance & have beaten the enemy well back. In these last two days our people have driven the enemy far back and have taken about 3000 prisoners. Of course we lost heavily, but we also inflicted heavy loss on the enemy & we are in possession of three covering trenches. The enemy are now very frightened. When our men without a thought for their own dear lives & loyalty to our dear

1. Arthur Wardle's 1915 recruitment poster, commissioned by Britain's Parliamentary Recruiting Committee, plays on the sense of imperial brotherhood that was fostered on the outbreak of war to encourage the 'young lions' of the dominions to come to the aid of 'old lion' of the British motherland.

2. The *War Deeds of Mike Mountain Horse*, created on calfskin, is a pictorial narrative of the war experiences of one Native Canadian, reflecting a tradition of the 'story robe'. In twelve panels, it records his exploits from August 1917 to the Battle of Amiens in August 1918. (From the Collection of the Esplanade Museum, Medicine Hat, Alberta, Canada.)

3. The racecourse at Marseilles (30 September 1914), transformed into a vast encampment for the Lahore Division of the Indian Corps, as photographed by Horace Grant. Their arrival brought new sights, sounds and even (**4**) the smells of new cuisine. As their commander Lieutenant General Sir James Willcocks (**5**) observed, 'Asia had dropped into Europe.'

6. Jemadar Mir Dast, the Pathan soldier presented with the Victoria Cross in August 1915 for his heroic actions in the Second Battle of Ypres. He is photographed, during his recuperation, on the terrace of the Royal Pavilion Hospital, Brighton.

7. Convalescing men of the Indian Corps pose with staff in the cavernous space beneath the dome of Brighton's Royal Pavilion (1915), after the building became a much-publicized military hospital.

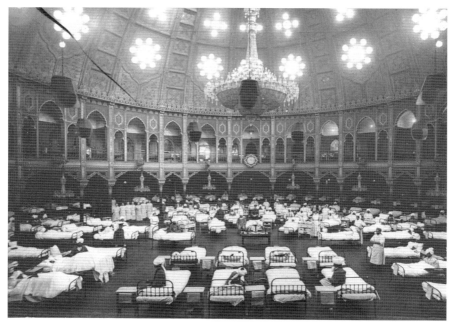

8. Indian Corps men and officers of the 2/2nd Gurkhas, 9th Gurkhas and 6th Jats who have been mentioned in dispatches (1915). Even white officers sometimes donned turbans.

9. Members of the Indian Corps prepare to leave Europe in late 1915, their faces and uniforms more creased than those of the smart arrivals of late 1914.

10. Alhaji Grunshi of the Gold Coast Regiment, pictured with his medals in a grainy photograph of 1918. He is credited with firing the first shot of any British-commanded soldier in the war.

11 (*opposite, centre*) *Askari* and their German officers on parade at the colonial station in Ebolowa, German Cameroon.

12 (*opposite, below*) Indian fatalities following the Battle of Tanga in German East Africa (November 1914), where poor British leadership and effective German machine guns combined to deadly effect.

13. (*right*) General J.C. Smuts, the South African politician-soldier who led the multinational campaign to subdue German East Africa in 1915–16.

14. A few of the hundreds of thousands of carriers who toiled, and died, for both sides in the East African war. This group were serving Lettow-Vorbeck's German and *Askari* forces.

15. A poster (1918) in aid of German colonial war funds idealizes Lettow-Vorbeck and his smartly uniformed *Askari*, though by this time his ragged forces were depleted and diseased.

16. The postwar myth of Lettow-Vorbeck and his loyal *Askari* was reinforced by his book *Heia Safari! Germany's War in East Africa* (1920), written with Walter von Ruckteschell.

Government reach the enemy's trenches, the Germans in fear throw down their rifles & come running towards us with their hands up. Now we hope that victory is very near. I expect you will see your son very soon ... Our losses have been great, but we died doing a good work. On the 11th & 12th our losses alone were a captain killed, six British officers wounded, three Indian officers killed & six wounded, & many men were killed.[59]

A day later, Sepoy Bigya Singh, a Garhwali, wrote to his family boasting that 'our regiment has exhibited great bravery. The fame of Garhwals is now higher than the skies. One of the Garhwals, a Havaldar [Sergeant], has won the honour of the Victoria Cross'.[60] On 14 March, the day after the battle had ended, Sir John French felt able to cable the Viceroy of India that 'the Indian troops under Sir James Willcocks fought with great gallantry and marked success in the capture of Neuve Chapelle', although he also had to acknowledge that 'the fighting was very severe and the losses heavy'.[61] Over the course of three days' fighting the Meerut Division suffered 2,353 casualties and the Lahore Division 1,694. Total British casualties numbered 11,652.[62] While some of the attacking Indian troops were exhilarated by the battle, others were becoming convinced that they had no chance of surviving the war.* One Sikh soldier concluded to his father that 'There is no hope that I shall see you again for we are

---

* While Captain Howell monitored the Indians' letters and watched for signs of impending collapse, the British High Command set out to see what tactical lessons could be drawn from Neuve Chapelle. The costly, three-day offensive and the loss of momentum at the end of the first day should have been interpreted as a clear demonstration of how recent German military reorganizations had placed far greater agency in the hands of junior commanders on the ground, who were able to adapt to circumstances, withdraw, and call in reinforcements, while British forces wasted time awaiting orders from distant commanders who were all too often beyond the easy reach of communications. The British had misinterpreted those German reorganizations, which increased the firepower of each regiment while at the same tine lowering the head count, as evidence that Germany was running out of men. This was one of the greatest feats of wishful thinking in the whole history of the war.

as grain that is flung a second time into the oven, and life does not come from it.'[63] Another soldier, a Rajput, warned his family: 'Do not think that this is war. This is not war, it is the ending of the world.'[64]

Six thousand miles away in India, the recipients of the letters were drawing their own conclusions. Among the so-called martial races, rates of recruitment dropped dramatically, just as quotas were hugely increased. As each affected community learnt of the scale of the suffering that its sons and brothers were being exposed to – at the First Battle of Ypres during the winter and now at Neuve Chapelle – the flow of young men willing to join up dwindled. This was another factor that led the British to recruit from peoples they had not traditionally considered to be martial races.

As for the depopulated village of Neuve Chapelle itself, it remained under British control until 1918, when it was once more lost to the Germans – this time by its Portuguese defenders. Their austere war cemetery – yet another enclosed square of granite headstones and tended lawns – stands amid the drab cabbage fields on the outskirts of Neuve Chapelle, within view of the memorial to the missing of the Indian Corps.

———

THE ROYAL PAVILION HOSPITAL, BRIGHTON, 1915. In Britain's best-known building in the 'oriental' style, convalescing Indian soldiers sit in bath chairs on the lawns. The wards – laid out in the former galleries of the Royal Pavilion – are filled with rows of neat, iron-framed beds with white, starched linen. The beds are interspersed with elegant pot plants, and plentiful light streams in through tall windows. In each bed sits an Indian soldier in a white turban. Nurses and doctors flit between them, tending to the most needy. To assist in their recuperation, the patients are given access to the grounds, and twice a week they are graced by recitals played on the grand pipe organ built into the southern side of the Pavilion's great dome. There are also electric lantern exhibitions and endless visits from well-wishers. For those patients who are mobile, there is outside seating. For Indian NCOs there is a separate recreational suite of rooms; on the wall of one of these hangs a signed photograph of King George V.[65]

Since December 1914, those convalescing soldiers fit enough have been permitted to go on sightseeing tours beyond Brighton. There are visits to the Tower of London, London Zoo and the Natural History Museum, and trips to view Buckingham Palace, the Houses of Parliament and more sites besides. Some Indian soldiers ride the London Underground or visit Selfridges for an hour's shopping.[66] It is sometimes hard for them to take it all in. One soldier writes home: 'Today I saw a museum in which all the living fish of the world were kept in boxes of water, and a magnificent palace which cost millions of pounds.'[67]

Once discharged from their treatment, the soldiers are presented with a *Short History* of the Royal Pavilion, which, among other things, records the royal visit to the hospital on 25 August 1915, when:

> ... *the King and Queen by their gracious sympathy gave many wounded soldiers a proud and happy memory that will be handed down to generations. In many an Indian village in the years to come these soldiers, their fighting days long over, will talk to their children's children of the Great War. Their faces will then glow with pride as they tell of that day when they were lying wounded in a Royal Palace and the King and Queen came to their bedsides and spoke to them words of tender sympathy and cheer.*

———— · ————

Among the Indian casualties at Neuve Chapelle were 1,495 wounded sepoys and 36 wounded Indian officers. The most seriously injured of these men were evacuated to six military hospitals that had been established in southern England, at Milford-on-Sea, New Milton, Brockenhurst, Bournemouth and Brighton, where two hospitals were set up very near one another. These facilities were in addition to the field hospitals behind the lines, which received men straight from the battlefield, and the clearing hospitals in France.

The Indian military hospitals in England were to treat almost 15,000 wounded Indians. The biggest was the complex of commandeered buildings in Brighton, including an old workhouse, which came to be known as the Kitchener Hospital. At its height this was the largest of all the military hospitals in Britain, with 1,736 beds and, as *The Times* put it rather indelicately, 'an asylum for 20 insane'.[68] Not as large, but more significant in terms of its propaganda role, was the Royal Pavilion Hospital, established within the faux-oriental seaside retreat built in the 18th century for King George IV. With only 724 beds it was far smaller than the neighbouring facility, but its setting, under mock Islamic domes and minarets, seemed the ideal location not only to treat the Indian soldiers but to demonstrate to the wider world the high level of medical and pastoral care they were receiving in British hospitals. These men of India were, after all, being treated in a 'Royal Palace', or so the propaganda claimed.

In 1915 the Brighton Corporation produced a widely distributed pamphlet – *A Short History in English, Gurmukhi & Urdu of the Royal Pavilion Brighton and a Description of It as a Hospital for Indian Soldiers.* This expensively produced booklet detailed the many wondrous medical facilities and architectural delights of the Pavilion Hospital. The dome, beneath which a great circular ward for the Indian troops had been established, was described as 'a lofty, spacious building of beautiful proportions' and 'with its fine proportions and rich colouring now mellowed with age would form at all times a good subject for a painter's brush, and a specially striking one now when filled with wounded Indians'. The whole palace, as the *Short History* explained, had been designed by a 'distinguished architect [who] had studied in India and had studied Eastern Architecture', so that 'with its domes and minarets and Pavilion [it] might have been designed as an Indian palace'. Fashionable Brighton had been chosen by George IV as the site for his oriental folly in part because the king had been influenced by the contemporary belief in the regenerative properties of sea waters and sea air. Similar considerations had influenced the military authorities in 1914. Again, the prevailing belief that Indians struggled in the cold suggested that they should be accommodated only in the warmer parts of southern England. The *Short History* promised that 'Everything has been done to make the wounded Indians as comfortable and happy as possible. Not only do they live in a Royal Palace, but the splendid grounds which surround it have been reserved for them, which goes far to promote their quick return to health and strength.'[69]

'Naturally,' explained a reporter from *The Times* who toured the Pavilion Hospital in May 1915, 'the conduct of a hospital for Indian wounded is a much more complicated business than the conduct of a hospital for Europeans.' There was some truth in that observation. As in the Indian Corps itself, the hospital was organized along lines of religion and caste. A Sikh temple was improvised in a marquee erected in the grounds, while a makeshift mosque was built on the lawns in front of the dome, enabling Muslim patients to face east during their prayers under the shadow of an Islamic-style structure. Enormous energies went into preparing appropriate food for men of the various faiths, and the hospital had nine strictly separate kitchens. To supply them, and the kitchens of the other Indian hospitals, the India Office sourced and imported huge quantities of Indian foods – flour, *dhal* and *ghee* as well as various spices. The *Short History* boasted:

> There are proper caste cooks, with a head cook in charge of each kitchen … Orders that none but these cooks are allowed in the kitchens are posted on the doors in Urdu, Gurmukhi, and Hindi. The food of the Hindus is handed out from the store to the different head cooks by a high caste Brahmin. He, of course has nothing to do with the meat store as he cannot touch dead flesh … In every ward there are two water taps used only for drinking water, one for the Hindus another for the Mohammedans.[70]

The segregation of amenities extended to the provision of water taps and the slaughter of animals. No beef was permitted within the hospital, lest it offend the Hindus, and pork was likewise banned out of respect to the Muslims. The Indian wounded were also shielded from the proselytizing of Christian groups. When a supply of envelopes arrived from the YMCA bearing the initials of that organization, the Censor's office decided that the four offending initials should be removed from each envelope. Similarly, when Christian-themed books were found to have been distributed by presumably well-meaning visitors, this breach in protocol was looked upon dimly by the hospital authorities, who were desperate to avoid any suggestion that the patients were the subject of any unwanted missionary work.

Even in death the faiths of the Indians were accommodated. The cremation of the dead required by the Sikh and Hindi faiths was, in theory, prohibited by the Cremation Act of 1902. However, the Home Office waived the law and three traditional cremation *ghats* were constructed on the South Downs outside Brighton. Between 31 December 1914 and 30 December 1915, fifty-three Sikh and Hindu soldiers were cremated there, their ashes scattered on the waters of the English Channel. The site where the cremations took place is today marked by the Chattri Monument, which has become the site of an annual act of remembrance. Similarly a Muslim cemetery was established at Horsell Common, near Woking, where the only mosque in Britain had been built. The remains of nineteen Muslim 'Tommies' of the First World War still lie in the cemetery, which is accessed through a Indian-style pavilion gate. Other Muslims who died in British hospitals were buried at the Brookwood Military Cemetery in Surrey.

The medical facilities and the medical care of Indian troops at the Pavilion Hospital were just as good as those provided to British troops elsewhere and far superior to those the Indians had known in the regimental hospitals in India itself. The hospital had two operating theatres and X-ray facilities. Mortality rates were low and recovery rates high. There were plenty of staff members, many of whom were rushed in from India to work as orderlies, dressers, cooks and clerks. Their numbers were bolstered after November 1914 when a little-known Indian lawyer, living in London, had a letter published in *The Times* in which he appealed 'to the Indian young men residing in the United Kingdom to enlist without delay' to work as orderlies at the Indian military hospitals: 'In my humble opinion,' wrote Gandhi, 'it ought to be a proud privilege to nurse the Indian soldiers back to health.'[71] Two-hundred Indians who had been studying and working in Britain when war broke out responded to his appeal. They worked not just as orderlies, but also as interpreters, easing the flow of information between the patients and the medical staff.[72]

Patients' letters, also transcribed by the Censor of Indian Mails, suggest that the Indians, both patients and staff, were impressed by their surroundings and the medical facilities in Brighton. One soldier wrote home to his family from his bed at the Pavilion Hospital: 'Do not worry about me, for I am in paradise. The King came down here last week and shook hands with all the Indians, and asked each one about his wounds and sufferings and gave consolation to each.' At the end of January 1915 a medical subordinate, in a letter to a friend in India, wrote: 'In my opinion it would not be amiss to describe England as a paradise on earth. In the evenings we always go for a walk. The people treat us very well indeed. Men & women alike greet us with smiling faces and take great pleasure in talking with us.'[73] To ensure that the flow of such positive reports bound for Indian eyes continued unabated, the patients at the Indian Military Hospitals were provided with copious amounts of free writing paper and envelopes.

After four months of the hospital's operation, *The Times* was pleased to report that:

> All ... difficulties have been overcome ... The results are worth the trouble. They seemed a cheerful and kindly set these dark-skinned patients of many races and creeds, as, clothed in the same hospital kit as issued to the British wounded, but clinging always to their turbans or their long hair, they sit in the sunny gardens, or wait in

their turn for a 'joy-ride' and a visit to a cinematograph, or get their
strength back in light fatigue duty. The visitor feels in the atmo-
sphere the smooth running of a complicated machine.[74]

Yet the 'complicated machine' inevitably contained stresses on
the conventional relationships of empire. While the differences
of caste and faith within the Indian Army had been addressed
through the clever design of the converted buildings, and written
into the administrative cultures of the institutions, the relationships between colonized and colonizer were to prove more
difficult to sustain. The most acute issues were those connected
to the roles of women. Within months of its outbreak, the First
World War, like no event before it, placed colonized men in positions of contact and intimacy with white women – circumstances
that would never have been permitted within the colonies themselves. It also brought black- and brown-skinned men into contact
with working-class white women, a group who were largely absent
from the colonies, where menial work was done by local people.
As in the military zones behind the lines in France and Belgium,
where men of many races encountered local women as both civilians and nurses, the Indian military hospitals in Britain became
places in which the boundaries of race, power and sexuality
became disturbingly blurred. One taboo – against deploying
non-white troops in a war between white Europeans – had already
been broken; another great taboo of empire, the deep opposition – even visceral revulsion – against contact between white
women and non-white men was now under threat. A powerful
mystique had been deliberately built up around white women in
Africa and Asia, which placed them strictly beyond the reach of
male colonial subjects. (The relationship between white male
colonizers and local dark-skinned women was, by contrast,
frowned upon but tolerated as an inevitable by-product of the
imperial venture.)

Even before the hospitals were fully active, the idea of white
English nurses caring for Indian soldiers, with all the inevitable
intimacies that involved, was regarded as a matter of deep

concern – so much so that in November 1914 a directive of the Army Council banned the employment of white English women on wards where Indians were treated. Although the ban quickly proved unworkable, and some hospitals found reasons to side-step it, the compromise many institutions adopted was to permit white nurses to work on the wards but only in supervisory capac-ities – this was aimed as much at preventing them doing menial tasks for men who were their supposed racial inferiors as it was intended to reduce contact between the races. When, in May 1915, the *Daily Mail* published a picture of a white nurse standing by the bed of a wounded Indian soldier, a minor scandal erupted. The soldier in question turned out to be Khudadad Khan VC, the sepoy who had garnered his honour at the First Battle of Ypres; while there was no suggestion of any impropriety, the picture may have influenced the Army Council in its issuing of another order, a month later, for the removal of *all* white nurses from three of the Indian military hospitals. The army was, however, unable to enforce its rules on privately run facilities.

Army authorities were equally concerned about the other forms of contact between the Indian wounded and white women. The patients received a great number of visitors, including white women, many of them well-born ladies involved in charitable work. The greatest threat, however, was identified not as these middle- and upper-class ladies, but rather the working-class women of Brighton and the other hospital towns into which the patients made trips, usually under the watchful eye of British officers. As it had been hoped that the sea and sea air might in some way aid their recovery, it seemed perverse to deny Indians the opportunity to take walks along the sea front; but the excur-sions caused alarm. Outings to the cinema and theatre seemed equally fraught. The ever watchful Censor's office was alert to any encounters with, or opinions about, white women in the Indians' letters – despite the fact that most references were inno-cent in the extreme. One soldier wrote: 'The women here have no hesitation in walking with us. They do so hand in hand. The men so far from objecting encourage them.'[75] Another recounted how he was 'standing outside a shop when someone touched my cheek. I thought it must be some old dear friend; but when I turned my face who should I see but a lady with a grand dress on and an ostrich feather, laughing.'[76] Other Indians, far from being the potential sexual predators of the authorities' nightmares, were themselves scandalized by British sexual mores. A Maratha clerk at Bournemouth wrote to his friend in the Indian city of Sholapur, in March 1915, describing his acceptance of the shocking fact that 'The men & women of this country go about boldly hand in hand. We feel ashamed, but such is the custom of the country. It suffices if one has a very slight acquaintance. They even some with us [*sic*] walks thus.'[77] All three of these letters caught the eye of the Censor, and any mentions or subtle hints at intimacies between Indian men and white women were excised from the letters of both Indian soldiers and staff.

Back in the 1840s, Queen Victoria had taken against the Royal Pavilion as a summer retreat because it lacked the privacy she sought for her growing family. By 1915 the Indian patients at the Pavilion Hospital might well have felt themselves subject to a comparable level of intrusion. In its first months of operation it became something of a tourist attraction. Day-trippers came down from London to see 'the Indians', and tram rides along the sea front now had the added benefit of offering a clear, if fleeting, view of the Indians convalescing on the Pavilion's lawns. The authorities' solution to what was seen as excessive contact between the Indian wounded and the people of the hospital towns was to effectively turn the hospitals into closed facilities. Fences were built around the Pavilion Hospital, and the walls that already surrounded the Kitchener Hospital – as a former workhouse – were made more imposing by the addition of barbed wire. This, unsurprisingly, proved to be a less than insuperable obstacle to men who had months earlier stormed barbed-wire entanglements on the Western Front. Ultimately, at both the Pavilion and Kitchener hospitals, police guards were posted to keep the patients in and would-be visitors out. It took a contingent of forty-five policemen to keep the Pavilion Hospital sealed off from the people of Brighton. One hospitalized Sikh soldier complained to a friend serving in France at the end of January 1915: 'They do not let me go outside this hospital at all, nor do they allow even the men of one's own village [to] come in to see one. There are British soldiers posted as sentries all round the hospital who neither permit us to go out or outsiders to come in.'[78]

With these tensions and difficulties brushed under the carpet, the splendour of the Pavilion Hospital and the high quality of the medical care dispensed there, along with the demonstrable British respect for the religious practices of their Indian servicemen, was a propaganda image that the British and Indian governments were keen to broadcast. Newspaper reports and photographs of the Royal Pavilion Hospital were distributed among Indian units at the front and within India itself. Images of recuperating Indian troops also made their way into American news reports. Postcards of various agreeable scenes of hospital life were produced, and Indian soldiers, on being discharged at the end of their treatment, were from late 1915 each given a copy of the *Short History*, which had been produced 'solely for its effect in India', containing its full-page photographic plates of the exterior of the building, with Indian soldiers milling around in the foreground, and a two-page image of the sea of beds arranged under the great dome.[79] Every photograph reinforced the message that the king and queen cared so deeply for their Indian subjects that they had dedicated one of their palaces to their care. Thousands of copies of the *Short History* thus made their way back to India, in the hands of once-wounded soldiers or distributed freely by the India Office. It was available to residents of Brighton, too – but at a cost of a shilling.

★

On the second page of the *Short History* were full-length photo portraits of King George and Queen Mary, and pages 13–15 described their second royal visit to meet the Indian troops (25 August 1915), a much grander affair than their first visit in January 1915. By 1914, the 'royal' building was in fact owned by the Corporation of Brighton, and it had been Kitchener, not the king, who had pushed for it to be turned into a hospital for the Indians.[80] None of these complicating details was permitted to muddy the waters of an otherwise clear propaganda message. The high point of the king's second visit took place not beneath the great dome, but on the lawns outside the Pavilion. 'The King had come,' the *Short History* explained, 'specially to decorate with his own hands, for conspicuous gallantry in the field, ten of his wounded Indian officers and one Indian non-commissioned officer. It was royal weather, and the investiture took place on the lawns on the west of the Pavilion, where over 1,000 wounded Indians were gathered to greet their King-Emperor.'

At the ceremony of investiture the recipients of eleven honours were brought forward one by one. 'The first to be decorated was Jemadar Mir Dast, 55th Coke's Rifles who had already won the Indian Order of Merit in India.'[81] Before the 1,000 Indian patients, King George declared: 'I have already bestowed with my own hands two VCs on Indian soldiers and I give this third cross with infinite pleasure. I earnestly hope that you will soon completely recover from your injuries and that you will live long to enjoy your honours.'[82]

As the soldier had the Victoria Cross pinned to his chest, in the summer sun on the west lawns of the Royal Pavilion, on the southern coast of England, his brother Jemadar Mir Mast, of the 58th Rifles – also a decorated war hero – was in Germany, working as an agent for the enemy.

Five months earlier, both brothers had been in the trenches. In the build-up to the attack at Neuve Chapelle, British preparations – though successfully concealed from the enemy – could not but signal to British and Indian troops that a major action was imminent. Battered units of the Indian Corps, not long recovered from the battles of November 1914 and the privations of the winter, began to sense their chances of survival once again diminish. On the night of 2/3 March, twenty-three men of the 58th Rifles, all of them Afridis from the Afghan frontier regions, crossed no man's land and deserted to the Germans. They were led by Jemadar Mir

Mast. This defection at Neuve Chapelle would be the greatest breakdown in loyalty among the Indian Corps in the whole war. Captain Howell, as Censor of Indian Mails, was well aware that some units were under severe stress. Just over a week before, on 23 February 1915, he reported on the 'big picture' of morale within the Indian Corps, cautioning that while it was difficult to ascertain the morale of an army from its letters alone, 'I should certainly say that if the strain is not to reach breaking point the "door of hope" must be opened somewhere before long.'[83]

Many of the men who deserted were from the same village, and some were related to each other. To them, and to Mir Mast, preparations for Neuve Chapelle may well have been the final closure of Howell's 'door of hope'. The 58th Rifles had suffered as badly as any unit on the Western Front. They had taken part in numerous raids as well as larger assaults at Givenchy and Festubert. Their officers had been decimated, the regimental 'family' slowly disintegrating under the sheer weight of their losses. They had also demonstrated numerous acts of gallantry and fortitude in the face of constant bombardment in the Ypres sector. Mir Mast and another deserter, Azam Khan, had even recently won the Indian Distinguished Service Medal for courage in the face of the enemy. On 9 March 1915, while both men were in German hands, their names were appearing in the supplement to the *London Gazette*, listing them as soldiers to whom 'His Majesty the KING-EMPEROR has been graciously pleased to approve of his undermentioned Rewards ... for gallantry and devotion to duty whilst serving with the Indian Army Corps'.[84]

The obvious portents of another, and larger, attack might well have convinced Mir Mast and the others that there was no possible means of surviving the war other than to desert to the German lines. But there might have been other reasons. There was some speculation that the desertions had been motivated by aggrieved men who had been denied promotion. It also appears likely that the 58th Rifles had been exposed to anti-British and Indian nationalist propaganda in the form of leaflets that the Germans were managing to get across the lines. The details of

Mir Mast's interrogation by the Germans strongly suggest that he had seen such literature. Those interrogations were carried out by Dr Paul Walter, a former missionary who had lived in India and spoke the local languages, and who had been posted to Lille precisely to debrief and assess Indian soldiers who were captured or deserted. On 6 March, three days after having crossed over to the Germans, Mir Mast in his interrogation offered his advice to German propagandists, suggesting to Walter that the most effective message the Germans could disseminate in their leaflets was '"We'll give you a Mauser pistol and a good German rifle." That's enough, all of them will come.'[85]

Stunned by the scale of the defection, the British held an investigation, undertaken by the Indian Corps Intelligence and the British Army Court of Enquiry. It concluded that the desertions were sparked by personal grievances. However, as a precaution the British sent home some men who were related to the deserters as well as halting the recruitment of Afghans from the frontier provinces – and thereby opening up further cracks in the martial-races theory.[86] As the British were investigating the mass desertion, Mir Mast was proving his value to his captors and new employers, by sketching a hand-drawn map of the Khyber Pass, which lay near his family home in the Tirah Valley on the Indian–Afghan border. He listed the positions and gave the rough numbers of the British troops that guarded this critical imperial artery. His extraordinary journey was, in some ways, only just beginning.

★

Between the Battle of Neuve Chapelle and the end of the year, the men of the Indian Corps had much else to endure. Photographs of their units taken late in 1915 are a stark contrast to the images that streamed from the camera of Horace Grant over a year earlier. The men in the later photographs have lost their formality as well as their naivety. No longer a Victorian army, they stand together in huddled groups rather than military lines. No two uniforms are alike. White officers and Indians stand alongside one another, the boundaries of race temporarily blurred, perhaps by shared horrors. All of them stare the camera down, some accusingly, some with haunted expressions.

The truth was that the Indian army that had been dispatched from Bombay and Karachi in the frenetic chaos of August 1914 had, by the end of 1915, effectively ceased to exist. The loss of so many white multilingual officers had had deleterious consequences, as had the denuding of the corps' Indian officers. The reserves sent to fill up the ranks of the sepoys had, in many cases, been men whose physical condition said much about the enduring poverty that blighted the regions from which the martial races were drawn. Even those who were fit and strong could no more be compared to the veterans who had landed in Marseilles in 1914 than Kitchener's volunteers and Pals Battalions could be regarded as soldiers of the same calibre as the career professionals of the BEF, who had died in the fields and canal banks of Flanders alongside the Indians.

The Indian Corps' depletion over fourteen terrible months was not simply in the loss of any one class of officer or soldier; it was in the catastrophic disruption to a whole *ecosystem* of relationships, traditions, expectations, unspoken understandings and cultural awareness that had, somehow, enabled the whole bizarre structure to work, and work well enough for it to be transplanted to Europe and thrust into a war the nature of which no nation or military commentator had accurately predicted. It has been argued that the Indian Corps probably never really recovered from its losses at Neuve Chapelle. Yet what really undermined its capacity as a fighting unit was the sheer relentlessness of the men's deployment. Just a month after losing the 4,047 casualties of Neuve Chapelle, they were again involved in action, at the Second Battle of Ypres. There they fought not in a long-planned and well-prepared British offensive, but as part of the desperately cobbled together defensive force rushed to the battlefield following the devastating German gas attack of 22 April. Two days later, the units of the Lahore Division were marched north to the Ypres Salient; they arrived on 25 April, and the next day were

involved in a concerted counter-attack that was itself checked by
more German gas. It was there that Jemadar Mir Dast won his
Victoria Cross, and there that the Indian Corps suffered another
3,899 casualties – around 20 per cent of those who had taken
part in the battle killed, wounded or missing. On 31 August 1915,
with the war one year and one month old, the Indian Corps
counted its losses. By that date, after having fought in the First
and Second battles of Ypres, and at Neuve Chapelle and innumerable smaller operations and defensive actions, 3,970 men
had been confirmed killed and 19,976 had been wounded.
Another 4,360 were 'missing' and 586 listed as 'other deaths'.
The previous day, as these figures were tallied, orders had been
issued for yet another attack in which the Indian Corps was to
play a role.

The mining town of Loos was renowned even before the war
as a bleak and dismal place, and after a year of fighting it was
pock-marked by artillery. The great slag heaps, the metal towers
of the pit heads and the ruins of the town itself made it one of
the worst places on the whole of the Western Front to launch an
attack; yet it was here that the British and Indian forces were to
assault the German lines while the French attacked to the north
in Artois. The Germans had learnt the lessons of the first year of
the war well, and they were already moving towards a system of
'defence in depth', which meant that attacking Allied troops who
breached the front lines would be drawn into killing zones commanded by German artillery and machine guns, many of them
concealed behind concrete emplacements. At Loos they had
established observations posts on the great mounds of mining
waste, from which they had commanding views of the battlefield.
To increase their chances of success, the British decided they
would retaliate in kind for the Second Battle of Ypres and use
their own chlorine gas in the attack.

The Battle of Loos would be the first major outing for units of
Kitchener's home-grown army of volunteers – fresh and enthusiastic, but untested. This time, having been involved in almost all
of the most costly British engagements of the war so far, the

Indian Corps was to have only a supporting role. The Indians were to take part in assaults of the first day, 25 September, as well as launching a series of feints intended to draw the German defenders away from the main areas of the line to be assaulted. That first day was as disastrous as those that followed. Once again, a lack of independence of action given to soldiers and officers on the ground undermined careful British preparations. The British gas was released at the allotted time of 05.50, but only because the Royal Engineers manning the cylinders were given no discretion on the matter – a critical flaw when dealing with a weapon carried by the changeable wind. Much of the gas blew back into the faces of the attackers. Ten minutes later, one British unit, fighting alongside the 2/3rd Gurkhas, attacked the German lines, but the wire had not been cut by the British artillery bombardment, and they found themselves funnelled towards the German machine guns, which fired blindly into the smoke and gas but with devastating results. The next day, men of the Garhwal Brigade made enormous progress, but, as was the case throughout the battle, the reserves were too far behind the lines to build on initial success. It was for this miscalculation that the British commander-in-chief, Sir John French, was to be removed from his post and replaced by General Haig.

It was at Loos that the full potential of the Maxim gun was unleashed. From a range of 1,500 yards, the German guns stopped the British attack in its tracks. The machine guns overheated from constant firing, and estimates vary, but they might have killed or wounded over 8,000 of the 15,000 attackers. German machine-gunners, appalled by the effectiveness of their work, were reported to have ceased firing when the British began their retreat, unwilling to add any more dead to the 'corpse field of Loos'.[87]

The Indian Corps alone suffered 3,973 casualties in a battle that achieved little. They were commended for their role by both Sir John French and General Haig, but it was clear that, in Howell's terms, the 'breaking point had been reached'. Conscious of the losses they had sustained, of the near breakdown of the

corps' regimental structure and the sheer exhaustion of the
men, Howell remained ever watchful for the signs of collapsing
morale or anti-British feeling in letters. Both the Lahore and
Meerut divisions were by now nothing like the fighting force they
had been a year earlier. When the 59th Rifles had landed in
France in September 1914, their strength stood at 13 British officers, 18 Indian officers and 810 other ranks. By the start of
November 1915, the regiment had no British officers at all, just
4 Indian officers and a mere 75 other ranks. The 47th Sikhs had
suffered even greater losses: they had no officers at all, British or
Indian, and only 28 men.[88] Critically, the regimental structure of
the Indian Corps had also come close to collapse. Men were
serving in *ersatz* units made up of the shattered fragments of once
cohesive regiments that had borne their own long traditions and
collective memories.

★

There was always a part of the British Army that distrusted the
Indian Army and feared the consequences of their deployment in
Europe. The longer men from India remained in France and
Belgium and watched the mighty British unable to defeat
Germany – a nation few Indians had heard of before 1914 – the
greater the potential damage to British prestige. Likewise, the
longer the Indians fought alongside white men, who were demonstrably as vulnerable, fragile, terrified and mortal as they, the
greater the damage done to white racial prestige in India. Their
potential contacts with white women – in Brighton, Marseilles
and elsewhere – seemed to threaten another of the most powerful
taboos of empire. And now units of Kitchener's volunteers had
been trained and were arriving in France and Belgium.

The mass home-grown army that Britain had lacked in 1914,
when the decision to send the Lahore and Meerut divisions had
been made, had rapidly and efficiently been forged. The Indians
had helped provide Britain with the time that Kitchener had
asked for during the War Council meetings of August 1914. With
the new armies surging into the front lines and re-invigorating

the British war effort, priorities changed, and the Indians were no longer needed. Their deployment in Europe had been an emergency measure, and the emergency had – it seemed – passed. Willcocks proudly concluded that the Indian Corps had 'done their full share of the work they were sent to do'.[89] In all 138,608 Indians had fought on the Western Front in the first 14 months of the war. Only the cavalry were to stay on until 1918, to fight mainly as mobile infantry.

The last ship carrying the last of the Indian Corps infantry regiments left Marseilles on 26 December 1915, exactly fourteen months to the day since the *Castilia* and the *Mongara* had arrived. This final transport, however, did not carry the Indian veterans back to Bombay or Karachi, from where they had departed in August 1914; it was bound for Basra – the main British military base in what was then known as Mesopotamia and today as Iraq. The Indian Army's war was to be as global as the British Empire itself.

CHAPTER 3

'NO LONGER THE AGENTS OF CULTURE'

Imperial dreams, African nightmares

——— · ——

12 AUGUST 1914. In eastern Belgium, four regiments of mounted German Cuirassiers descend upon the town of Haelen, charging with lances and sabres. In this 'Battle of the Silver Helmets', as it becomes known, they are repulsed at terrible cost by the Belgian defenders' rifle fire. No one in Europe can possibly know that this is the last mass cavalry charge that the German Army will ever launch. To the southwest, the first of the enormous 420mm shells fired from the Germans' 'Big Bertha' howitzers crash down upon the supposedly impregnable forts that ring the Belgian city of Liège. When *The Times* later prints reports of Germany's new super-weapons, they are dismissed as fanciful by British military experts, who disbelieve that such vast shells are technically possible.[1]

French troops – unwisely still dressed in their conspicuous but traditional red trousers and blue greatcoats – continue to surge across the border with Germany, in what will prove for them the calamitous Battle of the Frontiers. Meanwhile, in London the British Empire finally declares war on Austria-Hungary, which is in the process of invading Serbia. The British Expeditionary Force, having begun landing in northern France on 7 August, is marching into Belgium – and, unbeknownst to them, headlong into a German army several times its size. Also on 12 August, Germany itself is under invasion, as General Paul von

Rennenkampf, commanding the Russian First Army, crosses the border and captures a town five miles inside East Prussia. In Malmedy, Belgium, Obit Jahnow becomes the first German pilot to die in the conflict, after his plane crashes.

On the same day – 3,000 miles away and little noticed at the time – British and German units approach one another through the African bush, in the German colony of Togoland. A piece of history is made. Regimental Sergeant Major Alhaji Grunshi, of the British West African Frontier Force, fires the first British shot of the war on land, as he and his unit attack Lomé, Togoland's capital, before they move on towards the village of Kamina. It is not until ten days later that Edward Thomas, of the 4th Irish Dragoon Guards, becomes the first white British soldier to fire a round, in Europe. Incredibly, and against all the odds, both Alhaji Grunshi and Edward Thomas survive the full four years of the war.

For Britain and its empire, the land war has begun – not in Europe, but in Africa. For both the British and the Germans, it will end there too, at another half-forgotten clearing in the bush, surrounded by African fields and farms.

———— ·————

Europe's troubles ignited a conflict in Africa. Yet for much of the last quarter of the nineteenth century, European statesmen had worried – often with good reason – that some minor incident in Africa might become the spark for a European war. The most serious flashpoint came in 1898 with the 'Fashoda Incident', when a French expedition attempting to claim southern Sudan collided with British units from Egypt near the tiny, backwater village of Fashoda: for a few days, it became the focus of world attention and the obsession of two global empires. A tense stand-off ensued. It was only luck, circumstance and the skills of a gifted generation of diplomats and statesmen, who were acutely awake to the potential dangers, that avoided events like these leading to war. The idea that France and Britain might have gone to war in 1898 seems all the more bizarre to us now when we remember that all the leading officers who confronted one another in the Sudanese desert – Jean-Baptiste Marchand and a young ambitious lieutenant, Charles Mangin, on the French side, and Sir Herbert Kitchener and Horace Smith-Dorrien on the British – were, just sixteen years later, leaders in their nations' joint struggle against Germany on the Western Front.

By 1914, the concern that a clash over some slice of colonial African real estate might spark a conflagration in Europe had largely receded. The thick black lines that now cut across the map of the African interior had begun to acquire an air of permanence. Although it was generally recognized that some of those borders might – at some future date – require adjustments and refinements, there was a sense that it was in the interests of the European powers to cooperate with one another in the development of Africa and in the suppression of its indigenous peoples. This did not mean, by any stretch of the imagination, that the continent had been at peace. The list of wars, punitive raids and military expeditions unleashed against the peoples of Africa over this period by the colonizing powers is depressingly long. Outnumbered enormously by the black populations they ruled over, white settlers in Africa developed a strong sense of white comradeship across nationalities, which was paralleled – in a more cautious and qualified way – between governments in Europe. Britain in particular, which had the choicest slices of the African pie, was in a position to appear generous. Around a quarter of the land surface of the African continent was ruled by Queen-Empress Victoria, and the British ruling elites were able, in public at least, to sound magnanimous towards European nations who had more modest territorial claims. When those lesser colonial powers fought wars against their subject peoples, the British tended to see their actions as being in keeping with the advance of progress and the inevitable extension of white rule over black Africans – whom Rudyard Kipling described as Europe's 'new-caught sullen peoples'. Even when those wars expanded in scale and escalated in barbarism – as in the case of the German genocide against the Nama and Herero peoples in South West Africa (Namibia) in 1904–08 – the British did not often feel inclined to condemn the actions of a nation that many had come to regard as Britain's junior partner in the great mission to civilize. Indeed, German propaganda from 1919, after Germany had been stripped of its colonies by the Treaty of Versailles, went to great pains to collate and meticulously re-publish articles from the British press that had praised Germany's roles in Africa as colonizer, civilizer, educator and pacifier.*

This sense of common venture and racial comradeship was always strongest, though, among the settlers and colonial admin-istrators on the ground. In the southern and eastern portions of the continent, where the climate allowed for relatively comfort-able white settlement and the development of European-style farming, settlers tended to see one another as outnumbered pioneers, isolated and scattered over great distances, so they had to rely on one another in moments of crisis. White racial unity was reinforced by the experiences of war and uprisings, in which all whites – soldiers, settlers and farmers – fought alongside one another. Often these white communities were multi-national – Boers (Afrikaners) in German East Africa and British East Africa, alongside Swedes and other Scandinavians, for example. When it came to defending white rule and drafting laws and establish-ing economies that operated in the best interests of European settlers, appeals to white racial unity tended to trump the divi-sions of European nationalism. (The Boers of South Africa, whose own sense of nationalism existed independently of European rivalries, were the exception to the rule.)

Against this background, the outbreak of a war among the European colonial powers created a distinct conundrum. It threatened to tear apart the bonds of white racial community and potentially risked undermining all the other maxims of

* For a long, if self-interested, list of such articles, see 'English Pre-War Tributes to German Colonialisation Work Before the War', in *The Treat-ment of Native and Other Populations in the Colonial Possessions of Germany and England: An Answer to the English Blue Book of August 1918*, 1919.

colonial rule in Africa. A shared view emphasized the prestige of the white race – the threat to which was angrily voiced in a wartime essay entitled *England: Traitor to the White Race*, written by Bernhard Dernburg, the former German Secretary of State for Colonial Affairs, and published in the United States:

> *Just as the belligerents in Europe are divided by nationality, so people are divided by race in the colonies; and, just as closer ties bind nationalities and nations, so there is also a community of races ... in the colonial domain, every member of the white race is answerable to every other for the maintenance of his purity, culture, and prestige of this greater community ... But as, in the colonies, it is a question of dealing with great masses of undeveloped beings, far superior to the whites in number and not united among themselves, this task of the colonizer can be accomplished only if he succeeds in maintaining the prestige of the white race morally and culturally. If the white man is looked upon as mentally superior, on a higher plane economically, superior in weapons and power, the natives will decide that to render obedience to him is not only necessary, but wise. That is what is called the prestige of the white race. It is based on the native's belief that the will of the white man is good, unshakable, unconquerable.*[2]

Dernburg obviously had, in a war context, a propaganda axe to grind. Nevertheless, white setters – British, Boers, French, German, Belgian, Portuguese – all believed that if white men now fought one another in front of the Africans, the result would be to tarnish the white man's prestige and lead Africans to question the wisdom of paying 'obedience to him'. And therein lay a sense of dread. During the nineteenth century, all the powers had recruited black mercenary armies from among their local populations, with the sole purpose of repressing other black Africans. The prospect of now sending these men into a war in which they would inevitably fight and kill white enemy soldiers, and possibly occupy white farms and towns too, appalled many colonists. Not only would white prestige be damaged, but the spilling of white blood by black hands – for long cast as the greatest of all crimes in colonial Africa – would be condoned. The sanctity of white life had been a point reinforced through racially biased judicial systems, the widespread use of capital punishment, and through exemplary punishments and military retribution. If African men were now permitted to fight against whites, how would they ever again accept the notion that white life was uniquely valuable and precious?

Other fears entered the mix, too, based on the racial theories of the day. It was said that a war in Africa would awake within black soldiers their repressed, atavistic warrior instincts – the same savage forces that white colonization and the 'civilizing mission' had supposedly suppressed. There was the question of what role black veterans of an African war would claim for themselves in the post-war empires. German colonialists in South West Africa and the British and South Africans in southern Africa had spent much of the previous half century striving to take modern rifles out of the hands of the more worldly and militarily competent peoples of the continent. The prospect of thousands of African veterans, trained to use modern weapons, experienced in combat and having fought against white men, was widely considered to be anathema to the future security of white settlers.

Finally there was the bigger picture. Settlers in Africa and colonial ministers in Europe alike feared that the economic advances being made in their African colonies could be plunged into reverse by war. Across the continent, new farms had been established, and a great spate of railway construction was under way; all this seemed in jeopardy. Some argued that Africa's development stood at a critical moment, and that despite all these advances the process of colonial control was far from complete. There were, after all, huge swathes of the interior over which the writ of the colonial powers existed only on the map. The great carve-up of Africa as agreed at the Berlin Conference of 1884–5 was less a single decisive event but rather part of a process – one that was far from complete, and which was potentially reversible.

All of these arguments were aired in the years leading up to 1914; and most of them found audiences. But within days of the outbreak of the conflict, the idea that the colonial empires of Africa might escape being dragged into the conflict evaporated.

———— • ————

Togo, 2014. Surrounded by fields of crops and the mud and straw huts of the local Togolese farmers stand the ruins of a nerve-centre of European colonialism. Half-consumed by the vegetation lie huge rusted pieces of machinery. They are the heavy steel mounts on which enormous antennae once stood, along with giant water tanks which once cooled electric engines, and the remains of circular electric generators, brown with rust, some of them up-ended. All this detritus lies scattered – evidently by a huge explosion. Nearby are the concrete foundations of what once was a command centre, filled with weeds, overgrown with vines. The outlines of other buildings, perhaps outhouses or barracks, can still be traced in the red African soil. These physical manifestations are all that remains of a once vital hub for Germany's colonial communication: its radio station in Kamina – the *Funkstation Kamina*.

———— • ————

There was a reason why the first British land offensive of the war came in German Togoland, and a reason that the ultimate target of that offensive was the radio transmitter at Kamina. On 5 August 1914, within hours of the declaration of war, the British General Post Office ship the CS *Alert* carried out the very first British action of the conflict – the severing of five underwater telegraph cables that linked Germany to the United States.* What this

---

* This action is often reported as having been the work of the British cable ship the CS *Telconia*, reiterating a mistake that first appeared in Barbara Tuchman's 1959 book, *The Zimmermann Telegram*.

meant was that for the duration of the conflict, the German transatlantic telegrams were routed through neutral Sweden – but that effectively meant via London, since Sweden used the British Empire's vast cable network. That left the German communications susceptible to being intercepted, monitored and decrypted – as indeed they were, by the team of cryptologists in the British Admiralty's 'Room 40', Britain's First World War equivalent of Bletchley Park. However, foreseeing the vulnerability of its cable communications, Germany had, long before the war, commissioned the construction of a series of high-power radio transmitters capable of relaying Morse-code communications from across its colonial empire and beyond back to stations within Germany. By August 1914 that network was nearing completion and already spanned most of the globe.

In order to neutralize this threat, the instructions dispatched to Britain's colonial forces in Africa and Asia at the outbreak of hostilities included injunctions not only to capture German harbours, coaling stations and shipping, but also to attack and disable Germany's radio stations. On 8 and 9 August 1914, two Royal Navy warships bombarded the German transmitter in Dar es Salaam, capital of German East Africa. Five days later, and two days after Alhaji Grunshi had fired his historic shot against the German force in Togoland, the SS *Armadale Castle,* an armed merchant cruiser, appeared off the coast outside the town of Swakopmund, the main port of German South West Africa. After a short bombardment she slipped off into the mist of the Skeleton Coast, having destroyed another link in the enemy's chain of radio stations. Likewise, the station in Lüderitz Bay, in the south of that colony, was seized by South Africans. One by one, the transmitters were being silenced. The *Funkstation Kamina,* however, was the most important of them all, and the most valuable strategic asset in German Africa. It acted as a relay station, channelling communications between the Kaiser's wider empire and Berlin, and passed messages to and from German shipping in the southern Atlantic. In the event, as the British-led forces closed in, the station was dynamited on the night of 24 August

1914 by its German defenders, before it could fall into enemy
hands. By the end of September 1914, and without having to
fight for it, British forces had taken the coastal transmitter at
Doula, too, in German Cameroon.

Beyond the specific targets of radio stations, Alhaji Grunshi's
first shot represented the opening salvo in a series of wars that
– despite all the fears and pre-war lobbying of settlers and colonial ministers – spread rapidly across the continent, and which
would ultimately result in the systematic dismantling of Germany's
colonial empire in Africa and beyond. The war in Togoland –
along with the operations to capture Germany's scattered
territories in the Pacific, and the seizure by British, Indian and
Japanese forces of the German enclave at Tsingtao in China –
represented the only phase of the war in which the fighting really
was 'all over by Christmas'. With the destruction of the *Funkstation*,
German Togoland quietly ceased to exist.

The capture of German South West Africa – modern Namibia
– began just as decisively, but stretched on into 1915. There, the
German *Schutztruppe* ('Protection Troop') garrison was confronted by invading South African forces under the command of
Louis Botha, the Boer commander who had previously fought
against the British in the Second Anglo-Boer War. The South
Africans – a whites-only combat force – entered German territory
in September 1914, landing in the southern harbour town of
Lüderitz and crossing over the Orange River and into the southern deserts, in a far less successful land offensive than the French
and British achieved in Togoland. The progress of the invasion
was halted in September 1914 by an uprising by some Boers
against the British in South Africa itself. It was only after that
rebellion had been quashed, in February 1915, that the campaign in the Namib Desert recommenced. The hiatus had no
impact, however, on the ultimate result. By early May 1915 the
South Africans had taken the capital, Windhoek; by July the bulk
of the German forces had been pushed into the scrub deserts in
the north-east of the colony, and there they were forced into an
ignominious surrender near the settlement of Otavi.

Despite making great claims to this being a 'white man's war', the Germans in South West Africa mobilized three units of African troops on the outbreak of war.[3] They also pressed the mixed-race Baster people – descendants of settlers and indigenous peoples – to fight on their side. The Basters, who had been witness to the wholesale extermination and brutal repression of two of the colony's other ethnic groups in the previous decade, chose to rebel instead. They were saved from annihilation only by the advance of the South Africans. Yet the moment the fighting was over, considerations of race and white prestige quickly became pre-eminent. The South Africans permitted German settlers who had fought against them as reservists in the *Schutztruppe* to return to their farms; only the regular *Schutztruppe* were interned as PoWs. Louis Botha's peace terms were intended to ensure that nothing was done to impair what he called the 'standing of the white race' in the minds of the African peoples of South West Africa – a colony that Botha and the government in Pretoria were determined to wrest from German control at the end of the war and incorporate into an enlarged South Africa.

The campaign to capture and occupy German Cameroon (Kamerun) took longer to reach its conclusion. On 6 August 1914 French forces invaded from French Equatorial Africa to the east, while a force made up of 4,000 Nigerian troops under 350 white British officers marched in from the north. The French and British were supported by units from the Belgian Congo. All the invading armies wore European uniforms, but the vast majority of the fighting men were black Africans. The white Belgian officers found themselves in the unnerving position of leading a campaign from their nation's African empire, while their homeland itself was being overrun by a German army a million strong. The defending German forces in Cameroon numbered around 4,000, three-quarters of them *Askari* – native African troops. After abandoning the coastal ports without a fight, the defenders of German Cameroon retreated into the interior. The war in Cameroon dragged on miserably until spring 1916, despite the wide-scale and widespread hostility of a local population, resentful of thirty years of German aggression and punitive raids, and despite large-scale defections by the *Askari*. Eventually, the remaining *Askari*, Germans and their families escaped over the border into Spanish Muni (today's Equatorial Guinea), effectively surrendering the colony.

If events in the last-remaining German colony, German East Africa, had followed a similar trajectory, the final chapter in Germany's colonial venture in Africa would have been neatly concluded long before 1918. The fact that it was not is down to one man, the commander of the colony's *Schutztruppe*.

———— • ————

L ATE 1913. A steamer journeys to East Africa. Aboard is an old-style Prussian officer – the career soldier and son of a general, Lieutenant Colonel Paul Emil von Lettow-Vorbeck. He has already acquired a reputation as one of the German Army's colonial 'specialists'. For a start, he was part of the German-led international force sent to teach the nationalist 'Boxer' rebels a lesson in China in 1900. He has already fought against the Nama people, during Germany's war in South West Africa from 1904, where he was badly wounded, losing an eye. By most accounts, he is cultured, capable – and charming. The aim of his journey now is to take up command of the *Schutztruppe* in German East Africa. While on board, he makes the acquaintance of the young Karen Blixen, who will later write a memoir of her Kenyan life, *Out of Africa*, under the pen-name Isak Dinesen. She is struck by the force of his personality, and the two became travel companions. In her view, Lettow-Vorbeck belongs 'to the olden days, and I have never met another German who has given me so strong an impression of what Imperial Germany was and stood for'.[4]

———— • ————

The aspect of Lieutenant Colonel Lettow-Vorbeck's personality that Karen Blixen did not encounter, and upon which she left no remarks, was his obsessiveness. The *Schutztruppe* commander, forty-four years old in 1914, was a man driven by a fanatical belief in duty, a trait that made him prone to an extreme form of tunnel vision. From the moment war broke out, all non-military considerations seemed to evaporate from his mind. This might have been less of an issue had the civilian Governor of German East Africa, Heinrich Schnee, been a stronger figure; but from very early on in the war, Lettow-Vorbeck strongly asserted his belief that in the current circumstances he was the paramount authority in the colony, rather than Schnee. The conflict between the two men lasted until November 1918, but early victory and growing fame was to place Lettow-Vorbeck in the dominant position for most of that time. This victory of soldier over civilian in a battle of wills was to prove disastrous for millions of Africa's people.

The forty-two-year-old Schnee remained, at least in theory, the highest authority in German East Africa. The author of a number of books, and with a background in law and a career in the German colonies in the Pacific behind him, he had clear views on the peoples of Africa and Germany's colonial mission. He was, by the low standards of German colonialism in Africa, a liberal, and he was resented by the more thrusting and ambitious of the settlers and the *Schutztruppe*.

The colony over which Schnee now ruled was in many ways an oddity. The bulk of the African population lived in what is today Rwanda and Burundi, while along the coast was a zone populated by Swahili speakers. A great deal of racial mixing had taken place over the centuries between ethnic Arab populations and local African peoples, of whom there were over a hundred ethnic groups with their own languages, cultures and traditions. The offshore islands of Zanzibar and Pemba were under British 'protection', and the colony was surrounded on all sides by those of potential enemies. To the north was British East Africa, to the west the Belgian Congo, and to the south lay British Northern Rhodesia (Zambia) and Nyasaland (Malawi) and Portuguese Mozambique. There had been two extremely violent rebellions in the colony since 1885. The Maji-Maji rebellion of 1905–06 had been particularly bloody and was suppressed with appalling violence. The scorched-earth policies followed by the *Schutztruppe* resulted in a famine that had led to the deaths of perhaps as many as a quarter of a million Africans. Unsurprisingly, there was a deep-seated resentment of German rule among the colony's African population, almost 8 million strong.

Yet Schnee in 1914 was convinced that the colony, despite its bloody past, stood on the verge of the next phase of its development, one in which such repressive measures would not be required. Unlike many colonies, German East Africa operated at a profit. The white European population had swelled to over 5,000, and many of them lived in the healthier northern highlands, where they farmed and produced sisal, coffee, rubber and other goods for the German market. The colony had two railways: the Central Railway – 780 miles long and linking Dar es Salaam with Lake Tanganyika – had only been completed in July 1914. It was due to open formally on 12 August, and celebrations to mark this pivotal moment in the colony's economic development were being prepared when the war broke out. Along the rail corridors, European farms and tiny towns and settlements had begun to develop, the local people having been displaced or absorbed into the European economy as landless labourers. There had been great advancement in the provision of schools for Africans, and the slave trade that still existed on the Swahili coast was being effectively repressed. Governor Schnee was determined that any war in Europe would not be allowed to jeopardize German East Africa's economic progress or place the white settlers of the colony at unnecessary risk.

There had initially been some hope, during July and August 1914, that the colony might escape the war altogether, on the basis of what amounted to a legal technicality. As the great powers' alliance system pulled Europe into two armed blocks, Schnee and his opposite number in British East Africa, Governor Sir Harry Conway Belfield, both hoped that Articles Ten and Eleven of the General Act agreed in 1885 might be invoked. These stipulated that if war were to break out between nations with colonies in the Congo Basin – which included much of German East Africa, as well as German Cameroon – the region could be declared neutral and kept out of the fighting. In the immediate aftermath of the outbreak of war in Europe, neither Schnee nor Belfield sought conflict nor authorized any offensive actions that might provoke the other. The lawyerly Schnee even attempted to pursue legal avenues, through intermediaries, which might have led to the application of the neutrality clauses; but they came to nothing. And Belfield, even in January 1915, was declaring that 'the colony has no interest in the present war except so far as its unfortunate position places it in such close proximity to German East Africa'. Despite the caution of the two governors, the white settler populations of both colonies rushed to enlist or to don their reservist uniforms and take up arms. Nairobi, capital of British East Africa, in particular filled with white hunters and hot-headed settlers who had brought their own arms. They demanded to be incorporated into the army, given uniforms and a mission, forming themselves into militia units and planning for their part in the war against the Hun in Africa. Belfield hoped calmer heads would prevail, and that his counterpart in the German colony would have more luck dowsing the flames of nationalism.

From the start, though, Schnee was at odds in almost every respect with the plans and priorities of Lettow-Vorbeck. Assessing the military situation in August 1914, Lettow-Vorbeck looked far beyond the borders of the colony in which he found himself to the wider war. He could only be certain of a handful of factors. As he was surrounded by the colonial territories of hostile nations, he could count on the fact that any invading force would be far greater than anything he could field. At least the force available to him was a known quantity. The Germans had enforced their rule in East Africa by creating a local army of African soldiers.[5] The *Askari* – Swahili for 'soldier' – had been recruited initially from Sudan, and then later from among the tribes who had fought most determinedly against the first German invaders – the Wahehe, Wanyamwezi and Angoni – in accordance with what amounted to a German version of the British martial-races theory. They were in effect a mercenary, military elite, well paid and spared from menial tasks; they had their own traditions and a powerful sense of pride in their service and their abilities. Their self-belief was unquestionably justified as they were undoubtedly among the best-trained soldiers in all of Africa. However, like the indigenous armies of the other imperial powers, the *Askari* had been formed to crush local rebellions and not to fight Europeans or defend the whole enormous colony from external invasion. They were led by the officers and men of the German *Schutztruppe*, white colonial regulars of the German Army. The combined force was augmented by hundreds of German reservists. In a partly militarized white-settler society, German settlers were armed and used to being called upon to take part in military action. Many had formed local rifle clubs to hone their combat skills. The sett-ler-farmers also included a number of former soldiers, some of whom had taken part in past actions against the local tribes. By 1914 the entire German *Schutztruppe* force consisted of 2,542 *Askari* and 218 Germans, officers and men. The white reservists numbered 1,670, and there was a semi-military police force of 55 Europeans and 2,160 Africans.[6]

Lettow-Vorbeck could be confident about one other factor, too, in late 1914: that the prospects of receiving reinforcements or even basic supplies of food and war materials from Germany were slim. While the sea lanes were patrolled by the blockading fleets of the Royal Navy from the first hours of war, Britannia showed herself determined to rule the airwaves too. The completion of the destruction of German radio transmitters in Africa meant that, alongside the maritime blockade, by September 1916 Germany's empire was largely cut off from the fatherland.[7] Incredibly, Lettow-Vorbeck did manage for much of the war to learn of news on other fronts in Europe, and at times even communicate with Germany, through the use of an improvised telegraph network.

The generally haphazard and difficult communications with Berlin had another consequence: they left Lettow-Vorbeck free to devise his own strategy for war in German East Africa, side-stepping or simply ignoring Schnee. His plan was not, in essence, one for the defence of the colony; rather, it was a strategy designed to influence – as much as was in his power – events in the principal, European theatre of war. Lettow-Vorbeck hoped to draw into East Africa as many Allied troops and as much of the enemy's military resource as was possible, thereby denying Britain and France the opportunity of deploying them in Europe. It was an unquestionably brave and ambitious strategy; but it was far removed from that favoured by Schnee.

Thus, on the outbreak of hostilities in Europe, Schnee ordered Lettow-Vorbeck to refrain from aggressive actions. On 5 August, in another legalistic move, the governor declared the ports on the coast of German East Africa 'open', in accordance with the Hague Convention of 1907, and informed the Royal Navy that they would not be defended, in the hope of avoiding enemy bombardments to which the German navy would have no answer. The German garrison in Dar es Salaam was evacuated, but since, critically, the radio transmitter was left operational, it invited a British naval bombardment, which came three days later. Nevertheless, Schnee's strategy was still to follow the pre-war plans and have the *Schutztruppe* fall back to defend the interior of the colony along the railway lines. But in early September Lettow-Vorbeck began launching small-scale attacks into British East Africa. The most significant was on the settlement of Taveta, just a few miles over the border. As Lettow-Vorbeck's numerous apologists never tire of re-stating, this makes him the only German general to have invaded 'British' territory during the war. When Schnee heard that a German flag was fluttering provocatively over British territory, he became enraged and telegraphed Lettow-Vorbeck reminding him of the real priorities as Schnee saw them – among which the protection of the white population from 'possible native uprisings' was paramount.

———————

LONDON, 5 AUGUST 1914. On the same day that Governor Schnee declares all German anchorages in East Africa 'open ports', the British Committee of Imperial Defence meets in

London to discuss plans for the conquest of the German colonial empire. As well as agreeing to silence the radio station at Dar es Salaam, it is decided to capture the ports of German East Africa in order to deny German warships access to coal and provisions. The importance of this strategy becomes clear the next day, when the German light cruiser SMS *Königsberg* captures and sinks a British merchantman, the *City of Winchester*. Having slipped out of Dar es Salam some days earlier, to escape an impending British blockade, the *Königsberg* is now on the loose in the Red Sea.

Over a month later, on 20 September 1914, the *Königsberg* raids the harbour of British-administered Zanzibar and sinks the British cruiser HMS *Pegasus*. In order to neutralize German East Africa, prevent the *Königsberg* from re-supplying in a friendly port, and ensure that German forces in the region pose no threat to British East Africa, the Committee of Imperial Defence reconvenes and activates a contingency plan originally drawn up by the War Office in 1897. *The Scheme for Operations Against German East Africa* is a document that was drafted by the Director of Intelligence of the British Indian Army, because since 1897 the defence of Britain's East African territories has been subcontracted by Whitehall to the British Government of India.[8] Among those at the meeting is the Inspector-General of the indigenous King's African Rifles, Brigadier General A.R. Hoskins, who happens to be home in Britain on leave. He paints a picture for the Committee of the conditions in German East Africa, of the malarial heat of the coastal strip, of the lack of roads, of the suffocating humidity. His warnings appear to have little effect.

———

The plan initially adopted by the Committee of Imperial Defence involved the deployment of two Indian forces, one to attack Dar es Salaam, the other to defend British East Africa alongside the locally recruited King's African Rifles. However, the *Königsberg*'s raid on Zanzibar (and the disruption caused by another German cruiser, *Emden*, in the Indian Ocean) meant that this plan was expanded by

October to require the capture of *all* ports on the German East African coast. The first target was to be the most northerly, at Tanga, and it would involve two components of an Indian Expeditionary Force (IEF). IEF B would seize Tanga in an amphibious attack, while IEF C would march south from British East Africa, wind its way around Mount Kilimanjaro, and attack the settlement of Longido just a few miles over the border. IEF B would then proceed to march north along the railway to Moshi, on the slopes of Kilimanjaro, thereby trapping the Germans between the two forces.

As plans were laid, in Nairobi Governor Belfield remained avowedly disinterested in the war. But there were those in both Whitehall and Delhi who regarded the prospect of hostilities as a golden opportunity. German East Africa was the missing link in the 'red line', the continuous strip of British territories dreamed of by the arch-imperialist Cecil Rhodes and his followers ever since the 1890s. It was across this red line that Britain could drive a Cape–Cairo railway. Indeed, the British impulse to seize Sudan in the 1890s, which had led to the Fashoda Incident, was motivated by this dream, while what had taken the Frenchmen Marchand and Mangin to Fashoda was a comparable fantasy of a French railway running from Dakar in Senegal to the Indian Ocean.

In British India, in those same tumultuous decades, a different form of colonialism had gripped the imagination. The possession of German East Africa could open the way for the Government of India to realize one of its longest-held strategic ambitions of 'sub-imperialism', whereby the colony might become a region into which Britain could direct Indian emigrants. The British had already encouraged Indian immigration into British East Africa, albeit with mixed results. They now talked of extending this policy into conquered German territories creating a new zone of future colonization. It was thought that the development of Africa could be significantly accelerated by the importation of Indians, who were widely regarded as being racially and culturally superior to Africans. In 1901 the British colonial administrator and theorist Sir Harry Johnston had written that: 'Indian trade, enterprise, and emigration require a suitable outlet. East Africa is, and should be, from every point of view, the America of the Hindu'.[9] The idea was supported by voices in South Africa and by some in India itself. By 1916, Theodore Morison, a member of the Council for India in London, had no doubt that German East Africa was 'a colony for India', in which Indians could 'play a part in the civilizing of the wild' and 'share the white man's burden' in Africa.[10]

In August 1914, while the Lahore and Meerut divisions of the British India Corps were being readied for eventual service in Europe, the Government of India placed schemes for the future colonization of Africa to one side and prioritized preparation and planning for the conquest of German East Africa. By September 1914 most of the finest units of the British Indian Army had been dispatched to Europe, and a further force was being assembled for deployment in the Persian Gulf, for fear that Ottoman Turkey would enter the war. Thus, the units that the Government of India was able to cobble together to form IEF B and IEF C were made up from the less well-regarded regiments. Richard Meinertzhagen, a former officer of the King's African Rifles appointed as British Intelligence Officer to IEF B, and one of the singularly most unpleasant characters in the whole history of British colonialism, was dismissive of the Indians on first sight:

> They constitute the worst in India and I tremble to think what may happen if we meet with serious opposition. I have seen many of the men and they do not impress me at all ... Two battalions have no machine guns and the senior officers are nearer to fossils than to active, energetic leaders of men.[11]

Doing slightly better than their comrades destined for the Western Front, the Indian troops of IEF B were issued with the short-magazine Lee-Enfield rifle on leaving India, rather than on arrival in the theatre of war; but once again, the historical shadow of the Indian Mutiny loomed large, and a British Indian army was sent into combat carrying a weapon with which it was unfamiliar and on a continent of which they knew almost nothing.

While not all British officers were as negative as Meinertzhagen, serious doubts were raised in many quarters about the capabilities of many of the Indian units, especially those that had not been drawn from the peoples regarded as 'martial races'. Of the ten battalions that made up IEF B, only three units – the 101st Bombay Grenadiers, the 2nd Kashmir Rifles and the 2nd Battalion, Loyal North Lancashire Regiment (which had been based in Bangalore at the outbreak of war) – were looked on as effective combat troops units, while the 63rd Palamcottahs and the 98th Infantry Pioneers were regarded with particular suspicion.[12] Nevertheless, while the British commander, Major General Arthur Aitken, knew little about Africa or Africans, he was a firm believer in imperialism's racial hierarchies and remained convinced that even those Indians from the *least* martial of races, when trained and led by British officers, were superior soldiers to German-trained Africans. Despite not having served in Africa since 1885, and then only briefly, Aitken was in no doubt that 'the Indian Army will make short work of a lot of niggers'.[13] In a refrain that must have begun to ring hollow by November 1914 – after the British retreat from Mons and the catastrophic French defeats on the German frontiers – Aitken confidently assured his subordinates that the fighting in German East Africa would be over by Christmas.

British optimism was also fuelled by the belief that Tanga would not be defended. In the absence of the more cautious and knowledgeable local commander, Hoskins, others predicted that any attack would incite the downtrodden locals to rise up against the Germans; and it was widely believed that the German settler population would not put up much resistance. It was poor intelligence of this sort that encouraged Aitken to refuse the assistance of the 3rd King's African Rifles, men who were familiar with the terrain and the climate of East Africa.[14] With similar abandon, Aitken rejected the idea of blowing up the German railway lines between Tanga and Kilimanjaro. Most disastrously of all, he refused to allow the men of IEF B shore leave to rest and recover after their two-week-long journey in crowded army transport

ships from India, although the men were clearly in poor health
and lacking fitness. Aitken decided that these exhausted, disorientated men could be thrown straight into action after their
ocean crossing. Having stepped off the dockside at Bombay,
leaving their native soil for the first time in their lives, their next
step on land would be onto the sands of an enemy-held shoreline.

★

Tanga today is a nondescript city on the northern tip of Tanzania's
Indian Ocean coast. It boasts some moderately interesting colonial architecture, a railway station to which trains no longer travel
and a decaying German hospital that has become home to an
energetic roost of fruit bats. Its deep-water port is still active, and
the town has all the energy and dynamism of twenty-first-century
Tanzania; but most visitors are merely stopping over on their
journeys to and from Mount Kilimanjaro.

In 1914, Tanga was the second port of German East Africa and
the terminus of the shiny new Usambara Railway, which linked the
Usambara Highlands to the Indian Ocean. At dawn on 2 November,
a flotilla of fourteen transport ships with one escort, HMS *Fox*
(the expedition's other escort, HMS *Goliath*, had broken down at
Mombasa), gathered fifteen miles off the coast, lurking beneath
the horizon to avoid being spotted – though they had already been
given away. At this point in the story, blame for the impending
disaster shifts, if only temporarily, from Aitken to Captain Caulfield
of the *Fox*. Concerned about mines, and eager to avoid inflicting
civilian casualties with a naval bombardment, Caulfield sailed into
Tanga at 7am and gave the German District Commissioner, Dr
Auracher, the opportunity to surrender, which he politely declined.
Instead, Auracher promptly dispatched telegrams to Lettow-
Vorbeck informing him of the arrival of a British invasion fleet,
slipped into his own German reservist's uniform, and prepared to
take part in the defence of Tanga. With the advantage of surprise
now squandered, Aitken – for some unaccountable reason – waited
until late that evening before beginning to land. Even then, he
sent ashore only part of his force. The Indian and British units

landed some distance from the town and assembled on an increasingly disorganized beachhead, after having hacked their way through the thick mangroves that fringed the shoreline. The lights of Tanga were clearly visible.

Aitken had been right in that Tanga was poorly defended; but that state of affairs was rapidly changing as Lettow-Vorbeck was rushing his troops from Moshi, on the slopes of Kilimanjaro just 185 miles away, using the Usambara Railway. Even so, on the morning of 3 November the German defenders of Tanga still numbered only about 200 men. By 8am about half of the Indian and British force was ashore, and when Aitken heard from a patrol that the town remained lightly defended, he ordered an attack. The assault began tentatively on the morning of 4 November. Things went tolerably well until the lead units were about 2,000 yards from the town. There, the 13th Rajputs, one of the more favoured of the Indian units, came under heavy fire. At the height of this engagement the first of Lettow-Vorbeck's reinforcements arrived and entered the battle. A powerful counter-attack by *Askari* forced the Indians back, and under German machine-gun fire the whole time they were forced into a retreat. The attack had been a shocking failure.

It had been in the very early hours of 4 November that Lettow-Vorbeck himself arrived at Tanga, by train. He and his officers, at this point, still believed that they could probably not defend the town successfully against a British force several times larger than anything they could assemble. After speaking to the German wounded in the hospital and consulting with senior officers, Lettow-Vorbeck set off on a bicycle to reconnoitre the empty streets of Tanga and view the British positions, which he did almost unmolested. It changed his mind, for what he saw of the British beachhead convinced him there was some chance of success. He prepared to counter the next British attack.

Having allowed the Germans a full fifty-four hours to prepare their defences, Aitken, at about noon the same day, launched that second attack. He still outnumbered the German defenders, at this point by about eight to one. In the initial advance, the

Indians and British were slowed by the thick vegetation of the rubber and sisal plantations that ringed the town, and by the oppressive heat. Communications between attacking units was difficult, too. Advancing as one long line, in a formation that was as antiquated as it was ill-advised, the Indians got to within 600 yards of the town, before they were again cut down by machine guns. Aitken at this point was unable to reply with artillery support, as he had not landed his guns, and Caulfield was as reluctant as ever to bring HMS *Fox* close enough to shore for her heavy guns to be effective. By the time he relented, it was too late in the day for his bombardment to affect the outcome.

Although British and Indian forces did succeed in entering Tanga, where they became engaged in street-to-street fighting, they were driven back by ferocious defending and the massed firepower of the German machine guns. One unit of Gurkhas captured the Kaiserhof Hotel, and for a brief moment the Union Flag flew over the town; but once again it was the arrival of enemy reinforcements that drove the attackers back. The constant onslaught of machine-gun fire decimated whole units in the plantations. Some – most notably the 63rd Palamcottahs – panicked and began to disintegrate. Men threw away their rifles and ran into the ocean. At one point, machine-gun fire slammed into the hives that bees had excavated in decaying tree stumps by the water line: thousands of furious bees swarmed out and attacked the British and Indian soldiers, adding to their misery and lending the battle its informal designation: 'Battle of the Bees'. One signaller of the Royal Engineers, in what might well have been one of the most distinguished acts of bravery in the whole battle, stayed at his post throughout the bees' offensive. He suffered 300 bee stings, mostly to his head. *The Times* later accused the Germans of having planted the beehives as part of an elaborate insectine trap.[15] Amid the chaos, Richard Meinertzhagen, a man prone to uncontrollable rage and devoid of compassion, summarily executed a number of young and terrified Indian troops, as they took cover from enemy fire. He shot one terrified Rajput soldier for refusing to advance when ordered, reporting: 'I shot the brute as he lay half-crazed with fear.'[16] Later, in his diary, he condemned the Indian men he had executed as 'scum'.[17]

The defeat of the Indian and British force might easily have become a complete rout. Lettow-Vorbeck, like many of the German officer corps, dreamed of achieving a battle of encirclement; it was a collective obsession, which stemmed from their study of the celebrated Carthaginian victory over the Romans at the ancient Battle of Cannae. IEF B and the British units at Tanga were arguably only spared this fate because an *Askari* bugler mistakenly sounded a call that was interpreted by Lettow-Vorbeck's men as an order for a retreat, and *en masse* they moved to positions west of the town at the height of the battle. At that moment, as the Germans were rushing from the field of battle to their new lines, Aitken might still, against the odds, have won the day with a third attack, despite all his previous bungling. Yet instead of exploiting this unexpected and undeserved opportunity, he ordered his forces back to their assembly points on the beachhead. That evening, the battered, terrified, dehydrated and bee-stung remnants of IEF B gathered on the beaches or dug into their positions, trapped in small pockets by German rifle fire. The wounded were outnumbered by men who had simply lost their nerve. As with the Indian units then engaged on the Western Front, the fighting capacity of IEF B had been undermined by the loss of so many British officers who were fluent in Indian languages. Ill-prepared, badly provisioned, poorly led, and exhausted from a long and cramped sea voyage – and now lacking officers to transmit orders – the men of IEF B had been led to the slaughter. From the outset, Meinertzhagen had suspected Aitken was not fit for the command entrusted to him.

On 5 November, Lettow-Vorbeck – still outnumbered, although now with artillery support – prepared to counter a renewed British attack. But it never came. Instead, Aitken ordered a re-embarkation, and that evening the British ships were loaded and the shattered remnants of IEF B were evacuated. Aitken's final blunder – and perhaps the most inexplicable of all – was his order that the great bulk of the expeditionary force's equipment and stores be left behind on the beach. There, and in the plantations around Tanga, the British Empire left not only 817 dead but also 8 machine guns, 455 rifles and 500,000 rounds of ammunition. From the great hoard, the Germans salvaged a huge stock of uniforms and a number of field telephones too. For a German force cut off from the fatherland, the victory at Tanga brought with it a scarcely believable bounty.

To arrange the ceasefire necessary for the evacuation, Meinertzhagen had, on the morning of the 5th, been dispatched to the German lines, carrying a white flag and a bundle of medical supplies for the wounded British prisoners. He was taken to Tanga's German hospital, which had become a command centre. There, he handed over a note from Aitken apologizing for the accidental bombardment of the hospital the previous day. Meinertzhagen was greeted warmly and given a breakfast of 'good beer, ice, plenty of eggs and cream and asparagus'. Then he and a group of German staff officers excitedly discussed the battle as if, in Meinertzhagen's words, 'it had been a football match'. It was this moment of unlikely German victory, along with the image of an exotic, supposedly gentlemanly, war, in which opposing white officers could remain on cordial terms, that first drew the attention of the German public to the conflict in Africa. After a string of defeats in the other African and Pacific colonies, the victory at Tanga was seized upon by the German press. The Kaiser rushed to offer his personal congratulations, and the newspapers and state propagandists set about transforming Lettow-Vorbeck from a little-known colonial officer into a German legend.

The Official History of the war later described the Battle of Tanga as 'one of the most notable failures in British military history',[18] though British newspapers of the day were not given the opportunity to express a view. The press remained mute, muzzled by a government that believed – perhaps correctly – that in November 1914 the British public was already overburdened with bad news. On the German side, one effect of Lettow-Vorbeck's victory, and his elevation to the status of national hero, was that the balance of power between him and Governor Schnee tipped permanently in his favour. Although Schnee remained by his side for much of the war, and from time to time felt justified in reprimanding Lettow-Vorbeck for allegedly neglecting his duties to protect the white settler population, the *Schutztruppe* commander was to a great extent now freed from civilian oversight. Lauded by his troops and commended by his nation, Lettow-Vorbeck and his war in Africa were presented to an excited German public as a romantic, colourful and glorious distraction from the mechanized slaughter in France and Belgium. Not only had he recorded a spectacular victory against the most hated of Germany's enemies, Tanga had been the most delicious type of triumph – one achieved against the odds. In the Reichstag, one deputy described Lettow-Vorbeck as 'a German David' who was 'fighting alone against a British Goliath in Africa'. But then, putting his finger squarely on Lettow-Vorbeck's key vulnerability, he made an earnest appeal for the assembly 'to ensure that his gallant struggle shall not be lost for lack of encouragement to sustain him. If we cannot fight by his side, at least we must make sure that he is well supplied with shot for his sling.'[19]

★

Lettow-Vorbeck had indeed gathered a great deal of 'shot for his sling' from the beaches of Tanga. His next significant engagement, in January 1915 – a siege of the British forces that had captured the German border settlement of Jasin, to the north of Tanga – was another triumph, although one achieved at a cost in men and war materials that was unsustainable. There, the *Schutztruppe* expended 200,000 rounds of ammunition and, more worrying, sustained around 300 casualties, including many key officers. Lettow-Vorbeck himself was lightly wounded and was lucky not to have been killed. Like almost everyone else, Lettow-Vorbeck in early 1915 was still of the view that the war in Europe would be short. This assumption encouraged him to be far less cautious at this time than he was later to become. Rather, he remained determined to cause as much damage as possible to the British before a German victory in Europe brought hostilities to an end.

In July 1915 a second bounty fell into Lettow-Vorbeck's lap. SMS *Königsberg* had finally been hunted down and destroyed by two British, shallow-draft 'monitor' boats in the Rufiji Delta, south of Dar es Salaam. The ship's captain, in a moment of genius, had set fire to her wooden deck, giving her pursuers the impression that the damage they had inflicted had spread to her hold. He then scuttled the ship, leaving her listing to one side in the shallow waters. The next day, after the British had retired, the Germans were able to begin salvaging war material from the waterlogged but still intact hold. Their haul included six field-guns, a stash of rifles and literally millions of rounds of ammunition. In addition to the contents of the *Königsberg's* hold, the ship's ten guns were removed and set on mobile carriages, giving Lettow-Vorbeck heavy artillery. With these weapons and resources, the commander was able not only to re-supply his force of 1914, but in 1915 to equip and train more *Askari*. By the end of that year he had under his command an army of 2,712 Europeans and 11,367 *Askari*, along with another 2,000 auxilia-ries.[20] Lettow-Vorbeck was now in a position to fight a protracted war. But for now he did not have the opportunity.

★

By the summer of 1915, the German radio transmitters in Africa had been silenced, the German naval threat in the Indian Ocean and Persian Gulf neutralized, and British Imperial forces in Africa were otherwise engaged. German East Africa had slipped precipitously down Britain's list of priorities, and for much of 1915 Germany's new military hero was left to his own devices. It was a year of small skirmishes. The Germans launched raids against the British Uganda Railway, which put thirty-two trains out of action and destroyed nine bridges; but there were very few larger engagements. British forces generally contented them-selves with defending colonial borders as best they could. In both

London and Nairobi, blame for the disaster at Tanga was appor-
tioned between Aitken and the inadequately prepared men of
IEF B. Their poor performance encouraged the British to look
to their two most effective armies in Africa, the British West
Africa Frontier Force and the South African Defence force; the
local King's African Rifles, based in Kenya, were too small a force
to take on the Germans. Yet, in 1915 there was little chance that
either might be configured to confront the Germans in East
Africa. In February 1915 the South Africans recommenced their
stalled invasion of German South West Africa, while throughout
the year the West Africa Frontier Force remained mired in an
increasingly frustrating campaign against the *Schutztruppe* of
German Cameroon. It was only after the South Africans had
soundly defeated the *Schutztruppe* of South West Africa, in July
1915, that attention turned again to German East Africa. In mid-
November, a sub-committee of the Committee for Imperial
Defence agreed to place the conquest of German East Africa
back on the top of the agenda, and towards the end of 1915 the
South African Defence Force finally began to assemble in
Mombasa for this purpose.

The army now being put together in British East Africa con-
sisted of an initial force of 13,000 white South Africans and
Rhodesians. Among the South Africans was also a battalion of
Cape Corps – mixed-race soldiers of European and San origin,
the latter of a similar heritage to the Nama of German South West
Africa, whom Lettow-Vorbeck had fought a decade earlier. To this
force were added 9,000 Indian troops and the men of the King's
African Rifles, who between them were already defending British
East Africa from Lettow-Vorbeck's incursions during 1915. In
total the British Imperial army that was readied for action in
German East Africa reached 73,000 – an enormous force in the
context of the African war. It was equipped with 71 field guns and
123 machine guns, and supported by a Royal Flying Corps squadron. It was supplied by a huge and growing corps of carriers and
labourers. In the view of one commander it was as 'strange and
heterogeneous an army' as had ever been assembled – though in

reality a similarly heterogeneous army was at the same time serving in and behind the lines in France and Belgium.[21]

South Africa's willingness to embark upon a second major campaign was not motivated solely by loyalty to the British Crown and Empire. The Union of South Africa also nursed sub-imperialist ambitions as expansive as those of the government in British India, and which involved a radical re-drawing of the map of the southern third of the African continent. The defeat of German South West Africa in summer 1915 had been secretly regarded by Pretoria as the prelude to the post-war incorporation of that long-coveted territory into South Africa. Germans' past mistreatment of the territory's people fed this goal, for, having captured a huge haul of official German records and documents, the South Africans quickly began an investigation into the Germans' 1904–08 genocide against the Herero and Nama peoples: the information, collated into a devastating official report from 1917 onwards, was later used at the Paris Peace Conference to demonstrate German unfitness to be a colonial power or the guardian of 'primitive peoples'. Yet South West Africa – a desert colony of dubious economic value, despite the diamond fields of the far south – was not in itself enough to satisfy Pretoria's territorial appetite. Like the Government of India and the dominions of Australia and New Zealand, South Africa had other, long-suppressed ambitions that had been suddenly freed by the fluidity of war. South Africa's leaders, aware of the deep internal divisions between Briton and Boer, were only willing to be drawn deeper into the war if they were to be further rewarded for their loyalty.

One proposed scheme was for the outright annexation of German East Africa, which John X. Merriman, the former Prime Minister of the Cape Colony, believed would then become 'a colony with a planter aristocracy resting on black labour' – a description that could have been reasonably applied to much of southern and eastern Africa in the first decades of the twentieth century. An alternative plan, more diplomatically intricate, was for the southern half of the confiscated German colony to be awarded to the Portuguese, in return for their relinquishing of the southern portion of Portuguese East Africa – Mozambique – which would be absorbed into South Africa. This area included the ports of Beria and Delagoa Bay (now Maputo Bay), a natural harbour first claimed by the Portuguese in 1502. Such a revision of southern Africa's borders would, so Pretoria hoped, promote economic development in the Transvaal and thereby appease Boer opinion. The scheme – pushed energetically by Minister of Defence Jan Smuts – was no less grandiose than the Government of India's dream of creating an 'America for the Hindu' in East Africa, and far less ambitious than Berlin's plans for a post-war re-ordering of Africa should Germany win the war.

What mattered to London in 1915 was whether South Africa's long-term, sub-imperial plans could be squared with the immediate military needs of the war effort, so Britain's politicians kept all options on the table and did nothing to dampen South African ambitions. The British general who was to lead the conquest of German East Africa was the veteran of Fashoda (and later Mons, in 1914), General Sir Horace Smith-Dorrien; but pneumonia contracted *en route* to Cape Town, and a subsequent relapse, forced his resignation. Leadership passed to Smuts himself, a South African hero who – like General Botha – had led Boer commando units against the British in the Second Anglo-Boer War, and whose participation now added a dash of glamour to the coming campaign.

However, Smuts's previous military experience was of almost no relevance to the task he now faced. The commando tactics perfected by the Boers, and more recently successfully deployed in South West Africa, were those of fast-moving, lightly equipped, almost self-sufficient mounted units of just a few hundred men. Such tactics had outfoxed the British Army at the turn of the century on the veldt and had proved too much for the Germans in the Namib Desert in 1915. But Smuts now had the prospect of leading a campaign in a tropical colony, much of it covered in thick bush or forest, with limited infrastructure and endemic diseases dangerous to both men and animals. His forces were not going to be compact and mobile Boer commando units, but rather a large multi-national, multi-race, polyglot army, tens of thousands strong – and these numbers would be dwarfed by the hundreds of thousands of carriers and labourers attempting, against odds, to keep the campaign supplied. The political pressure for results was intense, too. Yet he was facing an elusive enemy, fighting on its home territory and led by a highly capable commander. Had Smuts recognized the extent to which these challenges would shape the conflict, he might well have sought better counsel and listened to in-country experts. Instead, he gathered around him too many South African commanders whose military experience was as narrow as his own, and he too often sidelined men who had a better understanding of the region and clearer insight into Lettow-Vorbeck's army and tactics.

The first phase of Smuts's strategy was to secure the border of British East Africa. It proved the only phase of the war in which the conditions and the terrain favoured Smuts's tactics, and things went well. By the end of March 1916 the Germans had been pushed out of the Kilimanjaro area; but the South Africans had been unable to force Lettow-Vorbeck into a decisive fight, and a pattern of confrontation and evasion was set in train that was to continue.

The total strength of Lettow-Vorbeck's force in 1916 stood somewhere between 15,000 and 20,000 troops, though Smuts and his intelligence officer, Meinertzhagen, remained convinced throughout the year that the Germans were far stronger. Now, Smuts's forces were drawn ever deeper into the malarial, tsetse-fly infested interior to pursue them. Converging on German East Africa from multiple directions – Portuguese troops were crossing the German colony's southern border in April 1916, and from June 1916 Belgians from the Congo were entering Urundi in the colony's north-west – the invasion forces very quickly began to stretch supply lines and break spirits, as the campaign developed into one that in many respects overthrows our vision of the First World War. Three-thousand miles away from the Western Front, the war in East Africa pitched armies of the continent's black and white tribes against one another in a campaign that was in truth more akin to nineteenth-century wars of colonial conquest. As he advanced, Smuts had to operate with maps that were unreliable and communications that were haphazard, carried along telegraph lines that were vulnerable to the ravages of the weather and even the attentions of giraffes. As the army under Smuts's command grew to its maximum strength, the problems of supply became almost insurmountable. When food failed to reach the troops, men who were already exhausted by long marches and sickness were further weakened by malnutrition. For months on end the fighting was simply an endless series of indecisive skirmishes or bloody ambushes. Small patrols encountered one another in the thick bush, often by accident, and there were cases of men firing on their own side. In this war of movement, advances were measured in miles, rather than in yards as on the Western Front; but the ground gained was easily lost and arguably not worth the fight.

The war on the Western Front was the first conflict in history in which the majority of casualties were victims of the battlefield rather than disease. In Africa, the old rules of war remained in force, and here the mosquito and the tsetse-fly killed far more men and animals than the bullet or the bayonet. At times, dysentery killed 40 per cent of those infected. Whole units were decimated by malaria and, to a lesser extent, yellow fever and sleeping sickness. Others fell victim to black-water fever, a deadly complication of malaria, or were infected with Guinea worms, whose ravenous larvae gather, agonizingly, in the lungs, eyes, joints or genitals, leaving men permanently crippled. The figures are stark. In July 1916, for every one combat casualty, thirty-one men were put out of action by sickness, disease, exhaustion or other non-combat-related factors.[22] The 9th South African Infantry were able to field 1,135 men in February 1916; by October, only 116 men were fit for service.[23] The 2nd Rhodesians recorded 10,626 cases of sickness, 3,127 of them malaria-related; they lost a mere 36 men killed in combat, yet by the end of 1916 only 30 of their number were designated fit for active service.[24] Meinertzhagen, a fierce critic of Smuts's campaign strategy, summed up the situation in September 1916: 'Our battlefield casualties have been negligible. What Smuts saves on the battlefield he loses in hospitals, for it is Africa and its climate we are really fighting, not the Germans.'[25]

The strategy began to disintegrate – in particular the notion of a mounted campaign. The virus and bacillus that had decimated his army had an equally devastating impact on the horses and mules they had brought with them. On the Western Front it was the machine-gun and fast-firing artillery that bought the age of cavalry to an end. In East Africa it was the tsetse-fly. Swarming down from the vines in their millions, and infecting horses with nagana fever, this tiny parasite proved itself a far more effective killer of horses than anything that had ever been produced by the great armaments factories of the Ruhr. In 1916 the monthly losses of horses ran at 100 per cent.[26] This bleak reality was one that the South Africans were disastrously slow to accept. Aware of his enemies' reliance on horses, Lettow-Vorbeck had calculatedly drawn the South Africans into regions in which the tsetse fly was most prevalent. Cavalry quickly became infantry, and supply trains ground to a halt. In the rains of spring 1916, the supply lines that were supposed to have fed and watered the advancing army became streams of black mud, littered with the bodies of tens of thousands of horses and mules.

Seasonal rains compounded the other problems, resulting in a campaign punctuated by periods of inactivity, in which armies were unable to reach one another. When forces did clash, they were often so depleted and exhausted by long marches that the fighting was short, as pursuit or encirclement across difficult terrain was beyond the capacity of even the victorious force. Nevertheless, despite the distances and the difficulties, there was a handful of set-piece battles. Although minuscule by the standards of the Western and Eastern fronts, such engagements were, in both tactics and spirit, of a piece with those being fought in Europe. When armies clashed over established positions in East Africa, the rapid fire of the Maxim machine gun and fury of artillery bombardments forced men to shelter in trenches and to protect those positions behind barbed wire. As in Flanders or Picardy, trenches in Africa had strongpoints and redoubts, and they witnessed frontal assaults, trench-raids and night-attacks. Despite the enormous logistical difficulties of massing a meaningful number of guns in any one place, there were still, on occasion, ferocious bombardments. At the end of 1916, at the Battle of Kibata, Lettow-Vorbeck besieged a force that was dug into entrenched positions. Using the guns stripped from the *Königsberg*, the Germans pounded the men of the British Gold Coast Regiment and the 129th Baluchis for days. Major Harold Lewis, who had served with the 129th Baluchis in France, now wrote to his mother on Boxing Day 1916 describing it:

> *We have had a very hard time, and for some days it was touch and go whether we should be able to hold our own against the Huns … all day long my left piquet [line of troops] was subjected to desultory bombardment from several guns, and also from heavy machine gun fire. An hour before dark, this developed into an intense bombard-ment, and except for the size of the shells, I never experienced such a hot one, even in France …*

Fighting alongside the King's African Rifles, Major Lewis and the 129th Baluchis sought to defend their lines by launching a night attack against the German positions. Lewis's vivid account of it could well have come from any of thousands of similar incidents on the Western Front:

> *We planned it so as to leave our trenches, and creep up to the Huns in the inky blackness, and to have moonlight as soon as we had the trenches. Accordingly at 11pm the line of bombers crept over the parapet and formed a line in the darkness … Bombs were thrown, the guns and machine-guns opened up and the still black night became pandemonium.*[27]

———— • ————

DAR ES SALAAM, 2014. Tucked away between a new office block and an industrial works on the edge of Dar es Salaam, in modern Tanzania, lies the city's War Cemetery. It is as well-tended and verdant as any in France or Belgium, and it is the resting place of 1,764 Allied victims of the East African campaign. Another 1,500 are remembered on a series of memorial walls. The long columns of neatly engraved names speak of a truly global conflict fought by men from opposite ends of the African continent. The names of men from Nigeria and Benin with Yoruba prefixes like 'Ade' and 'Olu' flow into clusters of Ashanti, Grunshi and Fante names – 'Kofi', 'Kobli' – men who left their homes in what today are Ghana and Burkina Faso to fight the Germans. The lists of the Indian dead – Sikhs, Muslims and Hindus – evoke the whole breadth of the subcontinent. Alongside them are the names of Arab riflemen from Zanzibar, poor peasant farmers of the Chinese Labour Corps, troops of the locally recruited King's African Rifles, engineers from the East African Railways, and translators from the East African Intelligence Department. Peppered among the soldiers is the occasional sailor – men who died on their transport ships while in transit or fell sick in Dar es Salaam. Beneath the symmetrical lines of headstones, clustered around a huge stone cross in the centre of one of the world's most multi-faith cemeteries, lie the remains of officers and men from the Burma Police, the South African Mounted Brigade, the East African Medical Corps and the Indian Veterinary Corps.

The defence of Kibata had fallen, in large part, to Indian and British African troops, and in this respect it was indicative of the way the war in German East Africa was developing. Although often thought of as the 'South African' phase, 1916 witnessed the increasing internationalization of the African conflict. As the campaign became more costly and logistically complex, and as more men became available from theatres elsewhere, the British drew in soldiers and labourers from across their empire – and even beyond. Alongside the South Africans were Indian units that had spent 1914 and 1915 on the Western Front. Among them were the 40th Pathans, the so-called 'Forty Thieves', who had fought at the Second Battle of Ypres and at Loos in 1915: hardened veterans of the war in Europe.* Despite the heavy casualties they had already endured, especially among their officers, the Pathans were still among the very toughest regiments in the Indian Army. They had been recruited from ethnic groups in what is now Pakistan and Afghanistan which the British still confidently regarded as true 'martial races'. Alongside them were the 129th Baluchis, the regiment of Major Harold Lewis and Khudadad Khan, the Victoria Cross recipient and hero of the First Battle of Ypres. The Baluchis brought to Africa the lessons they had learnt in the Ypres Salient and at Neuve Chapelle in 1915. But by 1916 they had a somewhat dubious reputation. After their withdrawal from the line in France, and following the murder of a British officer, they were suspected of having fallen under the influence of Ottoman propaganda, and they had refused to fight against the Turks in Mesopotamia, whom they saw as fellow Muslims. Weakened by their experiences in the trenches and, as far as the British were concerned, contaminated by enemy propaganda, they were nevertheless deemed suitable for East Africa, a theatre in which they might be useful, if not much more than that. As it turned out, the men of the 129th excelled in East Africa, as the letters of Harold Lewis demonstrate. Indian units like the Pathans and Baluchis found themselves in Africa serving alongside white Rhodesians, white South Africans and white volunteer units from British East Africa, for whom the concept of the Indian 'martial races' was at odds with prevailing racial attitudes in their home colonies, where both whites and black Africans had come to regard Indians as 'coolies' rather than soldiers. Early examples of Indian heroism under enemy fire went some way to undermining these prejudices.

As well as becoming more imperial in composition, the army that confronted Lettow-Vorbeck over the course of 1916 became

---

* Among the other Indian units in East Africa were the 2nd Kashmir Rifles, 3rd Kashmir Rifles, 130th Baluchis, 61st Pioneers, 27th Indian Mountain Battery, the 28th Indian Mountain Battery, 17th Cavalry, the Faridkot Sappers and Miners, and the 29th Punjabis.

more African. In July, the Gold Coast Regiment – men from
modern-day Ghana – were deployed in East Africa. In November,
four regiments of the West African Frontier Force arrived from
Lagos, their deployment having been delayed by concerns over
internal security in British Nigeria, where conscription of men
as military labourers had begun to grate. Other Africans,
recruited into the King's African Rifles, came from Sudan,
Rhodesia, Ethiopia and Nyasaland. These men, brought to a
distant, multicultural, multiracial military zone, hundreds of
miles from their homes, were – like most of the combatants
from outside German East Africa – displaced and dislocated.
Yoruba, Ibo or Hausa Nigerians, or Ashanti, Fante and Grunshi
men from the Gold Coast were now as far removed from their
own nations and cultures as any British soldier in the trenches
of Belgium – arguably more so. Perhaps most displaced of all
were the men of the Caribbean islands.[28] In 1916, the West India
Regiment, after having defeated the German-led forces in
Cameroon, were dispatched to East Africa. There, along with
elements of the recently formed British West Indies Regiment
(BWIR), created in the face of War Office hostility, they found
themselves now on the other side of an alien continent, about
which they knew very little and from which their ancestors had
been taken centuries earlier.

   Among the longest of the lists of names etched into the
memorial walls of the Dar es Salaam War Cemetery are of the
men of the King's African Rifles (KAR), the indigenous armed
force of British East Africa. Throughout 1916, and in the face of
constant objections and complaints from sections of the white
settler community in British East Africa, Britain expanded
recruitment into the KAR. Long neglected, and looked upon
with suspicion by the authorities in Nairobi before the war, the
regiment had been only 3,000-strong in 1914. By 1918 it had
expanded to over 35,000 men. As with the German *Askari*, the
KAR had been formed to put down 'risings of the native population'.[29] Both the KAR and the *Askari* were mercenary forces,
members of a respected profession. Both were relatively well

paid and far better rewarded and treated than the hundreds of thousands of their fellow Africans recruited or press-ganged into service as carriers. Military service offered an income, an impressive uniform and the chance to gain respect in their communities. For these reasons, and others, many young African men saw the war, even though it was not *their* war, as opening the door to possibilities – just as for the thousands of young Europeans who had rushed to the recruiting stations of 1914. But these colonial subjects were not being asked to fight for their nation, their liberty or their freedom. They were not the citizens of nations but the subjects of empires, and second-class subjects at that.

Understanding their true position, and fully aware that the colonial authorities showed little loyalty to Africans, there were those who made tactical and rational decisions about which side to fight for. When the 2nd KAR had been disbanded in 1911, a number of its former soldiers crossed the border into German East Africa and joined the *Askari*. This pattern was to be repeated throughout the war in East Africa, with men choosing to fight with the *Askari* for one season only to leave and change sides the next, if by doing so pay, prospects and conditions looked better. There was therefore an unknown number of African soldiers who fought for both the German and British empires.

The complex racial and cultural make-up of the force that Britain amassed for the invasion of German East Africa has been largely forgotten, however. It has been overwhelmed in historical memory by a popular narrative that focuses on the military talents of Lettow-Vorbeck.

★

Dar es Salaam – long abandoned by Schnee as German East Africa's capital – finally fell to the Allies in September 1916. It not only became the key port feeding men and materials into the war, it was also designated the logistical centre of the war in East Africa. A cluster of hospitals sprang up, despite the fact that the city was an infamously sickly and malarial settlement. Its capture

helped ease British supply problems, but also concentrated thousands of men in a city where disease was easily incubated and
infection spread rapidly. Among the most tragic stories of how
disease and climate conspired to wreak tragedy is that of the 800
men of the Seychelles Labour Battalion. Representing 15 per
cent of the entire population of those tiny islands, they arrived in
Dar es Salaam in December 1916 to work on the docks and in the
supply lines. Within six months, 335 of them had died, mainly of
malaria and bacillary dysentery.[30] Their deployment was so short,
and so disastrous, that little is known of them. The governmental
records themselves seem unable to agree even on units' official
names. Only one of the Seychelles labourers has a known grave
within the city. The remains of three others lie in cemeteries in
Bombay, while 289 have no known grave.

By September 1916, Lettow-Vorbeck's force had been pushed
into the southern fringes of the colony, and by now the ports of
Tanga, Lindi, Kilwa and Sudi had all fallen, in addition to Dar es
Salaam, as had the Central Railway on which the Germans had
long relied. Smuts's own East African war was almost over too.
On 27 December 1916 he was summoned to London to take up
a seat in the Imperial War Cabinet, and the remaining South
African forces were evacuated and later readied for deployment
on the Western Front. Smuts left for London on 20 January 1917,
having effectively declared victory, and with it – in his eyes – dem-
onstrating the supremacy of white soldiers over the *Askari*, whom
he had dismissed back in March 1916 as a force of 'damned
kaffirs'. Not only was this a misrepresentation of his own multinational force, but when the South Africans arrived home, their
emaciated frames and harrowing stories led to a public outcry
against Smuts, who was accused of having allowed his men to
starve and permitted medical facilities to slip into a state of crisis.
What success there was had been achieved at a high cost – indeed,
much higher than the welcoming crowds in Durban and Pretoria
yet knew. The virtual collapse of the lines of supply and the scandalous state of the army's medical infrastructure had exacted a
terrible toll on the fighting men. The catastrophic losses of

horses and mules had resulted in whole units going days without food. Rations were constantly short, and sick men died because they were not evacuated fast enough. The obliteration of the cavalry mounts and pack animals by the tsetse-fly not only undermined Smuts's campaign strategy; it was the prelude to the greatest human tragedy of all, which stemmed from the fact that the war could only now be carried to the enemy on the backs of human beings.

The largest 'army' of the East African war was neither the *Askari*, nor the South Africans, nor the King's African Rifles, but the enormous forces of carriers who laboured for all sides. Their conditions were for the most part far worse than those endured by the soldiers, and their death toll can be measured not in thousands, or tens of thousands, but in hundreds of thousands. It was a war in which the vast majority of victims were civilians – either the men drawn into the conflict as labourers or people through whose villages and fields the war passed, leaving devastation and famine in its wake. Even by 1916 the war had become what we would today call a 'humanitarian disaster'.

In the first months of the conflict, the British had been able to recruit carriers on a voluntary basis from among the peoples of British East Africa. They were needed only in relatively small numbers and were at this stage paid comparatively well. In those confident days, when the distances over which the war was fought remained manageable and almost everyone felt that the conflict would soon be over, the rations given to the carriers were mostly adequate and there was some effective oversight of their conditions. Things quickly began to change in 1916, when Smuts's campaign led to a renewed war of movement across the often inhospitable terrain. In anticipation of such an eventuality, the British in 1915 had passed the Native Followers Recruitment Ordinance, a law that allowed for compulsory recruitment of men from across British-ruled Africa to work as carriers.[31] It was in theory a wartime contingency measure, but few provisions of the conflict were as effective at servicing the needs of the war while simultaneously also tightening European domination over Africans and advancing the economic interests of the white minority. The ordinance allowed the military authorities to press-gang into service all African men except those already working for Europeans. This had the effect of funnelling the required 3,000 men a month into what was now officially called the Carrier Corps.

.The new law had another consequence, too – pushing thousands of men to attempt to escape the Carrier Corps by seeking employment on European farms, thereby abandoning their independence and their own plots. The law took men away from their homes, ripped African communal life apart, and was bitterly resented. With so many men seeking employment, laws of supply and demand came into play. Africans were compelled to accept longer, less-advantageous contracts from white civilian employers. Rather than three-month contracts, many had to accept year-long ones. The ordinance also slashed the wages paid to carriers by two-thirds, from 15 rupees per month at the start of the war to 5 rupees; carriers even had to pay 2 rupees for their own metal identification tags, which were introduced as a means to manage the huge numbers of men conscripted. (The tags were uncomfortably similar to those issued by the Germans to the inmates of their concentration camps in South West Africa a decade earlier.) The whole carrier system rapidly became a form of compulsory labour that was distinguishable from slavery only by its derisory wages. The decision, in 1916, to confront Lettow-Vorbeck across a potentially vast battlefield, with a large multinational force, ushered in an enormous rise in the size of the Carrier Corps. Government recruiters now scoured the continent looking for eligible men. Some black Africans sought escape by leaving their villages, squatting on European farms, or heading to the cities. Chiefs were threatened with fines or imprisonment if they attempted to evade the attentions of the recruiters.

Once the invasion of German East Africa was under way, the death toll among the carriers quickly rose. They were expected to march hundreds of miles, bearing loads of 40–60 pounds, over improvised roads and tracks beaten through the bush. The supply lines took men across different landscapes, forcing them to endure huge climatic changes. In the cold highlands men froze. It was not unknown for carriers to die from pneumonia while crossing the hills, while others, in the same column and on the same expedition, would later fall prey to tropical malaria when they reached the warmer, wetter regions. Things were made worse because of failures to supply the suppliers. From the earliest campaigns of 1914, sickness rates among porters had been worryingly high and sanitation poor. Carriers, weakened by exhaustion, were made yet more vulnerable by inadequate rations. Those for carriers were often of an especially low quality. Mealie meal that contained particles of grit caused diarrhoea, which in turn led to often-fatal dysentery, especially hundreds of miles away from medical assistance. Sudden changes in rations could be just as disastrous. Men used to eating green vegetables were given maize, badly cooked rice or mealie meal and beans. The history of European involvement in Africa, and the work of European anthropologists, had long demonstrated the poten-tially devastating effects that radical changes in diet could have upon men undergoing such arduous journeys. Yet these lessons were unlearned, and warning voices went unheeded.

The scale of recruitment to the Carrier Corps was vast. By the end of the 1917, the majority of men in the British colonies that bordered German East Africa had served as carriers. Nyasaland sent 86 per cent of its available manpower to carry the arms and materials of the British forces, while distant Nigeria was required to produce 4,000 porters each month. By the end of the war in Africa, over 1 million men had been forced – one way or another – to work on the British supply lines. From March 1916 onwards, as Lettow-Vorbeck was pushed back from the north of the German colony, the conquered regions became additional recruiting grounds as men who had served the Germans as carri-ers were now seized by the British.

There was a direct link between the enormity of the recruit-ment drive and the enormity of the battle zone, and here the cruel arithmetic of military supply stoked the fires of a human catastrophe. A carrier in East Africa had to bear not only the load he was supposed to deliver to the front, but his own food too. It meant that at a certain point, the law of diminishing returns made it virtually impossible to supply a distant army. This had two immediate consequences. The first was that the rations of carriers were maintained at levels that were inadequate for human health. The other was that in order to get food and ammunition to the most distant battle zones literally thousands of men were required for each ton of supplies, which increased the demand for men and widened the scope and scale of the recruitment drives. The vast size of the Carrier Corps had other unintended consequences. The greater the number of men on any march, the greater the risk that outbreaks of communicable disease would decimate their columns. The more men living together, and sleeping in the fields and forests at night, the more they polluted their own water supplies, spreading disease. The greater the distances marched, the higher the number of men who died because they were unable to reach distant medical centres.

The effect of mass mortality among the carriers was felt far beyond the supply lines, too. The greater the number of men who failed to return from their periods of service, the more their depleted communities at home struggled to work their fields and feed themselves. The inevitable and predictable consequence of the imposition of mass recruitment on communities whose food security was tenuous at the best of times was that when the rains failed – as they did in parts of East Africa in 1916 and 1917 – there was widespread famine.

Despite these immense depredations visited upon the British Empire's African subjects, for historic reasons the British were always fearful of being accused of slavery. In German East Africa, too, for political reasons they hoped to avoid, as much as was possible, offending the local population in a region they hoped to take control of after the war. Derisory wages for carriers offered the British a moral fig-leaf; but the Germans often did not even bother with this, resorting to the open use of forced labour. Moral qualms seem to have little troubled the minds of Lettow-Vorbeck and Schnee.[32] The Germans repeatedly, and in the end routinely, resorted to forced recruitment. While the carriers who were directly linked to each fighting company – often specialists who knew how to transport key pieces of military kit – were paid, the thousands of African men who found themselves forced to work the German supply lines were not. In the latter stages of the war, when Lettow-Vorbeck's *Askari* were increasingly prone to desertion and food was scarce, the Germans descended on villages and simply abducted men. There are accounts of carriers being tied together with rope and other reports of men being shot dead for attempting to escape their bondage. Schnee kept poor records of the number of carriers 'recruited' by the German forces. As most were not being paid, the incentive to even record names, dates of work or dates of death for them was minimal. Records of others – the forced conscripts as opposed to the virtual slaves – offer a far from complete picture. This lack of documentation allowed Germany after the war to confect ludicrously low official estimates of men press-ganged into service and those who died – a fiction maintained in the face of evidence to the contrary between the wars, when Lettow-Vorbeck and his apologists were mythologizing the conflict as one characterized by chivalry and decency, and in which Africans had willingly and loyally served their German masters. Behind closed doors there was more honesty, though. One post-war German estimate put the number of porters who had died servicing the Germans at between 100,000 and 120,000. The same source believed 250,000 had perished supplying British imperial forces.

The British kept some records, but then suppressed them after the war. The scale of the losses strongly suggests that carriers were treated, at times, as a disposable resource, far less valuable that fighting men. Anecdotal evidence also suggests that the high casualty rates were regarded by some as an acceptable and inevitable cost of the war. One colonial official admitted that the British record in East Africa 'only stopped short of a scandal because the people who suffered most were the carriers – and after all who cares about native carriers'.[33] In 1922 the British governor of what was by then known as Tanganyika Territory argued that for the dead of the Carrier Corps to be remembered with individual graves, as white soldiers were, would be a waste of public money. The notes of a meeting between representatives of the Imperial War Graves Commission and the governor recorded that he 'considered that the vast Carrier Corps Cemeteries at Dar es Salaam and elsewhere should be allowed to revert to nature as speedily as possible & did not care to contemplate the statistics of the native African lives lost in trying to overcome the transportation difficulties of the campaign in East Africa'.[34] Such an unwillingness to grant individual graves was influenced by ideas of race and religion, by a belief that as 'people of nature' Africans would not understand the significance of individual burials. But it was also motivated by a desire on the part of the British authorities and government not to draw to public attention, in Africa and elsewhere, to the numbers of carriers who had died in East Africa.

Yet even in the midst of war, there were British soldiers, missionaries, doctors and officials who were aware of the suffering of the Carrier Corps and regarded it as scandalous. And overall, it is difficult to read the history of the Carrier Corps as anything other than a scandal of neglect for their lives, conditions, and – after the war – for their memory.[35]

★

Lettow-Vorbeck's press-ganging of Africans was the darker side to what was trumpeted then and later as his capacity to live off the land. The legend created was that he fought what one commander described as 'the cheapest war in the world', in which his army took self-sufficiency to new and undreamed of levels – a make-do-and-mend war, that was fought at cost price. At the same time as the British naval blockade was forcing German civilians to drink coffee made of ground acorns, and tea made from linden blossom (and thereby bringing the word *ersatz* – 'substitute' – into common usage on the German Home Front), Lettow-Vorbeck and his army were learning how to create *ersatz* war materials. They fabricated the insulators for their telegraph wires from empty beer bottles with the bottoms removed, as well as from bones; they distilled a form of quinine, in drink form, that became known as 'Lettow Schnapps'. Although repulsive to taste, it was nonetheless effective. The undoubted resourceful-ness of Lettow-Vorbeck's men allowed him to overcome many of the challenges posed by the British blockade (though that was far from airtight), and such ingenuity was celebrated both during and after the war.

This colourful tale of human creativity in the face of adversity has a darker sub-plot, though, not limited to the procurement of forced labour. The British Carrier Corps system, calamitous as it was, had been deemed by London to be a lesser evil than a British attempt to live off the land. For what the term meant in East and Central Africa during the First World War was the wide-scale confiscation of food from civilians. Armies on all sides requisitioned food from the villages they marched through. British units were known to pay in cash for it. For the more remote communities, cash for their precious food supplies was not much use, especially when, with so many of their men already serving as carriers, their food security was already dangerously fragile. But, as the Germans had few other means of supply, the demands they placed upon civilians tended to be more costly. At times, the German columns paid for supplies with promissory notes given to village leaders, assuring them that all debts would be repaid after a German victory. But on other occasions food was simply stolen.

Lettow-Vorbeck's travelling contingent of doctors attempted, at times, to make up for requisition demands by helping to treat the sick in the villages they passed through. Their lack of medical supplies limited the effectiveness of these 'acts of kindness' (and were in any case outweighed by the underlying self-interest). However, alongside his self-sufficiency, the war-time and post-war mythologizing of Lettow-Vorbeck focused on the ingenuity of his medical staff. Although the rates of ill health between the two armies were not that divergent, historians of the East African campaign have been rightly impressed at the capacity of the

German forces, without access to proper supplies, to control the
levels of disease. Medical care within Lettow-Vorbeck's army was
very well maintained and advanced. His doctors were not only
competent, they were even innovative, exhibiting a professional
curiosity and always rising to the challenge of extremely testing
circumstances. The *Schutztruppe* had the advantage of inheriting
a large medical staff present in the colony when war broke out.
A research programme into sleeping-sickness was under way, and
these civilian doctors were added to the *Schutztruppe*, giving
Lettow-Vorbeck a total of sixty-three medical staff.[36]

Their expertise was much needed, given that disease and
epidemics played such a critical role in this conflict – and that
the war of movement itself became the means of the transmis-
sion of disease across a great swathe of the continent. There was
a widespread belief among the colonial powers that all Africans
possessed some degree of immunity to tropical disease. But as
the death rates on all sides demonstrated, this was a fantasy.
Men recruited from West Africa, or from the dry south of the
continent, were just as vulnerable to the diseases of East Africa
as any European. Immunity, as much as it existed, was highly
localized, and once men were forced to leave their own regions
they died in vast numbers from malaria and dysentery. There
had been a similar strain of climatic determinism in the decision to deploy the South Africans to East Africa in 1915: the
belief that Boer commandos, used to the arid lands of the South
African veldt or the acacia scrub of South West Africa, were
somehow naturally adapted to the tropical conditions of East
Africa went largely unchallenged. And as the armies marched,
the diseases marched alongside them, conquering new territories, such that the war changed the disease map of a continent,
introducing diseases into areas where they had never previously
existed. Sleeping sickness, which originated in West Africa, was
spread into new regions, beginning an epidemic that lasted
until the 1940s.

★

The cat-and-mouse game of Lettow-Vorbeck and his pursuers – and all that it entailed – had another two years to run after the capture of Dar es Salaam. Yet the First World War in Africa has often been dismissed as a 'side show', a minor footnote in the story of a European conflict. While the outcome of the First World War was unquestionably decided on the battlefields of the Eastern and Western fronts, the war's impact on Africa was enormous. For millions of Africans the war was a disaster. Two million Africans were dragged into the conflict; the number who died is unknowable. At least 100,000 of the 1 million carriers recruited by the British died; some suspect the actual figure was at least double that number. Around another 200,000 Africans died of the effects of the Spanish Flu – spread across their continent by the war. Millions more were affected by the fighting, their crops seized and their men conscripted by force and taken from their communities, leaving women, children and the elderly struggling to plant and harvest crops. At times, the forced conscription of men into the ranks of the European-led armies became disturbingly redolent of the slave raids of past centuries, while the scorched-earth policies followed by the German forces in East Africa were horribly in keeping with the decades of repression, exploitation and extermination that had characterized the Scramble for Africa.

By some estimates a million Africans died directly or indirectly as a consequence of the First World War. Disease, the famines that followed forced conscription, and the requisition of food stocks all killed far more Africans than the actual fighting. An official post-war German estimate suggested that around 300,000 civilians had died from starvation attributed to the conflict.[37] In 1917 it was estimated that one in twenty of the entire population of Africa had died as a result of the war.[38] Ludwig Deppe, a doctor who fought alongside Lettow-Vorbeck, admitted in his account of the campaign that the European-led armies had become a scourge on the continent, a force for devastation and death comparable to those that had ravaged Germany and Central Europe three centuries earlier. 'Behind us,' he wrote, 'we leave destroyed fields, ransacked magazines and for the immediate future, starvation. We are no longer the agents of culture, our track is marked by death, plundering and evacuated villages, just like the progress of our own enemies in the Thirty Years War.'[39]

Between 1914 and 1918, Africa and its people were viewed by the European powers primarily as a resource, as they had been for much of the previous century, and as they were to be again once the guns fell silent. One consequence was that from French North Africa, through the French and British colonies in West Africa, down as far south as British Nyasaland, the war sparked a series of uprisings and revolts as people attempted to resist the increasingly repressive policies of their colonizers. The end of the war in Africa did not herald a return to normality but rather ushered in another great carve-up of land and peoples. Under the terms of the Treaty of Versailles, and beneath a legalistic fig-leaf provided by the League of Nations, Africans of the former German colonies found themselves and their lands transferred to the empires of the victorious powers after 1919. New rulers arrived with new languages, customs, racial theories and their own interpretations of the civilizing mission. Often this meant little more than the local administrators wore a different uniform and spoke English or French rather than German; but these transferred territories, stripped from Germany and repackaged as 'mandates', were enormous in scale. 'Little Togoland' was certainly little compared to other African colonies; but it was larger than Belgium and the French provinces of Alsace and Lorraine combined.[40] German Cameroon was about the same size as pre-1914 Germany. German South West Africa was one-and-a-half times the size of the fatherland, and German East Africa twice its size.

In both its costs and its consequences the First World War in Africa was far from being a meaningless side show in Europe's war. It became the last phase of the Scramble for Africa.

CHAPTER 4

'LA FORCE NOIRE'

Africa in Europe – the 'races guerrières'

––––––––––

1887. In this year French artist Albert Bettanier completes his masterwork, entitled *La Tache Noire* – 'The Black Stain'. The principal figures of his painting are a geography master and his young pupil, who stand together, between the rows of desks to their backs and a great map of France in front of them, propped on an easel. As the rest of the class looks on intently, the frock-coated teacher rests one fatherly hand on the boy's shoulder and with his other hand points solemnly to the 'lost provinces' of Alsace and Lorraine – coloured black on the map. His focus remains on the wide-eyed face of the boy.

The painting exudes symbolism and allegory. Every detail of the boys and their classroom holds coded references ready for the viewer to decipher. The pupil wears the uniform of the school battalions, which train young boys of Third Republic France in military drill and rifle practice – hinted at by the gun-rack at the back of the classroom. The huge blackboard to the right of the French map represents Germany, while the scourge of Prussian militarism finds physical form in a war drum set on a table nearby. On the far wall, another map, that of the walled city of Paris as it was in the 1870s, reminds the viewer of the Prussian siege of the French capital at the end of the Franco-Prussian War. Casting an ominous shadow over that map is another symbolic representation of Germany, in the shape of a ceiling-lamp. Black and spindly, its arms appear to stretch threateningly around Paris, as if it were the eagle at the centre of the flag of Kaiser Wilhelm II's

Germany. The boys at their desks all play their roles, too. One, a blond-haired child seated in the first row, is dressed in a white military uniform and wears the *Légion d'Honneur*, the medal he is destined (one presumes) to win in some future war to restore French honour and territory, a war that will inevitably be the duty of his generation … .[1]

———— • ————

Bettanier himself had been born in Lorraine, in the city of Metz, and he and his family elected to remain French following the annexation of their home province by the Germans. By the 1880s, having moved to Paris, he had achieved fame for both his artistic talents and his determination to use those gifts to constantly remind France of its loss and humiliation in the Franco-Prussian War. *La Tache Noire* was but the most successful and powerful of a series of his paintings that were both a lament to loss and a call to arms. But it was a work that also – perhaps unconsciously – touched on the other great issue confronting Third Republic France: that the classes of boys such as he depicted were, quite simply, too small in size. In the years between the 1870s and 1914, French military cadets – boys not much older than Bettanier's – were often taken to the border and encouraged to gaze across at lost Alsace and Lorraine. Further east, beyond the horizon, lay Germany itself and for decades the French cadets who marched up the hills of the frontiers, to view the lands annexed by Germany, did so in the knowledge that the great enemy over that horizon was growing in strength and in numbers at a velocity that France was unable to match.

France had begun the nineteenth century as one of the demographic superpowers of Europe, second only to Russia, and by the time of its defeat in 1871 the population had reached 36 million. But that of the newly unified Germany, even before the absorption of Alsace and Lorraine, stood at 41 million, and by 1914 there were 67 million Germans compared to 40 million French. (Even in 2014, neither Britain nor France has reached the population that Germany attained by the time of the First World War.) To increase French anxiety, in 1897 Dr Jacques Bertillon, a celebrated demographer and Director of the Paris Statistical Bureau, wrote: 'It grieves me to say it, but I see firm proof of the imminent disappearance of our country.' The proof he was referring to was the latest national census, which demonstrated that for the last four decades the death rate in France had *exceeded* the birth rate.[2] In the same decades in which France had projected its power, trade, language and culture across the globe, its population growth had ground to a halt. Villages had been left deserted, and unwanted homes and farms abandoned. At the same time, France's population had been exceeded not only by Germany's but also by Britain's and Austria-Hungary's. The nation, at the end of the century, had sunk to fifth place in Europe's league table of populous nations.

Germany's unprecedented demographic boom, by contrast, was a trend that showed no sign of slowing down. The German anxiety was the mirror opposite of the French one: the inability of the Reich to find space, work and opportunities for its excess population, the so-called *Volk ohne Raum* – 'people without space'. Those in Germany who had led the clamour for colonies in the 1870s and 1880s, a campaign that pressured Chancellor Otto von Bismarck into the acquisition of Germany's four African territories, had argued that only with an empire would Germany be able to find living space for the *Volk ohne Raum*, millions of whom were being lost in emigration to America.

Thus, while Germans talked of the evident and natural vitality of their race, Frenchmen were reading predictions of their coming extinction and discussed ways of 'saving the race'. In the last year of the nineteenth century, the ailing Emile Zola caught the mood of his times with his novel *La Fécondité*. A joyous evocation of the power of life and a hymn to the community of nation, it was also – in part – an appeal to French womanhood. 'O French mothers,' pleaded Zola, 'make children, so that France may keep her rank, her strength and her prosperity for it is necessary for the world's salvation that France should live.'[3] To the consternation of politicians, generals and philosophers – as well as novelists – French women had gained access to contraception well before women in Germany and Britain. The better-off had managed to escape, almost completely, the animal cycle of repro-duction. Yet this liberation of French womanhood was looked upon, by Zola and others, as a calamitous threat to the very exis-tence of the nation. France's declining birth rate, and Germany's demographic boom, meant that when it came to men of military age, France could muster a mere 4.5 million men compared to Germany's 7.7 million (and rising). Reflecting on France's defeat in 1871, a chorus of voices sought to ascribe the calamity to a culture of decadence, of which the low birth rate was a symptom. (The superior tactics and leadership of the Prussian forces were brushed aside as minor details.)

Bettanier's paintbrush was animated by these the twin obses-sions of Third Republic France: the dream of revenge (*Revanche*) to regain the lost provinces, which mired France in a culture of awestruck militarism of a sort that even Prussians might have found excessive; and the fear that, with each passing year, this national mission seemed to be slipping beyond the nation's reach as a direct consequence of the birth-rate crisis. These two phenomena – and a potential solution – came together in the pugnacious, if diminutive, figure of General Charles Mangin, a soldier for whom *La Revanche* was the keystone on which his austere character was built, and a military theorist who believed that he had found a 'reservoir of men' that might tip the scales in France's favour.

———

PARIS, 23 JUNE 1940. Adolf Hitler – the former dispatch runner, who had spent four years in the trenches dreaming of reaching Paris as a mere foot soldier – arrives in the city as conqueror and *Führer*, nine days after his *Wehrmacht* has entered the capital. In six weeks Hitler's army has achieved what his own generation had previously failed to do in four years. In the warm light of a June morning, accompanied by architect Albert Speer, the sculptor Arno Breker and a gaggle of generals, all in their Sunday best, Hitler makes a triumphal tour of the city. Newsreel film shows the *Führer* and his generals standing at the Trocadero, with the Eiffel Tower as their backdrop; the scenes reverberate around a stunned world. If he wishes to, at this moment of triumph, Hitler can take revenge on Paris for the humiliations meted out on Germany after the earlier war. He might order the destruction of the Palace of Versailles, where the hated treaty of 1919 was signed. He might level Les Invalides and take Napoleon's body to Berlin, or strip the Louvre of its treasures.

Instead he orders the destruction of just two of the French capital's many statues. The first is of Edith Cavell, the heroic and humane British nurse, whose execution by the Germans in 1915 created a martyr and a potent propaganda figure for the Allies. The second is of Charles Mangin.

———— • ————

Charles Mangin, long dead by 1940, is largely forgotten today outside of France; but after the First World War his legend burned bright in both the French national consciousness and the minds of a whole generation of German statesmen and soldiers. Like Hitler, he had been consumed, motivated and energized by his hatreds. Short, whip-thin and constantly agitated, his bitterness and fiery lust for *La Revanche* was imprinted on the lines of his face. In most photographs his protruding jaw appears to be permanently clenched, as if awaiting some imminent blow. His thick black hair stuck up straight, giving him a somewhat thuggish appearance. In historian Alistair Horne's memorable words: 'Mangin was a killer, and he looked the part.'[4]

At the same time that Albert Bettanier and his family had abandoned their home in Lorraine, Mangin's own family – conservative, Catholic and deeply patriotic – had been forced to abandon their lives and property in Alsace. Mangin had then entered the army, serving as a lieutenant in Africa – first in Sudan, then Mali and French North Africa. Indeed, in the years before 1914 he was to spend two-thirds of his career in France's colonies, specializing in leading actions to pacify rebellious peoples. It was Mangin who had led a column of *Tirailleurs Sénégalais* during the Fashoda Expedition, the two-year-long and dangerously misconceived French mission in 1898, which had almost sparked an Anglo-French war on encountering Kitchener's forces in Sudan. Mangin breathed in the air of the continent more deeply than most colonial soldiers. In French West Africa he learnt Bambara, the *lingua franca* of that vast colony, and following his time in the French North African colonies he took to sleeping in a tent – irrespective of the weather. Wounded three times and decorated for his bravery, he had gradually come to regard himself as an African 'expert'. At some point in his early career, Mangin, it seems, also became influenced (or at least inspired) by the work of Count Eugène-Melchior de Vogüé.

De Vogüé was one of those figures, seemingly unique to the late nineteenth and early twentieth centuries, who were able to combine work as an amateur archeologist with a passionate orientalism, while at the same time serving as a diplomat. An *attaché* to the Ottoman Empire and later an emissary to Russia, de Vogüé became a notable expert on Russian literature, influencing the reading habits of many of his countrymen. But his influence on Mangin was more philosophical than literary. De Vogüé's ideas on nationhood and empire, for the most part, ran along well-worn grooves. Like many others, he looked to the example of Rome in the hope of identifying the forces that caused great powers to decline and empires to collapse. By contrast with some, though, who put Rome's fall down to racial mixing, de Vogüé saw it as a consequence of cultural and civilizational decline – and all around him in *fin-de-siècle* France he detected the same cancer at work. He postulated that Rome might have saved itself by infusing the blood and savage energy of Barbarian tribes to counter the crippling decadence of the Romans themselves. France, de Vogüé suggested, could harness the life-energy and warrior spirit of the culturally inferior peoples of its empire, forging their menfolk into new legions dedicated to the defence of France.

In 1899, the year of Zola's *La Fécondité,* de Vogüé published *Les Morts qui parlent* ('The Dead Who Speak'), a novel that embraced these thoughts. Exposed to the 'school of action and responsibility' that was life in the West African colonies, Pierre Andarran, a young officer, becomes a new sort of Frenchman, freed from the decadence of metropolitan France and its corrupting politics, one of the 'cadres of our national regeneration'. In many ways, Pierre is a romanticized fictional version of what Charles Mangin was to become.[5] In conversation with his politician brother, Pierre predicts that when his generation of colonial officers finally take command of the French Army their masculine vitality will 'make our European adversaries think twice before trying to push the French around'.[6] Having fought alongside black Africans, Pierre is also convinced of their great martial potential in a French national rebirth. In one crucial passage, Pierre appeals to his brother:

> *If you would like to provide us with the means, we could put at your disposition tomorrow one hundred thousand, two hundred thousand incomparable soldiers, Senegalese, Sudanese, Hausas; bayonets who do not reason, retreat, or forgive; submissive and barbaric forces ... England subjugated the world with a few regiments of Sepoys. We can give you the same tools for the same service.*[7]

In fact, France had begun to recruit *Troupes Coloniales* in its African colonies as early as the 1820s, and by the end of the century all the colonial powers in Africa, including the Germans, had created similar armies of local mercenaries. In 1857, the Governor General of French West Africa, Louis Faidherbe, established a new force, the *Tirailleurs Sénégalais* ('Senegalese Riflemen'). He envisaged they would enable him to police and then expand French control in the region, and they were repeatedly deployed during the conquest and 'pacification' of the two federations of French West Africa and French Equatorial Africa.

Despite their name, the *Tirailleurs Sénégalais* were recruited from right across the enormous French colony, and not just Senegal. Some of the earliest 'recruits' were slaves bought from local owners; but some were volunteers, attracted by the offer of regular pay and the excitement of military service. Like the sepoys of India, the *Tirailleurs Sénégalais* were eventually deployed beyond their homelands, sent to suppress revolts and police the local populations of France's other African colonies: Madagascar, French Congo, Chad and North Africa.

By the early twentieth century the *Tirailleurs Sénégalais* were well established as a professional mercenary army, which had proved itself an effective fighting force; but they were still regarded as only being suitable for service in the colonies. France, during the same decades, had recruited units of North African soldiers in Algeria and Tunisia, and in its great moments of peril in the Franco-Prussian War had brought these men, Arabs and Berbers, onto the European battlefield. It was the first appearance in modern times of fighting units from Africa on the European continent. Yet the thought of deploying black men from sub-Saharan Africa on European soil was seen as a step too far.

In 1907, Mangin became Commandant Supérieur of the *Troupes du Groupe de l'Afrique Occidentale Française*. In that capacity, he began from 1909 onwards to set out a new vision for the *Tirailleurs Sénégalais*, and they were a radical departure. He became the key spokesman for an informal group of army officers, most with colonial service under their belts and personal experience of leading Africans in battle. What Mangin argued for was not only the expansion of the *Tirailleurs* into a force hundreds-of-thousands strong, but that this black army be used to defend France and perhaps one day help reclaim the lost provinces from Germany. Black Africa, in Mangin's conception, would become France's 'reservoir of men'. He justified this radical policy – in the face of enormous opposition – by energetically arguing that the *Tirailleurs Sénégalais* were a potential solution, though not a comprehensive one, to France's birth-rate crisis. (On the latter issue, Mangin was able to point to his own efforts in that area. As true French patriots, he and his wife had rejected birth control and done their bit in the demographic race against Germany by having eight children.)

In 1910, Mangin published his book *La Force Noire* – in effect his manifesto for the expansion of the *Tirailleurs Sénégalais* and the French North African forces. With little in the way of hard demographic data to support him, and in the face of practical objections from many of France's colonial experts, Mangin claimed that France would be able to recruit 10,000 West Africans each year; it was after all France, and not Britain, that possessed the most extensive empire in Africa.[8] Mangin confidently asserted that despite France's recent practice of purchasing slaves to serve in the *Tirailleurs Sénégalais*, he could persuade thousands of men from West Africa to volunteer for service. Tantalizingly, he also suggested that his estimates were perhaps conservative and that even greater numbers of men might be drawn from the region.[9]

The rationale behind the *Force Noire* theory was not just that Africa was a huge and easily tapped reservoir of fighting men, but that racial factors – both physiological and psychological – made some of them specially suited to modern, industrialized warfare. Mangin argued that Africans, as members of allegedly primitive races, had 'warrior instincts that remain extremely powerful'.[10] He suggested that Africans were naturally capable of carrying heavier loads than other soldiers and were better able to survive and fight in harsh climates. Mangin and others of a similar view cited dubious anecdotal evidence, including the suspiciously opportune accounts of French surgeons who reported that they had successfully operated on African men without the aid of anesthetics. Slipping into the idiom of racial anthropology – one of the most influential pseudo-sciences of his age – he claimed that Africans had an underdeveloped nervous system, which, in some unspecified way, enabled them to withstand the shock of battle, rendering them conveniently immune to the post-traumatic, psychological conditions that blighted white European troops. With all the over-assured confidence of an amateur psychologist, Mangin maintained that the low intellectual abilities of Africans meant that they were unable to rationally analyse their chances of survival in a combat situation, and so they believed only in fate. This lack of analytical aptitude meant that Africans were consequently less distressed by the thought of impending combat, and less psychologically damaged having gone through the experience. Later, he even claimed that African troops were so unperturbed by the experience of modern warfare that they were able to sleep through bombardments, if so ordered. In one of the more infamous passages of *La Force Noire*, Mangin wrote:

> *The black troops ... have precisely those qualities that are demanded in the long struggles in modern war: rusticity, endurance, tenacity, the instinct for combat, the absence of nervousness, and an incomparable power of shock. Their arrival on the battlefield would have a considerable moral effect on the adversary.*[11]

This idea that the real power of Africans on the battlefield was as shock troops – men who would lead the attack, and through their military prowess and sheer impact on the nerves of their opponents overwhelm them physically and psychologically – stood at the heart of Mangin's theory. In one of the more portentous passages, which perhaps betrays the influence of de Vogüé, Mangin foresaw that 'In future battles, these primitives, for whom life counts so little and whose young blood flows so ardently, as if avid to be shed, will certainly attain the old "French fury", and will reinvigorate it if necessary.'[12]

It was this assertion that savage and fatalistic African troops had the capacity to overwhelm their enemies by the shock of their attack that was later to prove so disastrous for them. Yet in this view, Mangin was not a lone voice. General Hippolyte Langlois, of the Ecole de Guerre, averred:

> *Those who belong to the black race take their qualities as warriors from their heredity, because, as far back as we can go in history, the state of war has been normal in Africa – their social situation that*

teaches them discipline; the harsh conditions of their existence which render them persistent, their carelessness, which makes them tenacious in the long struggles that characterise the modern battles; their bloody and fatalist temperament, which renders them terrible and shocking ... .[13]

While serving in the colonies, Mangin had concluded that these qualities were shared by all the peoples of West Africa – that they were all, to some degree, warrior peoples. Like Langlois, he concluded that this was a consequence of history, as Africa had been for centuries one 'vast battlefield'. However, Mangin had also become convinced that some Africans were more martial than others. Viewing disparate African societies, their traditions and cultures, through the prism of European values and the current racial theories, Mangin blithely ranked, categorized, praised or dismissed the peoples of French West Africa. His French concept of *les races guerrières* was in many respects identical to the British notion of the martial races of India. The British themselves were perfectly happy to concede that such classifications were just as pertinent to the peoples of West Africa's forest belt as they were to the hill tribes of the North-West Frontier. (Indeed, in the 1890s, when the British and French were at times bitter rivals for territory in West Africa, both nations feared the prospect of the other annexing the lands of the most martial peoples of the region.[14]) In Mangin's hands, these ideas went on to determine which African societies found themselves drawn into the World's War. Mangin's theories often decided who lived and who died.

There was, however, much opposition to the *Force Noire* theory and a heated debate in the press. Mangin and his supporters were able to marshal, in support of their campaign within France, the fact that these ideas provoked immense hostility in Germany, on the part of both its right-wing and left-wing press.[15] There was visceral German opposition to the mere suggestion that a black French army might, in some future conflict, be deployed in Europe. In the febrile atmosphere of Third Republic France, such loud squeals of opposition was taken as proof that Germany feared the men of France's African colonies and that, therefore, Mangin was onto something.

★

When the German Army crossed into Belgium in August 1914, and the French launched their own invasion over the German frontiers in the hope of finally seizing back Alsace and Lorraine, the French High Command was nevertheless convinced (as much as anyone) that the war would be a short affair, in which French national spirit and the legendary *élan* of its fighting men – pent up since the defeat of 1871 – would carry the day. In August 1914, France had around 90,000 *troupes indigènes* in her ranks – non-white soldiers from West and North Africa. Although it was widely expected that they would play only a marginal role in this short war in Europe, they were quickly mobilized. When the Lahore Division of the British Indian Corps landed in Marseilles in late September 1914, they encountered colonial soldiers from across the French Empire on the streets of that port city. Just weeks later, the *Tirailleurs Sénégalais* were in battle in Picardy and Belgium, some under the command of Mangin himself. Like the Indian Corps, the *Tirailleurs Sénégalais* were thrown into the front lines near Ypres – used piecemeal to plug gaps and shore up improvised defensive lines. In those desperate days, when it seemed entirely possible that the Germans might break through and reach the coast, four battalions of *Tirailleurs Sénégalais* fought on the bend of the River Yser. At the Belgian town of Dixmude (Diksmuide), they were routed by a German attacking force four times their size. One battalion of Africans was reduced from over 1,000 to just 30 men and 2 officers.[16] In November, three further divisions of *Tirailleurs Sénégalais* were committed to the defence. By the end of 1914, the *Tirailleurs Sénégalais* had won praise and had played perhaps a greater part than had been initially expected in the battles of outflanking manoeuvres that saved France in 1914 – but which, in doing so, created the trenches of the Western Front.

The cost of France's salvation in 1914, however, had been little short of catastrophic. Over a third-of-a-million French soldiers had been killed. More Frenchmen died in 1914 than in any other year of the war – even though there were only five months of fighting. Half of all the French soldiers who were to die in the First World War – around 1.3 million – fell in the first fifteen months of the conflict.[17] Suddenly, the demographic nightmares that had haunted the nation loomed larger than ever.

In late 1914 and early 1915, modest recruitment drives were undertaken in the French colonies – West Africa, North Africa, Madagascar and French Indochina. Yet still the plan was that these recruits would, for the most part, be tasked with garrisoning duties in North Africa, allowing white French troops to defend their mother country. But towards the end of 1915, around the time that the now exhausted British Indian Corps was leaving Marseilles, French policy shifted decisively. Finally convinced that the war would be longer than anyone had dared imagine in the summer of 1914, the High Command cleared the way for a series of mass recruitment drives in the French colonies. Throughout 1915 Mangin had been working behind the scenes. In preparation for what he was convinced would be the decisive phase of the war, he had vocally argued that France should urgently raise a colonial army 700,000 strong, 300,000 of whom would be drawn from the warrior tribes of West Africa – this despite the continuing lack of any reliable population statistics for the regions in question. To harry the government into action, a law calling for the recruitment of troops from West Africa was introduced into the French Parliament. One of the Parliamentary sponsors stated that France not only had the moral right to recruit men from its colonies, but also that the country had a moral obligation to do so:

We have the right to call on the aid of our colonial subjects. We have brought to our colonies prosperity and peace. We have delivered them from epidemics, raids, periodic famines, and civil wars. We have shed the most precious of our blood in order to spare them from

powerful invaders and slave traders. Today, we struggle for them as
well as for us. The yoke of the invader – they know it – would weigh
as heavily, more heavily, on them than on us. France overseas fights
for its own cause. We have the right to call on our colonies – and we
have a duty.[18]

Before the new law could even be passed, the government acted.
Two decrees, on 9 October and 14 October 1915, set out a scheme
for a hugely expanded recruitment drive in West Africa, with a
goal of 50,000 recruits in 1916. What followed was one of the
great scandals in the French conduct of the First World War.

The recruitment in West Africa was, for the most part, carried
out by African intermediaries – who were expected to meet
quotas and were paid by results. Although there were recruits
who volunteered for service, many were coerced.[19] The majority
of the earliest recruits were drawn from what are now Senegal
and Niger, then later the levies fell heavily on the peoples of Côte
d'Ivoire, Guinea and Dahomey.[20] The recruiters carried out their
work with vigorous brutality. When quotas of men were not forth-
coming, whole villages were subjected to collective punishments.
Crops were destroyed, livestock killed, homes and entire villages
set alight. The relatives of men who had fled to avoid being conscripted were taken hostage, and chiefs who refused to cooperate,
or who sought to shield their peoples from the attentions of the
recruiters, were imprisoned or fined. Conversely, those chiefs
who acquiesced, often because they owed their position to
French patronage, were given financial rewards. In the recruitment drive of 1915, half-a-million francs were set aside for
payments and bounties to compliant chiefs, described as 'com-
pensation' for the men they provided.[21] In the initial stages, men
were forced to take part in lotteries to determine who would stay
with their families and who would be sent to war. Later, a one-
son-per-family rule was introduced – a policy that was bizarrely
similar to the Devshirme system of the Ottoman Empire, the harvesting of Christian boys in the Balkans, which had been a favourite
target for the moral outrage of anti-Turkish propagandists of the

nineteenth century. Oral histories carried out among former *Tirailleurs Sénégalais* by the pioneering historian Joe Lunn, in the late twentieth century, confirmed both the existence of this policy and revealed that the burden tended to fall on younger sons, sparing the elder boys who were better placed to care for their parents. A predictable consequence of this method of forced conscription, when imposed upon highly stratified and hierarchical societies, was that the men and boys coerced into the French Army tended to be the most powerless and the poorest in their societies. Some were orphan boys, who had no-one to protect them from the recruiters. Others were slaves.[22]

The African recruiters, who worked either for local chiefs or directly for the French colonial authorities, acted as a moral fire-wall between the French and the grim process of recruitment. This permitted the French to claim that they were merely the beneficiaries of the process, rather than its agents. Yet there is considerable evidence that the French were fully aware of what their intermediaries were up to. French colonial *commandants* in the field and their superiors in the urban centres fretted about the damage being done to the social fabric and economic poten-tial of the region. Their reports, cataloguing the consequences of the recruitment drives, are clear proof that they were cogni-zant of what was taking place. *Commandants* spoke not only of how the recruiting drive was threatening the economic potential of the French colonies, but also listed incidents of armed resis-tance against the recruiters. They spoke of mass abscondings into the bush by whole villages and of men who had resorted to self-mutilation to save themselves from abduction by recruiters. An unknown number fled to neighbouring colonies – to the British Gold Coast (Ghana), American-protected Liberia, Gambia, or Portuguese Guinea – to place themselves beyond the reach of the recruiters and the French authorities.[23] Living in the shadow of recent famines and epidemics, a high proportion of the region's men were in ill health, as the French and their inter-mediaries discovered. The logical corollary of those findings, that the French might reasonably have reached, was that the region could ill afford to lose its most fit and capable men, and local *commandants* right up to the governor-generals reached exactly that conclusion. They rightly feared the results of the recruitment would be shortages of food and local rebellion. But in 1915 and 1916 Paris gave little heed to their warnings, and the harvest of men continued unabated.

While the local chiefs acted as a filter between their societies and the recruiters, exercising power over which men and boys were to be offered up, some men were 'recruited' more directly. They were simply seized from their villages or captured in the fields by armed recruiting gangs. The raids were most common in those areas furthest from the French centres of power, where their authority was diluted by distance and terrain. There, recruiters embarked on expeditions that amounted to man-hunts. There were reports that men and boys were marched to the collecting stations, bound by ropes or chains or bound together in coffles. In September 1917, the new Governor-General of French West Africa, the sensible and far-sighted Joost van Vollenhoven, wrote:

> *Since the beginning of the war, recruitment has become a hunt for men … Out of recruitment has resulted an unpopularity that has become universal from the very day when recruits were asked to serve in Europe and grim, determined, terrible revolts started against the white man, who had hitherto been tolerated, sometimes even loved, but who, transformed into a recruiting agent, had become a detested enemy, the image of the slave hunters he had defeated and replaced himself.*[24]

As van Vollenhoven was well aware, French colonialists had justi-fied their take-over of much of West Africa – to themselves and to Africans – on the grounds that the French *mission civilisatrice* would bring an end to the slave trade in that part of the conti-nent. Yet the truth is that during the First World War African men were seized from their villages, held prisoner and marched in chains, and were then shipped to the battlefields of France to fight in the name of liberty and civilization. The French even had a phrase for enforced recruitment of Africans: *l'impôt du sang*, 'the tax in blood'.

★

In December 1915, not long after the mass recruitment drive in French West Africa had got under way, the German High Command made a strategic decision of its own, one informed by the French manpower crisis and the stalemate on the Western Front. A year and a half into the war, there were those on both sides who were ever more convinced that the struggle on the Western Front had become, above all, a demographic conflict, in which numbers counted perhaps above all else. Every British and French offensive on the Western Front in 1915 had failed. As things stood, it appeared impossible to achieve a breakthrough. Such considerations led the German High Command to a brutal conclusion.[25]

Erich von Falkenhayn, German Chief of the General Staff since Moltke's fall in September 1914, had never believed that the war would be short. By December 1915 he concluded that while some grand strategic victory might be out of reach, perhaps the wholesale slaughter of the enemy, leading to their exhaustion and a collapse of the will to fight, might achieve the same end. There is evidence that Falkenhayn had, from the start, imagined the war as a conflict of attrition in which racial strength and Darwinian fitness would be among the deciding factors.[26] In the infamous Christmas Memorandum that Falkenhayn claimed in his memoir to have written at the end of 1915, he summarized the military situation: 'France has been weakened militarily and economically – almost to the limit of what it can stand.' As the Russians on the Eastern Front seemed unable, for the time being, to launch a major offensive, Germany was in a position to dictate the terms of the fighting in 1916. 'There are targets,' Falkenhayn went on to explain:

> ... *lying within reach behind the French section of the Western Front for which the French leadership would need to use their very last*

man. Should they do this, then France would bleed to death, for
there is no retreat, regardless if we ourselves reach the target or not.
Should they not do this, and should these targets fall into our
hands, then the effect on morale in France would be enormous. For
these operations, which are limited in terms of territory, Germany
will not be compelled to expend itself to a degree that would leave it
seriously exposed on other fronts … The targets being spoken of are
Belfort and Verdun. What was said above applies to both of them.
All the same, Verdun is to be preferred.[27]

Verdun, the great fortified citadel that protected the approaches
to Paris, had stood firm against the German attacks of 1914; it
now presented the perfect symbolic target that he believed the
French would be compelled to defend.[28] Verdun sat in a large
salient, created by a loop of the River Meuse that jutted out from
the French lines into German-held territory. Assembling a vast
arsenal of 1,220 guns of all sizes, calibres and types, and laying
railway lines to feed them with shells, Falkenhayn planned to
turn Verdun into the graveyard of the French Army, the place
where – as he supposedly told the Kaiser – 'the forces of France
will bleed to death'.[29]

Operation Gericht ('Judgement'), the German assault on
Verdun, began at exactly 7.21am on 21 February 1916. After a
colossal bombardment the Germans advanced through the snow,
pouncing upon obliterated French positions. 'Storm-troopers',
following newly developed battle tactics, hunted down terrified
French survivors with flame-throwers. By the fourth day of the
battle much of the outer zone of French trenches had been captured. Then, at around 3.30 on the afternoon of 25 February,
Falkenhayn met with a completely unexpected success. The
mighty fort of Douaumont was captured without a fight. On
paper, Douaumont was the most formidable of the sixty fortresses, of various sizes, that defended the approaches to Verdun.
In reality she had been stripped of most of her guns and was
manned by fifty ineffectual and poorly-led reservists. Months
earlier, the French High Command had understandably

concluded that the age of the fort had been decisively brought
to an end by the destruction of the Belgian forts that had failed
utterly to defend towns like Liège in the first weeks of the war,
hammered into submission by Germany's enormous Krupp guns.
Some of the forts in the Verdun sector had even been earmarked
for demolition. That military assessment, although entirely
logical, turned out to be completely mistaken.

The humiliating loss of Fort Douaumont, which was seized
with apparent ease by men of the 24th Brandenburg Regiment
– who wandered into the poorly defended stronghold and duped
the bewildered defenders into surrendering – goaded the French
people into outrage and the French High Command into action.
News of its capture resonated across Europe. There was panic
among the defending forces at Verdun itself and talk of a great
retreat. German newspapers crowed with national pride and
overflowed with near ecstatic editorials prophesying the impending collapse of the old enemy. Pragmatic voices in the French
High Command, which had calmly assessed the situation and
offered a reasoned and balanced analysis of the situation, suggesting alternative strategies to an all-out defence, were almost at
a stroke marginalized.

Two days after Douaumont fell, French reinforcements
began to arrive at Verdun in real numbers. The icy ground
thawed and turned to mud, and a steady, unremitting pageant
of deadly attrition began. It was not to stop for ten months.
Both the French and Germans committed ever more men and
resources to the crucible of Verdun. There, artillery bombardments were launched that were so titanic that not only were
enemy positions obliterated, the hills into which they had been
dug were reduced in height by up to twenty metres. Millions of
tons of earth and thousands of men were atomized by the
approximately 10 million shells fired by both sides – 2.5 million
alone had been stockpiled by the Germans just for the initial
assault. Throughout the spring and summer of 1916 offensive
followed offensive. A spider's web of railway lines was built by
both armies to feed men and materials into the inferno and

bring up the vast railway howitzers that crushed through the concrete of forts and obliterated strongpoints. Deadly gas attacks were launched, designed to wipe out whole battalions, while overhead the largest aerial battle the world had ever seen was fought out, the Germans and French both drafting in their elite squadrons and legendary air aces. Every hill of the Verdun battlefield, every trench line, strongpoint and fort was contested, with terrible losses. All told, 70,000 men were dying each month. The French kept the casualty figures from their newspapers, while Falkenhayn withheld the German death toll from even his fellow generals. Under the command of General Pétain, the French developed the 'Noria' system, by which men were rotated through the fighting zones around Verdun, lest their nerves be shattered by the ferocity of the bombardments and the intensity of the carnage.

In May 1916, command of the French Second Army at Verdun passed from Pétain to General Robert Nivelle, a man whose career had begun in the colonies. He had served in both Tunisia and Algeria and was a veteran of the French force sent to crush the Chinese Boxer Rebellion of 1898–1901. He had made his name during the First Battle of the Marne in September 1914. Nivelle was not the only new arrival. He brought with him the man who was now Commander of the 5th Division: Charles Mangin. By now, as a general on the Western Front, Mangin had acquired two telling nicknames – the 'Butcher' and the 'Eater of Men': he had led Frenchmen and his *Tirailleurs Sénégalais* into battle, and their terrible casualties under his command had already been noted. Fighting for the survival of his nation rather than merely for the pacification of its colonies, Mangin had shown himself to be as fanatically dedicated to the principle of attack as he was to his *Force Noire* theory. Soon after his arrival at Verdun, Nivelle ordered Mangin to prepare for an assault to retake Douaumont. Although it reached the fort, the attacking units were unable to break into the catacombs within and take on its German defenders. They seized parts of the great structure but were forced by heavy losses to retreat.

In June 1916, before the French could launch a new operation, the Germans attacked with diphosgene gas, delivered in over 100,000 shells. It was not until October that Nivelle and Mangin were in a position to launch another, all-out offensive to retake Fort Douaumont. The final stage of that assault was led by a 'colonial' regiment of Moroccans – white settlers with a fearsome reputation as fighters. They were supported by the 43rd Battalion of *Tirailleurs Sénégalais* and two companies of Somali soldiers.

Douaumont, even today, remains a shocking sight. The subterranean fort appears like a great tor erupting from the earth, but made of concrete and rubble rather than living granite. Its thick, steel gun emplacements, observation posts and retractable turrets look like armaments stripped from a battleship of the nineteenth century, rather than the defences of a twentieth-century fortress. The forests that have grown up around the battlefield hide, under their shade, a lunar landscape of craters and ditches. Despite the softening effects of vegetation, Verdun is one of the few places on the Western Front where the ferocity of First World War artillery bombardments can still be seen and even vaguely appreciated. Above the single entrance to Fort Douaumont hangs a plaque. It reads, in translation:

> *On 24 October 1916, the Moroccan Colonial Infantry Regiment reinforced by the Senegalese 43rd Battalion and by two companies of Somalis, seized, with admirable élan, the foremost lines of German trenches and then advanced under the energetic command of Lt. Colonel Régnier breaking the enemy's successive waves of resistance to a depth of two kilometres and inscribed a glorious page in their history by seizing in an irresistible assault the fort of Douaumont and holding it in spite of the enemy's repeated counter-attacks.*

Although they had not been the spear-point of the French attack, when the 43rd Battalion of the *Tirailleurs Sénégalais* marched out after the assault, to head through the towns and villages behind the lines, they were ordered by their white officers not to wash the mud from their uniforms, so that civilians would know that they were the Africans who had taken part in the recapture of Douaumont.[30] Ultimately, it was Charles Mangin, the champion of the *Force Noire*, rather than Falkenhayn who enjoyed the last flourish of symbolism at Verdun. In the aftermath of Douaumont's recapture, Mangin was depicted on the cover of the popular illustrated magazine *Le Rire Rouge* surrounded by the *Tirailleurs Sénégalais* he had helped make famous. The caption read '*Un Noir vaut deux Boches*' – 'One black is worth two Boches'.[31] And in the afterglow of these events, much of the opposition to Mangin's *Force Noire* was temporarily silenced. He and the French Army were free to set about determining, through experiment and according to theory, the best ways of deploying Africans troops on the Western Front.

★

There was, of course, one other expansive African empire in the Allied camp. One of the most perplexing questions raised by the French recruitment of the *Tirailleurs Sénégalais* for the Western Front is why the British did not do likewise. There had been British figures who, before the war, had argued for the raising of an African army for use across that continent and perhaps elsewhere. And the British, too, felt they had identified which of their subject Africans had the martial qualities needed – the Hausa of Nigeria, the Sudanese, and the Zulu in the south all passed muster in this respect. There were those at the top of the British Army in the latter half of the nineteenth century who were so impressed by the martial abilities of Africans that the 1859 Indian Army Reorganization Committee, set up in the aftermath of the Indian Mutiny, had toyed with the idea of garrisoning India not just with loyal local troops but also Africans, who might prove more reliable and be less likely to find common cause with the disgruntled voices of the subcontinent.[32]

In his tract *The Colonies and Imperial Defence,* published just a year before Mangin's *La Force Noire,* the British colonel and 'African expert' P.A. Silburn condemned the British government's position that 'native races are not to be considered seriously in the organization of Colonial troops for Imperial service,' asking: 'Can the Empire afford such magnanimity?' He continued: 'Will reciprocity in this respect be shown by the Power or Powers we have to fight in the future? If any Power approves of our self-denial it will be because of the old advantage of fighting against one who has voluntarily tied up one of his arms.'[33] Like others who feared for the future security of the empire, Silburn was adamant that 'To be the decisive fighting machine the size of the Empire demands, the Army must include every available man, irrespective of race, creed, or colour ... Native races, the subjects of His Majesty, must then be considered in the organization of our Army.'[34] The first step in that process, he suggested, was that 'The South African Colonies should between them ear-mark from among the tribes within their borders a force of 30,000 men.' Here Silburn, who had strong views on South Africa and the threat posed by the menace of racial mixing, cautioned that 'In the case of the Zulu it would perhaps be unwise to teach him the use of small arms ... [as] there remains the fear, not ground-less, that to teach and encourage the use of the rifle by the native races may result in trouble if not disaster.'[35] In West Africa the absence of a large white population reassured Silburn that recruitment could be carried out with less caution. The men of that region were, in his analysis, especially valuable; after all, 'The negro has proved himself a most excellent gunner; the Hausas in this respect are hard to excel.'[36]

Pre-war opposition to Silburn's analysis, and more vocally to Mangin's *Force Noire* theory, was nevertheless as strident in pre-war Britain as it was in Germany. A digest of recent articles (1911) written in English on *La Force Noire* noted the French War Department's 'sense of relief' at the prospect of this extra man-power, but described the potential African recruits as 'a new source of supply of what Napoleon called "cannon food"'.[37] There was even disquiet in Britain at the formation of indigenous forces for use in Africa itself, something that every colonial power had pursued. In 1902, J.A. Hobson, in his influential *Imperialism: A Study*, warned of the terrible danger:

... whereby the oppressor at one deprives himself of the habit and instruments of effective self-protection and hands them over to the most capable and energetic of his enemies. This fatal conjunction of folly and vice has always contributed to bring about the downfall of Empires in the Past.[38]

Others, rather than looking to the imperial past for cautionary tales, envisaged dystopian futures. In 1898, H.G. Wells published his science-fiction novel *The Sleeper Awakes,* in which the hero (Graham) awakes after having fallen asleep for two centuries. He finds London ruled by the dictator Ostrog, a tyrant who enforces his rule through a militarized police force of black Africans – men recruited from Senegal and South Africa. Graham escapes from the monied elite he finds himself part of to explore London, and he finds a city where the white industrial poor live a troglodyte existence. They are, it seems, like the Morlocks of *The Time Machine* (a novel Wells had completed only three years earlier) but before the process of de-evolution has stamped itself upon their bodily frames. And the jailors are the Africans. Thus, in the same years when the French were using *Tirailleurs Sénégalais* to enforce their colonial grip on North Africa, Wells was envisaging a future age in which Africans would become the agents not of colonial repression but of class war, deployed by the rich to enforce their rule over the working class. In the climactic chapter, waves of African soldiers converge on London in a vast fleet of aircraft, and Graham encourages the white workers of London to construct anti-aircraft guns to defend themselves.

Like all great science-fiction writers, Wells was playing with exaggerated versions of ideas that were current and with phenomena that were at least vaguely conceivable. If the soldiers of French West and Equatorial Africa could become the guard-dogs of empire, why could they not also become the protectors of industrial wealth or the privileges of the ruling classes? French socialists nursed similar fears, believing that black French colonial troops might be used to repress the French working class. Yet the fear of armed Africans *en masse* seemed to have taken a deeper hold in Britain than in France, despite the lack of any such force within the British Army.

In August 1914, with Britain struggling to hold a modest stretch of the Western Front and to find the men to defend the empire, such racial fears were clearly at odds with harsh demographic realities. An MP, R.P. Houston, was one of the first to challenge official reluctance to raise a mass African army. He called for the recruitment of a regiment from the 'martial races' of South Africa – most notably the Zulu – and for its rapid deployment to the battlefields of Europe. Houston's plan was ill-conceived, as the Union of South Africa was the least likely part of British Africa to allow the arming, training and deployment of black Africans. The issue re-emerged in the summer of 1916, in the weeks after the Battle of the Somme. With the military and political leadership of Britain plunged into crisis, there was near panic within official circles at the catastrophic losses the British Army had suffered. Kitchener's home-grown volunteers were being decimated and the nation faced a fresh manpower crisis. By that point, of course, tens of thousands of Indians had come and gone on the Western Front; the Indian cavalry were still there. Yet the government steadfastly resisted the military logic of recruiting Africans for the Western Front, despite what was now a chorus of loud voices demanding that the empire emulate the French and consider not just recruitment but conscription in Africa.

That year, what was dubbed the 'Black Army Lobby' emerged. Its most vociferous spokesman was Major Darnley Stuart-Stephens, a career soldier who had commanded the Lagos Battalion of British Nigeria in the 1880s. In October 1916, during the protracted Somme campaign, Stuart-Stephens published an article in the *English Review* entitled 'Our Million Black Army'. In it he promised to use his experience of Africa to personally recruit a force of 20,000 Africans in just two months. Describing Africa as an 'almost unlimited reservoir of African man-power', he projected that if a full-scale recruitment drive were initiated across the British-controlled territories of Africa a force half-a-million strong could be raised, trained and thrown into battle against the German line, all within just nine months.[39] What Stuart-Stephens called the 'black fighting material' of Africa consisted of tribes who, he argued, were every bit as martial as the martial races of India. 'In northern Nigeria alone,' he believed, 'there are to-day more than 700,000 warlike tribes-men. Let them be used! These "bonny fechters" are now engaged in the pastoral arts of peace. But I would make bold to assert that a couple of hundred thousand could, after six months' training, be usefully employed in daredevil charges into German trenches.'[40] The first Africans the major wanted to see dispatched to the Western Front were Sudanese battalions, '70,000 big, lusty coal-black devils, the time of whose life is the wielding of the bayonet, and whose advent would not be regarded by the Boches as a pleasing omen of more to come of the same sort'.[41] Tapping into this vast human resource would allow Britain to man the Western Front with an army whose natural propensity for war would simultaneously save white lives and help overcome the awesome military might of Germany.

While Stuart-Stephens was certainly the most energetic member of the Black Army Lobby, the most influential voice was that of Winston Churchill. In May 1916 he argued in the House of Commons that a force of Africans be recruited and deployed (in addition to extra Indian regiments). 'Let us … think,' he warned Parliament:

> … *what historians of the future would write if they were writing a history of the present time and had to record that Great Britain was forced to make an inconclusive peace because she forgot Africa: that at a time when every man counted … the Government of Great Britain was unable to make any use of a mighty continent … It would be incredible but it is taking place … What is going on while we sit here, while we go to dinner, or home to bed? Nearly 1,000 men – Englishmen, Britishers, men of our own race – are knocked into bundles of bloody rags every twenty-four hours … Every measure must be considered, and none put aside while there is hope of obtain-ing something from it.*[42]

Ranged against Churchill and Stuart-Stevens was an unlikely alliance of humanitarians (concerned about exploitation), military theorists (who dismissed the abilities of black troops) and white settlers supported by the leadership of South Africa (who had refused to countenance any policy that led to guns being placed in the hands of black Africans). Churchill and others supported calls for missions to be dispatched to the French Army to explore how the French had been able to forge the *Tirailleurs Sénégalais* into such an effective fighting force; but nothing came of such enquires.

The conclusion to the whole debate had one final irony. In East Africa, Lettow-Vorbeck's *raison-d'être* for his dogged guerrilla war was to try and bog down Allied men and resources that might otherwise be used on the Western Front. In one sense he need not have bothered. British policy decisions meant that no black Africans under arms would ever be heading from British Africa to the Western Front.

★

There had been seventeen battalions of *Tirailleurs Sénégalais* on the Western Front during 1916; they also fought on the Somme, the offensive conceived in part as a way of drawing German forces away from Verdun. Over the course of 1917 the number of battalions leaped to forty-one, and by war's end it had reached no less than ninety-two.[43] Their actual deployment was, like their initial recruitment, heavily shaped by French racial thinking. The firm conviction that Africans were naturally suited to the attack both encouraged and justified their use as shock troops, particularly in the last two years of the war, after Charles Mangin had been elevated to the High Command. Eventually the *Tirailleurs Sénégalais* were so synonymous with frontal assaults that white French soldiers learnt to recognize the arrival of black units in the front lines as the portent of an attack.

In 1918 the High Command issued its *Notice sur les Sénégalais et leur emploi au combat,* a manual for officers leading *Tirailleurs Sénégalais.* It was an attempt to summarize tactical thinking on

the use of the African units and offer white officers a better
understanding of the men under their command. For the most
part it simply regurgitated the *races guerrières* theory, and once
again the various peoples of French West Africa were listed, eval-
uated and ranked. Apparently impervious to empirical evidence
and blind to recent experience, the authors of the *Notice* asserted
that the peoples of the African interior were born-warriors while
men from the coast were mediocre soldiers. Wolof, Serer, Tukulor
and Bambara men were all defined as being especially warlike
and among the best soldiers.[44] But the *Notice* did not focus solely
on martial abilities; it went on to catalogue and explain the limi-
tations that the French had come to ascribe to their African
troops, the root cause of which was the supposedly limited intellect of Africans – as compared to Frenchmen and other colonial
troops. One consequence of these purported inadequacies was
an alleged propensity among the *Tirailleurs Sénégalais* to panic.
This had been noted by French commanders in previous encounters, from the Second Battle of Ypres in 1915 to some of the
fighting at Verdun in the summer of 1916. Specific reasons why
African units might have performed poorly on these occasions
were brushed aside in favour of explanations based on race. One
conclusion drawn was that Africans struggled in defensive operations. The explanation for this went roughly as follows: while it
required moral courage and skill to defend a trench, to assault
an enemy position required only the sort of innate unthinking
courage Africans were known to possess. The Frenchman, supposedly more intelligent than the African, and fighting for a
cause he understood and a civilization he appreciated, could be
better relied on to stand and fight as a defender, and to intelli-
gently use the terrain to his advantage while doing so. Africans,
despite all their natural warrior instincts and unthinking courage,
lacked the intellect to acquire the more nuanced skills in defence
and therefore had to be supported in this task by white officers
and other white companies appended to their battalions. Without
the stiffening presence of white soldiers, Africans could be put to
flight by the enemy. The deployment solution designed to solve

JOURNÉE DE L'ARMÉE D'AFRIQUE
ET DES TROUPES COLONIALES

DEVAMBEZ, PARIS

17. A poster for the 'Day of the African Army and Colonial Troops' (1917) celebrates France's *Tirailleurs Sénégalais*, who are shown eager to rush into the fight alongside the white French *poilus*.

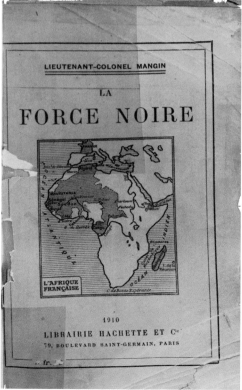

18. Albert Bettanier's *La Tache Noire* ('The Black Stain'), painted in 1887, was an exercise in artistic symbolism, dripping with *revanchism* for the loss of the provinces of Alsace and Lorraine in 1871.

19. *La Force Noire* (1910), written by Charles Mangin, encapsulated the view that the martial manpower of France's colonies could revitalize the French Army. It was a controversial proposal.

20. The uncompromising General Charles Mangin (1866–1925). His unswerving belief in throwing his African troops into the forefront of the battle – testament to both his confidence in their usefulness and his recklessness with their lives – earned him the nickname 'the Butcher'.

21. Members of the 43rd Battalion of the *Tirailleurs Sénégalais*, heroes of the recapture of Fort Douaumont in October 1916, pose with their banner.

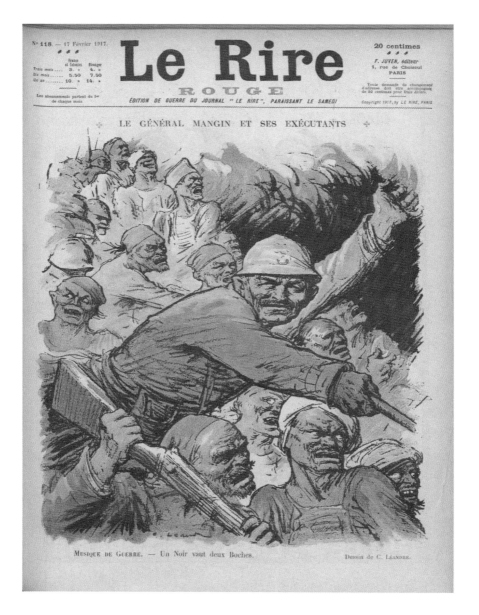

22. Continuing the celebratory vein after the recapture of Douaumont, the cover of *Le Rire Rouge* (17 February 1917) depicted Mangin directing some stereotypically fierce-looking *Tirailleurs* accompanied by the slogan 'Music of War – One Black is worth Two Boches'.

BANANA

EXQUIS
DÉJEUNER SUCRÉ

ALIMENT DÉLICIEUX
POUR LES ESTOMACS
DÉLICATS
En vente partout
USINE à COURBEVOIE

y'a bon

23 and 24. Among the otherwise contrasting French and German propaganda about African troops were comparable portrayals that stressed primitiveness, whether in a presumed childlike simplicity (as in the 1915 French advertisement for the chocolate drink Banania) or, more extreme, as *ersatz* fighters barely out of the jungle (in this image from the German satirical magazine *Lustige Blätter*).

LUSTIGE BLÄTTER

5 GORILLA-REGT.
I. ERSATZ
BATAILLON
SENEGAL

Trier.

s Aufgebot der „Grande Armee".
Parole: Für die „Zivilisation" gegen die Barbarei!

25. Max von Oppenheim (*centre*, in suit) in a Bedouin tent in 1899. The German orientalist and archaeologist became – come the war – an eager proponent of *Jihad*.

26. Kaiser Wilhelm II greets the Sheikh ul-Islam, accompanied by Sultan Mehmed V (foreground) and Ottoman War Minister Enver Pasha, in 1917.

27. The Sherif of Medina preaches *Jihad* to a local throng in late 1914.

28. Ottoman infantry in the campaign to wrest the Suez Canal from British control pause for rest and a photograph (1915)

29. The Senussi, newly armed with German Mauser rifles, prepare to attack British Egypt from the west in late 1915.

30 (*above*). Mir Mast (*left of group*) with other ex-Indian Corps Pathans of the German–Ottoman expedition to win over the Emir of Afghanistan. Their epic trek (**31**, *left*) in 1915–16 took them through eastern Persia.

32. The luminaries of the Afghan expedition: (*left* to *right*, seated) Kasim Bey, Werner Otto von Hentig, Mahendra Pratap, Oskar Niedermayer and Maulawi Barakatullah sit awkwardly for the camera in Kabul.

this was to position, behind black battalions, one white reserve battalion, whose task it was to prevent the blacks troops from fleeing and, if possible, to exploit the breaches in the enemy lines created by the attacks of the African battalions. The obvious and inevitable corollary of this policy was that the Africans would suffer heavier losses than the white battalions supporting them.

Some of the reports that came into the French High Command outlining the weaknesses of African soldiers were written by commanders who had never subscribed to the *Force Noire* theory and who were hostile to Mangin and his growing influence. There had long been tensions between the followers of Mangin and French North African officers who regarded the Arabs and Berbers under their command as better soldiers than the *Tirailleurs Sénégalais*. The bitter debate that had raged between these two opposing camps ever since the publication of *La Force Noire* back in 1910 continued, in peaks and troughs, throughout the war. Although partly silenced by the symbolic successes at Verdun, Mangin's opponents, in the latter years of the conflict, developed new arguments with which to dismiss the abilities of the West African troops. As the weapons on the Western Front became more advanced and as operations became more complex and integrated, the supposedly limited intellectual capacity of the *Tirailleurs Sénégalais,* it was said, rendered the troops increasingly unsuited to modern warfare.

Another effect of the widespread belief that Africans were of low intellect was that the military authorities refused to offer the *Tirailleurs Sénégalais* proper instruction in French. Despite the fact that some of the African troops came from societies that were traditionally multilingual, the army remained wedded to the supposition that they were incapable of learning the French language. This became a self-fulfilling prophecy, because it hampered the capacity of African troops to follow complicated orders or receive effective instructions in the use of the more advanced weapons, and so merely confirmed the negative views of their detractors. The army's attempt to answer the question of language was a form of pidgin French, known as *Français tirailleur* or *petit-nègre.* It formed the basis for a list of orders and questions drafted by the army and issued to white officers in an official army instruction pamphlet.[45] This reductive and infantalizing argot was deemed appropriate for men of 'rustic intelligence'; but *Français Tirailleur* had the effect of hindering the efforts of Africans to acquired the language skills they needed in an increasingly technical war.

In a wider context, the lack of a proper education in French also denied African troops freedom of expression when dealing with wider French society.[46] That society was one that the authorities were keen to school in the theory of the *races guerrières*.

FRANCE, JANUARY 1916. An edition of the magazine *La Dépêche Coloniale Illustrée* is published. It is, in fact, a special edition, which celebrates the service of the *Tirailleurs Sénégalais*. Included is a map of French West Africa, onto which are superimposed portraits intended to represent the various 'races' recruited into the *Tirailleurs*. Men from Senegal itself, Mauritania, Liberia, Côte d'Ivoire and Niger are shown in profile – in accordance with current conventions of anthropological photography. Accompanying the map is a descriptive page headed: 'Types of the principal races of West Africa, whence the *Tirailleurs Sénégalais* have come'. It names each of the men whose portraits are shown and explains where they have come from and the role they are now playing in the war.

When compared to the United States, or to much of the colonial world, France in the early twentieth century was a racially liberal society. Certainly, as with other Europeans, the French held deep cultural prejudices against the people of Africa; but what was different about French racism was that it was arguably more cultural than biological. It ascribed to Africans a whole array of negative traits, and questioned their intelligence, but tended not to regard racial 'blackness' as an insurmountable obstacle to preventing Africans from becoming 'civilized'. The French colonial mission in Africa was built on the foundations of the nation's republican traditions and revolutionary ideals. France justified the violent conquest of other peoples and their lands by claiming that, through assimilation or association with French culture, Africans could eventually be raised up from barbarism.

Racism of such a kind was widespread and shared by much of the ruling elite. It was, however, not to be permitted to interfere with the military service of the half-a-million non-white, colonial troops France was to recruit for the war effort. The French authorities therefore faced the task of somehow reconciling French racism with the official line, that black Africans were now soldiers of France come to defend the motherland. The powerful contemporary stereotypes of Africans as savage, violent and unrestrained were useful when promoting the idea that the *Tirailleurs Sénégalais* were a powerful force that France could unleash on Germany; the same stereotypes were profoundly unhelpful when trying to reassure the French public that their presence within France, behind the lines and billeted in towns and cities, was in the nation's interest.

There were other elements of the popular racialized view of Africans that posed a challenge, too. African men were widely viewed as both uncontrollable and highly sexual. One official response was to juxtapose the image of the *Tirailleur Sénégalais* as a warrior in the trenches with an image of 'le Grande Enfant' behind the lines. This incarnation of the *tirailleur* saw him as childlike and naive, an overgrown boy, astonished by the wondrous society in which he now found himself, childishly amused by the simple pleasures of European life, and in the slow process of being guided slowly towards the light of civilization by France. *Tirailleurs* were at times depicted smiling and playful, but as physically giant figures, often set alongside tiny French children, hammering home their loyalty to France and the unthreatening simplicity of these *bons sauvages*. This was a comforting image to balance against that of *Tirailleurs* as savage warriors capable even of decapitating German soldiers.

Yet official propaganda, and then commercial advertizing, was seemingly unable to resist the temptation of amalgamating these two contrasting images. In 1915 the image of the *Tirailleur Sénégalais* as 'le Grand Enfant' became imprinted onto French culture in an advertising campaign for the drink Banania. Posters showed a happy, smiling *tirailleur* in uniform, carrying the slogan '*y' a bon*' ('it's good') in the *petit-nègre* form of pidgin French. A French wartime postcard then subverted the advertisement, using all the visual signposting to deliver a grimmer propaganda message. In this version, hinting at the old preconception of the African as cannibal, the *tirailleur* has a German *Picklehaube* helmet as an improvised cooking pot, hanging over a roaring fire. The implication was reinforced by a caption that played on the Banania slogan: '*Y' a bon! C'est le boche qui régale!*' ('It's good! This is a treat from the Boche!')

Yet what is most striking about French propaganda images of the *Tirailleurs Sénégalais* are the similarities with the work of German propagandists, whose task it was to portray the Africans as savages and their deployment as a war crime. Both repeatedly depicted the *Tirailleurs* using their rifles as clubs, as if too animalistic to accurately fire them; in both, African faces are shown in distorted grimaces, with white staring eyes that seem to owe their inspiration to caricatures of the American South in the segregation era. Some of the most unpleasant German propaganda is unambiguously and viciously racist; yet there are these other, more ambiguous efforts, which – were it not for language differences – would be difficult to identify as either French or German.

Among the most pervasive and long-lasting effects of German propaganda against the *Tirailleurs Sénégalais* was the myth, generated in the trenches as well as in the propaganda offices, that they did not take prisoners and mutilated or killed those who fell into their hands. While there may well have been incidents of illegal killings or other atrocities, there were innumerable accounts of German prisoners being well treated by black French units. German troops were, however, so convinced of this particular myth that they feared being taken prisoner by black units, trying to surrender to whites whenever possible. The memoirs of Bakary Diallo, *Force Bronté*, one the handful of first-hand accounts of the war written by *Tirailleurs Sénégalais*, includes his encounter with a German prisoner:

> *A German who had mistaken our lines for his own, was captured with his load of coffee by a Senegalese sentry. When he saw himself surrounded by tirailleurs, he began to shake. Poor man, couldn't you have expected this possibility just as well as the gold of glory? The blacks that you took for savages captured you in war, but instead of cutting down your life, they made you prisoner. May your fear not prevent you from proclaiming in your country, tomorrow, after the battle, the sentiment of justice which will rehabilitate the name of the human race of which we are all savages.*[47]

The German fear was, particularly, of being dispatched by a *tirailleur*'s *coupe-coupe*, a kind of machete. Like the *kukri* carried by the Gurkha regiments of the British Indian Corps, the *coupe-coupe* was a weapon of war that developed into a sort of regimental insignia.[48] In the regions of French West Africa that were covered in thick vegetation, the utility of the *coupe-coupe* was obvious. Less well understood is that in the desperate hand-to-hand fighting, which was an all too common feature of both trench raids and major assaults, the *coupe-coupe* was a highly effective weapon. In the dog-legged trenches, in which men had to fight to take each corner, the French Lebel rifle was an unwieldy weapon. For the *Tirailleurs Sénégalais*, therefore, the *coupe-coupe* was their equivalent of the maces, knives, axes and coshes to which soldiers of all armies resorted in the enclosed confines of an enemy trench. In the hands of propagandists, however, the *coupe-coupe* became both emblem and ultimate proof of the innate and uncontrollable savagery and barbarism of France's African soldiers – European innovations with poison gas, for example, notwithstanding. But this argument, made loudly and repeatedly by the Germans throughout the war, had real and lasting effects, well into the next war. And when German soldiers took French officers prisoner, they were known to wield a captured *coupe-coupe* as physical evidence of France's degeneracy, an unfitting weapon for a civilized nation.

The obsessive fear of the *coupe-coupe* symbolized the evolution of German attitudes towards non-white colonial troops into a deep loathing, which permeated the nation's propaganda.

★

The initial German victories on the Western Front throughout August and into early September 1914 had generated a great wave of optimism. In this atmosphere, the appearance on the European battlefield of non-white, colonial troops fighting in French and British uniforms was dismissed by German newspapers as merely an oddity or interpreted as a symptom of the Allies' military weakness.[49] It is perhaps not coincidental that the German press hardened its line and began to energetically condemn the deployment of African and Indian troops at the moment when German fortunes took a turn for the worse with the Allied counter-attacks of the Battle of the Marne. The change was particularly noticeable after the so-called 'race to the sea', by late October 1914. The end of mobile warfare and the beginning of static, trench fighting ended all possibility of a short war, and in doing so allowed the French and British time to do what Germany feared – draw in men and materials from their colonial empires.

By the end of October 1914, the corresponding attitude of the German press to the deployment of non-white troops on the Western Front and the strategy of the German propaganda machine had shifted to something approaching hysteria. Africans and Asians in the British and French ranks were now said to represent an attack on civilization – and to be a betrayal of the white race. Max Weber, later in the war, raged against Britain and

France for having unleashed 'a refuse of Africans and Asiatic savages'.[50] After the war, he regretted that German propaganda had not more effectively tapped into the groundswell of outrage and used the simple and emotive issue of race to forge greater national unity 'to say this and only this all over again: that Germany continues to struggle for its existence against an army of Negroes, Gurkhas and sundry other Barbarians from all nooks and corners of the world, who wait in the wings to turn our country into a desert'.

Despite Weber's disappointment at what he felt was his nation's insufficient propaganda response, German magazines from the time remain shocking to the modern reader. The cartoons in the popular graphic magazines portrayed Asians and (especially) the black Africans of Mangin's *Tirailleurs* as savage monsters, cannibals, rapists and sub-human thugs of pitifully low intelligence. At various times and in various publications German writers, cartoonists and journalists condemned the colonial soldiers as 'dehumanized savages', 'a motley crew of colours and religions', an 'African exhibition', a 'black flood', 'dark mud', the 'black shame' and an 'auxiliary rabble of all colours'.[51] The word 'auxiliary' was used repeatedly to suggest that non-white troops were not true soldiers.

German propaganda railed not just against the supposed savagery of the colonial troops but at the fact that men from so *many* nations and races had been brought to Europe to fight. A German sense of geographic encirclement transmuted into national and racial victimhood, as if the whole world really were conspiring against Germany. In a post-war essay, German linguist Wilhelm Doegen complained that 'Germany did not fight against a world of armies ... but rather against a world of races.' It was, however, a Swede – the celebrated explorer Sven Hedin – who perhaps best expressed the sense of moral outrage and indignation felt by Germans. *With the German Armies in the West* was Hedin's propagandist and unashamedly biased account of scenes behind the German front lines as he encountered them in late 1914. In one of the most emotive passages, he wrote:

... there are five continents – supporting the gospel of war and hatred. The two Western powers of the Entente bear the responsibility for having caused the Dance of Death to involve the whole globe, for they are bringing into the fight masses of men raked together from all parts of the world : Canadians come in their ships from America, Turcos and Senegalese negroes from Africa, and poor Hindus and Ghurkhas, bronzed by the sun of India, lie freezing in the trenches – these are the representatives of Asia – and lastly, Australia and New Zealand are sending their contingents, over land and sea, from the Antipodes. And what is the purpose of which the attainment is thought worth such a world-wide levy of warriors? Why, Germanic culture is to be uprooted from the earth. And it is the bearers of this culture, the people of Luther, Goethe, Beethoven, Helmholtz and Röntgen, that are called barbarians and Huns – a danger to the future and civilisation of the white race! It is therefore fit that Ghurkhas and Senegalese should come and save us from relapse into the dark ages.[52]

Hedin's contention, that the deployment of colonial soldiers was a means not only to win the war but also to destroy German culture, was repeated elsewhere. But the Swede also voiced a wider German contention that the black and brown men fighting for the Allies were themselves the victims of British and French treachery: savage and uneducated, they were the unknowing tools of an immoral strategy.

When the German press launched its campaign against the deployment of colonial soldiers on the European battlefield, the newspapers claimed that not only was it a crime against Germany but also a profound threat to global racial order and the dominance of the white race. German wartime propaganda exploited what was indeed, for the British in particular, a genuine concern – that soldiers from the colonies, having been trained in the use of modern weapons, ordered to kill white men, tended to by white nurses, and even lionized by white civilians while in Europe, would not then be willing to submit themselves to imperial domination when they returned home at the end of the war. The

German argument that the Allies were undermining the prestige and position of the entire white race was not only for domestic consumption but directed also at those in neutral countries, particularly the United States, who feared for the stability of the established racial hierarchy.

The official response of the German government to the colonial troops on the Western Front came in the summer of 1915, when the Foreign Office in Berlin issued the British and French governments with a memorandum of protest. Translated into English, French, Spanish, Dutch and Italian, this *Employment, Contrary to International Law, of Coloured Troops upon the European Arena of War by England and France* was widely distributed. The opening passages set out Germany's case. 'In the present war,' it complained:

> *England and France have not relied solely upon the strength of their own people, but are employing large numbers of colored troops from Africa and Asia in the European arena of war against Germany's popular army. Ghurkhas, Sikhs and Pathans, Sepoys, Turcos, Goums, Moroccans, and Senegalese fill the English and French lines from the North Sea to the Swiss frontier.*

Not only was this strategy deemed unfair, it was criminal. Germany's enemies, the memorandum argued, had dispatched to Europe men from 'countries where war is still conducted in its most savage forms'.[53] While the authors of the memorandum conceded that 'The laws of nations do not, indeed, expressly prohibit the employment of coloured tribes in wars between civilized nations,' they argued that this was only the case if such troops were 'kept under a discipline which excludes the possibility of the violation of the customs of warfare among civilized peoples'. Such constraints, the memorandum asserted, had not been maintained and thus it proclaimed that:

> *... the German Government sees itself compelled in the present war to enter a most solemn protest against England and France*

bringing into the field against Germany troops whose savagery and
cruelty are a disgrace to the methods of warfare of the twentieth
century. The Government bases its protest upon the spirit of the
international agreements of the past few decades, which expressly
make it a duty of civilized peoples 'to lessen the inherent evils of
warfare,' and 'to serve the interests of humanity and the ever-
progressing demands of civilization'.

In the interest of humanity and civilization, Berlin therefore
demanded that 'coloured troops be no longer used upon the
European arena of war'.[54]

Up to the summer of 1915, when the memorandum was published, Germany had mostly fought a dire propaganda war. The
incredible violence unleashed against Belgian civilians in 1914,
along with the needless destruction wrought upon the medieval
town of Leuven (Louvain) and the execution of the English
nurse Edith Cavell, could almost have been designed in London
or Paris to make it easy for British and French propagandists to
portray the Germans as the 'Beastly Hun' and their Kaiser as a
'criminal', 'lunatic' and a 'monster'. Following the 'Rape of
Belgium', the German Army was condemned in the Allied and
neutral press alike for allegedly killing babies and cutting off the
hands of Belgian children – often unsubstantiated cruelties
which, nevertheless, gained credence. By 1915 French newspapers were no longer even writing banner headlines for each
new German war crime, but merely listing them under the semi-
permanent banner '*Les Atrocités Allemandes*'.[55] But with the issue
of race and the deployment of colonial soldiers, the German
Foreign Office believed that it had found a cause that enabled
Germany to portray itself as victim and characterize the Allies as
transgressors of international law and of the conventions of civilized warfare. Furthermore, with the German gaze now on the
issue of non-white soldiers, propagandists set out to demonstrate
to domestic and international audiences that the colonial soldiers had committed their own war crimes against German troops
and white civilians.

On 1 December 1914 the newspaper *Norddeutsche Allgemeine Zeitung* published a report claiming that Gurkhas and Sikhs had begun to sneak across no man's land at night, enter the German lines and slit the throats of the German soldiers. For good measure the Indian troops would then, it was claimed, drink the blood of their victims.[56] Ironically two months earlier, in September 1914, a newspaper in the Punjab had reported the similarly incredible rumour that 'the Germans have cut off the heads of some Gurkha and Sikh soldiers and have sent them to the Powers with the complaint that the English are sending Indian soldiers to the front'.[57] The official German memo of 1915 contained a long appendix listing alleged war crimes by non-white soldiers. Each of the incidents was backed up by 'the sworn testimony of approved witnesses, and also extracts from diaries and letters of citizens of hostile countries', all of whom claimed to be either the victims of, or witnesses to, the incidents. According to the German Foreign Office, these documented atrocities represented 'only a selection from the comprehensive material at hand illustrating the barbarous behaviour of the mercenary coloured troops of England and France'.[58] The memorandum asserted that among the war crimes that were routinely carried out were 'the barbarous practice of carrying with them as war-trophies the severed heads and fingers of German soldiers, and wearing as ornaments about their necks ears which they have cut off'. The later appendices detailed how colonial soldiers:

> ... *creep up stealthily and treacherously upon the German wounded, gouge their eyes out, mutilate their faces with knives, and cut their throats. Indian troops commit these atrocities with a sharp dagger which is fastened in the sheath of their side-arms. Turcos [North Africans], even when wounded themselves, creep around on the battlefield and like wild beasts murder the defenceless wounded.*[59]

One alleged witness, civilian Susanne Ullrich, claimed that a white French officer had told her that 'the clearing up of the battlefield was assigned chiefly to Moroccans and negroes; in

France it was said everywhere that this was done purposely because it would promote the murder of the wounded Germans'. Another, the Bruges merchant Victor Schmier, testified to have:

> *... met in a valley among the dunes black North-Africans wearing white turbans. They called themselves Goumiers. I spoke to them and asked whether they had already seen much of the war, and whether they had shot many Germans. They replied in the affirmative, and one drew out from the pocket of his baggy trousers a string of putrid fragments of flesh. He raised it proudly aloft and counted the single pieces, to the number of twenty-three. He told me that these were all the right ears of Germans whom he had shot; and he meant to carry them home as trophies of victory.*

Schmier added that 'A second man took out from his trousers a head with red hair and a stubble of beard; it had been severed from the neck diagonally. He said it was the head of a German soldier whom he had shot. The eyes were half open and full of sand.'[60]

Such stories gained currency, and not only in the German media. Julius M. Price, the war artist and correspondent for the *Illustrated London News*, recorded in his war memoir *On the Path of Adventure* two very similar 'grim yarns' about the Senegalese troops, though in his version twenty-three ears were 'all from the left or "heart side," which it appeared gave them more value, as it indicated he had captured them from the enemy'.[61] In other wartime retellings of similar stories, the ear tally is twenty-one or twenty-two. While the dates change, as do locations and the races of the soldiers involved, the central details remain remarkably consistent; there is a strong suggestion, therefore, that the stories were essentially folkloric.[62]

One explanation put forward for the potency of the severed-ears story is that some French officers might have offered African troops rewards for every German killed, monies paid on presentation of these war trophies as proof of each kill. If true, it suggests how the French also fell back on preconceptions of their West African troops as barbarous and bloodthirsty. Certainly, French authorities and civilians alike resorted to the same stereotypes when celebrating the service of African soldiers as the German propagandists did when condemning it. When units of *Tirailleurs Sénégalais* arrived in France in 1914, excited crowds had shouted: '*Bravo les Tirailleurs Sénégalais! Couper têtes aux allemands!*' ('Well done, *Tirailleurs Sénégalais*! Cut off the Germans' heads!').[63] A few months later the French periodical *Midi Colonial* carried a cartoon of a French Muslim soldier with a necklace made of human ears and the caption 'Be silent, be careful, enemy ears are listening!'[64]

The wartime atrocity stories that poured off the production line of the German propaganda machine were, to some extent, built on the foundations of recent historical memory. Similar claims had been made by sections of the press during the genocidal wars fought by the German Army between 1904 and 1908 against the Herero and Nama peoples of German South West Africa. Reports that the Africans had mutilated the corpses of the German dead – both soldiers and civilians – were for the most part newspaper inventions. Some reports were so exaggerated that the army itself felt compelled to refute them; but such accounts had a deep impact at the time and firmly established black Africans, in the folk culture of late Wilhelmine Germany, as savages who were incapable of adhering to the rules of civilized warfare. This folk memory made it easier for wartime propagandists, a decade later, to bring Indian and North African soldiers into a category similar to that occupied by Africans in the popular German imagination. The weapons that were carried by the non-white troops were seen to substantiate, or at least add credence to the propaganda stories: and thus the *kukri* and the *coupe-coupe* were, in German propaganda, not traditional weapons but instruments of torture and mutilation.

In the end, the full truth about human war trophies, the mutilation of the dead and the killing of prisoners will probably never be known. It is inevitable in a war in which millions of men were mobilized that atrocities took place; it is equally clear that while such incidents were rare, reports of them were common and exaggerated.* Atrocity stories, on both sides, were amplified and duplicated, distorted by constant telling and re-telling. But the sheer weight of German propaganda convinced both German soldiers and civilians that the taking of war trophies, the killing of prisoners and even acts of cannibalism were not rare aberrations but the standard practice of Asian and more particularly black African soldiers. Unable, ultimately, to prove that colonial soldiers were illegal combatants, Germany's propaganda machine instead encouraged the belief that men from Asia and Africa were incapable of fighting according to the rules and conventions of war and instead fought according to their innate savage instincts. In this way they were portrayed not so much as fighting in a war, as hunting German soldiers as if they were some sort of prey.[65] But still, France recruited.

★

The consequences of France's *races guerrières* theory reached their apotheosis early on the morning of 16 April 1917. In the shadow of the great ridge at Chemin des Dames on the Western Front, twenty battalions of *Tirailleurs Sénégalais* – around 15,000 men – huddled together in icy, water-logged trenches shrouded in thick mist. They had come from across French West Africa – Senegal, Benin, Mali, Côte d'Ivoire, Burkina-Faso, Niger, Guinea and Mauritania, from thousands of tiny villages as well as from the towns of the region such as Bamako, Abidjan, Cotonou and – literally – Timbuktu.

---

* There exists very real and grim evidence that body parts were taken as war trophies. In 2002 the mummified head of a Turkish soldier, a war trophy that had been taken from battlefields of Gallipoli, was brought into a police station in Echuca, a small town in Victoria, Australia. It was handed over to the authorities by the grandson of an Australian soldier who had fought with the ANZACs. The Australian journalist Jeff Sparrow described this horrific relic of the war: 'The head lay in a red velvet display case. The eyes had rotted away, as had the lips, but the ears remained and tufts of a moustache clung to the black, leathery skin. A 3-centimeter impact hole gaped in the crown, with a matching perforation punched roughly through the bone on the other side.' *See* Jeff Sparrow, *Killing: Misadventures in Violence* (Melbourne University Press, 2009), p. 1.

These were the men, boys, orphans, slaves, abductees and volunteers who had been 'recruited' during 1915 and 1916. Even before
the new offensive began, the *Tirailleurs* had begun to suffer badly
in the freezing conditions: 1,100 of them had been already been
withdrawn from the trenches, suffering from pneumonia or other
complaints caused by the cold.

The Battle of Chemin des Dames – known as the Second Battle
of the Aisne to British historians – was the main component of
the great offensive promised by generals Nivelle and Mangin
ever since their victory at Verdun. This was their moment. Nivelle
was supremely confident that French artillery and his unswerving
faith in the power of a shock assault would achieve what no Allied
general on the Western Front had managed in three years of
fighting – a complete rupture of German lines and breakthrough
into the open country behind. What the attackers were supposed
to have done upon reaching open country – by which time they
would have gone beyond the range of supporting artillery – was
not clear. Yet Nivelle's infectious bravado swayed his colleagues.
The attack was to take place along a front twenty-five miles long,
immediately following an enormous barrage. Nivelle projected
that there would be only around 10,000 French casualties –
modest by the standards of the war. Fearing that the general's
faith in his own strategies might have got the better of him, the
more cautious men of the French Medical Services prepared
themselves to receive fifteen-thousand. In the end, the total was
ninety-thousand.[66]

Opposing the French and the *Tirailleurs Sénégalais* was the
German Seventh Army, which was dug into some of the most
formidable defensive positions on the whole of the Western
Front. Improved, refined and reinforced since they were first
excavated in the weeks following the First Battle of the Marne in
1914, the German positions were further strengthened by the
deep quarries that had been dug into the Chemin des Dames
ridge over the preceding centuries. These the Germans now
used as underground bunkers to protect them from French artillery. The Germans also had good views over the French positions

below, and the land over which any attackers would have to come was waterlogged and already churned by artillery. Furthermore, the Germans had adopted a system of defence in depth. The front lines were only lightly defended and most troops were held in reserve. By the time any French attackers reached the real centres of German resistance, they might well have already exhausted themselves and lost contact with their own artillery.

Charles Mangin, by now elevated to the High Command, inevitably deployed the *Tirailleurs* as shock troops, in the first waves of the attack. A German officer, Reinhold Eichacker, who left a vivid and horrifying account of the assault, recalled that the first waves of attackers were indeed black Africans. Only when they had been decimated by German artillery and machine-gun fire did 'finally the whites themselves charge'. As they approached the line of dead and dying Africans, lying in heaps in front of the German trenches, Eichacker had no doubt that 'The same thing will happen to the whites. We are waiting for them.' His account is not only revealing about how the French deployed their African soldiers; it drips with racial hatred:

> *At 7:15 in the morning the French attacked. The black Senegal negroes, France's cattle for the shambles ... Let them come, the blacks! And they came. First singly, at wide intervals. Feeling their way, like the arms of a horrible cuttlefish. Eager, grasping, like the claws of a mighty monster. Thus they rushed closer, flickering and sometimes disappearing in their cloud. Entire bodies and single limbs, now showing in the harsh glare, now sinking in the shadows, came nearer and nearer. Strong, wild fellows, their log-like, fat, black skulls wrapped in pieces of dirty rags. Showing their grinning teeth like panthers, with their bellies drawn in and their necks stretched forward. Some with bayonets on their rifles. Many only armed with knives. Monsters all, in their confused hatred. Frightful their distorted, dark grimaces. Horrible their unnaturally wide-opened, burning, bloodshot eyes. Eyes that seem like terrible beings themselves. Like unearthly, hell-born beings. Eyes that seemed to run ahead of their owners, lashed, unchained, no longer to be*

restrained. On they came like dogs gone mad and cats spitting and yowling, with a burning lust for human blood, with a cruel dissemblance of their beastly malice.

The first blacks fell headlong in full course in our wire entanglements, turning somersaults like the clowns in a circus. Some of them half rose, remained hanging, jerked themselves further, crawling, gliding like snakes – cut wires – sprang over – tumbled – fell. Nearer and nearer rolled the wall … Our artillery sent them its greeting! Whole groups melted away. Dismembered bodies, sticky earth, shattered rocks, were mixed in wild disorder. The black cloud halted, wavered, closed its ranks – and rolled nearer and nearer, irresistible, crushing, devastating! And the rifles were flashing all the time. A dissonant, voiceless rattle. The men still stood there and took aim. Calmly, surely, not wasting a single shot. The stamping and snorting of thousands of panting beasts ate up the ground between us.

And now came the gruesome, inconceivable horror! A wall of lead and iron suddenly hurled itself upon the attackers and the entanglements just in front of our trenches. A deafening hammering and clattering, cracking and pounding, rattling and crackling, beat everything to earth in ear-splitting, nerve-racking clamor. Our machine guns had flanked the blacks![67]

The assault by the *Tirailleurs Sénégalais* on the left-hand end of the ridge was but one disastrous element of the wider catastrophe that was Nivelle's Offensive of 1917. It was a calamity that destroyed the general's reputation: he was replaced by Pétain within days. It also tarred the already dubious fame of Charles Mangin. Now more than ever, 'the Butcher' was perceived as a commander who was frivolous with men's lives. When Mangin had heard that troops, including the *Tirailleurs*, were unable to advance in the face of German barbed-wire entanglements that should have been neutralized by the French guns, he was reported to have barked: 'where the wire is not cut by the artillery it must be cut by the infantry. Ground must be taken.'[68] The failures at Chemin des Dames and elsewhere sparked within the

French Army the most serious and widespread military mutiny of the First World War, one of which the Germans somehow remained almost completely unaware. More a military strike than a violent uprising, the exhausted, disillusioned French troops declared themselves willing to hold the front-line trenches but unwilling to take part in any further attacks. The battle also raised question marks in the minds of some over the effectiveness of the *Tirailleurs Sénégalais*.

The reasons for the French failure at Chemin des Dames were legion. Not only had the Germans seized a copy of the French plans during a trench raid in Champagne in February, they had got hold of even more up-to-date and specific plans from a hapless French NCO captured just two weeks before the battle. They had thus readied fifteen counter-attacking divisions behind the lines, using the deep quarries (known as the Dragon's Cave) to conceal and protect them. Today the Dragon's Cave is the site of a moving memorial to the thousands of *Tirailleurs Sénégalais* who died there. These casualty rates were not solely a consequence of the Africans having been deployed as shock troops, nor the failure of the French High Command to prevent the battle plans from falling into enemy hands. By 1917 the *Tirailleurs* were dying in such numbers because they were being very deliberately used as cannon fodder, placed in the first waves of attack and set against the most difficult of objectives. This was done in order to reduce casualty rates among white French units. The evidence for this policy is overwhelming.

Not long after he had taken up his post, Nivelle himself had a signed note suggesting the army should ensure that it was 'not being gentle with Black blood', because the higher priority was to ensure 'that White blood can be saved'. In a letter to the Ministry of War written in February 1917, he had demanded 'that the number of [African] units put at my disposition should be increased as much as possible. [This will] increase the power of our projected strength and permit the sparing – to the extent possible – of French blood.'[69] But Nivelle was merely the most high-ranking of many commanders who made calls of this kind. A report written in 1918 openly described how the French had come to regard their West African soldiers as *chair à canon* ('cannon fodder') and suggested that they should be used even more intensively 'in order to save whites'. The general attitude was perhaps most honestly and frankly summarized by Colonel Eugène Petitdemange, the commander of the camp in which the *Tirailleurs Sénégalais* trained while in Fréjus, the town on the Côte d'Azur to which the Africans were dispatched each autumn to spare them the worst months of the French winter (the system known as *Hivernage*). In a letter to Pétain, who by now had replaced Nivelle, Colonel Petitdemange wrote:

> *My aim is to seek to increase the use of the Senegalese ... in order to spare the blood of French servicemen, France having already paid a heavy tribute during this war. It is essential to try by all means possible to diminish their future losses through the enhanced use of our brave Senegalese ... The Senegalese have been recruited to replace the French, to be used as cannon fodder to spare the whites. It is essential then to use them in an intensive fashion... .[70]*

Most damning, though, were the words of the French prime minister, Georges Clemenceau. He was defending his decision to begin yet another recruitment drive in French West Africa, the need for more troops for 1918 being considered to outweigh the risks of further revolts in the colonies or even their potential destruction as functioning economies. On 20 February 1918 he told the French Assembly:

> *We are going to offer civilization to the blacks. They will have to pay for that ... I would prefer that ten blacks are killed rather than one Frenchman – although I immensely respect those brave blacks – for I think that enough Frenchmen are killed anyway and that we should sacrifice as few as possible.[71]*

To find more 'brave blacks' to take the place of Frenchmen at the front, France in 1918 thus embarked upon another recruitment drive in its colonies. In Africa, France was faced with peoples who had grown resistant to the activities of the army and its recruiting agents. Mangin, ebullient as ever, remained confident that France's reservoirs of African men were still able to offer up yet more of their sons, perhaps as many as a third-of-a-million. The first obstacle, though, was not the resistance of the Africans but the opposition of the white French colonial administrators, who feared further recruitment would leave their territories financially ruined and socially devastated. Enticed by the enormous manpower figures Mangin set out in a report, but hoping to avoid inciting outright rebellion in Africa, Clemenceau turned to a man who was the very personification of the French ideals of equality and assimilation, the concepts upon which the whole imperial project was supposedly founded.[72]

In 1914, Blaise Diagne had become the first black African elected as a deputy in the French Parliament. Born in Gorée, in Senegal, he was a remarkable figure. Highly educated, well travelled within the French Empire and remarkably energetic, Diagne believed earnestly and passionately in the French *mission civilisatrice*. For him, the war was not just an epic struggle but a great opportunity – for France to demonstrate to the peoples of its empire that French egalitarian values were paramount over considerations of race, and for Africans to offer to France what he described in 1916 as a 'harvest of devotion'. Diagne had spent the first years of the war touring the army camps. With all the powers and status of his position as a deputy, he had demanded better treatment for colonial soldiers and confronted racist white officers. In the French Chamber of Deputies, he pushed through a new law that realized a longstanding demand: the *Loi Blaise Diagne*. It secured full French citizenship for African soldiers from the most integrated regions of French West Africa. There were to be rewards for military service, and Diagne's task was to convince his fellow Africans of his own conviction: that France and its colonies were destined to become integrated and unified 'above any question of origin or race'.[73]

Arriving back in West Africa in early 1918, Diagne set about the task of recruitment with characteristic fervour. The sight of a black French politician, one of their own, accompanied by three black officers, all decorated war veterans, had a powerful impact. Communities who had come to regard recruitment as a death sentence, or at the very least as a form of military servitude, now encountered black veterans who had not only survived the conflict but attained, through their service, new status and authority – authority that even extended over white men of inferior rank. By September 1918, Diagne and his team had recruited 77,000 Africans, by persuasion rather than coercion, and had far exceeded the target set for them by Clemenceau. The Diagne mission was looked upon with horror by the Governor-General of French West Africa, Joost van Vollenhoven. It was he, the white governor, rather than Diagne, the black politician, who pleaded with Paris to end the recruitment, complaining: 'This African empire is poor in men but rich in products, so let us use its miserable population for food supply during the war and for post-war times! This country has been ruined just to recruit another few thousands of men.'[74] Van Vollenhoven resigned and volunteered for service on the Western Front himself, where he was killed in the Second Battle of the Marne. Blaise Diagne was appointed Commissioner General in the French Ministry of Colonies.

That France was willing to grant full citizenship to some of its colonial subjects reinforces the fact that French racism was distinctive from that which prevailed within other European nations and the United States. Yet the French faith in the ideals of assimilation and eventual equality existed in parallel with an unshakable belief in the supposedly innate racial characteristics of black Africans, a belief that had disastrous consequences for the men recruited from West Africa.

★

As with the British view of 'martial races' of India, the implication of the French concept of the *races guerrières* was that there were *races* that were *non-guerrières* – a phenomenon that can perhaps best be demonstrated by comparing the wartime experiences of the *Tirailleurs Sénégalais* with that of men from other parts of the

French Empire. During the war, French deployment of the almost 500,000 men recruited from their colonies was in accordance with these prevailing racial theories – and where evidence from the front seemed to contradict the theories, it was usually explained away as an anomaly or simply ignored. Thus while West Africa was regarded as the home of the most spirited and ferocious of the *races guerrières*, matters were more complex when it came to the peoples of North Africa, Madagascar and the French colonies in Asia. Sometimes they too were written off as men of low intellect, and it was claimed that North Africans were, for the most part, poor marksmen because they lacked 'notions of precision, indispensible to soldiers in specialized branches'.[75] The experience of men recruited from French Indochina was, however, in many ways the mirror opposite of that of the *Tirailleurs Sénégalais*.

Throughout their deployment, the French military authorities remained convinced that the Indochinese were members of a *races non-guerrières* – an essentially feminine and passive people, who generally did not make good soldiers. Their relatively small stature came to be seen as physiological evidence of a lack of martial qualities. The army went as far as designing a special rifle, shorter than the standard model, for issue to them. While supposedly frail and passive, the Indochinese had other virtues of use to the army. They were deemed to be more intelligent than black Africans and suited – in ways that Africans were not – to specialized and technical roles. During the Battle of the Somme, Indochinese were deployed as military drivers, and by the war's end 4,000 of them were driving trucks behind the lines. Their ability to remain focused, for long periods, in this role was put down by one French commander to their vegetarian diets.[76] There were also two battalions of *Tirailleurs Indochinois* on the Western Front, and two more on the Salonika (Macedonian) Front; but the Indochinese were for the most part deployed as support units, behind the lines, rather than as front-line combat troops.

Despite their generally *races-non-guerrières* status, some Indochinese did face the full horrors of trench warfare, fighting at Verdun, on the Somme and at the Chemin des Dames. As was the case with other colonial armies, the Indochinese arrived full of confidence in the power of the empire of which they were part, only to be stunned by the military might of Germany. Like the men of the British Indian Corps they wrote letters home to relatives describing the unimaginable scale of the conflict and, at times, warning their comrades still in Indochina not to join up. Even when *Tirailleurs Indochinois* did fight as combat troops, and acquit themselves well in battle, it did little to change French attitudes. One company of the 6th Battalion *Tirailleurs Indochinois* took part in the assaults to retake Fort Douaumont in October 1916. The men were said to have performed well and remained a cohesive force despite sustaining losses. They fought again at the Battle of Chemin des Dames (1917) and in the defence of Reims, winning awards for their service. Yet the power of racial theory was such that none of this had much impact on the prevailing assessment that the Indochinese were not natural warriors. Forty years after the start of the First World War, when an army of white French troops, North African units and *Tirailleurs Sénégalais* were decimated by the North Vietnamese Army at Dien Bien Phu – in a battle that descended into trench warfare – the nonsense of such racial categorizations was comprehensively and painfully demonstrated to the French nation.

The most telling example of the power of the idea of the *races guerrières* and *non-guerrières* was to be found behind the lines. In the *Commis et Ouvriers d'Administration*, men from France's empire worked as office clerks, performing skilled and semi-skilled tasks behind the lines, including everything from butchering animals to working as mechanics on vehicles. While a high proportion of Indochinese and Madagascans, and smaller proportions of French North Africans, worked in the *Commis et Ouvriers d'Administration*, not a single West African spent the war behind a desk or in any other auxiliary role.[77] This unwavering devotion on the part of the French Army to racial theory, over and above any empirical evidence, shaped almost every aspect of the experiences and deployment of West Africans in the French Army. They remained shock troops, deemed of insufficient intelligence for other roles. One consequence was that West Africans were almost completely absent from those parts of the army that suffered the lower casualty rates – cavalry, artillery and engineering units.[78]

During the last two years of the war, French racial theory fused with the growing determination to deploy Africans in ways that would save white lives. Race became a determinant of who was likely to live and who was likely to die. The results can be seen in the casualty figures. Over the four years of the war, around 140,000 West African soldiers served in combat. According to the official estimate, around 31,000 or roughly 23 per cent of them died; but the real number is almost certainly higher. Several historians have examined the casuality statistics of the *Tirailleurs Sénégalais*,[79] the most exhaustive analysis being that of American historian Joe Lunn. His work has demonstrated that when deployed in combat in 1917 and 1918 – the period when they suffered the majority of their casualties – the probability of a West African soldier being killed at the front was two-and-a-half times higher than for a white French infantry-man.[80] Life expectancy was even lower for men from the West African tribes whom Mangin and the other 'colonial experts' had defined as being especially warlike: men from the Wolof, Tukulor and Bambara ethnic groups were about three times as likely to die in combat as a white French soldier recruited in the same years.

Numbers measured in the tens of thousands seem small when compared to the total losses of the metropolitan French Army – 1.3 million men. In *pure* terms, many more white Frenchmen from the mother country died than did men from France's empire. There is also much truth in the argument that when compared to its British and American allies, France – boasting its republican, egalitarian values – was in certain respects less racist towards troops with an African lineage. However, the widespread acceptance of the theory of the *races guerrières,* and the willing-ness of the French – traumatized as they were by the losses of 1914 and 1915 – to use Africans only as shock troops eventually translated into a higher rate of *proportional* loss and proved disastrous for thousands of young African men and the communities from which they came.

———————

FRANCE, 10 MAY 1940. Nazi Germany unleashes *Blitzkrieg* against France and the Low Countries. For the third time in seventy years, a German army has crossed the frontiers, its pincers stretching out to the coast and threatening Paris. The old battlefields of the Western Front that have stood quiet for twenty-two years are once again contested by British, German, Belgian and French troops. At Neuve Chapelle, the memorial to the dead of the British Indian Corps, built in the 1920s on the site of the trenches from which the Indians had advanced, is peppered with machine-gun fire and struck by shrapnel – scars that survive into the twenty-first century. In 1914 the German Schlieffen Plan to knock out France in weeks failed. This German invasion will have quite different results.

As *Blitzkrieg* thunders across France, German forces very quickly come into contact with around 40,000 *Tirailleurs Sénégalais*. It soon becomes clear that when coming up against Africans, the German Army is adhering to set strategies and military policies that are dramatically different from those they employ when facing other enemy units. In numerous engagements, Germans refuse to take black prisoners. In combat, the *Tirailleurs* battalions suffer a casualty rate far higher than most of their white comrades. It is when Tirailleurs *are* captured, or encircled or surrender, that the full dimension of German policy is revealed. Thirteen days into the Battle of France, the *Oberkommando der Wehrmacht* (OKW) – the German High Command – orders its propaganda operatives to scour the makeshift prisoner-of-war pens and there to 'quickly take photographs showing particularly good-looking German soldiers alongside particularly bestial-looking Senegalese Negroes and other coloured prisoners of war ... Sharp racial contrasts are of special importance.'[81]

Six weeks later, on 20 June 1940, a group of sixty *Tirailleurs Sénégalais* and their eight white officers surrender near the French village of Chasselay. They are marched, *en masse*, to a field outside the nearby village of Chères. Under the gaze of two Panzer tanks, the officers are instructed to lie down, while the black soldiers are ordered to assemble in the centre of the field with their hands raised in surrender. Huddled together, the *Tirailleurs* are then ordered by the Germans to run. At that moment, the Panzers open fire with their machine guns and canon, shooting into the backs of the fleeing men. Fifty of the *Tirailleurs* are killed. The Panzer commanders then run their tanks, back and forth, over the bodies of the fallen, crushing to death the wounded as they lie helpless.[82]

The incident at Chères was just one of many, ranging from the battlefield executions of captured individuals to orchestrated mass-murders, that took place in May and June 1940. In those months, French African soldiers were systematically sought out by German units, separated from their white comrades and officers, and summarily killed. The accounts collated by the historian Raffael Scheck – found in both local French archives and the archive of the German Army – describe an orgy of murder and abuse, motivated by a widespread and intense racial hatred. Witnesses – often white French officers – described how German soldiers justified these summary executions by dismissing Africans as savages, sub-humans who had no legitimate place within a European war. All the myths of the First World War appear to have been inherited by a new generation of German soldiers – the hatreds of one generation effectively passed down to their sons like family silver, a bequest that was eased by Nazi propagandists. Particularly feared, again, was the *coupe-coupe*, seen as an 'illegal weapon' (it was not): German soldiers were genuinely convinced it would be used in an appalling fashion should they fall prisoner to the *Tirailleurs Sénégalais*. The *coupe-coupe* in itself was sometimes regarded as justification for the murders of Africans. Their French officers were beaten and berated for having supposedly betrayed both the white race and European civilization by fighting for a nation that had brought into its army, and on to its soil, such savage peoples. Some white French officers were even shot and killed for the crime of having led Africans into battle.

The policy of executions was directed unambiguously against black Africans from the French colonies below the Sahara, rather than at all non-white combatants. On one occasion a group of Moroccan soldiers were gathered together with the white prisoners while their black comrades were segregated and taken to a separate location. There, the black Africans were massacred. The Moroccans and the whites were accorded their legal rights as prisoners of war.[83] In all, over 3,000 Africans, subjects of the French Empire and soldiers of the French Army, were murdered by the Germans in 1940. After the war there were some investigations into the killings, mass graves were unearthed, and bodies exhumed; but there were no trials and none of the killers was ever held to account.

Germany's little-known race war against Africans in 1940 complicates a neat division of the Second World War into the 'decent' war in the West, fought by the rules of the Geneva Convention, and the war in the East from 1941, a vicious fight to the death witnessing brutality and genocide. Yet to understand the forces that inspired the murder of 3,000 black Africans in the spring of 1940 – and which compelled Hitler to single out Mangin's statue for destruction – requires us to look backwards in time to 1914, rather than forward to 1941.

CHAPTER 5

'INFLAME THE WHOLE MOHAMMEDAN WORLD'

The Kaiser's Jihad

———

ISTANBUL, EARLY NOVEMBER 1914. In a city that most of Christian Europe still calls Constantinople, and which many of its Greek Orthodox residents still wilfully and wistfully know as Byzantium, Ürgüplü Mustafa Hayri Efendi, the Sheikh-ul-Islam – second highest religious authority in the Ottoman Empire – presides over a ceremony at the city's Fatih Mosque. For this auspicious event the sacred relics of Islam, held in the Topkapi Palace, have been transported across the city, and the empire's dignitaries and power-brokers have gathered together. Under the great vaulted dome of the fifteenth-century mosque, the banner of the Prophet Mohammed is ceremoniously unfurled and the Sheikh-ul-Islam solemnly presents the sword of the Prophet to Mehmed Reshad V, the thirty-fifth Ottoman sultan.

Mehmed is not only sultan of a secular empire; he is also the Caliph of Sunni Islam, the religious title first held by the immediate followers of the Prophet after his death in AD 632, and which has been inherited by Mehmed V from his sixteenth-century forefather Sultan Selim I. It is a position reinforced by Ottoman possession of Islam's sacred relics and by the sultan's role as protector of the *Hajj* and defender of the holy places of Mecca and Medina.

The sultan – a squat, portly figure – speaks the words written for him by the leading politicians. After a few sentences elaborating on the empire's recent grievances, he reminds his audience that 'Russia, England and France have never for a moment ceased harbouring ill-will against our great Caliphate to which millions of Muslims suffering under their tyranny are religiously and whole-heartedly devoted.'[1] Omitting to mention Britain's role as defender of the Ottoman Empire against Russian ambitions in the nineteenth century, he continues: 'it was always these powers that started every disaster and misfortune that came upon us'. A litany of historic injustices, Mehmed declares, has now left the empire with no choice but to declare not just war against Russia, England and France, but a Holy War – *Jihad*. 'This Holy War which we are undertaking will put a definitive end to the attacks made against the glory of our Caliphate as well as against our sovereignty.' Sultan Mehmed now addresses his army and navy, urging them 'Never even for a single moment abstain from strenuous efforts and self-sacrifice in our cause and this holy war we have opened against enemies who dared to undermine our religion and our beloved homeland.' But, as *Jihad*, this must be war waged in the name of the worldwide Muslim population: 'Throw yourselves against the enemy,' Mehmed declares:

> ... *as lions for the life and existence of both our country and 300 million Muslims, whom I have summoned by sacred decree to a supreme struggle ... Prayers and good wishes of the hearts of 300 million aggrieved and innocent believers, whose faces are turned in devotion to the Lord of the universe in mosques and the holy Kaaba, are with you.*

To help them, he reassures his audience that in this effort they not only have 'the divine help of God and the moral support of our glorious Prophet,' but also that they will be 'comrades-in-arms with the two bravest and [most] magnificent armies of the world'.[2]

———— ▪ ————

With his speech, Mehmed V signalled the Ottoman Empire's entry into war. Although widely dismissed as 'the sick man of

Europe', the empire still ruled over 22 million disparate people, from the southern Balkans to the fringes of the Arabian Peninsula. Now, driven on by their German allies, and themselves groping for a rationale that might explain the purpose of the war to their own people, the leaders of Ottoman Turkey permitted Islamic Holy War to become one of the forces to spread the violence and misery of the First World War across the globe. The ruling political party, the Committee for Union and Progress (CUP), was dominated by a cabal of ambitious 'Young Turks', many of whom were secular modernizers of shallow faith; they were now evoking the religious authority of the sultan-caliph in order to cloak their political ambitions in religious garb, and in doing so were attempting to draw into the war the 300 million Muslims who lived beyond the crumbling frontiers of the Ottoman Empire.

What resulted was a tale of holy war and unholy alliances, espionage and counter-espionage, and global ambition on a breathtaking scale. The weaponization of religion helped cast the seeds of war, revolt and discord across parts of Africa, Asia and the Middle East. Under the shadow of the banner of the sultan-caliph, Germany dispatched U-boats loaded with arms and ammunition to the coast of North Africa and sent gifts of gold to local Islamic leaders – men to whom the sultan addressed elegant parchments calling upon them to take up the call of *Jihad*. German money bankrolled secret military expeditions across the Islamic world to ignite the resentments of Muslims living under British rule. Led by warrior-intellectuals – officers regarded as the German equivalents of T.E. Lawrence – and planned in Berlin and Istanbul, these expeditions involved a bizarre cast list of German propagandists and orientalists – most of them either romantic fantasists or wealthy playboys. Other parts in this global drama were played by local rabble-rousers, stateless gun-runners, devout tribal leaders, corrupt emirs and sheikhs, and soldier-defectors from British India and French North Africa.

Yet perhaps the most remarkable aspect of the whole story is that the real driving force behind this bizarre and unlikely scheme was neither the sultan, nor the Sheikh-ul-Islam, nor even the Young Turks. This was the Kaiser's *Jihad.* In the words of Allied propagandists, it was a 'Holy War made in Berlin'.[3]

★

The *Jihad* strategy was not a knee-jerk reaction to events of 1914; rather, it had emerged out of the strange alliance of mutual self-interest that had begun to develop in the last years of the nineteenth century, between a buoyant, unified and expansive Germany and a decrepit, humiliated and disempowered Ottoman Empire. It was a marriage of convenience, consummated by two state visits made by Kaiser Wilhelm II to the Ottoman sultan – not Mehmed V, but rather his older brother and predecessor, Sultan Abdülhamid II. As the last of the 'Lords of the Horizons', he was the last sultan to exercise *real* power over this intercontinental empire, until he was overthrown.

By November 1914, as Mehmed V declared *Jihad,* across the Bosphorus his older brother was being held in permanent captivity, within the baroque gaudiness of the Beylerbeyi Palace. There the former sultan worked on his memoirs and brooded. In November 1889, Sultan Abdülhamid II had been at the Yıldız Palace, another of the many royal residences, awaiting the arrival of the SMY *Hohenzollern,* the royal yacht that brought the German Kaiser through the Dardanelles and into the Golden Horn for his first visit to Istanbul. The Kaiser and sultan, through mutual flattery, seem to have formed a bond on their first meeting. There followed tours of the city, boat trips on the Bosphorus, the exchange of gifts and mutual declarations of friendship.

Nine years later the Kaiser returned, this time for a full tour of the Ottoman Empire. To accommodate the return of his royal friends, the sultan had ordered the construction of a new wing of the Yıldız Palace. The Kaiser's itinerary was planned, in meticulous detail, by the British firm Thomas Cook & Son, the inventors of the package tour.[4] It was during this longer, more exhaustive tour that Wilhelm seems to have become captivated by Islamic culture and to have developed real respect for the Islamic faith. So effusive was Wilhelm in his praise of Islam that in the first years of the twentieth century a rumour swirled around the Middle East and British India that the Kaiser had secretly converted to Islam. The German intelligence services did nothing to correct that mistaken view. Perhaps the more austere aspects of Sunni Islam and the faith's strict moral code appealed to a man brought up amid the iron discipline of the Prussian Officer Corps. Whatever the case, it seems likely that Wilhelm's interest in Islam was not an affectation. In a private letter to the Tsar, written on his visit to Jerusalem, the Kaiser claimed that if he were an atheist, able to select a faith, he would choose Islam.

It was in October 1898 that Wilhelm travelled to Jerusalem, entering on a white horse through a breach knocked into the walls near the Jaffa Gate. His next stop was Damascus. There he visited the tomb of Saladin, the great Muslim warrior of the Crusades. After a fulsome eulogy to the greatness of Saladin, and yet more praise for his friend Sultan Abdülhamid II, Wilhelm declared that the '300 million Muslim subjects scattered across the earth ... can be assured that the German Kaiser will be their friend for all time'.

The Kaiser was infamously prone to short-term obsessions with certain policies or issues, for which he later lost enthusiasm. Yet Wilhelm's fascination with Islam and the Orient was not the product of naive romanticism about the East. The sheer amount of attention and interest he seems to have shown towards Ottoman Turkey and the potential power of Islam lends credence to the idea that on this issue he was more involved, and paid more attention, than with the many other schemes and issues that grabbed his attention only to later fall by the wayside. There is certainly no doubt whatsoever that the Kaiser's declarations of friendship to Ottoman Turkey and the Muslim world garnered the full attention of the governments of France, Russia and Britain.

What was it that Germany had to gain from an alliance with the Ottoman Empire that could be worth antagonizing Russia and causing dismay and distrust in France and Britain? Militarily, the Ottoman Army was, as one British general claimed, 'a non-entity', although under German tutelage this was fast changing. Germany's interest was primarily strategic. By dint of its geographic position, the Ottoman Empire was uniquely able to threaten two of Germany's most likely enemies in a future war – Imperial Russia and the British Empire. The Ottoman state shared a border with Russia in the Caucasus and would, in some future war, be able to draw a proportion of the Tsar's forces southwards towards that region and away from the German frontiers. Perhaps more significantly, the Ottoman Army, by marching through Syria and Palestine, could threaten Egypt and the Suez Canal, Britain's supply line to India – critical to both British trade and military capacity. If Ottoman Turkey was able to train and field a modern army, and transport those forces to its strategic borders using a German-built rail network, the empire would become a very significant potential ally.

Yet there was something of a self-fulfilling prophecy about German diplomacy. Two years after the Kaiser's second Ottoman visit, Germany allowed the so-called Reinsurance Treaty with Russia – the traditional enemy of the Ottoman Empire – to lapse, despite Russian interest in its renewal.* It was a significant factor in drawing Tsarist Russia, looking for new allies, into the diplomatic embrace of Third Republic France, which in turn would come to convince Germans that the encirclement they had long feared was now a reality.** When, in 1907, Britain formed

---

* In this secret treaty, negotiated by Bismarck, Germany and Russia both agreed to remain neutral if involved in a war with a third power, with two exceptions: should Germany invade France, or should Russia invade Austria-Hungary. Germany also implicitly acknowledged Russian spheres of influence, in Bulgaria and the Black Sea.

** It is too easy to imagine that Wilhelm, a man known for emphatic pronouncements and telling gaffes, was the captain of the German ship of state, always directing policy. Yet, as many historians have warned, most recently and compellingly Christopher Clark, this is a dangerous presumption. Wilhelm's was a butterfly mind. He made statements that were mutually contradictory and often later reversed by changes of policy. He was one key player in a ruling elite, which contained rival factions vying for influence, money and patronage. He was not the author of all German policy and at times hardly involved in key decisions. There is much evidence that his role in the decision to allow the Reinsurance Treaty to lapse may have been a marginal one. *See* Christopher Clark, *Kaiser Wilhelm II: A Life in Power* (London, 2009).

the Triple Entente with France and Russia and that encirclement appeared complete, Germany's desire for an Ottoman alliance was strengthening. Finding a way to bolster and modernize Ottoman Turkey though trade, railway construction and re-armament had already become a feature of German foreign policy. Even in 1898, one German newspaper was predicting:

> *The sick man will be cured, so thoroughly, that when he wakes up from his sleep of recovery he will be difficult to recognize. One would think he has got blond hair, blue eyes, and looks quite Germanic. In our loving embrace we have injected so much German essence into him that he will be hard to distinguish from a German.*[5]

In these same years, by contrast, the British and French came to believe that their best interests were served by keeping the sick man on his deathbed and planning for his eventual demise.

German designs were not, however, focused solely on strategic military planning in advance of any war. Germany imagined an alliance with Ottoman Turkey also as a key aspect of a post-war re-ordering of the world. At their most expansive, the geo-strategic fantasies entertained by sections of the German Foreign Office (along with the far right Pan-Germanic League and pro-colonial and ultra-nationalist writers) foresaw an empire stretching across the sands of Arabia and beyond. There were those in Germany's ruling elite who envisaged an empire funded by oil and fuelled by trade, its main artery being a railway of German steel, running from the port of Hamburg, through the heart of Europe and across Arabia and Mesopotamia to the port of Basra – a second choice after British machinations had pushed Kuwait beyond Germany's reach. The famous Berlin–Baghdad Railway was, in the minds of some, to be a new Silk Road, an umbilical link between Europe and Asia that would reverse the long decline of Asia. The fast train to Berlin would outpace, by up to three days, the slow boats that slipped through the Suez Canal. Along the same 2,000 miles of track would pour into Germany the raw materials and oil of the Near East. Flowing the other way would be train-loads of German manufactured goods. The key concession for the Berlin–Baghdad Railway was agreed by Abdülhamid II in 1899, the year after the Kaiser's second visit. In Whitehall the railway was regarded not just as an economic rival to the Suez Canal, but also as a direct strategic threat to India – and therefore to the empire as a whole and to Britain's primacy in the world. The railway could – in theory at least – enable Germany to dispatch its armies to the Persian Gulf within one week.[6]

If German ambitions were for a re-ordered future, the rulers of Ottoman Turkey fantasized about regaining the power and influence of the past. Despite the grandeur of the setting and the solemnity of the event, the true condition of the empire was apparent to all those who witnessed the sultan's declaration of *Jihad* in November 1914. The Fatih Mosque (Mosque of the Conqueror) stands on the site of the Church of the Holy Apostles, formerly the second most important place of worship of the Byzantine Empire, which had been demolished in 1461 to make way for the Islamic edifice. It was built in honour of Sultan Mehmed II, the twenty-one-year-old conqueror of Constantinople, who had brought to an end the 1,500-year-old Byzantine Empire. In 1914, the burning legend of Mehmed II could not have stood in greater contrast to the enfeebled seventy-year-old puppet Mehmed V: the perfect metaphor for the decline of Ottoman power. In the five intervening centuries since the glories of Mehmed II, the Ottoman Empire had been eclipsed in almost every regard by the Christian states of Europe, which had once lived in fear that the Ottoman fleet might appear off their shores or that the elite Janissary Corps of the sultan's army might breach the walls of their cities. Although Ottoman decline lasted longer than the rise and fall of most other empires, it was, by the last quarter of the nineteenth century, inexorable – and seemed to be approaching its conclusion.[7] Since the 1870s, the empire had experienced a string of disastrous military defeats in the Balkans as the Christian nationalities fought to create their own nation states, often with the support of Russia. Even within its contracted borders, the 'sick man of Europe' had, like all invalids, lost a great deal of his independence. The great powers of Europe had forced upon the Ottomans an open-door trade policy, and European traders and agents were exempt from prosecution and taxation within the empire's borders. Moreover, in 1875 the Ottoman Empire had declared itself bankrupt, and six years later was forced to accept the Ottoman Public Debt Administration, a bureaucracy of 5,000 employees by means of which European creditors seized Ottoman tax revenues at source.

With Ottoman death looking inevitable, for some decades the great powers of Europe had all staked claims (often justified on religious grounds) to their chosen cuts of the Ottoman corpse. The British wanted control of Mesopotamia, the French Syria and Palestine. Italy had already fought a war for control of Ottoman Libya, and the Russians wanted Istanbul itself and control of the Dardanelles, through which much of their trade flowed. During the last thirty years of the nineteenth century, European treatment of the Ottoman state had not *quite* descended into gun-boat diplomacy; but the European warships that slipped up and down the Bosphorus and into Ottoman waters with impunity were physical reminders of Ottoman powerlessness in the face of voracious and circling enemies.

The only European power that *appeared* to have no imperial designs on Ottoman lands or an interest in Ottoman demise was Germany.

———————

ISTANBUL, FRIDAY 14 NOVEMBER 1914. Ali Haydar Efendi, Custodian of the *Fatwa*, addresses a vast crowd from a balcony of the Fatih Mosque that is bedecked with the red pennant flags of the Ottoman Empire.[8] He proclaims a series of *fatwa* – religious judgements – signed by twenty-nine religious authorities and approved by both the sultan and the Ottoman Chamber of Deputies. Probably drafted three days earlier, they have been written in a question-and-answer format and intended to legitimize the *Jihad* according to Koranic scripture. In doing so they stretch Islamic jurisprudence to its limits – and beyond.

The first asks: 'If several enemies unite against Islam, if the countries of Islam are sacked, if the Muslim populations are massacred or made captive … is participation in this war a duty for all Muslims, old and young, cavalry and infantry?' The answer read out is 'Yes.' The second asks whether the 'Muslim subjects of Russia, of France, of England and of all the countries that side with them in their land and sea attacks … against the Caliphate for the purpose of annihilating Islam must … too take part in the Holy War against the respective governments from which they depend?' The answer again is 'Yes.' A third *fatwa* asks: 'Those who at a time when all Muslims are summoned to fight, avoid the struggle and refuse to join in the Holy War, are they exposed to the wrath of God, to great misfortunes, and to the deserved punishment?' The answer again is 'Yes.' The fourth *fatwa* is also a warning, this time addressed to the Muslim soldiers and would-be soldiers of the Allied powers: 'If the Muslim subjects of the said countries should take up arms against the government of Islam [the Ottoman Empire and its allies], would they commit an unpardonable sin, even if they had been driven to the war by threats of extermination uttered against themselves and their families'? Unsurprisingly, the answer is 'Yes.'

The final *fatwa* is addressed to Muslims already fighting on behalf of the Allies. These soldiers 'who in the present war are under England, France, Russia, Serbia, Montenegro and those who give aid to these countries by waging war against Germany and Austria, allies of Turkey, do they deserve to be punished by the wrath of God as being the cause of harm and damage to the Caliphate and to Islam?' The answer is 'Yes.'[9]

——— · ———

The proclamation of the *fatwa* was but one of a series of remarkable and clearly choreographed public events in Istanbul that day.* With the Jihad declared and the *fatwa* issued, an official Holy War demonstration, which had been organized by the Ottoman government, assembled outside the Ministry of War. There, as the Dutch orientalist Christiaan Snouck Hurgronje recorded, 'Prayers were said, long speeches were held, there was no end to the jubilation.' From the Ministry of War, a 'procession passed through the main parts of the city, waited upon the Grand Vizier, and demonstrated in front of the German and the Austrian Embassies.'[10] It was when the procession reached the German Embassy that the most theatrical, ominous and telling events of the day took place. While a band played, the enormous figure of German Ambassador Baron Hans von Wangenheim appeared above the heads of the throng, on the large balcony at the front of the embassy. From this vantage point, and speaking through a member of the German diplomatic staff fluent in Turkish, Wangenheim addressed the crowds. Although not one of the more committed believers in the wisdom of the *Jihad* policy, Wangenheim promised the crowd German support in the Holy War and offered his salutes to the sultan. According to Hurgronje:

> ... *the German ambassador did not only speak of Germany and Turkey, but of their common struggle for the real welfare of the Mohammedan world; of Germany's friendship for the Empire of the Ottomans, but especially for the adherents of Islam, before all of whom, as soon as the German and Turkish arms have achieved victory, there lies a glorious future.*[11]

Wangenheim's address was followed by yet more speeches, by the ruling CUP party, which solicited enthusiastic cheers from the crowd.

The greatest *coup de théâtre* of the whole stage-managed day was yet to come. A group of Muslim PoWs was dramatically

* For an overview of the complex debate over the dates of both the *Jihad* and the *Fatwas, see* M. Aksakal, '"Holy War Made in Germany"? Ottoman Origins of the 1914 Jihad', in *War in History* (online serial), Vol. 18, No. 2 (April 2011), pp. 84–199.

paraded on the embassy balcony – fourteen men who had been captured during various engagements in France and Belgium earlier in the war, or who had come over to the German lines as deserters. All were originally from the French colonies of North Africa – Algeria, Tunisia and Morocco. They now read aloud, in Turkish and Arabic, declarations of their support for the sultan and personal affirmations of their intention to join the struggle against their former colonial masters. Behind them stood Karl Emil Schabinger von Schowingen, their translator as well as recruiting officer. He was on hand to prompt the prisoners to shout the agreed slogan 'Long live the sultan and caliph!'[12] At least one of the prisoners, a Moroccan, spoke in Arabic. He thanked Germany for 'liberating' him from the clutches of the French oppressors and condemned the treatment of Muslim soldiers in the French Army.[13] Anna Grosser-Rilke, a German resident of Istanbul who was witness to these scenes, doubted that 'much of what he said was understood down there. People will hardly have understood his gibberish.'[14] Summing up the whole of the day's events, Hurgronje compared them to a 'musical comedy of Offenbach'.[15]

Indeed, a sense of theatre had infused the journey of the North Africans to Istanbul. They were recruited directly from PoW camps (established in occupied France) by Schowingen, who was an orientalist, a diplomat and an agent of the German Foreign Office. They were then secretly transported across Europe on the *Orient Express*, accompanied by Schowingen and under a cover-story of being acrobats in a travelling circus. On arrival at Istanbul's Sirkeci Station, the prisoners had been placed in the care of the Ottoman police, who had presumably helped ready them for their big moment.[16] Their appearance on the German Embassy's balcony was the first public indication that German–Ottoman operations to inspire *Jihad* would be intertwined with the fate and treatment of PoWs from the British and French empires, men who – disorientated, conflicted and vulnerable though they undoubtedly were – came to play a critical propaganda role in Germany's global *Jihad*.

Once the fourteen PoWs had been ushered off the balcony and the invited dignitaries had exhausted their condemnations of Britain, France and Russia, the crowds moved on to the Austrian Embassy for a similar rally. This was followed by a disorderly procession through the streets of the Beyoğlu district of European Istanbul – then known by the name Pera and regarded as the 'Paris of the Orient'. There, in the wide French-style boulevards, the frantic crowd attacked and looted French- and British-owned businesses. Churches on the Grande Rue de Pera – the heart of the most cosmopolitan district of one of the most diverse, multi-ethnic cities on earth – were attacked and damaged. However, the only confirmed 'Western' casualty of the day was a grandfather clock, which stood in the lobby of the Tokatlian Hotel, a luxurious establishment owned by a family of wealthy Armenian Christians. Schowingen had ordered his escort of Ottoman policemen to storm the lobby and fire a single, symbolic shot into the old clock.[17] The crime, for which this clock was symbolically executed, was that it had been manufactured in England. After this strange assassination, the mob then set to work. 'Six men who have poles, with hooks at the end, break all the mirrors and windows, others take the marble tops of the tables and smash them to bits. In a few minutes the place has been completely gutted.'[18] Very quickly Istanbul was becoming a very different city.

On the next day, the *fatwas* were distributed in pamphlet form. According to one account, the document that now circulated around the city concluded with a call to arms:

Oh, Moslems … Ye who are smitten with happiness and are on the verge of sacrificing your life and your goods for the cause of right, and of braving perils, gather now around the Imperial throne, obey the commands of the Almighty, who, in the Koran, promises us bliss in this and in the next world; embrace ye the foot of the Caliph's throne and know ye that the state is at war with Russia, England, France, and their Allies, and that these are the enemies of Islam. The Chief of the believers, the Caliph, invites you all as Moslems to join in the Holy War![19]

Even before *Jihad* had been declared, Christian and European residents of Istanbul had begun to fear for their safety. As early as 3 November, a Hungarian newspaper was reporting pro-*Jihad* demonstrations in which 'Large numbers march through the city waving large green flags, dervishes howl and wave blood-soaked pieces of cloth.'[20] In the aftermath of the *Jihad* declaration, British, French and Russian residents suddenly found themselves enemy aliens in the city in which they had made their homes or set up their businesses. The diplomatic staffs of the various embassies were rapidly evacuated, and there was a great clamour among civilians to get out before the borders were closed, or before they were interned by the Ottoman police. The seizure and ransacking of schools and hospitals run by Allied nationals added to the growing sense of panic. The final escape for many was coordinated by American Ambassador Henry Morgenthau, who spent much of his time at Sirkeci Station pleading with the authorities to allow the trains packed with frightened Europeans to depart for neutral nations in the Balkans.

Morgenthau's dispatches captured the febrile atmosphere that took hold of Istanbul, but also the mechanisms by which news of the *Jihad* spread across the Islamic world:

> *The religious leaders read this proclamation to their assembled congregations in the mosques; all the newspapers printed it conspicuously; it was broadcast in all the countries which had large Mohammedan populations – India, China, Persia, Egypt, Algiers, Tripoli, Morocco, and the like; in all these places it was read to the assembled multitudes and the populace was exhorted to obey the mandate. The* Ikdam, *the Turkish newspaper which had passed into German ownership, was constantly inciting the masses. 'The deeds of our enemies,' wrote this Turco-German editor, 'have brought down the wrath of God. A gleam of hope has appeared. All Mohammedans, young and old, men, women, and children, must fulfil their duty so that the gleam may not fade away, but give light to us forever. How many great things can be accomplished by the arms of vigorous men, by the aid of others, of women and children! … The time for action*

*has come. We shall all have to fight with all our strength, with all
our soul, with teeth and nails, with all the sinews of our bodies and
of our spirits. If we do it, the deliverance of the subjected Mohammedan
kingdoms is assured. Then, if God so wills, we shall march
unashamed by the side of our friends who send their greetings to the
Crescent. Allah is our aid and the Prophet is our support.*'[21]

★

In both the tone and content of the various declarations made in
Istanbul in November 1914, Morgenthau detected 'a German
hand' exercising 'an editorial supervision'. For one thing, the
fatwas, and the accompanying religious commentaries written by
Muslim jurists, had been printed and distributed with subsidies
partly provided by the German government.[22] The *fatwas*, like
the *Jihad*, had strained Koranic jurisprudence to breaking point
– and in the eyes of many Muslims beyond credulity. As
Morgenthau noted, both proclamations had emphasized that
'only those infidels are to be slain, "who rule over us", that is,
those who have Mohammedan subjects'. Rather conveniently for
Germany, few in 1914 were aware that in its African colonies
Germany fell into the category of an 'infidel' power ruling over
Muslim subjects. There were around 2 million Muslims in
German East Africa, while the small Muslim communities in
Togoland had already been subjected to the sort of routine bru-
tality that German colonialism had visited on Africans of all
confessions. Yet, despite this record, and these hypocrisies,
Germany was able to portray itself as a nation innocent of subju-
gating Muslims – indeed, even as an enemy of imperialism and
defender of the 'slandered peoples' of the European empires.
Things were more complex for Austria-Hungary. Ambassador
Morgenthau commented that 'The Germans, with their usual
interest in their own well-being and their usual disregard of their
ally, evidently overlooked the fact that Austria had many
Mohammedan subjects in Bosnia and Herzegovina.'

If anything, the ambassador probably underestimated the
extent to which the *Jihad* of 1914 was a joint German–Ottoman

policy. The Ottomans had much to gain by evoking faith to justify their political war. Nevertheless, the specific 'German hand' at work was that of Baron Max von Oppenheim, a half-Jewish son of a Cologne banking family. To the profound disappointment of his father, the young Oppenheim had rejected the world of finance for a life of travel and intrigue in the Orient. Entranced by the cultures of the region he became another of those strange, Edwardian-era figures – in turn archaeologist, orientalist and diplomat, although long before 1914 the British had concluded that Oppenheim was more spy than diplomat. His story had begun in the 1880s when he had started to travel in the Middle East. By 1892 he had visited North Africa, Mesopotamia and Morocco, before finally establishing himself in Cairo. There he learnt Arabic and became a well-known society fixture among the small European and American community that drifted in and out of the city's wealthier districts and hotels. Throughout his time in the Middle East, Oppenheim was in the habit of taking 'temporary wives', an exotic, erotic predilection that only added to his reputation as a true orientalist, a man who lived his life in the borderlands between European and Islamic culture. It was an image he sought to cultivate, and although by no means one the greats of German orientalism he had enough standing for T.E. Lawrence to cite his work. Yet, despite his regional contacts, language skills, private wealth and powerful friends in Berlin, Oppenheim was twice rejected by the German Foreign Office due to his Jewish ancestry. Throughout his life, Oppenheim was a man desperate to prove his loyalty to Germany.* From 1900 onwards he had become associated with Kaiser Wilhelm himself, whom he had first met when both were young men. The Kaiser became fascinated by Oppenheim's descriptions of life and culture in the Middle East and by his reports on the growing

---

* Despite claiming to have adopted his mother's Catholicism, Oppenheim remained half-Jewish according to the definition established in the Nuremberg Laws, and in the 1930s and 1940s was to be the target of Nazi persecution. Yet he was a committed patriot and worked on schemes to enhance German influence in the Middle East right up until 1940.

potential of Pan-Islamism and the authority of the Ottoman sultan as the twin forces that might unify and mobilize the Islamic world. The two men met on numerous occasions, with Oppenheim being invited each year for dinner to regale the Kaiser with the latest developments in the region.

Pan-Islamism was then a minor obsession with political thinkers in Europe and a force that had attracted the attention of Sultan Abdülhamid II. It took many forms, but at its heart was a call for unity among the *Ummah* – the worldwide community of Muslims. Pan-Islamists saw their faith as the flag around which the peoples of the Islamic world might be marshalled against European imperialism. Abdülhamid II regarded it rather differently – as a force that would allow him, as caliph, to entrench his power, save his empire from European encroachment, and force the Christian powers to respect his status and potential global influence. While there was a great deal of justifiable scepticism about the potential power of Pan-Islamism among Europeans, Oppenheim was a vocal advocate of the idea that it, in combination with the religious authority of the sultan-caliph, could be harnessed by Germany to devastating effect in a war against the empires of either Britain, France or Russia. Oppenheim predicted (in prescient terms for the twenty-first century) that 'the demographic strength of the Islamic lands will one day have a great significance for European states. We must not forget that everything taking place in one Mohammedan country sends waves across the entire world of Islam.' In an article written in 1899, the German nationalist Friedrich Naumann shored up Oppenheim's theories, warning that:

> It is possible that the world war will break out before the disintegration of the Ottoman Empire. Then the Caliph of Constantinople will once more uplift the Standard of the Holy War. The Sick Man will raise himself for the last time to shout to Egypt, the Sudan, East Africa, Persia, Afghanistan, and India, 'War against England.' It is not unimportant to know who will support him on his bed when he utters this cry.[23]

On 2 August 1914, the day after Germany mobilized against Russia and two days before Britain declared war, Oppenheim was summoned to the German Foreign Office. This was his moment. On the same day a secret alliance treaty was agreed between Germany and the small but powerful war faction of the leading Young Turks within the Ottoman government, led by the 'Three Pashas' – Enver Pasha (Minister for War), Talat Pasha (Minister of the Interior) and Djemal Pasha (Navy Minister). The treaty was kept secret, not just from the Ottoman people and the wider world, but even from most of the Ottoman Cabinet; when the rest of the government discovered the truth, there was a wave of resignations. In late October 1914, the Ottoman Empire abandoned its formal neutrality and, in a naval attack involving warships donated by Germany, attacked Russian bases in the Black Sea. There was no turning back – and Oppenheim could take centre-stage, to nurture his strategy of a *Jihad* that he had promoted so energetically, now with official backing and state funding.

In late October 1914 Oppenheim drafted a memorandum – *Denkschrift betreffend die Revolutionierung der islamischen Gebiete unserer Feinde* ('Memorandum Concerning the Fomenting of Revolutions in the Islamic Territories of Our Enemies'). It called for the creation in Berlin of an Intelligence Bureau for the East (*Nachrichtenstelle für den Orient*), where Oppenheim would draw together Germany's orientalists and regional experts. It then set out the targets for the German *Jihad*. Summarizing the numbers of Muslims in the various colonies of Britain, France and Russia, it explained which branches of the faith they adhered to and outlined the attitudes and concerns of their leaders. From the very start, demographics dictated that the main target was Britain and its empire, within the bounds of which one-third of the world's 300 million Muslims lived. The British Empire was, in these terms, the greatest Muslim power in the world, and so George V ruled over more Muslim subjects than the Shah of Persia, the Khedive of Egypt or indeed the Ottoman sultan.[24] (In fact, only around 30 million Muslims lived in Muslim-ruled states.) It was a statistic that reinforced a prevailing German

resentment which held that Perfidious Albion had, in the nineteenth century, prevented the newly unified Germany from
taking up its rightful place at the top table of imperial powers.
The prospect now that, via a German–Ottoman alliance, restive
Muslims could convert the economic strength and military manpower of Britain's colonies into a large Achilles heel was an
extremely appealing one to large sectors of the German ruling
elite. A German economist, Werner Sombart, captured the fever-
ishly anti-British mood in an essay of November 1914, *Unsere
Feinde* ('Our Enemies'), describing how anti-British feeling had
come to supplant all other antagonisms in Wilhelmine Germany.*
While taking a moment to denounce the Japanese as 'clever half-
apes' and the Serbs as 'mouse-trap peddlers', the author claimed
that 'Fundamentally we have nothing at all against the French'
(since they were 'chivalrous opponents … dying for their fatherland') and that the German people harboured 'no real hatred'
towards Russia, despite its being contaminated by 'Mongolism'.
Turning to the English, however:

> *We perceive England to be the enemy. We wage the war against
> England. We will not consider the war to be finished, before England
> lies shattered and above all humiliated to its innermost depths at our
> feet. Were England to be granted an honourable peace, I almost believe
> that this alone would drive the peaceful German people to revolution.
> For I have never at any time found the German temperament more
> passionate as now, when the word 'England' is pronounced.*[25]

Catching the temperament of his nation in late 1914, Oppenheim's
memorandum prophesied that once Turkey formally entered the
war, and the prestige of the sultan-caliph had drawn the faithful
millions to the banner of Islam, then the *Jihad* could be focused
upon the hated British to deadly effect. 'Only when the Turks
invade Egypt and revolts break out in India,' he predicted:

---

* This same title was to be used again later in the war by another of Germany's wartime propagandists.

... will England be made to yield. Public opinion in 'greater England' will force the government in London either to send as much as half the fleet to India in order to protect the many Englishmen living there, as well as the billions invested in the country, and to sustain Britain's place in the world, or – since it can be expected that England on its own [that is, without her empire] will be unable to achieve that last goal – to make peace on terms favourable to us.[26]

The Kaiser was clearly in agreement as to which of Germany's enemies was the main target of the *Jihad* strategy. On 30 July 1914, five days before Britain had entered the war and three days before the signing of the secret alliance between Germany and Ottoman Turkey, Wilhelm had written:

Our consuls and agents in Turkey and India must inflame the whole Mohammedan world to wild revolt against this hateful, lying and conscienceless nation of shopkeepers. If we are going to shed our blood then England must lose India.[27]

To unleash the power of *Jihad*, Oppenheim's October memorandum foresaw local revolts as well as military campaigns launched by the armies of Muslim states that lived under enemy domination. It envisaged the Emir of Afghanistan marching his army over the Khyber Pass and into British India, and the Suez Canal being closed when the Egyptian people rose up to support an Ottoman Army that would sweep down through Syria and Palestine. Oppenheim painted an intoxicating picture of both the British and French armies riven by insurrection, revolt and sabotage, as the Muslim contingents of their colonial forces turned against their masters; and he cast the Muslim PoWs being accumulated in German camps as an *avante-garde* of insurrection: converts to the cause, they would spread hatred of the Allies among their countrymen and march alongside German and Ottoman soldiers on secret missions to spread the word of *Jihad*.

In the late summer of 1914, when the war had seemed to be
going Germany's way, the sheikhs of Arabia, including the legendary Ibn Saud and Hussein bin Ali, the Sheriff of Mecca, had
sent their sons to meet the Germans and the Turks in Istanbul.
They arrived bearing gifts and promises to support any *Jihad*
against the British and French. In November 1914, the events in
Istanbul and outbreaks of violence elsewhere in the Islamic world
seemed to suggest that Oppenheim's predictions were beginning
to prove correct. Within two days of the sultan's call for *Jihad* in
November, the news reached India: there British Army officers
were lynched on the streets by Muslim crowds. Riots broke out,
too, in French Algeria; and at the other end of the Mediterranean,
cinema audiences in Cairo cheered the newsreels that announced
German victories.[28] Stirrings of discontent were reported among
the hundreds of thousands of Muslim soldiers in the British
Indian Army, and in London, Paris, Brussels, Washington and
Moscow the newspapers schooled Europeans in the meaning of
an unfamiliar word – *Jihad*.

★

The Kaiser's rant of 30 July 1914, although written during a
period of acute stress when British entry into the war looked
imminent, gave voice to one of the great paradoxes of the conflict: that Britain, with its vast empire, had most to gain by
restricting the conflict to Europe, while Germany, the continental power who lacked extensive colonies or a fleet capable of
dominating the oceans, had the most to gain from spreading the
war as widely as possible. The *Jihad* was one pillar of a wider
German strategy to globalize the conflict, sowing the seeds of war
and revolution beyond Europe.* When, in mid-September 1914,

* As well as pursuing *Jihad*, Germany also aimed to stoke nationalist/ethnic
resentments of Ukrainians, Finns and Georgians (along with the Crimean
Tartars and Kurds) against Russian rule, and foster anti-colonialism among
India's Hindus. The mastermind – if that is the right word – overseeing
much of the strategy was Arthur Zimmerman, Under Secretary of State at
the German Foreign Office, who ran a programme titled *Unternehmungen*

Allied victory on the Marne terminally derailed the German strategy of quickly defeating France, the prospect of a protracted war on two fronts became real – a war in which Britain would have the time to draw further men and materials from its enormous empire. Cutting off Britain's supply line to India was no longer merely a potential means of forcing her to the negotiating table. It might even become a requirement for Germany's survival against an enemy capable of marshalling the wealth and power of one-third of the world.

The ultimate aim of the *Jihad* strategy was to make real the Kaiser's demand that 'England must lose India'. This, along with the lesser aim of driving the Russians out of the Caucasus by inciting revolt among the Tsar's 20 million Muslim subjects, was what Oppenheim had assured the Foreign Office his strategy could deliver. On receiving official backing and official funding in November 1914, he established two bases of operation. One was in Istanbul, while in Berlin's Wilhelmstrasse Oppenheim set up his Intelligence Bureau for the East – the '*Jihad* Bureau' – as outlined in his October memorandum, and it was here that many of Germany's leading orientalists, most-celebrated adventurers and most-shameless charlatans rushed to volunteer their services. It was from here, too, that *Jihadi* propaganda was disseminated. Oppenheim's staff – most of them white, Christian Germans – set about writing propaganda pamphlets in Arabic, quoting verses from the Koran, and calling for Holy War against other Christians. Oppenheim himself wrote a pamphlet that contained the passage 'The Blood of the infidels in the Islamic lands may be shed with impunity' and which called for Muslims to 'slay' unbelievers. Under Oppenheim's direction, the *fatwas* of November 1914 were translated into Persian and Urdu, and

und Aufwiegelungen gegen unsere Feinde (Seditious Undertakings Against Our Enemies). Zimmerman's offices supported Russian revolutionaries, Irish republicans and (ironically in the light of later history) Zionists too. Zimmerman's enduring fame, however, is as the author of the 'Zimmerman Telegram', which offered German support for Mexican aggression against the United States.

into Arabic and French, and distributed to agents and contacts across the world.

To the men of the German Foreign Office who were financing Oppenheim's activities, one of the great appeals of his schemes was that compared to conventional warfare the *Jihad* strategy represented war on the cheap. Although not insignificant amounts of gold and arms were to be made available to the leaders of various missions sent out to foment revolt, or sent directly to wavering Islamic leaders whose acquiescence Germany and Turkey sought, such costs – when weighed against even the price of a single day's fighting on the 475 miles of the Western Front – were near to insignificant.

Alongside the religious propaganda, the Intelligence Bureau for the East ran a sideline in false war reports, designed to convince would-be Jihadists and indecisive local leaders that Germany and its allies were on the verge of winning the war, and that the military power of Britain was waning. To this end, the Intelligence Bureau generated fake accounts of great German and Ottoman victories on the battlefield and concocted detailed narratives of the near collapse of the British Army. In this alternate reality, George V abdicated his throne and fled his realm, and the colonial soldiers of Britain and France turned their guns on their own officers and *en masse* turned their minds to the cause of Holy War. The general plot-lines and *leitmotifs* in the Oppenheim-approved re-imagining of the war were strikingly similar to those of pre-war German novels that had speculated on how Germany might win an enhanced place in the world at Britain's expense. The scenarios conjured up in the Intelligence Bureau were no less fanciful than those penned by nationalist pre-war authors like August Wilhelm Otto Niemann, whose *Der Weltkrieg: Deutsche Träume* ('The World War: German Dreams') of 1904 imagined an invasion of a collapsed Britain, precipitated by its loss of control over India and the Indian Army. Sigmund Freud might have classified them all as examples of *Wunscherfüllung* – wish fulfillment.

In order to fulfil the Kaiser's ultimate wish of seeing the British lose India, Oppenheim left no stone unturned and no potential source of revolution or discord untapped. In Berlin, he also formed the 'Indian Revolutionary Committee'. Its mission was to incite a second Indian Mutiny, by radicalizing soldiers in the Indian Army – those deployed on the Western Front and in the Middle East, as well as their comrades who had remained on garrison in India itself. These types of revolutionary toxins, synthesized in a Berlin suburb, were political in nature rather than religious, the dream of national self-determination rather than holy war. The Indian Revolutionary Committee was manned by Indian students and revolutionary exiles from the Raj, who energetically tapped into the growing surge of nationalist sentiment in their homeland. As well as generating propaganda and their own false accounts of the progress of the war, they devised schemes to run guns to India, distribute anti-British literature, and destabilize the economy of the Raj by flooding the subcontinent with counterfeit 10-rupee notes.

While the propaganda war was waged from Berlin, the Ottoman capital became the jumping-off point for the missions and expeditions that were to be dispatched to the Islamic world to inflame passions and incite revolt. As nervous British, French and Russian civilians flocked to Istanbul's Sirkeci railway station in November 1914 to leave the country, arriving on trains coming in the opposite direction was a procession of German soldiers, diplomats, intelligence officers and spies. Sirkeci became their entry point into Istanbul, and the fashionable Pera Palace Hotel – located conveniently near to the German Embassy – became their residence.* There they gathered their equipment, assembled their teams and prepared cases of bribe money, which, along with letters from the Kaiser and sultan, were intended to ease their passage and impress local Islamic leaders. Then they and their Ottoman co-conspirators would cross the Bosphorus to the jetty of Istanbul's other rail terminal, the huge, beautiful and

---

* Built to entertain passengers travelling on the *Orient Express*, the Pera Palace features in Graham Greene's *Travels with My Aunt* and Ernest Hemingway's *The Snows of Kilimanjaro*, and it was the creative starting-point for Agatha Christie's *Murder on the Orient Express*.

German-built Haydarpasha Station. From this gateway to the East they would slip away into Mesopotamia, Persia and beyond.

The list of agents and missions dispatched by Oppenheim is a long one. Although the German–Ottoman *Jihad* has rarely been a focus of great attention in histories of the war, when it has been explored most attention has tended to be lavished on the stories of these daring expeditions.* Led by small groups of highly educated, highly literate, middle-class European officers, travelling across exotic lands of classical tradition – Arabia, Persia, Mesopotamia – the expeditions have a powerful allure. They came to fame soon after the war when the dramatic memoirs of the officers who ventured into the deserts of Asia and the Middle East, to fight either for or against German and Ottoman interests, began to appear. T.E. Lawrence's *Seven Pillars of Wisdom* is the most famous of many such accounts, which formed their own sub-genre within the European orientalist tradition, the same tradition that had inspired men like Lawrence in the first place. But these romantic desert odysseys have perhaps overshadowed the wider story of the *Jihad* and obscured the fact that the whole scheme was a mechanism designed to bring yet more nations and societies into the most calamitous war the world had ever known.

★

There was, however, only one part of the British Empire against which Germany, in alliance with the Ottoman Empire, was able to directly launch a land attack: Egypt. In September 1914 the German agent Robert Mors had been sent to Alexandria on board a ship loaded with *Jihadi* literature and dynamite. Along with Egyptian co-conspirators, his mission had been to spread Holy War and launch terror attacks against infrastructural targets, including the Suez Canal; but the scheme in the end had come

---

* Hew Strachan's *The First World War*, Volume 1, *To Arms* (2001) was one of the first major books to dedicate chapters to the *Jihad* strategy (as well as the war in Africa).

to nothing. Its failure did little to dampen the belief of Oppenheim and others that the Muslim peoples of Egypt, and the Muslim contingents of the British colonial forces stationed there, were ripe for *Jihadi* conversion and liable to revolt. Here, Oppenheim's strategizing fused with conventional military strategy. An attack on the Suez Canal by the Ottoman Army had been Berlin's first demand of its Ottoman allies, and Oppenheim convinced many that such an assault, bolstered by *Jihadi* volunteers and Mujahideen from North Africa, would be the spark that would ignite a general anti-British rising in Cairo and elsewhere.

The British had been preparing for a possible attack since October 1914, but, despite having a force of 70,000 to defend the canal, its size – a hundred miles from the Bitter Lakes in the south to Port Said on the Mediterranean – still made it vulnerable. Most of the potential reinforcements from India had, from September, been diverted on to Marseilles to shore up the Western Front. Targetting the canal was the Ottoman Fourth Army, equipped, partially funded and fitted out by the Germans and commanded by Young Turk Djemal Pasha, one of the prime movers behind the German–Ottoman alliance. Assisting him was the head of the German military mission to the Fourth Army, the highly competent Lieutenant Colonel Kress von Kressenstein. Before leaving to take up his command, Djemal Pasha gave a speech in Istanbul that, although containing the requisite amount of fiery righteousness, was perhaps not the oration of a commander confident of success:

> *I am fully aware of the greatness and of the difficulty of my task. If our endeavours fail, if my corpse and those of the brave men who accompanied me will remain on the shores of the canal, the friends of the fatherland will have to march over us in order to liberate Egypt, which is by rights the property of Islam, from the hands of the British usurpers.*[29]

On 20 December 1914, the holy green flag of Islam was taken from Mecca and sent to Jerusalem; on 10 January 1915 an

Ottoman force numbering 20,000 set off from that holy city towards the Suez Canal, with the green flag at its head.

Between their railway terminus in Palestine and the canal area itself, the men had to march the full 300-mile distance across the Sinai Desert. The heat and the terrain restricted the size of the attacking army, as everything from drinking water to shells for the artillery had to be hauled by pack animals. It was, by the standards of any era, a brilliantly executed crossing, down in part to the skills of Lieutenant Colonel von Kressenstein. As well as their food, water and ammunition, the Ottoman soldiers dragged across the desert howitzers and the pontoons with which they aimed to cross the canal. They marched at night to escape the terrible heat and avoid aerial observation by British pilots, and after three weeks they emerged from the desert in good spirits and with the canal before them.

The Ottoman army was as multiracial and polyglot as the British Imperial forces dug in along the canal, comprising Anatolian Turks, Circassians, Syrians, Kurds, Druzes, Bedouin men who were native to the Sinai itself, Arab *Jihadi* volunteers and, of course, a contingent of Germans. The British fielded an army dominated by Indians: men from the Punjab, along with Baluchis, Gurkhas, Sikhs, and Rajputs. Alongside them were Egyptian soldiers, and officers and men from Britain itself.

In the early hours of 3 February 1915, the Ottoman Fourth Army succeeded in lowering onto the still waters of the canal steel pontoons, of German manufacture. Teams of military engineers were even able to cross the canal; but once the morning light exposed their positions, the British and Indian machine gunners, who had been readied to expect the assault, brought Ottoman operations to a halt with a murderous blaze of fire. A second nocturnal attempt to bridge the canal was similarly repulsed, and after other smaller actions, the Ottoman force, having lost around 800 men, began a long retreat back to the Holy Land. Not only had the canal held, the *Jihadi* uprisings that Oppenheim had promised would erupt in Cairo had failed to materialize. Although the Egyptian capital had been tense and watchful, the city had remained quiet. Neither the Egyptian people nor the Muslim troops in the British defending forces showed any sign of revolt. There were a handful of Indian desertions, but the assertion peddled in Berlin and Istanbul that Indian Muslims, when confronted with an army of fellow believers carrying the banners of Islam, would join forces with their co-religionists had been proven fanciful.

★

The dream of severing the Suez Canal and driving the British out of Egypt was also the ambition behind the other German–Ottoman mission to North Africa – the attempt to co-opt the Senussi sect.

The desert region to the west of Egypt, but east of Tripoli, was known as Cyrenaica – today the eastern province of Libya – and in 1915 it was a somewhat lawless zone, home to the Senussi. A religious order rather than an ethnic tribe, they were in effect a brotherhood of the strict Islamic Sufi sect, with followers in North Africa, Arabia, Sudan and elsewhere. To most outsiders, the sect was an enigma – which was enough to ring alarm bells with the British, who had bitter memories of confronting Islamic Mahdists in nineteenth-century Sudan. Indeed, men in Whitehall, surveying the Islamic world in 1914, might well have reminded themselves that Britain's own national warrior-hero, the man whose pointed finger stretched out accusingly from thousands of recruiting posters, had in large part built his reputation fighting against Islamic rebels. Secretary of State for War Kitchener was, after all, Earl Kitchener of Khartoum, and as well as battling the Sudanese Mahdists he had fought in Somalia. The French, too, had their own experience of a long, protracted and highly costly series of colonial wars during their struggles to take full control over Algeria. The Italians had learnt similar lessons fighting against none other than the Senussi themselves, during the 1911–12 Turco-Italian war fought for control of Libya. In August 1914, the still neutral Italians and the rest of Europe had been reminded of Senussi military prowess when they had attacked an Italian baggage caravan, killing Italian troops and seizing arms and supplies.

There were therefore those in London and Cairo who regarded the Senussi as an unquantifiable but real danger to their geo-strategically vital hold on Egypt. And that the British later regarded the Senussi as a potential threat was good enough for Oppenheim. In his October memorandum, he identified the Senussi as prime candidates for the *Jihad*; but even before that, in early August 1914, the German agent Otto Mannesmann was sent to Tripoli to try and stir the Senussi into action against the British. His attempts floundered on his inability to deliver to them the arms they desperately needed and the military assis-tance they wanted. Despite this early setback, the Ottomans had good links to the Senussi, and in late 1914 Enver Pasha dis-patched his half-brother Nuri Bey to Libya, with instructions to persuade the Grand Senussi Sayyid Ahmed ash-Sharif to embrace the sultan's call to *Jihad*. Alongside Bey was Jafar al-Askari, a Mesopotamian Arab and senior officer in the Ottoman Army. (He had an eventful career: he was later captured, defected to the British, joined the Arab Revolt and ended up as prime min-ister – twice – of post-war Iraq.) They landed on the Marmarican coast from German U-boats and brought with them good-will money and a small quantity of rifles and ammunition, a sample of the huge stocks of arms the Germans and Ottomans promised to provide, should the Senussi join the Holy War and attack British Egypt.

Like all the local Islamic leaders caught up in the German–Ottoman *Jihad*, Sayyid Ahmed ash-Sharif sought to play his hand as best he could. Caught between competing empires, which all now came knocking as potential suitors, he wanted the best price for his neutrality – or involvement – in the war. To British offi-cials, the Grand Senussi spoke unctuously of his determination to remain neutral and not offend Britannia. To the Ottoman delegations and German agents in his midst, he made reassuring noises about *Jihad* and religious duty, while biding his time to see which way the tide of war turned. He skilfully played these suitors off against one another, ultimately sparking what amounted to a bidding war for his alliance, all the while fearing that one miscalculation or premature move would land him on the losing side in the war. The Senussi, however, could not play the waiting game for long; their people were hungry, and their armies depleted and lacking all the materials of war after their long fight against the Italians. In November 1915, with the British defeated at Gallipoli, and following deliveries of weapons and gold – and promises of more to come – the Grand Senussi finally threw in his lot with the Ottoman sultan and proclaimed *Jihad.*

The Allied failure at Gallipoli was a serious reputational blow as well as a military reversal, and that defeat was more visible in Egypt than anywhere else, as it was to Alexandria and Cairo that the defeated armies and the many sick and wounded were evacuated. With the beaches of Gallipoli being slowly abandoned, British prestige sank to a new low. Under the shadow of this defeat, the British now began to sense rising tensions on Egypt's western borders. In November 1915 Senussi warriors, armed with German Mauser rifles, attacked the coastal settlement of Sollum, on the edge of the Western Desert. A German U-boat supported their advance, sinking British ships in Sollum harbour. The small British garrison escaped by sea, but, worryingly, three-quarters of the Egyptian troops went over to the enemy.[30] In the south a series of oases was also captured, and fears about the loyalty of the Egyptian population again gripped the British in Cairo. The Senussi, with around 5,000 men, in white robes and bandoliers, then rushed along the coast, overrunning the settlements of Baqbaq and Sidi Barrani and threatening Alexandria. Kitchener feared for the defence of Cairo, with news of new attacks inland adding to the growing sense of alarm. Armed and equipped by their Ottoman and German allies, the Senussi now had light artillery and machine guns, were led by experienced Ottoman officers, and outnumbered the defenders of the western regions of British Egypt. These last consisted of a cobbled-together Western Frontier Force, made up of troops stationed in Egypt but not required to garrison the Suez Canal: a regiment of the Australian Light Horse, which had suffered terrible losses at Gallipoli; the 15th Sikhs; the Gurkha Rifles; the Bikanir Camel Corps from India; men of the Egyptian Army; and New Zealanders and South Africans. The campaign to defend Egypt was as international as the defence of the Suez Canal nine months earlier.

The war in the Western Desert turned out to be one of the most exotic and decisive of the First World War. After the Senussi's initial success, the British Empire forces won a string of victories, pushing the enemy back. By early 1916, men straight from Gallipoli could be thrown into action against the Senussi, and the tide of the campaign shifted. Although almost completely forgotten today, at the time the war against the Senussi gripped the attention of a British press desperate for a distraction from the slaughter in France. The war saw aircraft attacking mounted Bedouin fighters, and German U-boats off African shores. The British press swooned over the Duke of Westminster, who commanded a Light Armoured Car Brigade equipped with six bulletproof Rolls Royces fitted with machine guns. In the recapture of Sollum on 24 March 1916, the armoured cars cut through the enemy ranks, 'shooting all loaded camels and men within reach'.[31] The fighting on the coast was over in this month, though it continued in the deserts until early 1917. Although the British won decisively, the Senussi and their foreign backers did succeed in leeching desperately needed men and materials away from other theatres of war. And for the people of Libya, the Senussi campaign had profound, long-term implications. In 1918 the cousin of the Grand Senussi, Sayyid Muhammad Idris, seized power, eventually becoming King Idris. He remained on the throne until overthrown by Colonel Gaddafi in 1969.*

Had the Ottoman attack on the Suez Canal and the Senussi campaign succeeded and sparked a wider Egyptian revolt, as Oppenheim had hoped, Britain may well have been cut off from

---

* During the Libyan Revolution of 2011, thousands of Senussi fought against Gaddafi. Some carried into battle images of King Idris, and one of the leaders of the revolution was the British-educated Mohammed As-Senussi, a direct descendant of the late king.

India, at least temporarily. However, the ultimate prize demanded by the Kaiser, and energetically pursued by Oppenheim and his Intelligence Bureau, was to incite a revolution on the subcontinent itself.

———

ISTANBUL, SEPTEMBER 1914. Oskar von Niedermayer, a highly educated, highly capable German artillery officer, arrives at Istanbul's Sirkeci Station, in the part of the city that lies on Europe's mainland. He has crossed Europe on the *Orient Express*. Although he is a pragmatic and ruthless soldier, what makes Niedermayer unusual is his education. As confident in the lecture hall as he is on the battlefield, he has a strong command of languages and a deep knowledge of Islam. He has already travelled extensively in the Middle East and Asia, visiting Persia, India and the Ottoman province of Syria. Like Oppenheim, he is entranced by the Orient – and like Oppenheim, he has been a spy. In later life, Niedermayer will often be compared to T.E. Lawrence, and in truth the German is a more accomplished soldier and a more gifted linguist. It is, perhaps, inevitable that Niedermayer's unique set of skills are now called upon by Max von Oppenheim and the German Foreign Office to serve their evolving *Jihad* strategy.

Accompanying Niedermayer is a small team of fifteen officers. They are all disguised – less than convincingly – as a travelling circus. Their bags and equipment are supposed to follow on later, but in fact never arrive. After Romanian customs officials examine baggage described on the inventory as 'tent poles', they identify the contents – accurately – as the aerials of field radios. That discovery leads to a full search, which turns up machine guns, rifles and all the paraphernalia of a military expedition rather than a season under the big top.

Deprived of their equipment, the German contingent is forced to wait in the Pera Palace Hotel in the European quarter of Istanbul, while they are re-equipped. Eventually, on 5 December

1914, on the same day that French aircraft drop bombs on the ancient German city of Freiburg and German guns resume their bombardment of the beautiful French city of Reims, Niedermayer and his men slip across the Bosphorus to Haydarpasha Station in Asian Istanbul, and they board a train on the railway to Baghdad. Their ultimate destination is, however, much further beyond: Afghanistan. And their goal is to incite the collapse of British India.

———— · ————

An uprising in India, whether inspired by Islam or Indian nationalism, might well – the theory went – force the British to choose between fighting against Germany in Europe and fighting in India to save their empire. To achieve this critical objective of their joint global strategy, Germany and the Ottoman Empire adopted a twin-track approach. In Berlin, the exiles and activists of the Indian Revolutionary Committee concentrated their efforts on spreading nationalist propaganda within India, while their comrades in the United States attempted to dispatch shiploads of rifles to their homeland in order to equip an armed uprising. They were thwarted in this endeavour.

The other approach was to persuade the Emir of Afghanistan to march his army over the Khyber Pass and launch an invasion of British India. A mission to win over the emir and convince him to join the Central Powers was thus to be undertaken, and it was this task that fell to Oskar von Niedermayer. In the event, he would lead a small, multinational, disunited and unlikely group of soldiers, diplomats, defectors, agitators and mercenaries in what was the most daring and potentially world-changing of all the expeditions to foment *Jihad*.

The theory that Emir Habibullah Khan might easily be induced into declaring war against the British was promoted not just by Oppenheim but also by Enver Pasha, who wanted to ensure that any agreement to that end was negotiated through Ottoman officials.[32] Oppenheim had assured his masters in Berlin that the emir could muster an army perhaps 50,000-strong. By August 1914, three months before the Ottoman Empire's formal entry into the war and the sultan's declaration of *Jihad*, Enver had already sent a delegation to Kabul. At the same time, in Germany the embryonic core of the expedition team was being formed.

After leaving Istanbul, Niedermayer's entourage passed through Baghdad in December 1914, a city that had become a nest of spies. From there they headed for Persia. Technically neutral, Persia was in effect a failed state in which the rule of its shah counted for little, after decades of British and Russian interference. War-time Tehran was a hive of frenetic intrigue, terrorism and espionage. While awaiting an Ottoman Army escort that never materialized, Niedermayer became energetically involved in the destabilization of Persia, launching sabotage operations against British interests and spreading *Jihadi* literature. In July 1915, after it had become clear that the expedition would have to go on without Ottoman military support, Niedermayer and his men left the city.

The party now took on its final configuration. Niedermayer was joined by Werner Otto von Hentig, a lieutenant in the 3rd East Prussian Cuirassiers. With a background in law and a career in the German Diplomatic Corps, Hentig was in command of the diplomatic aspects of the mission. The Ottoman state was represented by Kâzım Orbay, a Turkish liaison officer who had served in the Ministry of War. To help convince the emir to invade India, two leading Indian figures were attached to the expedition. Mahendra Pratap was an aristocratic Marxist and a highly intellectual Indian nationalist leader. He had recently had audiences with Kaiser Wilhelm, the exiled Khedive of Egypt and Enver Pasha. Alongside Pratap was the twenty-eight-year-old Pan-Islamist firebrand Abdul Hafiz Mohamed Barakatullah, who had spent much of the war in PoW camps in Germany attempting to persuade Indian prisoners of war to defect and join the *Jihad*. Accompanying them on the expedition were six other Indians. They included none other than Jemadar Mir Mast, the Indian officer who had led twenty of his countrymen

over to the German trenches the night before the Battle of
Neuve Chapelle.*

The expedition carried £100,000 in gold bullion and an
unwieldy haul of gifts for the emir, along with formal letters from
the Kaiser and the sultan. To add firepower, their numbers were
bolstered by a contingent of Persian mercenaries. The journey
from Persia to the borders of Afghanistan involved a crossing of
the *Dasht-e Kavir*, the Great Salt Desert, a barrier that observers
in London regarded – over-optimistically – as almost impassable,
especially in the appalling heat of the summer. To reach Kabul
and avoid being intercepted by the British and Russian patrols
that had got wind of the expedition and were forming an East
Persian Cordon, Niedermayer divided the expedition into two
parties, each of about a hundred men. Following the route of
Alexander the Great across Persia, they crossed some bitterly
inhospitable terrain. Always fearful of being betrayed by their
own Persian mercenaries, or sold out by local villagers, they never
stayed long in any of the potentially hostile villages they came
across. To avoid contact with the growing number of enemy
patrols, which now included several mounted Cossack units, the
expedition often travelled at night. Although their progress was
hampered by every imaginable form of discomfort – unbearable
heat, lack of water and even plagues of insects and scorpions –
they made surprisingly good time. One reason for this was that
Niedermayer chose to abandon most of the gifts they had brought
for the emir. Thus, despite all their hardships, on 21 August 1915
the expedition slipped through the East Persian Cordon, evading
Russian and British patrols, and entered Afghanistan. The military phase was over, and the diplomatic phase about to begin.

The party, having lost only one man in the trek, was eventually
escorted to Kabul. As they entered the city to enthusiastic crowds,
all of the confidence invested in the mission by Oppenheim and

---

* A photograph of the six Indians, probably taken in Baghdad, and which
is part of the Hentig Collection of photographs of the expedition, is preserved in a Swiss archive. The annotation on the reverse confirms the presence of Jemadar Mir Mast.

Enver Pasha seemed justified. Here in Kabul, on the very borders of the British Raj, was the tinder-box of anti-British sentiment and religious fervour that might be ignited. The mood in Afghanistan in the period was unquestionably and violently anti-British, a bitter residue of Anglo-Afghan wars in the 1840s and 1870s. However, the £400,000 annual stipend paid by Britain to the emir had been buying his support. What the British authorities feared now was not just that they might be outbid by Germany, and the emir persuaded to change sides by the German and Ottoman emissaries, but that the near universal anti-British sentiments among the emir's people would either force his hand or lead to his overthrow.

Having been cheered through the streets, Niedermayer, Hentig and the rest of the expedition had high hopes. But, rather than being ushered into an audience with the emir, they were settled into a smart villa on the edge of the city and told to wait – which they did for a whole two months. It was not until 26 October 1915 that Emir Habibullah Khan agreed to receive the delegation. At the meeting that day, Kâzım Orbay presented him with a copy of the Ottoman sultan's declaration of *Jihad*, while the German diplomat Hentig handed to him personal letters from Kaiser Wilhelm promising independence for Afghanistan and German military assistance for an attack on British India. The audiences with Hentig, Orbay and the Indian revolutionaries then continued on an almost daily basis for weeks.

By 1915, the emir had been on the throne for fourteen years. He was an intelligent, calculating reformer and a cautious operator. With one eye on events on the Western Front and Gallipoli, he carefully weighed up his options. In January 1916 he eventually signed an agreement with Germany and the Ottoman Empire, whereby he was willing to forego his £400,000 annual stipend from London and attack British India – but in return for a payment of £10 million, supplies of German arms, German military assistance and the usual guarantees of independence. Although Germany would have been willing to stump up the money, any offers of German military assistance were unrealistic and impractical, given the inability of Germany to actually supply any arms or march its armies to Kabul. Both parties were silently aware of this, and in the final analysis the emir's willingness to enter into an agreement on these almost hypothetical terms amounted to another stalling tactic. Habibullah Khan, even more than the Grand Senussi, was playing a double game. Worldly and well-informed, he was not the naive, irrational creature of Oppenheim's orientalist imagination. The emir kept the Germans believing he was always on the verge of agreeing to an alliance, while he watched the progress of the war and hoped for a better offer from London. Disheartened and disempowered, the expedition slowly began to fall apart, its members beginning their long and separate journeys home. The emir's invasion, never mind rebellion throughout British India, was not to be.

'FURLING', A COUNTRY HOUSE IN HAMPSHIRE, 1915. Major Richard Hannay, of the Lennox Highlanders, is convalescing from injuries sustained at the Battle of Loos on 25 September 1915, when he receives a telegram summoning him to the Foreign Office. There, he is briefed by Sir Walter Bullivant on German and Ottoman attempts to incite Holy War. Bullivant warns Hannay: 'There is a dry wind blowing through the East, and the parched grasses wait the spark. And that wind is blowing towards the Indian border. Whence comes that wind, think you?' As Hannay remembered:

> *Sir Walter had lowered his voice and was speaking very slow and distinct. I could hear the rain dripping from the eaves of the window, and far off the hoot of taxis in Whitehall. 'Have you an explanation, Hannay?' he asked again. 'It looks as if Islam had a bigger hand in the thing than we thought,' I said. 'I fancy religion is the only thing to knit up such a scattered empire.'... There is a jihad preparing.*[33]

Continuing his sermon on *Jihad*, Bullivant went on:

I have reports from agents everywhere – peddlers in South Russia, Afghan horse-dealers, Turcoman merchants, pilgrims on the road to Mecca, sheikhs in North Africa, sailors on the Black Sea coasters, sheep-skinned Mongols, Hindu fakirs, Greek traders in the Gulf, as well as respectable Consuls who use cyphers. They tell the same story. The East is waiting for a revelation. It has been promised one. Some star – man, prophecy, or trinket – is coming out of the West. The Germans know, and that is the card with which they are going to astonish the world.[34]

———— ✦ ————

In late 1916, the novelist John Buchan reprised his hero Richard Hannay (of *The Thirty-Nine Steps*) for his new espionage thriller, *Greenmantle*. It proved a best-seller. A friend of T.E. Lawrence, Buchan was directly involved in Britain's wartime intelligence programme, working at the War Propaganda Bureau. As events showed, the fictional Hannay was arguably more believable – or at any rate no less believable – than the exotic cast of characters that reality served up: Baron Max von Oppenheim, the half-Jewish, orientalist fantasist; Oskar von Niedermayer, the polyglot intellectual and artillery officer; Emir Habibullah Khan, playing empires off against one another while driving around Kabul in his Rolls Royce. They demonstrated that the *Jihad* strategy pursued by Wilhelmine Germany and Ottoman Turkey was all too real.

It was, for the most part, thwarted; but it diverted arms, men, effort and money away from the decisive theatres of war. Where the fire took hold, it spread the violence and the instability of the First World War through towns, villages and communities in North Africa and parts of Asia. There were few winners in the Kaiser's *Jihad*. It cost thousands of men their lives, altered the borders of nations and the balance of power between clans, tribes and communities. And eventually, the empire that *was* toppled by the fatal alliance between Germany and Turkey was not that of Britain or France, but that of the Ottoman sultans itself.

The men who took part in the Afghan expedition emerged from the war better off than most. Oskar von Niedermayer returned safely to Germany. He travelled back the way he had come, through Persia and back into Ottoman territory. Arriving home in 1918 he was knighted and awarded the Military Order of Max Joseph. In 1919, in the aftermath of Germany's defeat on the Western Front, he joined the infamous *Freikorps* unit of Franz Ritter von Epp, a veteran of the Germany genocides in South West Africa, whose forces led the brutal suppression of communists in postwar Munich.

After being rebuffed by the Emir of Afghanistan, the diplomat Werner Otto von Hentig crossed the Pamir Mountains and made his way to China. From there he took a ship to Hawaii and handed himself over to the authorities of the still-neutral America. Once repatriated, he was personally awarded the House Order of Hohenzollern by Kaiser Wilhelm.

Perhaps the most unlikely home-coming of all was that of the Indian deserter and former PoW Jemadar Mir Mast. Held in the British Library is a report marked 'Secret' and entitled *Nominal Roll of Indian Prisoners of War Suspected of having deserted to the enemy or of having given information to or otherwise assisted the enemy*, revised on 24 October 1918. Mir Mast appears as Number 19 on the list of Indian deserters. In a column giving the latest information on him and two others, the report states: 'These three accompanied the Turco-German mission to Afghanistan and are reported to their homes in Tirah in June 1916.'

The home to which Mir Mast returned was in Tirah's Maidan Valley, today on the Afghan–Pakistan border, and which is nominally part of Pakistan. Some time after the failure of the Afghan mission, Mir Mast seems to have slipped away from Kabul and made his way back there. And at some unknown date after that Mir Mast, reputedly a winner of Germany's Iron Cross, must have been reunited with his brother and hero of the Allied war effort, Mir Dast VC, whom he had last seen in March 1915. It must have been an interesting encounter. Together they had sailed with the Indian Corps for France in

August 1914, and they had fought in the trenches of France and Belgium during the terrible winter of 1914–15. On 26 April 1915, seven weeks after his brother had defected, Mir Dast and the 57th Wilde's Rifles fought the vicious engagement against German forces in which he won his medal for (as his citation read) leading 'his platoon with great bravery during an attack' and then collecting 'various parties of his regiment when no British officers were left, until the retirement was ordered. He then helped carry eight British and Indian officers to safety under heavy gun fire.'[35] As with other recipients of the Victoria Cross, Mir Dast had his portrait depicted on British wartime cigarette cards. He was mentioned in dispatches and photographed meeting Lord Kitchener and General Jan Smuts, and his name is today etched into the Memorial Gates at Hyde Park Corner in London.

As the historian Santanu Das has pointed out, it is difficult to find a category or definition for Mir Mast – brave soldier of the British India Corps, then deserter, prisoner and Jihadist.[36] Certainly he was nothing like the stereotypical image of the passive, unworldly sepoy, incapable of independent action without the paternal hand of a white British officer. He was a dogged survivor, a man who somehow navigated a path between the competing demands of global empires. Surviving the Western Front as well as capture and internment, he demonstrated to the Germans his value as a native of the Khyber region of Afghanistan with local knowledge and contacts. This is what almost certainly led to his recruitment into the Niedermayer expedition, which took him back to his homeland, via the *Orient Express*, Istanbul, Baghdad, Tehran and Persia's Great Salt Desert. Although a pawn in someone else's 'Great Game', he found his own strategies and used the ambitions of those who sought to exploit him to find his way home. That home is today part of Pakistan's Federally Administered Tribal Areas. In truth, it remains as disconnected from twenty-first-century Pakistan as it was from the British Raj a century before. But still it is a region contested by empires and drawn into global conflicts, as the American drones that patrol the skies above testify.*

———— • ————

ISTANBUL, 2014. Towards the northern end of the ancient Hippodrome stands a large, neo-Byzantine fountain, which shelters under the shade of a stone gazebo that is held aloft by eight stone columns. Dismissed by one commentator as 'a lumbering commemorative fountain, which according to experts is an insult to good taste', the *Alman Çeşmesi,* or German Fountain, was a gift to the Ottoman Empire from Germany.[37] It was even said to have been designed by Kaiser Wilhelm II himself, and in 1900 it was erected on a site of huge symbolic importance. Deep in the soil beneath its marble base are the ossified roots of the Bloody Plane tree – the Janissary Tree – the ancient gathering point for the Janissary Corps, the elite military sect of soldier-slaves who made the Ottoman Empire feared across three continents. Recruited mainly from the Christian provinces of the empire, the Janissaries became a rival locus of power within the empire, and they ultimately turned upon their masters. On three occasions the Janissaries came close to bringing down the House of Osman: in the seventeenth century they rebelled, imprisoning and finally executing Sultan Osman II; in the early nineteenth

* Among the descendants of the family of Mir Mast and Mir Dast is Dr Shakil Afridi who, in 2011, allegedly assisted the CIA to set up a fake vacci-nation programme in the Pakistani city of Abbottabad – a programme that eventually helped lead to the location, and subsequent killing, of Osama bin Laden in May 2011. A year later, a Pakistani court sentenced Afridi to thirty-three years in prison for treason. In response, in January 2014, Presi-dent Obama withheld $33 million from US funds for Pakistan – a million dollars for every year of Dr Afridi's sentence – until such time as he was released. In 2012, bills were also introduced into the US House of Repre-sentatives asking for Dr Afridi to be declared a naturalized US citizen and to award him the US Congressional Gold Medal. If granted, Dr Afridi's family would add that American award from a global conflict to the haul of medals – British and allegedly German – won by an earlier generation in the global war of 1914–18.

century they rose again, deposing Sultan Selim III before he too was murdered. In the 1820s, though, the wily Sultan Mahmud II lured the Janissaries into another revolt, which he used as the pretext for their disbandment and annihilation, in a bloody struggle in the heart of Istanbul itself. The Janissaries were then outlawed and all reminders of their presence eradicated. Seventy years later, on the now vacant site of the Janissary Tree, the German fountain was constructed to celebrate the Kaiser's second visit to Istanbul, its inscription on the base reading: 'The German Kaiser Wilhelm II presented this fountain in 1898 autumn, in thankful remembrance of his visit to the Ottoman Sultan Abdülhamid II'.

———— • ————

It was this relationship between a young Kaiser and an old sultan on which the fatal alliance was constructed. The ambitions of the German–Ottoman *Jihad* begun in 1914 were global and total. At their most grandiose they envisaged the toppling of the British Empire, or a British retreat from the war in Europe to cling onto the great colonial jewel of India. Even as the crowds in Istanbul had joined in the orchestrated celebrations of *Jihad* in November 1914 it had been made clear, on the battlefields of Europe as well as in the forests of West Africa, that empire was one of the great strengths possessed by Germany's enemies. Imperial manpower had assisted the British in defending Ypres in the battles of October and November 1914. Empire gave the British and French great reservoirs of men, who could be brought to Europe as soldiers or sent to other far-flung battlefields of the ever-expanding war. Empire was a source of money and raw materials. It was copper from the Congo that was smelted to make the brass casings of the hundreds of millions of shells that British and French guns fired at the German lines over four years.

Long before 1914, German strategists, including critically the Kaiser himself, understood also that empire might be turned into an Achilles heel – that the religious loyalties and the embryonic stirrings of nationalism among subject peoples might be exploited and harnessed to disrupt, even destroy, imperial might, forcing a diversion of men and resources away from the war against Germany in Europe and undermining the will to fight. And in 1915 and 1916 the Ottoman summons to *Jihad* travelled among the Muslims of British Nigeria and the Belgian Congo; it swept across Sudan, through German East Africa and reached as far south as Nyasaland – modern-day Malawi.[38] It was known of in British India and among the various leaders of the peoples of Arabia.

Although, for the most part, the *Jihad* and the missions it spawned failed to spark the great revolutions their authors dreamed of, they did succeed in dragooning into the conflict peoples and communities that might otherwise have been spared the agony of the First World War. At times, events descended into farce, undone by conflicting egos and the realities of geography. From the start, the *Jihad* was undermined by the dubious religious authority of the sultan-caliph and by Germany's poor grip on the complex web of competing loyalties, schisms and internecine conflicts among the 300 million Muslims whom they sought to marshal to their cause. When the call to *Jihad* fell – mostly – on deaf ears, it was more often than not because local leaders were perfectly capable of acting in their own best interests and were not the malleable unworldly beings of the German orientalist imagination. In the end, the German–Ottoman embrace succeeded in doing what the Janissaries had never been able to achieve – bring down the House of Osman and topple a 600-year-old empire.

The *Jihad*'s ultimate failure has led some to dismiss it as a non-event. Yet across Africa, Asia and the Middle-East are the graves of British, German and Turkish men who died in the expeditions, revolts and small wars ignited by the *Jihad* schemes; alongside them, beneath the sand, lie the remains of Senussi fighters from Libya, Sudanese who fought in the army of Ali Dinar, the Sultan of Darfur, Egyptians and Indians who defended the Suez Canal, and men from Australia, South Africa and elsewhere. These men were just as much combatants in the First World War as the French *poilu* in the forts of Verdun or the British Tommy lumbering across the deadly fields of the Somme. Where the spark of *Jihad* took hold, the fire was real, and its potential was rarely underestimated by the British and French. The files of the British intelligence services contain innumerable references and reports on the impact of the call for *Jihad* on their subject peoples and the Muslims in the army. Indian soldiers on the British front lines, and North and West Africans fighting for the French, were monitored carefully for signs of disloyalty or expressions of sympathy to the Ottomans or to the sultan-caliph. When units were believed to have fallen under the influence of *Jihadi* propaganda, they were distrusted by the military authorities, as was the case with the 129th Baluchis, who would not fight fellow Muslims of the Ottoman Army.

The *Jihad* of 1914 not only made the First World War more costly and more global, it left in its wake the political, geographic, religious and ethnic instabilities that became the foundations on which some of the most intractable disputes of the modern age stand. The names of the nations and regions to which Germany and its Ottoman allies dispatched their *Jihad* missions, targeted their propaganda and attempted to foment rebellion seem uncannily like a roll-call of twenty-first-century trouble spots and places of international worry: Egypt, Libya, Iraq, Afghanistan, Iran, Darfur and even Pakistan's tribal areas, to which Mir Mast and Mir Dast returned.

CHAPTER 6

'OUR ENEMIES'

Polyglot PoWs and German schemes

——— ——

BRANDENBURG, GERMANY, 2014. Wünsdorf, near Zossen and twenty-five miles to the south of Berlin, is a town whose layout and geography is unlike any other. Nothing about it makes sense. It seems to have no proper town centre, there are too many homes and not enough people, and it has more railway lines and sidings than a settlement of its size could possibly need. The town is ringed by a series of huge but empty facilities – great civic buildings, huge dormitories, abandoned colleges and decaying sports fields. Unidentifiable concrete relics, half-demolished and graffitied, stand in the middle of otherwise empty fields, and there is a web of abandoned roads, some terminating in dead ends, almost all of them slowly crumbling to dust, or being colonized by weeds and saplings. The main roads are in better condition, and lined with neat houses and clusters of suburban streets; yet right beside these oases of domesticity are areas that are overgrown, consumed by forests and sealed off by high walls. There is little here that a town planner would recognize as normal.

Wünsdorf's strangeness stems from the fact that it was not shaped by the normal demographic and economic forces of human settlement, but instead by great global forces – military, strategic, and ideological. It has seen too much history, and it has become bizarrely misshapen by it. The great dormitory buildings are former barracks, built in different eras, to house different generations of soldiers, of different nationalities, for different wars. The derelict concrete structures are abandoned military facilities – stations for the testing of rocket engines, tank work-shops and the largest surviving cluster in Germany of 'Winkel' Towers – bizarre blast-proof bomb shelters. Huge, brutalist and conical with thick walls and small doors, they survive in part because they are too expensive to demolish. The twentieth century weighs so heavily on Wünsdorf that the twenty-first century seems unable to gain much purchase. What to do with the place? The local tourist office, adapting an idea from the UK, now markets it incongruously as 'the Book and Bunker Town', a tourist destination offering the dual attraction of antiquarian bookshops and military ruins.

The layers of history at Wünsdorf are a palimpsest of a century's militaria. The most recent stratum is also the one buried deepest underground – bunkers and subterranean command centres for the Red Army in the former German Democratic Republic – augmented by a new quarter of the town above, which once represented the biggest Soviet military base outside the USSR ('Little Moscow' as the German locals called this sealed off community). A direct, daily train service even connected it with the Russian capital. Then, in August 1994, a fleet of railway wagons was assembled on those same tracks and the last Soviet tanks were loaded for the journey home. The remaining Russian in Wünsdorf is Lenin, whose statue, unkempt and discoloured by green lichen, stands on a high plinth, forlorn in a long overcoat, arm outstretched and forsaken by his countrymen.

Before the Russians, Wünsdorf was the location for a Nazi communications centre code-named 'Zeppelin' as well as Maybach I and Maybach II: the Nazi command centres for the regime's competing military hierarchies of the *Oberkommando des Heeres* (OKH; the Supreme High Command of the German Army) and the *Oberkommando der Wehrmacht* (OKW; Supreme High Command of the German Armed Forces). The whole complex was disguised to look from the air like a cluster of tradi-tional, high-roofed German villas, no different to thousands of others in the surrounding area, complete with terracotta roof tiles and whitewashed walls. Today they lie dynamited, their spines broken, their heavy roofs collapsed in on themselves, crushing the floors beneath, the remaining innards of ducts, inlets and outlets for the ventilation system rusting away. Yet it was from here that Operation Barbarossa, the invasion of the Soviet Union, was planned in 1941.

But there is a further layer, too. On the outskirts of the town, overlooked by empty, crumbling barracks with broken windows and leaky roofs, is a great cleared expanse of wasteland, slowly being colonized by saplings. Across these empty acres spans a network of old pathways and the vague outlines of buildings demolished long ago. In 1915 this space was the *Halbmondlager* (Half-Moon or Crescent Camp), housing prisoners of war, and named after the crescent moon of Islam. The facility was a show camp, brought into existence as much for propaganda reasons as to warehouse enemy PoWs. What took place behind its barbed-wire fences, between 1915 and 1917, is one of the most bizarre and least known stories of the First World War.

——— • ———

The inmates at the *Halbmondlager* were mostly from India and the French North African colonies. At any one time there were between 4,000 and 5,000 of them, living in rows of tidy wooden barracks. Another 12,000 men from the Muslim minorities of the Russian army were housed at the nearby Weinberger Camp. Most of the men in the *Halbmondlager* were Muslims, but there were also Sikhs, Hindus and a few Indian Christians. In the early months of the war, captured colonial troops had been housed by the Germans in makeshift interment camps, and later they were interned in general camps, alongside men of other British and French army units; but in early 1915 construction of the *Halbmondlager* and Weinberger Camp was begun, and in the summer of that year the Germans began to move prisoners to Wünsdorf. The *Halbmondlager* was built to demonstrate to both the prisoners and the wider Muslim world that Germany was a friend of Islam, a nation that was generous and respectful towards the Muslim soldiers who had fallen into its hands. The camp was yet another of the many schemes of Max von Oppenheim, the strategist of *Jihad*. In his October 1914 *Memorandum Concerning the Fomenting of Revolutions in the Islamic Territories of Our Enemies*, he outlined in detail how Indian prisoners were to be processed, from the moment they were captured:

> *Indian prisoners are to be presented as soon as possible to Mr Walter [a former missionary working as an army translator on the Western Front] or other people of trust so as to be thoroughly questioned by them about: their origins, the (military) formations they belong to, which Indians had at all come to Europe, their fellow countrymen in Egypt, who their officers are, the position of native officers, how the food supply for the Indians is organised in the enemy army etc. … Thereupon the Indian prisoners are to be transported speedily to a single prison camp in close proximity to Berlin, which, similar to that of the French Mohammedan soldiers, is to be completely cordoned off from other prisoners and any attempt made by our enemies to influence them. They should, if possible, be separately housed according to religious community, race, and caste. Already during transport, in prison camps and in hospitals, religious duties and practices of individual Indian races should, to the extent possible, be taken into account. Most of them are vegetarians; Hindus are forbidden to eat beef, Mohammedans to eat pork. Funerals are to be carried out in compliance with their customs, and places for prayer established. Furthermore, accommodation should of course be warm. Both German and Indian agents are to be kept in the camp at all times to act as interpreters, to observe the people, to assess who could be of use to us, who would be suitable as a leader etc.*[1]

Max von Oppenheim's Intelligence Bureau for the East later provided the camp authorities with more detailed reports, outlining the religious, dietary and cultural requirements of the prisoners. This document covered everything from prayer to burial rites and became the foundational text upon which the camp was run, influencing almost every aspect of its administration. The faith, military rank, caste and nationality of each of the inmates determined in which of the long wooden barracks they would be billeted. The main avenue of the *Halbmondlager*, named *Kaiser Wilhelmstrasse* (Kaiser Wilhelm Street), along which the barracks were built, led to communal areas shared by all. The food of the prisoners was a subject to which a great deal of attention was paid. Meals were prepared in separate facilities according to the requirements of each faith, and from the propaganda pictures and even archive film that was produced of camp life it is clear that the prisoners themselves were involved in the slaughter of animals and the cooking of their own rations. The inmates were actively encouraged to celebrate their religious festivals. Eid was marked and the strictures of Ramadan observed. Indian Hindus marked their spring festival of Holi, while Nepalese Hindus celebrated Fagu Purnima, their own variant of the event. Among the many communal facilities provided were workshops, in which men could learn or practise the arts and crafts of their homelands. With materials and tools provided by their captors, they produced ornate furniture, decorated pottery, embroidered wall hangings and even elaborate wooden signposts showing the distances between local landmarks. These were erected at the designated crossroads and intersections of wartime Wünsdorf, reminders to the bemused locals of the thousands of exotic strangers hidden away from view on the edge of their town.

The German officers who oversaw the camp became attuned to the taboos and observances of each of the nationalities under their charge. They learnt the complexities of caste, faith and clan, and displayed towards the prisoners a degree of what we would today call 'cultural sensitivity'. The many propaganda photographs taken in the *Halbmondlager* create the impression of a strange flourish of frenetic activity and culture in the midst of the most terrible war the world had ever known, all taking place in what was little more than a large clearing in the Brandenburg Forest near a small backwater town.

On the advice of Oppenheim, the more favoured of the Indian prisoners were taken on excursions into the surrounding countryside; in September 1915 some were even taken to nearby Berlin. These field trips were intended to win the confidence of the more cooperative prisoners and to impress upon them the power and order of German society and industry.* However, the most dramatic, well-publicized and expensive outward expression of Germany's concern for the wellbeing of its Muslim prisoners was the erection in the *Halbmondlager* of a mosque, the very first on German soil. It was built, on Oppenheim's recommendation, in an Ottoman style with a broad round dome and a single minaret. Of wooden construction, it was erected by a local Berlin contractor and decorated in stripes of a dark, earthy red and a muted grey.

We know the mosque's colour scheme from the photographs of it that were reproduced as postcards and distributed across the world. German propaganda even spread the rumour that the cost of the mosque had been borne personally by Kaiser Wilhelm himself. Other postcards of the *Halbmondlager* show Muslim prisoners praying outside the mosque in summer, in orderly rows with their German guards cheerily looking on. There are images of the prisoners milling around in front of the ornate arched doorways or being led in prayer by Muslim mullahs specially brought in to tend to their religious needs. Other images depicted religious festivals, prisoners playing sports and games, or engaged in the slaughter of animals. Few of the photographs show the barbed-wire fences that ran the circumference of the camp or the menacing machine-gun towers, the high vantage points from which many of the propaganda photographs were taken. Indeed, some of the *Halbmondlager* images are almost comically contrived. In one, of the Halal slaughter of livestock, the mosque is perfectly framed in the background and two

---

* This was a standard device in the armoury of colonial powers. When Cetshwayo, King of the Zulus, had visited London in 1882, he had been taken on a tour of the Woolwich Arsenal and on a trip to see the ships of the Royal Navy off the south coast – a show of might, intended to cow into subservience an African king who had defeated a British army at the Battle of Isandlwana in 1879.

German soldiers stand by the butchers, their faces plastered with unctuous, approving smiles.

As a show camp, the *Halbmondlager* was in effect the propaganda counter-ploy to Britain's Royal Pavilion Hospital for Indian troops, at Brighton. The wide diffusion of the *Halbmondlager* images allowed German propagandists to constantly trumpet Germany's respect for Islam and the rights of Muslim peoples. Indeed, with each side engaged in a battle for the hearts and minds of the world's Muslim population, these two facilities became trump cards. Formed for identical propaganda purposes, they came to mirror each other. Both the Brighton hospital and the *Halbmondlager* went to enormous efforts to respect the strictures of faith and the traditional cultures of their patients and inmates. But the men of both facilities had their letters monitored and were provided with officially sanctioned newspapers – effectively propaganda. The pictures of both institutions were distributed across the world, as two Christian powers competed to demonstrate who was most attentive and sensitive to the needs of the Muslims in their midst. From both facilities, Indians were taken on tours of the nearby national capitals, as Britain and Germany both hoped to awe these men from Asia with the might, order and wealth of their great metropolis. But just as the Pavilion Hospital became sealed off from the public, its patients prohibited from wider contact, the *Halbmondlager* concealed a darker truth – and another function.

★

One of the propaganda films made at the *Halbmondlager* shows a marching band, in full procession with drums and brass instruments, heading through the camp and out of the main gates. It passes the huge wooden watchtower that guarded the entrance. Above the gates and the barbed-wire fences fly two flags, the eagle tricolour of Germany and the red crescent flag of Ottoman Turkey. In another part of the film Ottoman officials, wearing fezzes and carrying umbrellas, can be seen milling around among the prisoners or chatting with the guards and with German officers in their heavy greatcoats and pointed *Pickelhaube* helmets. The *Halbmondlager* was much more than a PoW camp; it was at the same time a recruiting station, a place of indoctrination and part of Germany's strategy of *Jihad* and global revolution. The Muslim prisoners were not expected simply to sit out the war in the shade of the Brandenburg Forest. It was hoped that many of them – perhaps most of them – through a process of persuasion and education, could be converted into Jihadists. Re-directed and re-armed they would re-enter the conflict and fight their erstwhile colonial masters. Their Hindu and Sikh comrades were to be similarly encouraged to take up arms against Britain and fight for Indian self-determination.

The indoctrination and recruitment of the prisoners was overseen and directed by Oppenheim's Intelligence Bureau for the East, which appointed propaganda officers to work with each of the nationalities represented within the camp population. Some of these officers were Muslims who had been living in Germany before the war; others had been drawn into Oppenheim's orbit when the net was cast for anti-British agitators in the summer of 1914. These intermediaries were able to translate propaganda material, hold classes and transmit the required message. There were also Ottoman propaganda agents at work in the camp, and physical reminders of Germany's alliance with the Muslim empire – the crescent flag flying over the gate post, a portrait of the sultan-caliph. In the hope of winning their trust, prisoners were given books in their own languages and encouraged to take part in educational activities, including the learning of German. As many were understandably interested in learning more about the country they now found themselves in, and in whose hands their fate rested, education and indoctrination to some extent fused, as prisoners submitted willingly to lectures on Germany and German culture.

The other means of disseminating the *Jihadi* message was through the camp newspapers. The driving force was again Oppenheim, whose officials oversaw their production too. For the Hindu prisoners a nationalist newspaper, the *Hindostan,* was produced, appearing in both Urdu and Hindi editions. The Muslim newspaper – Oppenheim's principal interest in this sphere – was unsurprisingly named *El-Dschihad* ('The Jihad'). As a rule, PoW newspapers were amateurish and often light-hearted efforts, the work of the prisoners themselves; *El-Dschihad* was, by contrast, a professionally produced propaganda tract. Printed in Arabic as well as in the languages of the Russian Muslim minorities, it contained incessant appeals to reject Britain, France and Russia and to embrace the German and Ottoman strategy.

In 1916 the camps at Wünsdorf were able to dispatch to Ottoman Turkey the first contingent of converted Jihadists willing to fight for the sultan and the Kaiser against their former masters. Ultimately 1,084 Arabs and 49 Indian prisoners travelled across Europe and into Ottoman Turkey to do so.[2] Among them was Mir Mast, who had spent time at the *Halbmondlager*. What became of the other men he had led over to the German lines at Neuve Chapelle in 1915 is less clear. But if, up to that stage, the recruitment policy at the *Halbmondlager* had been a moderate success, it seemed to collapse on contact with the waters of the Bosphorus. Would-be Jihadists, who had grown used to being treated with a degree of tolerance and sympathy, found themselves in an Ottoman Army that did not know how to deploy them and was unwilling to fully trust them. Jihadists deserted back to the British, and their evidence suggests that some of them had been subjected to severe mistreatment while in the ranks of the Ottoman Army, while many more had suffered what might best be described as neglect. Indeed, by the time that Germany's great ambition was realized, to field Indian and French North Africans on the battlefields of Mesopotamia, the men from the Wünsdorf camps had been so starved and abused that the majority crossed over to the British lines at the first opportunity.

By 1917 the *Halbmondlager* experiment was deemed a failure, and along with much of the rest of the *Jihad* strategy it was quietly wound down. But the question remained as to how to treat colonial prisoners among the hundreds of thousands of Entente PoWs now held by the Central Powers.

★

The rules for the treatment of prisoners of war had been codified in 1907 at the famous *Hague Convention Respecting the Laws and Customs of War on Land*.[3] Despite being created and approved by the great imperial powers, whose armed forces included African and Asian soldiers, the Hague agreements established no rules on how captured soldiers of different races were to be interned. Within weeks of the outbreak of war, the issue was confronted by a bewildered Germany. After just six months of fighting, Germany and its allies, fighting across two fronts, had captured 625,000 enemy troops; and a year into the war, more than 1 million Allied troops were in German and Austrian custody, among them soldiers from Africa and Asia, Aboriginal men from Australasia, and troops from South-East Asia, Mongolia, Japan and the Russian minorities.[4]

Among the initial German responses was a policy designed to punish British and French soldiers, directly and collectively, for the deployment of non-white troops by their governments. In October 1914 the Prussian War Ministry, despite some internal opposition, set forth its intention to create a series of camps in which there was to be 'a thorough mixing of the different races (*Volksrassen*) among our opponents in the field'.[5] The ministry calculated that imprisoning white French, British and Belgian troops alongside dark-skinned men from the colonial empires would be understood as a form of humiliation. The pro-German Swede Sven Hedin picked up on this sentiment. He reported that French wounded at a German hospital behind the lines were attempting to prolong their stay on the wards, 'For it is pleasanter to lie in one's comfortable bed and be coddled in every way, than to live in a barracks or a concentration camp with crowds of other prisoners, including Senegalese negroes, Moroccans and Indians.'[6] Whether this desire to avoid contact with colonial troops was expressed by the French prisoners themselves, or whether it came from the two German army doctors who showed Hedin around the wards, is not clear.

If the intention of the Prussian War Ministry had been to provoke anger and resentment in London and Paris, though, it

succeeded admirably and rapidly. The British Army and government lodged formal protests – as did the Americans, who were the
neutral power responsible for protecting British prisoners held in
Germany. When these failed, the British retaliated in kind, informing the German authorities in early November 1915 that Britain
was to begin holding German prisoners alongside captives of other
races. The British even invited the Germans to 'consider what
would be the position … [of] a few German soldiers interned
amongst large numbers of prisoners of alien race, say, for instance,
with Ottoman troops'. The effect of this blatant threat was almost
immediate. On 12 November – just nine days later – the Prussian
War Ministry ended the practice of racial mixing in the PoW
camps.[7] From then on, colonial soldiers were housed in separate
facilities in Germany, including the camps at Wünsdorf.

The camps constructed to house the non-European prisoners
were a wholly new phenomenon, because never before had so
many men from so many nations, and of so many different races,
been gathered together. In 1915 Dr Rudolf Martin, a physical
anthropologist from the University of Munich, who was to
become one of the most powerful figures in the German tradition of *Anthropologie* between the wars, sensed an opportunity in
the fact that 'The practice of our enemies, to pull in auxiliaries
from everywhere, has resulted in representatives of the most
varied people coming to Germany, who under natural circumstances would never have set foot on German soil in such
numbers.'[8] The only comparable phenomena in popular German
memory were the *Völkerschauen* – 'people shows', a series of colonial exhibitions that had been held in the late nineteenth
century. The *Völkerschau* had brought together men and women
from the various peoples and races of the German colonies and
beyond, and placed them on display in German cities, in what
were in effect human zoos. The most spectacular had been the
Berlin Colonial Show of 1896, a public–private partnership
between the German Colonial Department and the Colonial
Society. It formed part of the city's Great Industrial Exhibition.
The organizers had transported to Berlin's Treptow Park more

than a hundred people of different races from across the German Empire. The official brochure boasted that the show had 'transplanted a piece of natural savagery and raw culture to the centre of a proud and glamorous metropolis, with its refined morals and fashion-conscious people'.[9] On the Western Front, suddenly black and brown men were out of this 'zoo' and on the battlefield, armed and wearing the uniforms of enemy nations; they were no longer human exhibits, safely fenced off from white Germans by rope barricades. But in the PoW camps, 'normal service' could be resumed, as men from the colonies of Germany's enemies were once again disarmed, pacified and controlled.

If it had not been for the fierce resistance of the Germany Army authorities, the camps that housed colonial prisoners might easily have become major wartime tourist attractions, and there is evidence that civilian day-trippers did venture down from Berlin by train to get a closer look at the strange mix of peoples held in Wünsdorf. The photographs and cartoons depicting the camps and their inmates, in official propaganda and the general press, went some way to making up for the fact that the real thing was off-limits. Many of these publications used the folk memory of the *Völkerschau* to make sense of the huge array of men now in German internment and the thousands more still fighting at the front. Leo Frobenius, an anthropologist and African explorer, on returning to Germany in 1915 (after a failed expedition to foment *Jihad* along the Red Sea) turned his attention to the colonial troops in the PoW camps. He visited them and presented a series of lectures that condemned the Allies for having dispatched their colonial armies to the war in Europe. In 1916 he published *Der Völkerzirkus unserer Feinde* – 'The People Circus of Our Enemies'. This short tract was a racial satire on the Allies' use of colonial soldiers, denouncing Britain as the manipulative ringmaster in a vile racial circus. The book was illustrated with photographs captured from the enemy and portraits of men held in the PoW camps, and it made specific reference to the idea of the *Völkerschau*. In 1915 a Berlin newspaper described the colonial PoWs in German camps as 'a Hagenbeck Show', a reference to Carl Hagenbeck, the great impresario, who procured rare wild animals for nineteenth-century zoos as well as coloured people as exhibits for the various *Völkerschauen*;[10] and the Austrian anthropologist Rudolph Pöch saw obvious similarities between the pre-war human zoos and the wartime camps, describing the latter as an 'unparalleled *Völkerschau*'.

As a leading member of the one group of civilians who were getting extensive access to PoW camps, Pöch's interest was purely professional. Even before the final camp barracks had been constructed and the barbed-wire fences put up, German and Austrian scholars – anthropologists, ethnographers, musicologists and linguists – had all come to appreciate that the huge racial and cultural diversity among Allied PoWs represented a unique opportunity for study. The camps they were dispatched to, especially those at Wünsdorf, had the potential to revolutionize whole disciplines, make careers, inspire doctorial theses and build academic reputations. For decades, German anthropologists had been forced to make long journeys to the colonies in order to locate the exotic peoples whose cultures or bodies they sought to measure and classify. On occasion, their research had been thwarted or undermined by local peoples who had proved unwilling, or at least reluctant, to submit themselves to examination or to answer questions about their cultures and languages. Physical anthropologists in particular had encountered firm resistance. Some of the measurements their studies depended upon were physically uncomfortable and even painful. The calibration of the shape of the human skull, for example, involved the use of metal callipers, which caused painful bruises; while the process of making facial plaster-casts could, by all accounts, be an extremely alarming and unpleasant experience for the subject. Within weeks of the outbreak of war, German scholars were cut off from these difficult fields of study as Germany's colonies, one by one, fell into the hands of the Allies. With Germany's ports blockaded by the ships of the Royal Navy, the pursuit of science risked grinding to a complete halt.

Then, in 1915, when the first of the camps for colonial prisoners was opened, German science was presented with literally thousands of diverse peoples – on home soil. This great throng of humanity had little choice but to submit and cooperate with scientific enquiry. But the camps were not just more convenient than field study in the colonies; they offered a wider range of people than had ever previously been assembled in one place – in the words of one leading German anthropologist, 'an almost incalculable quantity of the most different races' who could suddenly 'be better and more comfortably studied here than in their homeland'.[11] Men whose nations were separated by thousands of miles were now housed in barracks only metres from one another. This made it possible for the scientists to carry out comparative studies of the various races of mankind – as they defined them – in ways that were inconceivable in any other setting. Research projects that would once have been considered laughably impractical almost overnight became straightforward and easily affordable. Not only were the prisoners from a highly diverse range of ethnic backgrounds, there was also a reasonable mix of ages, with the older career soldiers mixed in with younger, recent recruits. Women, of course, were missing; but the anthropologists blithely dismissed them as unnecessary for their studies. And thus the camps at Wünsdorf became a vast field laboratory, just twenty-five miles from Berlin and the German capital's many universities, institutes and learned societies.

Anthropology in the early twentieth century was still a relatively new science, and German *Anthropologie* differed from the variants studied elsewhere in that it focused not primarily on culture but on the physical and racial differences between peoples across the world. Its practitioners sought to define and categorize the races. Among the leaders in the field was Felix von Luschan, Professor of Anthropology and Ethnography at the University of Berlin. He had studied the human exhibits at the 1896 Berlin Colonial Show and now regarded the PoW camps as potentially the greatest professional opportunity his science had ever been presented with. Working with the authorities, he coordinated scientific access to the prisoners at Wünsdorf and elsewhere. The study of PoWs became not simply an academic sideline but the *dominant* activity of German anthropology during the war.

German studies looked at the colour and shape of a prisoner's eyes, measured his height and weight, and classified the shape of his mouth and nose. Prisoners were interviewed to determine their place of origin, and a series of standardized anthropological photographs was taken to allow comparisons to be made between men of different races. As definitions of what constituted a 'race' and what constituted a 'nationality' were fluid in this period, the scope of the study increased, with men from enemy nations within Europe being examined and compared to non-whites from the colonial sphere. East-European Jews from the Russian Army were examined and set alongside Africans, and while no English prisoners were examined, Scots and Irish were.

Photography was central to anthropology; but the images taken of prisoners were published not just in academic articles and papers but in popular books and in newspapers too, often with official backing. Luschan published the book *Prisoners of War* in 1917, but many of the books that emerged using the anthropological photographs (or approximations of them) were not the work of the anthropologists. In 1915 Alexander Backhaus, with all the authority of a professor of agriculture, published a collection of photographs under the title *The PoWs in Germany*. A year later Otto Stiehl, a historian of German architecture (though he could also claim to be a member of the Berlin Society of Anthropology, Ethnology and Prehistory and an officer at the *Halbmondlager* itself) brought out *Unsere Feinde* ('Our Enemies'), a compilation of ninety-six of his own photographs of PoWs from the Wünsdorf camps. Ironically, as an amateur, unschooled in the craft of anthropological photography, Stiehl proved himself a far better photographer than a propagandist. His photographs failed utterly to reduce his subjects to racial types. By accident rather than design, he produced some of the most powerful photo-portraits of the First World War, capturing the individuality of each of the prisoners studied.

While the professional anthropologists tended to reject the idea that character – individual or racial – could be read from faces, that idea was widely held by the public and it informed many popular publications such as those by Stiehl and Backhaus. To make the photographs of the prisoners more menacing, and assist the viewer to reach a judgement about each prisoner and the race he represented, some publications added descriptions, explaining how primitive or uncivilized each of the enemy races was and pointing out tell-tale signs of inner savagery that could be discerned in the shape of faces or skulls. Portraying the Allied imperial armies as a flood of savage and backward races offered to German propaganda – both amateur and professional – a means to undermine the Allied arguments that they were defending civilization from German militarism.

The expertise marshalled by Luschan and others was increasingly put to work in the name of patriotism rather than science, as anthropology began to fuse with propaganda. The war on two fronts created, within Germany, a powerful sense of national encirclement by numerous enemies, which accentuated a mood of both hyper-nationalism and condemnation of 'alien' cultures. It was a mood expressed in public meetings, in the press and in books. It was in such an atmosphere that German and Austrian science became an instrument of war.

Scientists received grants and access to the PoW camps from a government increasingly aware of the propaganda potential of the conjunction of the huge array of races and nationalities held prisoner with the young science of anthropology. But, as historian Andrew D. Evans has shown, the driving force behind the ever-closer bond was the *anthropologists* and not the government (or the army).[12] German anthropologists willingly weaponized their science, making it available to the war effort. Through this process, a discipline that in Germany was known before the war for its internationalism and relative liberalism knowingly transformed itself into little more than a propaganda tool.*

---

* Before 1914, there had been a tendency among some German anthropologists to place their science at the service of Germany's imperial project. See Andrew D. Evans, *Anthropology at War*, p. 8, and Andrew Zimmerman, *Anthropology and Antihumanism in Imperial Germany* (University of Chicago Press, 2001).

Within Germany, the multiplicity of races behind the fences of PoW camps became one of the defining images of the conflict. Photographs taken and published by the anthropologists were transformed by the pens of German graphic artists into a vision of a world arrayed against Germany. In one cartoon, a German soldier appears in front of a multiracial group of PoWs huddled behind the barbed wire of a camp; every enemy race is represented, and every face is a racial stereotype. The contrast between the purity of the German soldier, fighting for his own nation, and the multi-ethnic horde set against him was intended to be stark and emotive. In 1918 one newspaper article claimed that 'every single race is represented in the support troops of the Entente … There is no race on the planet that would not stand against us in the service of England.'[13] Such a view of the *Weltkrieg*'s internationalism is a long way from the early German satisfaction that colonial forces were a demonstration of the Entente's weakness; now it was a global conspiracy. The PoW camps became the place where Germany could demonstrate this theory and prove to its public the mendacity of her enemies.

——— ————

THE *HALBMONDLAGER*, WÜNSDORF, 4PM ON 11 DECEMBER 1916. Mall Singh, aged twenty-four and from the village of Ranasukhi in the Punjab, is ordered to stand in front of the funnel of a microphone. He has little choice, having arrived on the Western Front as part of the Indian Corps only to subsequently find himself a German prisoner of war. But at least he can choose his words. He recites a poem, which he has composed himself, into a machine that etches his voice directly onto a wax disc. Clearly the poem is autobiographical; but it is phrased in the third-person, as if Mall Singh is already disembodied.

> *There once was a man. He ate butter in India. He drank milk.*
> *This man came into the European war. Germany captured this*
>   *man.*

He wishes to go to India. He wants to go to India.
He will get the same food as in former times.
Three years have passed. One does not know when there will be
*   peace.*
If this man goes back to India, he will get the same food as in
*   former times.*
If this man has to stay here for another two years – he will die.
*   If God has mercy, he will make peace soon.*
We will go away from here.

In the last days of December 1915, while the anthropologists at the Wünsdorf camps continued their measurements of bodies and facial features, and as Max von Oppenheim's *Jihad* propagandists maintained their busy schedule of lectures and observations, another programme got under way. Earlier that year, Professor Carl Stumpf of the Berlin Phonogram Archive, along with the well-connected language expert and teacher Wilhelm Doegen, had come together to form, in a round-about way, the Royal Prussian Phonographic Commission. Gathering around them a group of ethnographers, linguistics experts and musicologists, they garnered official backing for a full-scale study of the various languages and musical traditions of the Wünsdorf prisoners. The project was personally approved by the Kaiser, who even helped find the money to fund it.[14] The aim of the Phonographic Commission was to record and then preserve the diverse range of languages in the camps. Doegen dreamed of a collection that would constitute a museum 'of the voices of all the peoples'.[15] The recordings were also to be used to advance ethnography and language teaching.*

From the end of 1915, and continuing past the end of hostilities into late December 1918, the commission meticulously made

---

* Doegen was indeed later to pioneer the use of voice records in the teaching of foreign languages.

2,677 separate recordings of prisoners, recording around 250 different languages or dialects. Their activities took them far beyond Wünsdorf, too. In total they made forty-nine field trips to thirty-one different camps.[16] The expedition teams recorded not just speech samples, but also poems, local folk-tales and music, along with the personal words of the prisoners, poems of the prisoners' own composition – and tragic, plaintive pleas made by disorientated, dislocated men, as if their appeals might be answered, rather than merely studied. The researchers on occasion even had X-rays produced of the larynxes of prisoners, in an effort to determine how certain language-sounds were physically formed. Before each recording was made, a form was filled out noting the language of the speaker, his level of education, his social class, his place of origin and military rank. Then, a transcription of the agreed text was made, and only then were the PoWs allowed to speak.

All the activities of the commission were kept secret for the duration of the war. Today, the voices of the colonial prisoners are held on thousands of heavy shellac discs, stored in a line of green, steel cabinets in the *Lautarchiv* (Sound Archive) of Humboldt University in Berlin. The final fate of many of the men whose voices are preserved is unknown.

The recordings are unedited and raw. The voices – thin and compressed by the simple recording technology of the day – have to fight their way through the heavy bass static. But once audible they are haunting and tragic. These voices of the war are unmistakably those of young men, speaking not as veterans repeating familiar war stories, worn smooth by over-telling, but as men still trapped at the moment of recording in the unfolding conflict, still in its grip, with uncertain futures. Many speak with a sing-song intonation, delivering appeals and poems as if their words are folk-songs or oral epics. Their mistakes, false starts and hesitations are all held in magical preservation alongside their words. Men clear their throats and fight back the revealing waver of nervousness in their voices. Even if all that had been recorded by the linguists had been merely these voices, repeating standard texts as was sometimes the case, the recordings would still be remarkable and moving. But that the prisoners were permitted and encouraged to write their own texts and deliver their own messages to the world beyond the barbed wire and the Prussian forests that surrounded them, and ultimately to future generations, gives them a far greater power and significance.

One prisoner, recorded as Bela Singh from Amritsar, delivered his poem in Punjabi, a poignant lament on his own experiences of war:

> *When we arrived in the city of Marseilles we ate well. Thus, all were happy. We were placed in cars and the major gave the order: 'Go now, oh Lions, in the trenches, go! Fight the Germans, why do you walk backwards?' For two months we sat in the trenches. A few lions had had enough of fighting. The German cannons hurled their artillery with great force. All ran off as they noticed the force. I was a hindrance as I could not run away. When the Germans saw me, they needed their entire strength against me. They took me with force. Where – they did not tell me....*

Another PoW, a Punjabi Sikh called Sib Singh, spoke of his own political awakening:

> *The German Emperor is very wise. He wages war against all kings. When the war is over, many stories will be printed. In India, the Englishman rules. We had no knowledge of any other king. When the war began, we heard of several kings. In India this is a problem: The people know nothing.*

The voices that pour forth from the shellac discs are those of men who are almost never recorded by history – the poor, the powerless, the cannon fodder of empire. They are the voices of men who almost always went to their graves silently, leaving no other record of who they were or the lives they lived. The recordings in the *Lautarchiv* are more even than this, though. They preserve the thoughts and words of men who were born in the last years of the nineteenth century, when empires were being built rather than sliding into decline. Their voices are not just those of colonial soldiers of the First World War – though that in itself is miraculous enough – they are also the unheard voices of the poor of rural Africa and rural India in the early twentieth century. It is ironic that in this respect, German science, so often suborned to the military, political and propagandist imperatives of the war effort, should have almost inadvertently left such a moving and unique repository. These words and the haunting voices that speak them are among the most beautiful artefacts left behind by any soldiers of the First World War.

CHAPTER 7

'BABYLON OF RACES'

The Western Front – a global city

———————

THE ENGLISH CHANNEL, 21 FEBRUARY 1917. In the early hours of the morning, two ships approach one another in the English Channel. It is still dark and patches of heavy fog have settled over the water. The SS *Mendi*, a British passenger steamer pressed into military service by the government, is heading for Le Havre, one of the ports into which the British are pouring men and materials bound for the Western Front. The ship bearing down on her in the winter darkness is not a German destroyer but another British vessel, the cargo ship SS *Darro*, heading to Falmouth; her holds are almost empty, apart from some meat that has spoiled in transit. At 11,000 tons the *Darro* is almost three times the size of the *Mendi*, and despite the heavy fog she is cruising at her maximum speed of thirteen knots. In contravention of regulations, her crew are not sounding the ship's whistle at the required one-minute intervals. Blind to the danger, the *Darro* cuts through the black water in near silence.

It is the whistle of the *Mendi* that alerts the Fourth Officer and the lookouts on the *Darro* to the impending catastrophe. Moments later they catch sight of a green starboard navigation light emerging rapidly from the foggy darkness. Orders to put the engines into reverse are given, the siren is sounded and evasive action taken. But with the siren still wailing, the great bow of the *Darro*, towering over the *Mendi*, looms out of the fog and slices into the flank of smaller ship. The *Darro* strikes the *Mendi* almost at a right-angle, in the middle of her starboard side, cutting an enormous gash in her hull, an incision so deep that it almost cleaves her in half. With engines thrown into reverse, the *Darro* pulls away from the shattered *Mendi*, revealing a fatal wound. The impact has lacerated the ship from her deck to below the water-line; two of her watertight bulkheads are breached, and sea-water is flooding in. The *Mendi* is doomed.

The *Mendi* and the *Darro* are about twelve miles south of St Catherine's Point on the Isle of Wight. There is no hope of any help coming from the shore. As the *Mendi* starts listing heavily to her starboard side, the order to lower lifeboats is given. But the radio operator is not at his post, so no SOS signal is sent. Inside the *Mendi* hundreds of men, almost all of whom had been asleep in the dark of the ship's cabins, now begin to rush towards the exits to the deck and to the lifeboats. They fight past debris strewn across the lower decks by the impact and wade through the freezing water that is now surging everywhere and inching higher. Perhaps as many as 140 men never reach the upper deck; an unknown number have been killed in their beds by the initial impact.

The men on board the SS *Mendi* are not soldiers, not in the strict sense. They are a contingent of the South African Native Labour Corps, men from the various ethnic groups of the British dominion of South Africa – Swazi, Pondo, Zulu, Xhosa, Mfengu and others. They number 802, plus 22 white officers and NCOs. On board are also the eighty-nine members of the crew of the *Mendi* and fifty-six other military passengers. There are spaces in the lifeboats for a mere 289 men. As the South Africans gather on the deck, the operation to lower the lifeboats begins. Boats Number 1 and 3 are lowered into the water on the starboard side and, despite the difficulties of evacuating from a now heavily listing ship, they fill with their complement of men. Boat Number 2 is also lowered successfully into the water, but it capsizes, casting the men and crew into the water. Boat Number 5 launches, but panicking men on the deck of the *Mendi* begin to jump and clamber into it, and in the chaos that lifeboat capsizes too, throwing yet more men into the freezing sea. Lifeboat Number 4 suffers a similar fate. Lifeboat Number 6 is lowered but is caught

by a wave and smashed to pieces against the side of the *Mendi*.
The fate of lifeboat Number 7 is unknown.

The bulk of the remaining passengers of the *Mendi* are, at this
moment, still on the deck. The ship lists more heavily, and then
an explosion shakes it, signalling the beginning of her death
throes. The order to 'abandon ship' is given, and the men are
urged to throw themselves into the sea and swim away from the
sinking steamer in order to escape the vortex that might drag
them underwater. Only around a hundred men have made it
into the lifeboats. Others jump into the sea and hang on to
pieces of wreckage or float as best they can on rafts or using their
life-vests for buoyancy.

Now, twenty-five minutes after the collision, which occurred at
around 4.57am, the last traces of the *Mendi* slip beneath the water.
Hundreds of men are in the icy water, clinging to rafts and wreckage. Some are fainting with exhaustion and cold, and then
disappearing under the waves. Over the next two hours, 110 men
from the *Mendi* lifeboats are brought aboard the *Darro*. Another
137 are plucked out of the sea by HMS *Brisk*, a Royal Navy destroyer
that has been escorting the *Mendi*. The SS *Sandsend*, a ship that
answers an SOS made by the crew of the *Darro*, rescues another
23 men. The total number of survivors is two-hundred-and-sixty-
seven. Of the men of the South African Native Labour Corps, 618
meet their death; 9 of their white officers and 33 crewmen are
also lost. The bodies of most will never be recovered.

As the Board of Trade's Court of Inquiry later notes, the
captain of the *Darro*, Henry Stump, chose not 'to send away a
boat or boats to ascertain the extent of damage to the *Mendi*, and
to render her, her master, crew and passengers such assistance as
was practicable and necessary'.

———— • ————

By the 1940s, the story of the loss of the *Mendi* had become a
feature of black South African history and folklore, heavily
mythologized in its retelling. The tragedy had acquired

a symbolic meaning and become part of the long narrative of suffering, exclusion and exploitation that inspired and informed the freedom struggles of South Africa's black majority. The 21 February became 'Mendi Day', on which services were held in memory of the dead, and the wider story of the South African Native Labour Corps was in this way remembered. The fate of the *Mendi* remains part of the tradition from which emerged black political and national consciousness, one tragedy in a long list that acted as milestones along the troubled road to the new South Africa.[1] Today, the Order of the Mendi is the nation's highest award for courage, bestowed only on those South Africans who have performed outstanding acts of bravery. In Europe, even in Britain in whose seas she was lost, the fate of the *Mendi* has been almost completely forgotten. The names of the men whose remains were never found are listed in the Hollybrook Cemetery in Southampton, and there has been some renewed interest in their story, but the loss of the *Mendi*, along with the wider story of the South African Native Labour Corps, has largely been obscured – overwhelmed, like so much else, by the dominant narratives of the 'literary war'.

The *Mendi* had left Cape Town on 16 January 1917, its passengers – most from the Eastern Cape – bound for the most diverse and dangerous place on earth. France and Belgium in 1917 witnessed the greatest gathering of peoples and races in the history of the world. Perhaps only Ottoman Istanbul, at the very height of that empire's global reach, could compare to the Western Front in the penultimate year of the First World War. This prodigious gathering of peoples was utterly new and nothing like it would be seen again until after the Second World War.

In the trenches, the armies of two vast inter-continental empires fought side by side. Men from almost every continent, different in their skin colours, were unified in either the khaki of the British Army or the horizon-blue of the French Army. Behind the lines – within the militarized zones of encampments, billets, depots, rail-hubs, rest areas, *estaminets* (improvised canteens), official kitchens, brothels, hospitals, supply dumps, ports and stations – an

33. This poster for the 'Day of the African Army and Colonial Troops' (1917) celebrates France's North African fighters: Moroccan and Algerian infantry plunge forwards under the *Tricouleur*, and beside them ride the flamboyant Spahi light cavalry.

34. A propaganda postcard (1916) depicts the *Halbmondlager*'s mosque with an inset group of its Muslim PoWs.

35. An ornate page from the *Lagerzeitung der Halbmondlagers Wünsdorf,* the PoW's camp's newspaper, dated 5 March 1917.

36. A striking portrait of a wounded *Tirailleur Sénégalais* in German captivity conveys a distinct sense of fearful discomfort, whether as a reaction to his recent experiences or his current situation – or both.

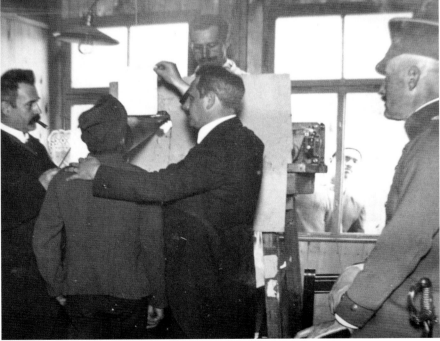

37. A Gurkha PoW in the *Halbmondlager* speaks into the recording equipment as part of the wartime German academic project to record the diverse inmates' voices and languages.

38. The Kaiser, with Carl Hagenbeck and assorted dignitaries, converses with some Ethiopian 'exhibits' at Hagenbeck's zoo in Stellungen, Hamburg (1909). In some ways, the camps at Wünsdorf seemed to echo these 'people shows'.

39. Lines of mainly North African PoWs at Wünsdorf, the diversity of their origins and units suggested in the variety of clothing and uniform on display.

40. A rifleman, probably of the *Tirailleurs Algériens*, who were known as 'Turcos', waiting to board a French troop train (1914).

41. Fijian Labour Corps volunteers *en route* to the Western Front pause in front of a well-known redwood tree in Vancouver's Stanley Park, having crossed the Pacific (1917).

42. Men of the South African Native Labour Corps queue to take a bath near Dannes, north of Etaples (March 1917). Their lives were some of the most circumscribed on the Western Front.

43. Members of the Chinese Labour Corps, near Etaples, interrupt their usual routines to mount entertainments – here including performers on stilts – for British and Asian onlookers (June 1918).

44. Riveters of the Chinese Labour Corps carry out essential repairs at the British Tank Corps' Central Workshop, in the latter part of the war.

45. Labourers from French Indochina prepare to do some digging.

46. King Vajiravudh (Rama VI) of Siam, on his throne of state (*c.* 1915). When he joined the war in 1917, he sent a select expeditionary force of specialists to the Western Front.

47. A recruitment poster (1915) for the recently founded British West Indies Regiment responds to the genuine enthusiasm for the war effort that emerged in the Caribbean islands.

even greater encounter of world peoples was taking place. In its mixture of races, religions, languages and nationalities, the French, British and – more recently – American sectors of the Western Front and their support networks were in many ways a foretaste of a multiracial Europe that would later emerge, after another global conflict. The spectacle of the world brought together in rural France fascinated the newspapers of the Allied nations and the neutral states alike. There are innumerable articles, photo-essays and illustrations of the 'types' of the various armies. Posters and collectable cards were produced for the young boys of Europe, to teach them to distinguish a sepoy from a *tirailleur*, an Indochinese Annamite from a Nepalese Gurkha. Although the poets and canonical memoirists of the war seemed little interested, journalists and diarists were eager to record this exotic and inherently transient moment of globalism. It was an event that – as many commentators noted – would be remembered by all those who witnessed it, whether they were residents of rural Belgium and France or the soldiers and labourers sent there.

For the local civilians, living amid a sudden kaleidoscope of peoples, races, languages, traditions and faiths, the experience was almost overwhelming. They encountered new peoples as temporary neighbours, as customers in their shops and restaurants, and as men billeted in their homes, sometimes living in intimate closeness with them. The responses to these encounters cover the full gamut of human behaviour. There were outbreaks of racial violence, murders and riots in various parts of France in the summer of 1917. There were also liaisons between colonial men and French and Belgian women that ended in marriage and mixed-race families. Indian soldiers reported being treated almost as sons by bereaved French ladies in whose homes they were billeted, while in hospitals doctors and nurses cared for men who, in normal circumstances, they would never have met.

Within the armies themselves, even before they had begun to meet the civilians of Europe or the men of other regiments, there were moments of unprecedented encounter. When the Gurkha regiments of the British Indian Corps marched through

Bombay, in August 1914, on their way to the ships that would carry them to Marseilles, some residents concluded that the strange men from the mountains of Nepal must be elements of the Japanese Army rather than soldiers of their own Indian Army. Likewise, there were white Australians from the growing cities of that country's south-east who had their first encounters with Aboriginal men in the camps and canteens of wartime France and Belgium. In the decisive year of 1918, African Americans from Harlem and the Deep South, rejected by their own white officers, found themselves serving in the French Army alongside West African *Tirailleurs*. For black Americans, men from a nation in which it was commonly believed that Africa was a continent of uneducated savages, their meetings with the *Tirailleurs Sénégalais* – the officers of which were often the well-to-do and well-educated sons of African chiefs – would have been a profound shock. In the same front lines, and under similar conditions, soldiers recruited by the French from the paddy-fields of Vietnam donned the blue uniform of the *poilu* or the overalls of the labour battalions only to find themselves serving alongside labourers from China. In Europe, the Asian soldiers and labourers seem to have at times forged a common bond and put aside historic conflicts and differences.

As men from all corners of the world were brought together on European soil, so too were their religious practices. During the four years of war, Muslim prayers were held in the fields of Flanders. In July 1917, 1,500 Indian soldiers observed the Eid prayers and afterwards sat down to share a celebratory meal with their Indian comrades of other faiths. Ramadan was observed in the trenches, and troops from the Punjab marked the Sikh festival of Vasiakhi. At the vast complex of barracks, hospitals and depots the British had built at Etaples, near the coast south of Boulogne-sur-Mer, Chinese labourers entertained British troops and their fellow countrymen in an open-air theatre. Beneath dragon-emblazoned banners, the Union Flag and the now almost forgotten multicoloured banner of pre-communist Republican China, men on stilts in traditional costumes performed for the crowds. Both Chinese New Year and the Dragon Festivals were celebrated in France and Belgium – and both were filmed and photographed. There were great public demonstrations of Asian martial arts and *tai chi* put on for the entertainment of the French troops. Traditional Chinese opera was performed with instruments specially brought over. British and French newspapers – desperate for some light relief – effused over the colonial troops and foreign labourers with their exotic handicrafts and cultures. They became one of the great spectacles of the war – but not one that was remembered long after 1918.

Equally forgotten is the fact that the diversity of the men and women who served and laboured in the First World War was not just racial in nature. Within the broad categories of 'white' and 'European' – even more nebulous in the early twentieth century than they are today – lay a great array of peoples and nationalities, all of whom were caught up in the war to some extent. The German Army, which we have come to imagine as one huge, grey homogenous military machine, was made up of various peoples, many of whom were, in 1914, unused to thinking of themselves as Germans – this despite an energetic propaganda effort that stressed the racial unity of the German *Volk*. There were 30,000 Danes in the German Army, men from the disputed region of Schleswig, seized by Germany in the 1860s. Many of the young Danes who fought for the Kaiser did so unwillingly. Over 2,000 of them refused to take up arms for a nation to which they felt no allegiance and fled north to neutral, welcoming Denmark. Five-thousand of those who *did* fight in German uniforms did not live to see the northern half of Schleswig reincorporated into Denmark after the war. Alongside the German Danes were the other minorities: Serbs, Lithuanians, Frenchmen from annexed Alsace and Lorraine, and 3 million Poles, who had clung on to their identity, language and Catholicism in the face of Bismarck's *Kulturkampf* of the 1870s.[2] When Luxembourg was occupied by the Germans in August 1914, the men of the Grand Duchy were likewise subject to conscription into the German Army, despite Luxembourg's supposed independence. By contrast, almost

3,700 Luxembourgers, who were outside their homeland when the Germans marched in, volunteered to serve in the French Army. Even Germany itself in 1914 was a patchwork nation, consisting of twenty-five federal states, four kingdoms, five duchies, six grand-duchies, seven principalities, the cities of the old Hansa League and the annexed French provinces of Alsace and Lorraine. The German Reich was less than fifty years old and the extent to which each of its nationalities considered itself German varied enormously. The German Army was therefore, in essence, an army of minorities, some of them less enthusiastic than others about their young nation or the course it had followed under Prussian domination and the rule of Kaiser Wilhelm II.

Between 1914 and 1917 there was another complex and ethnically diverse war being fought on the other side of Europe. The Russian Army on the Eastern Front was also the product of a multi-ethnic empire of various peoples. Within the vast legions of the Tsar were ethnic Russians, Ukrainians, Latvians, Armenians, Muslims from the Caucasus and men of Mongol origin from the far east of the empire. There were over 100,000 Estonians in the Russian Army, along with an unknown number of men from Finland, then a Grand Duchy within the Russian Empire. There were Poles in the Tsar's army, as well as in that of the Kaiser and the Emperor of Austria-Hungary. Russian Jews and ethnic Germans both served in the Russian Army, but both groups were distrusted and were the subject of crude propaganda attacks.[3]

In the snowy expanses of the Eastern Front the Russian armies confronted not just the Germans but the army of the Austro-Hungarian Empire, another multi-ethnic, polyglot state, ruled from Vienna, the city that Adolf Hitler was later to condemn as 'that Babylon of races'.[4] Fighting on two fronts, like their German allies, the army of Austria-Hungary was as heterogeneous as the empire from which it was drawn. Although three-quarters of the officers were German-speaking Austrians, of their men only around one-third were from a similar background. The rest were Magyars, Romanians, ethnic Italians, Poles, Ukrainians, Croats, Czechs, Serbs and Bosnians.

Russia, the great colossus and itself a continental empire, had no need for additional labour or manpower in its war effort. A little of Russia's great ethnic diversity instead flowed in the opposite direction during the war. Calculating that Russia had an abundance of manpower but a lack of materials and munitions to arm them, the French suggested that Russian troops be sent to the Western Front in exchange for French munitions. In early 1916, ships carrying the men of the Russian Expeditionary Force were dispatched to France. The first contingent landed in Marseilles, in 1916, just three months after the last troops of the Indian Corps had left for Mesopotamia from the same harbours. The Russian troops were city men, factory workers from Moscow and Samara, and peasants from the Volga. Three brigades of Russians were also sent to the front in Salonika, to fight against German, Austro-Hungarian and Bulgarian forces. The brigades deployed in France were, by early 1917, in the line near Reims, manning the Fort de la Pompelle, one of the many defensive forts built by France after the defeat of the 1870s, its architects never imagining that it would one day be defended by men from the Russian steppe. The Russian cemeteries on the Western Front are among the many little-visited and half-forgotten memorials to a global war. After the October Revolution, in 1917, one battalion of the Russian Expeditionary Force mutinied and was attacked in its camp by French forces and loyal Russians. The Russian troops who remained loyal to France formed the Russian Legion – a unit that was eventually incorporated into the 1st Moroccan Infantry Division, perhaps the most hybrid of all the divisions that fought in the war. This bizarre formation consisted of the Moroccan *Tirailleurs*, the *Tirailleurs Malgaches* (black Africans from Madagascar), the French Foreign Legion and the displaced Russians. At the end of the war, some of the Russian survivors chose not to return to their homeland and simply slipped into French society, along with thousands of other displaced former soldiers and labourers from across the world.

★

By the summer of 1917, the British Army, bolstered by contingents from the dominions and swelled by conscripts from within Britain itself, was approaching its maximum size. Over the course of the war, 5.4 million men would pass through its ranks on the Western Front alone. The British Army had never been bigger and, even at the height of the Second World War, it would never be so large again.[5] The maintenance of so vast a force in France and Belgium, and engaged in operations in Africa and the Middle East, was one of the greatest logistical undertakings in British military history. The French Army of 1917, exhausted by the gargantuan effort of the Battle of Verdun the previous year, was a similarly complex organization and one as desperate for labour and logistical support as it was for fighting men. Despite the losses at Verdun, the French Army stood at around 2 million in 1917. To sustain armies of this scale over 475 miles of the Western Front, as well as in the other theatres of war, required the British and French to draw on the labour of hundreds of thousands of the world's poorest people. Peasants and villagers from Africa, Asia and remote islands were recruited to feed the war machine. Across the world, men who otherwise would never have left their villages, never mind their home countries, travelled across oceans. The Great European War – as it was then still being called – became the greatest employment opportunity in history, and hundreds of thousands of men, some of them from the most beautiful lands and islands on earth, descended upon Flanders and northern France, one of the most drab and featureless landscapes in Europe. They came from Bermuda, Macedonia, Malta, Greece, Arabia, Palestine, Singapore, Mauritius, Madagascar, Vietnam, Fiji, the Cook Islands, the Seychelles – anywhere that there were unemployed men who could find a ship to the war zones. They served not just in France and Belgium but across the world, transported to wherever they were needed.

Many came enthusiastically, inspired by notions of duty and motivated by a sense of belonging to a family of nations, represented by the British and French empires. Others were induced to serve only by the prospect of work and wages. The men of

British-controlled Fiji actively pressured the colonial authorities to be allowed to leave their beautiful islands and serve in France. So strong was the determination of the Fijians to play a role in the defence of Britain and the empire that after their initial offers of assistance had been rejected in 1914, the Governor of Fiji, Sir E.B. Sweet-Escott, noted that there were great 'difficulties in keeping them back from going "home" to England to serve'.[6] The government finally relented, and in 1917 the first contingents of the Fijian Labour Corps arrived in Boulogne, after having sailed across the Pacific Ocean, travelled the whole length of Canada by train, and traversed the Atlantic on troop ships. After their epic journey, they were employed loading trucks. While in France, they experienced persistent racism and, as with most non-white labourers, were at times barred from entering certain facilities. There was also a concerted effort to keep them separated from Chinese labourers, who it was feared might undermine the status of Britain in the eyes of the men from Fiji.[7]

Among the Fijians was Lala Sukuna, the son of a chief, who had been studying at Oxford University in 1914, the first Fijian to attend a university. When war broke out, Sukuna presented himself for enlistment at a British recruiting station, but was rejected on the grounds of race. Undaunted, he joined the French Foreign Legion. Britain's loss was France's gain. Sukuna fought on the Western Front and was decorated for his service until being wounded in 1915. Repatriated to Fiji he then returned to France, despite his wounds, to serve in the Fijian Labour Corps. Although a decorated war hero, he was content to work on the docks at Calais. Sukuna went on to become one of the statesmen whose work led to Fijian independence in 1970.

Recruitment from the colonies often exposed the concealed workings of racial systems that operated behind platitudes of imperial brotherhood. In the British colony of Bermuda, white men formed the Bermuda Volunteer Rifle Corps, which was welcomed into the ranks of the Royal Lincolnshire Regiment. Black Bermudans were only permitted to join another unit, the Bermuda Militia Artillery, which was commanded by white officers. Both units were sent to Europe, but the black men were relegated to labour duties in the ammunition dumps, a task that still exposed them to enemy shell-fire, which led to casualties. South Africa's even more elaborate systems of racial segregation, although at this time prefiguring the full apparatus of *apartheid* in later years, demanded even greater degrees of racial separation. While black South Africans served in the South African Native Labour Corps, coloured men were recruited into the separate Cape Coloured Labour Battalion, which was also deployed to France and Belgium. White South Africans fought in their own units, in the trenches of France and Belgium, as well as against the Germans in German South West Africa and German East Africa.

The demand for labour on the Western Front was so great in 1917 that, long after the British had evacuated the two infantry divisions of the Indian Corps to Mesopotamia, partly in the belief that conditions in France and Belgium were too cold for them, the men of the Indian Labour Corps were deployed to these same cold regions. The Indian Labour Corps was partly made up of Nagas and Kukis – minority peoples of the Raj. That the war was able to stretch its tentacles into the remote homelands of the Naga, a tribal people who lived in the hills on the India–Burma border, illustrates both the vastness of the British Empire and the enormity of the need for labour. Five-thousand miles from the Western Front, British officials in 1916 travelled the Naga Hills demanding that every village make available a number of men to work as labourers in a war that must have seemed inconceivably remote to them.

In September 1917, the British archaeologist Sir Henry Balfour encountered a group of Naga labourers in Eastern France, who were working on the repair of a road. They were within artillery range and appeared to Balfour 'to be quite at home and unper-turbed'. Later he speculated: 'One wonders what impression remains with them from their sudden contact with higher civilisa-tion at war. Possibly they are reflecting that, after what they have seen, the White Man's condemnation of the relatively innocuous headhunting of the Nagas savours of hypocrisy.'[8]

Most Indian labourers served not in France, though, but in Mesopotamia. The British were so desperate for labour to support the Indian Army fighting the Turks in that theatre that, in October 1916, they formed the 'Jail Porter and Labour Corps', which consisted of 16,000 prisoners who had been flushed out of the Indian prison system and put to work in gangs.[9] These convicts laboured alongside men from Persia, Arabs from Egypt, and Mauritians from that tiny island in the Indian Ocean. When even this great phalanx of men was not enough, local Iraqi women, displaced by the fighting, were put to work.

In every theatre of war there was never any shortage of work for these armies of labourers to do. The historian Paul Fussell estimated that the total miles of trenches on the Western Front dug by the British alone – which included front-line trenches, communications trenches and reserve trenches – reached almost 6,000 miles by the end of the war. Between them, the warring sides dug perhaps 25,000 miles of trenches. It was possible, in theory, to walk from the English Channel all the way to the village of Pfetterhouse on the Swiss frontier, where the lines ended, and remain below ground-level for the whole 475 miles. Every mile of this great labyrinth of trenches, strong-points, saps, and dug-outs had not only to be dug by hand but then maintained – shored-up in winter, and drained during heavy rains. While much of this work was done by soldiers, a vast amount was carried out by men of the labour battalions. And the actual trenches were only part of what made up the Western Front. From north to south, from the front-line fighting trenches to the rear rest areas, the Western Front was in effect a great linear city, one with its own railways, roads and logistics systems, post offices, police forces and health services. By 1916 the cost of all this for the British alone had reached £5 million per day. The Western Front had its own slums and ghettos too, with generals lodging in elegant châteaux far behind the lines, troops huddled together in the cold of the trenches, and the poorest non-white labourers living under canvas and behind barbed wire. It was a city with a disparate population of millions, and to feed and supply it was an enormous and constant undertaking. The repair of those roads, the building of the railways and the supplying of ammunition and artillery shells for daily use and periodic offensives was an epic task. It took labourers deep into the fighting zones, within the reach of enemy artillery. Thousands of them were killed; thousands more died of disease.

In a newspaper article of 1914, Georges Clemenceau had described France as 'nothing more or less than a great battle-field'. What in 1914 had been something of an exaggeration had, by 1917, become a concrete reality. While the battle zone itself, known after the war by the French as the Zone Rouge, was a narrow strip of intensive destruction within the range of the guns, the infrastructure required for what was effectively total-siege warfare ranged across much of France. To hold the line, and launch the great attacks to free France of the invader, required the militarization of much of the nation and much of the nation's industrial production. Factory towns became dormitory towns, in which thousands of foreign workers were housed. To meet the demands of war, large numbers of other Europeans migrated to France to work in industry, munitions, food production and supply. They came from impoverished Spain, Greece and Portugal, as well as from Italy, which, from 1915, was an ally of the Entente powers. These guest-workers laboured side-by-side with almost 200,000 workers who arrived from France's colonies, including 5,000 from Madagascar and around 50,000 from French Indochina (Vietnam, Cambodia and Laos). By far the largest contingent consisted of North Africans, men from the same colonies from which the fighting men of the Spahis and Goumiers had come – Algeria, Morocco and Tunisia. Around 130,000 North Africans worked in industry during the conflict as every sinew of France's industrial strength was strained by the unnatural effort of total war.

★

One effect of the great mixing of men on the Western Front, in Africa and the Middle East, and in the factories of the industrial zones of France, was that the First World War enabled colonial peoples to see their rulers in ways that would never have been possible, or permissible, under normal circumstances. The British and French authorities in Paris and London, and in the colonies themselves, fretted endlessly about the unforeseeable consequences of allowing the subjects of empire to see their colonial masters in a struggle against an enemy who was equal to them in strength. They feared that men who had tasted new freedoms in Europe, and seen that continent in a new light, would never again submit to being dominated once they returned home. The concocted racial mystique that was a central element of colonial rule risked being exposed for what it was. In May 1916, a letter from a Frenchman living in French Indochina was cited in a report by the Marseilles postal censor's office. He spoke for many when he expressed his fear that the service of colonial men might help save France but in the process sow the seeds for the destruction of its colonial empire. 'At this moment,' he wrote:

> ... they are recruiting Annamite volunteers. 50,000 more are needed. I do not know where they will find them, nor what will result from this ... certainly nothing good, without a doubt; this will eventually create malcontents and revolutionaries, as well as the upsetting of our beautiful colony. They will no longer feel like planting rice in their fields after they have seen in France a number of things that one must not let them see or hear. This will be terrible, and this is not only my humble opinion, but that of all who know their race well.[10]

One way of addressing these concerns was to attempt to limit the extent to which colonial soldiers and labourers could interact with European soldiers and civilians. Various schemes of segregation and separation were attempted, with varying degrees of success. Some of the methods of recruitment, employment and segregation were imported into the war zones and the industrial areas from the colonial world. When the opportunity arose, men from the colonies were placed in barracks and isolated from their French co-workers and the French public. In places they were housed in conditions more akin to those endured by PoWs or inmates in a forced-labour camp than those of civilian, volunteer labourers who had signed contracts of employment. While the stated aim of the British and French authorities was to avoid 'spoiling' or corrupting their colonial subjects, there was also a desire, especially among the French, to avoid interaction. There were fears that contact would lead to racial violence between local peoples and colonial soldiers and labourers. And there was concern about the inevitable sexual contact between French women and the huge number of male colonial subjects living and working in France, a nation whose own young men were away at the front.

There developed an enormous gulf between French attitudes towards non-white labourers and non-white soldiers. There is ample evidence of the routine racism to which African and Asian soldiers in the French army were subjected. However, there was never any question that the *Tirailleurs Sénégalais,* or the North African or South-East Asian troops, were sharing in the privations of the war and risking their lives in the defence of France. The non-white labourers were less readily comprehended. Their work in industry, although essential, was regarded by many as work taken away from Frenchmen. It was possible to imagine the colonial worker as an alien, who was exploiting rather than defending France, someone benefitting from the war and doing so in safety, far behind the lines and away from the dangers faced by the troops. That these outsiders were sleeping in beds (albeit ones in barracks or dormitories), while the sons of France slept in the trenches, rankled with some. To those inclined to view them as such, the foreign non-white worker joined the ranks of the shirker or the war profiteer: living off France while its own sons were dying at the front in horrific numbers. That the colonial workers were paid lower wages and were used to break strikes further antagonized white workers and their unions.

The spring of 1917 saw these tensions erupt into a wave of racial attacks and even race riots. At a moment when France suffered defeats on the battlefield that threatened to tip over into a national crisis, non-white labourers were attacked by both French civilians and French front-line soldiers home on leave. Events were, in part, motivated by tensions over inter-racial relation-ships. In the wartime factories, two groups – African men and white women – who had both been largely excluded from the French industrial economy, and separated from one another by distance and convention, were suddenly brought together. The factory – the peacetime preserve of the white man – became both a feminized zone and a place of racial interaction, 'manned' by non-whites from Africa and Asia and by French women enjoying new freedoms (although accompanied by the burdens of long hours and hard, sometimes dangerous, work). Not only was it believed that colonial workers were taking French jobs, and thereby lowering industrial wages, it was now clear that some were having relationships with French women. The fear was made all the more acute by the fact that French women and colo-nial workers laboured, in some cases, literally side-by-side in the factories, to the amazement of men from Africa and Asia, for whom white women were normally off-limits. A labourer from Madagascar working in Toulouse, perhaps unaware that wartime opportunities available to French women were exceptional, expressed some of this shock when he wrote to a friend: 'Would you believe that white women, who at home love to have us serve them, here work as much as men. They are very numerous in the workshops and labor with the same ardor as men.'[11]

Official fears of miscegenation were realized when French women met and married men from the colonies and had mixed-race children. The outright refusal of French authorities to even contemplate recruiting non-white women from the colonies for war work in France helped ensure that the racial mixing they were so eager to avoid took place on an even larger scale. In effect, they created a situation that was in many ways the inverse of that in the colonies, where mainly white colonists routinely had relationships – and children – with local women.[12]

★

In the factories and in the military zones behind the line, the sheer numbers of foreign soldiers and labourers meant that it proved impossible to prevent an unprecedented mixing of peoples and races. There were efforts made by both the British and French authorities, partially successful in some cases, to limit the contact between civilians and non-Europeans, but a complete separation was never fully practical, and efforts at segregation (for reasons of expediency) focused primarily on groups about which the British or French had particular concerns.

The soldiers and labourers from all over the world were young men who, no matter what their role, were engaged in what was unquestionably a great adventure. They were travellers in a world turned upside down, in which old rules had been set aside and the barriers of distance and race temporarily breached or at least lowered. New experiences, sights, relationships, and opportunities were possible, at least for some. But most of the contacts between French and Belgian civilians and the armies of exotic foreigners who had come to their nations went unrecorded. We know very little about what the visitors themselves made of Europe, the only real sources being the censored letters of Indian and African troops augmented by a handful of war memoirs and the efforts of post-war oral historians. Similarly, there are only a tiny number of European diarists who were in the right locations at the right time, and had the right mindset to offer historians a broad picture of what this strange invasion meant to local peoples, and how it affected their lives. The most compelling and expansive of the few accounts that do exist is that that of Pastor Achiel Van Walleghem, a priest in the Belgian village of Dikkebus, just three miles from Ypres. Dikkebus and much of the surrounding region fell within German artillery range, and whole communities were engulfed within a world of billets, encampments, depots and rest posts.

Pastor Van Walleghem was in many ways the perfect diarist. Thirty-five-years old in 1914, he was a man who, by both profession and nature, was entwined in the grapevine of chatter, rumour and village news. Inquisitive to the point of rudeness, and a figure who was trusted with sensitive information, he was evidently an incorrigible gossip. Van Walleghem's diary runs to 1,240 pages, contained in 13 separate notebooks, all written in the same neat, consistent script. It is the diary of an unworldly man struggling to make sense of the extraordinary times in which he found himself.[13] It presents the First World War as seen from behind net curtains, and it contains not only his own voice, opinions and prejudices, it also acts as a conduit for the voices, experiences and stories of local farmers, shopkeepers and villagers. Through Van Walleghem, who stood at the heart of his community, we hear second-hand its views and learn of the strategies that were developed as the people of a tiny, inward-looking rural region adapted to their strange new lives in a global war.

Throughout Van Walleghem's diary we are also privy to the gossip and rumours of the soldiers and officers of many nationalities who passed through his region. The pastor, a man well within the age range for conscription (but from which his vocation exempted him), was fascinated by the troops from Britain and France and the men from Britain's white dominions. In late August 1916, on a trip to nearby Poperinghe, he had the opportunity to compare the British with their Australian cousins, and found he much preferred the men from Down Under. 'The town is full of Australian soldiers,' he reported. 'The Australians always have lots of money; little wonder that they are so popular with the local people. What's more, they seem more decent than the English. Above all, they are politer and less pretentious.'[14] It was, however, the sudden and repeated appearances, in rural Flanders, of men of other races that most captivated him. His diary abounds with stories of a rural population entranced by the arrival of peoples only previously seen on postcards or in books. Many of his observations are tainted by his own unthinking racial assumptions; yet at other times he reveals himself willing to be surprised and a man capable of recognizing the qualities of men of other races and cultures.

In December 1914, the pastor was witness to what must have been among the most sobering sights of the first months of the war.

On 9 December, the depleted and exhausted Allied armies that had
survived the First Battle of Ypres were rotated out of the lines and
sent behind to rest and to be reorganized. The men who marched
through the Ypres Salient, through Dikkebus and the other villages,
had witnessed the birth of the Western Front. 'The soldiers coming
from the trenches look terrible,' Van Walleghem wrote:

> ... *covered in mud from head to toe. In some places the trenches are*
> *full of water. Many of the men have frozen feet from the constant*
> *cold and wet. How pitiable they are! In general, the local people*
> *have a good deal of sympathy for them. However, because many of*
> *the soldiers are angry, and sometimes behave badly, this sympathy*
> *is perhaps less than it once was. I suppose we have to take the good*
> *with the bad.*

That day also represented Van Walleghem's first encounter with
troops from beyond Europe, and it was perhaps his first indication that the area around Ypres was rapidly becoming the
encampment of an international army. 'At the moment we have
all different kinds of troops around the village,' he noted:

> ... *including plenty of zouaves, with their wide red trousers, short*
> *tunics and Turkish caps. There are also lots of Tirailleurs Algériens,*
> *men with brown-black faces and dressed in grey trousers and a*
> *hooded cape. (These Algerians are half savage and it is not safe to*
> *leave them alone; there has been more than one complaint about*
> *their wild antics.) We have not yet seen much cavalry around here,*
> *although several different types have passed through; mainly chas-*
> *seurs and hussars, but also some dragoons and cuirassiers, and*
> *even a few spahis (Algerian cavalrymen).*[15]

Van Walleghem was quick to believe rumour and often overly
eager to fall back on comforting racial stereotypes, but his insa-
tiable curiosity also made him, at times, a sympathetic observer.
He first encountered the Indian Corps in 1915, when they were
rushed to the Ypres sector to stem the German onslaught (with

poison gas) at the Second Battle of Ypres. In the summer of 1916, the pastor met another contingent of Indian troops, probably cavalry units. On 6 June he commented on the 'new troop movements in the streets of the village'. To his confusion, units of Scottish Highlanders, who had until recently been encamped nearby, disappeared and suddenly:

> ... there are currently quite a lot of Indian troops in the parish, most of them out towards Vlamertinge. Dark-skinned, but otherwise dressed as English soldiers, apart from their distinctive turbans, wrapped elegantly around their heads from a single cloth. They speak English and some of them also know a few words of French. They are very curious by nature and ask questions all the time.

With his customary lack of self-awareness, Van Walleghem went on to demonstrate that his own curiosity put that of the Indians to shame. 'They are quite prepared to walk for half an hour to find milk,' he was surprised to note, 'and then watch everything around them while they are being served':

> They are very suspicious of everyone. Yet they themselves are not to be trusted, and if you give them half a chance to run off without paying, they will be gone in a flash! And if they do pay, they offer their own Indian money, rupees, and are angry when the local people refuse to accept them. They don't understand – or they pretend not to understand – the value of our money, and when they try to exchange it they always want to get back more than they give! Our people prefer not to do business with them.

Towards the end of this entry, Van Walleghem felt compelled to point out that the Indians were:

> ... in general ... friendly and polite. But their curiosity continually gets the better of them, and they will examine you from head to foot right in front of your very own eyes. And they just love looking through the windows of houses! They bake what look like pancakes

and they also eat a very strong-tasting seed. It seems that they will
be here for a number of weeks.[16]

Pastor Van Walleghem may well have been among the first residents of West Flanders to have sampled Indian food.

The Belgian historian Dominiek Dendooven has worked most closely with Van Walleghem's long diary, and he has demonstrated that many of the events described by the pastor's accounts can be substantiated by official records or the accounts of other diarists. While the pomposity of his tone and his tendency to regurgitate simplistic stereotypes grates on the modern reader, Van Walleghem's constant curiosity has been a boon for modern historians exploring life behind the Western Front. While Van Walleghem never questioned, or thought to question, his belief in the innate supremacy of European culture and values over all others, he was able to recognize the virtues of the colonial soldiers and labourers who passed by his door and through his community. In his tendency to vacillate between judgemental racism one moment and universalist sympathy the next, Van Walleghem was not unusual. Jozef Ghesquiere, a Belgian schoolteacher, describing a battalion of *Tirailleurs Sénégalais* on the march in Flanders, reveals how people caught in extraordinary times similarly lurched between the same extremes:

> *There are about eight hundred of them. On their heads they wear a red fez with a black tassel. With their tanned faces, their jet-black hair, black moustache and eyebrows, they look quite scary. They are looked at with a degree of fear. And yet they smile at the bystanders in a friendly manner and the fear soon dwindles away. Indeed, they have come to help liberate our country. Poor boys! So far from their home country. How many will never see it again?*[17]

Maurice Duwez, a doctor in the Belgian Army, wrote another account of life behind the lines and was witness to the great influx of the armies of empires and beyond into the tiny corner of his nation that remained under Allied control. He described one group of French North Africans, which he encountered in 1915, as a 'strange mix of races. Arabs and Jews with tanned skins, black beards and the profile of an eagle.' As with many of the Belgian population, Duwez became adept at guessing the origins of the armies he saw marching past him – although he was confused upon encountering a group of men he took to be the Chinese Labour Corps, but who turned out to be Japanese Canadians of the Canadian Corps.

Just as with the Indian hospitals on England's south coast, the military hospitals of France and Belgium had became another zone of intimate contact between non-white soldiers and European civilians. Jane de Launoy, a nurse at the L'Océan Hospital in De Panne, southern Belgium, recorded her experiences in a diary that was published after the war. Walking in the sand dunes by the sea, in between shifts in late 1914, she found herself transported, in her mind, to Arabia when coming across a group of Spahis – Algerian horsemen of the French Army: 'An Arabian fantasy on the beach. At least fifty horses in a row take off at a gallop in various successive waves. With their bright uniforms it is indeed a fabulous spectacle.'[18] Two days later, on Christmas Day 1914, her diary recorded how North African soldiers had propositioned other nurses and even an 'honourable lady'. De Launoy confided to her private pages that she 'probably did not look kind enough, as no one has propositioned me'. But by the end of the year she had concluded that 'On the whole Muslims have great respect for women in uniform.' In a truly remarkable passage, she admitted to her own attraction to one of the North African soldiers with whom she had been having innocent, but sensual, liaisons:

> For the past few nights a beautiful Goumier has asked me for coffee at one o'clock in the morning. Shrouded in his burnouse he enters from outdoors and comes up to my office. I am not easily unnerved but when this large devil with his dammed seductive eyes appeared before me I was not at ease. He enjoyed his coffee, muttered a few words and looked at me like a sacred object, incomprehensibly taboo.[19]

The opposite perspective is less well known. What did the non-white troops and labourers think of communities like that of Pastor Van Walleghem in which they found themselves? Many, but not all, will have come to war with some notion of what Europe would be like. How different was the reality from those expectations? The effects of total war presented them with a distorted picture. The nations into which colonial troops and labourers arrived were societies in shock – culturally, economically and demographically disfigured by war. Vast numbers of young Frenchmen were at the front, while women performed new tasks and were employed in unfamiliar roles. The evidence is that non-Europeans were repeatedly astonished at both how hard French and Belgian women worked and the level of independence they enjoyed. Many of the freedoms and economic opportunities available to women in France were, unbeknownst to the outsiders, novel, often temporary wartime exigencies, which would be contested after the war when the men returned to their homes and jobs.

Colonial arrivals in the encampments and billets behind the Western Front also encountered individual trauma as well as collective, societal shock. One Indian soldier wrote, in a letter of 1915, of how a well-born middle-class French lady, in whose home he had been billeted, took on the role of surrogate mother, as her own boys were all in the front:

> ... *she comforted me to such an extent that I cannot describe her kindness. Of her own free will she washed my clothes, arranged my bed, polished my boots, and washed my bedroom daily with warm water. Every morning she gave me a tray with bread, milk, butter and coffee ... When we left the village, the old lady wept on my shoulder and gave me five Francs.*[20]

★

There were units working behind the lines in France and Belgium that were comprised of men who had volunteered to fight rather than labour, but for reasons of race were not permitted to do so. Just as in London and Delhi, the outbreak of war in 1914 had

been greeted with enormous enthusiasm in the British West
Indies. The people of Jamaica, British Honduras (Belize),
Barbados, Trinidad and Tobago, British Guiana (now Guyana),
the Bahamas, Grenada, the Leeward Islands, St Vincent and St
Lucia regarded themselves as subjects of the empire, and the
general feeling that prevailed was that the islands and their
people should do their bit. There were immediate calls for a new
regiment of men from the Caribbean to be raised and sent to
France. The men of Jamaica were asked somewhat insensitively,
at one public meeting, if they were going 'to sit down and be
slaves' or take part in the war as men and soldiers.[21] At war rallies
on that island and others, the image of Britain as the emancipa-
tor of the enslaved Africans – the cornerstone of the limited
history education on offer to pupils in Caribbean schools –
became the call of the many self-appointed recruiting sergeants
who emerged. The young black men of the Caribbean were
asked if they were willing to defend the nation that had emancipated their ancestors. That it had been the same nation that
enslaved them was left unsaid.

The clamour among some to come to Europe and fight for the
British Empire got under way even before the war rallies had
been organized or the fiery speeches delivered. 'War fever' was
so strong that there were Caribbean men who sold their belongings to pay for passage to Britain, where they hoped to enlist.
Others, who could not afford a ticket, stowed away on ships
bound for Europe. Patriotism and the war fever of 1914 fused in
the Caribbean with the suffocating poverty under which most
islanders were forced to live. On islands like Jamaica in the early
years of the century, there were precious few opportunities.
Thousands of Jamaicans had left their island looking for work in
Panama and Cuba, where work on sugar plantations offered a
meagre income, if not a way out of poverty. The First World War
represented an outlet for the skills and energies of a dynamic
people who had for too long been denied work and hope.

None of this delighted the War Office, whose officials looked
upon the prospect of black men arriving in Britain *en masse*,

intending to enter the ranks of the volunteer army, with deep antipathy. In late 1914, the War Office set out to prevent Caribbean men from enlisting and threatened to repatriate all those who arrived in Britain. In May 1915, nine men from Barbados, who had hidden aboard the SS *Danube*, were found in the London docks. Before they could make their way to a recruiting office, they were arrested. When they appeared at West Ham Police Court they were mocked by the magistrate, who then had them sent home. Other West Indians who made it as far as the recruiting offices were simply rejected. Unwanted and penniless, they then found themselves destitute in a 'mother country' about which, they discovered, they knew little, and in which they had no friends and few prospects. There were deep concerns, though, within the Colonial Office at how the wholesale rejection of earnest and honest offers of service by the men of the Caribbean, on grounds of race, would be interpreted by the peoples of the islands. Fearful of causing deep and damaging offence, the Colonial Office intervened and – with the support of King George V himself – they approved the establishment of the British West Indies Regiment (BWIR) as a new infantry formation within the British Army. The first contingent arrived in Seaford training camp, in Sussex, in September 1915.[22] Twelve battalions were raised and ultimately almost 16,000 men served in the new regiment. However, when they were deployed on the continent, the men of the BWIR were segregated from white British troops and reduced to the status of labourers, despite being armed and trained for combat. In the few tiny snippets of film footage held by the Imperial War Museum in London that show the regiment in France and Belgium, they are busy transporting ammunition in a field depot. This was important work; but their exclusion from active service was understood as a racial slur, and it was deeply resented.

In 1916, long after the initial wave of war fever had subsided, in the Caribbean islands support for the war and enthusiasm for local men playing an active role in it was catastrophically undermined by an incident that is still remembered with anger today. In March of that year, 1,140 men left Jamaica bound for Britain on the SS *Verdala*. Diverted away from her normal route by German U-boats, the ship headed to Halifax, Nova Scotia. In the freezing northern waters, the unheated *Verdala* was battered by blizzards from the Arctic. The Jamaican troops, wearing only their tropical uniforms, began to freeze. By the time they reached Halifax, five had died of hypothermia and six-hundred men were suffering from frostbite and exposure. The reaction in the Caribbean was one of outrage. Recruitment in Jamaica was immediately halted, and faith in Britain and the war was permanently damaged. When a conscription law was passed in Jamaica, the authorities never dared seriously enforce it for fear of stoking resentment over what islanders called the 'Halifax Incident'.

In May 1917, Pastor Van Walleghem of Dikkebus came across a unit of British troops, most likely members of the BWIR. 'A number of negroes have come to work at Alouis Adriaen's farm and the Drie Goen,' he wrote in his diary. 'They are from Jamaica, in the West Indies. They are dressed like English soldiers, are polite and speak softly.' Despite their politeness, Van Walleghem explained that among the local people the Jamaicans were 'not very popular, because of their long fingers. In general, the local people prefer to see the back of them rather than the front, because if they drop in somewhere, say for a cup of coffee, they are just as likely to stay for a few hours as for a few minutes!' Pastor Van Walleghem himself seems to have taken a more favourable view of the Jamaicans, despite the supposed length of their fingers. He was pleased to discover that 'Many of them are Catholic,' and was extremely taken by a letter he found, 'belonging to one of the blacks, written to him by his mother. Such fine, upright and Christian motherly feelings! None of our mothers could write any better.'[23] Always alert to the little cultural differences between the men he encountered, Van Walleghem was interested to note that the Jamaicans, men from an island that produced tobacco, 'like to smoke cigars, whereas most soldiers prefer cigarettes'.[24] In his entry for 27 May 1917, the day after he had first come across the men from the Caribbean, Van Walleghem reported that:

Alouis Adriaen's farm was heavily shelled. Two shells landed on the stable and another fell on the house. The people inside were lucky. When the shell hit, they were all down in the cellar. All they had were a few scratches and bruises from bits of falling masonry. The animals were also lucky; by the time the stable was hit they had already run off in fright towards Hallebast. The negroes billeted at the farm were less fortunate. Four were killed and three were wounded.[25]

The men of the BWIR were ultimately permitted by the British Army to take part in active operations, but only outside Europe. In East Africa, for example, they participated alongside black Africans from Nigeria, Ghana, Kenya, Nyasaland and elsewhere.

Although the army authorities were successful in preventing them from fighting on the Western Front, there were a small number of black men in British uniforms who did see action in France and Belgium. In 1914, an Act of Parliament had ostensibly made clear exactly what it meant to be 'British', in the eyes of the law. The British Nationality and Status of Aliens Act was passed on 7 August 1914, three days after the outbreak of war, and it came into force on 1 January 1915. It defined 'natural-born British subjects' as 'any person born within His Majesty's dominions and allegiance'. In practice, however, officialdom took the position that to be British was to be white. Both the Army Council and the War Office, operating largely under military law, determined that black men, whether from within Britain itself or from the empire, were not to be permitted to serve in the regular British Army. Neither were they to be conscripted. The men from the Caribbean who had been drawn into the BWIR could easily be kept segregated from their white comrades – funnelled into labour-battalion work or deployed to other theatres. It was far more difficult for the army authorities to prevent men from Britain's small black population from enlisting in the regular volunteer army. A tiny percentage of these men, most of them apparently mixed-race, did manage to cross the colour line. During the great recruiting surge of 1914, huge discretion was given to recruiting officers with regard to which men they could pass as fit for service. Age and height restrictions were both, at times, overlooked by recruiters who were just as caught up in the fevered patriotism of the moment as the eager volunteers who stood in front of them. That the recruiters were paid a fee for each man who enlisted may have also influenced the degree to which some were willing to bend rules or turn blind eyes. While there are reports of discrimination against black Britons by some recruiting officers, there were clearly other recruiters who were willing to look beyond race.

In December 1914, Walter Tull, the star midfield footballer who played professionally for Northampton Town Football Club (and before that Tottenham Hotspur), travelled down from Northampton and presented himself at a recruiting office in Holborn, in London. The son of a Barbadian carpenter and a British woman, Tull was unquestionably fit enough to do duty and was demonstrably intelligent. He was also willing to give up his fame and career to volunteer for active service, so he was accepted into the 'Footballers' Battalion' of the Middlesex Regiment, a battalion made up of supporters and officials as well as players.[26] After training, Tull served on the Western Front, rising to become a sergeant and surviving the Battle of the Somme. In May 1917, he won a commission, becoming second lieutenant. This was theoretically in contravention of the 1914 *Manual of Military Law,* which stipulated that 'alien soldiers' were prohibited from 'exercising any actual command or power'. The HM Stationary Office publication *Short Guide to Obtaining a Commission in the Special Reserve of Officers* (1912) explained in more detail that all officer candidates 'must be of pure European descent'.[27] Yet by 1916, when Tull applied for officer training, the catastrophic level of losses the British Army had endured exposed the impracticality, if not the inequity, of these rules, and they were quietly relaxed. Service record, education, fitness and combat experience all, for the moment, took precedence over race, and black men were permitted to apply for temporary commissions 'after serving with credit in the ranks of the Expeditionary Force'.[28]

Second Lieutenant Walter Tull was killed in action in late March 1918, near the village of Favreuil in the Pas-de-Calais, during the opening of the German Spring Offensive of that year. His remains are not among the 385 men buried in the Favreuil British War Cemetery, as his body was never recovered.

———•———

NOYELLES-SUR-MER, PICARDY, 2014. Near the estuary of the River Somme, on the edge of the village of Noyelles-sur-Mer, a long, straight dirt road runs through the centre of a broad field of tall maize. Flanking the road on the way into the village are two Chinese stone lions, gifts to the village (population 860) from the People's Republic of China (population 1.35 billion). At the end of the dirt road, surrounded on all sides in summer by the billowing seas of maize, is one of the most incongruous sights on the whole of the former Western Front. The Chinese Cemetery at Noyelles-sur-Mer is entered through a grand Chinese-style archway, shaded by two tall evergreen trees. Within the low walls of the cemetery are the graves of 841 Chinese men – labourers who came to France and Belgium to work behind the lines of the First World War. On the day they 'signed' their contracts of employment in China, with an inky thumbprint, they were promised that they would 'work on railways, roads, etc., and in factories, mines, dockyards, fields, forests etc.,' and that they would not be 'employed in military operations'. But nevertheless here they lie, victims of shells fired from distant guns, or of bombs dropped from the German aircraft that attacked their camps. Many more died of cholera or had their short lives snuffed out by the Spanish Flu epidemic that followed hard on the heels of the war itself.

The war cemetery is as well tended and as sombre as any of the hundreds in France and Belgium. Each headstone is engraved with the name of the fallen man and the serial number he was allotted upon signing on with the Chinese Labour Corps. In some cases, the name is unknown and the victim is commemorated only by the serial number, retrieved from the metal identification bracelet that each man wore, attached around his wrist with metal rivets. Each headstone bears one of four proverbs, in both Chinese characters and English letters, which have been cut into the standard Portland limestone as used for all British war graves. They read: 'Faithful unto Death', 'A noble duty bravely done', 'Though Dead He Still Liveth' and ' A Good Reputation Endures For Ever'.

Many of the dead in the small Chinese Cemetery of Noyelles-sur-Mer, which today is surrounded by farmers' fields, were themselves farmers – poor peasants mainly from Shandong province, on China's north-east coast. They were for the most part young men, some of them very young, and they came to Europe in the hope of making some money and seeing something of the world. In many cases they had little to keep them at home. As with so many who came to Europe from afar, the conflict offered a way out of grinding poverty. War work was potentially the key to a better life, or at least a temporary means of supporting children, parents or both. What is unique about the men from China, though, is that they were not from one of the warring nations or its empire; China did not declare war against the Central Powers until August 1917, long after most of the 140,000 labourers had signed up. The men whose remains lie at Noyelles-sur-Mer, and the thousands more who survived and returned to China, were economic migrants. Of all the many peoples who ventured to the Western Front, the Chinese are among the most forgotten. Almost from the moment the gunfire stopped, their part in the story of the war was airbrushed out, and their presence in France and Belgium – which continued into 1919 and 1920 on the orders of the military authorities – was almost instantly resented.

In 1914 Republican China was a nation only three years old – a revolutionary state, emerging from the ruins of recent turmoil and the traditions of a civilization that stretched back five millennia. The country was 'semi-colonized', having over the years submitted to twenty-seven foreign territorial concessions – one-sided trading deals, which opened up China to the trade and industries of the European powers and America, for little in return. China had been further weakened by the 'Boxer Indemnities' – enormous sums that flowed out of China and into the treasuries of seven European nations and the United States, the countries that had dispatched a joint military force to suppress the nationalist Boxer Rebellion at the turn of the century. China's ruling elites were desperate to modernize the nation and they aimed to do so, in part, through a process of internationalization. By playing some role in the war, China, they hoped, would demonstrate to the great powers of Europe that it was a modern, or at least modernizing, nation, and one worthy of being treated more as a partner. The leading Chinese thus came to regard the outbreak of war in Europe as an opportunity, a chance for China to win a place within what we would today call the 'international community' and, perhaps, take back some of the powers and territories wrested from its control by the foreign concessions.

Among those concessions was Tsingtao in Shandong, territory that in 1898 China had been forced to lease to Germany on unfavourable terms for ninety-nine years. Tsingtao had become the base for the East Asian Squadron of the German navy, which was an important strategic asset and a danger to British naval and merchant shipping in the event of war. In the first months of the war, the Chinese ruling elite, led on this matter by the brilliant and worldly diplomat Liang Shiyi, made two far-sighted calculations. First, they concluded that despite initial German successes it would be the Allied powers that would emerge from the war victorious. Second, they understood that the post-war world would be shaped at the following peace conference – whenever that might come. Only those nations with a seat around the conference table would be in a position to influence the future. Rightly fearful of rising and expansionist Japan, their rapidly modernizing neighbour across the East China Sea, the rulers of China sought a means by which their nation might secure a place at the peace conference and reverse the decline in their status. In

August 1914 Liang Shiyi proposed to the representatives of Britain that China raise an army of 50,000 men, which would then be deployed to assist British forces in expelling the Germans from Tsingtao.[29] This approach was rather brusquely rebuffed by the British, who felt it was not even worth consulting their French and Russian allies on the matter. China's military assistance would not be required, even for operations conducted on Chinese territory. In 1914, China was a military nonentity and financially almost a failed state. Rather, it was to modernized, dynamic Japan – the nation and growing maritime power that had defeated the Russians a decade earlier in the Russo-Japanese War – that the British looked for assistance in East Asia. Honouring its existing pre-war alliance with London, Tokyo declared war on Germany (and later in August, on Austria-Hungary too) and agreed to assist the British in removing the Germans from Tsingtao – but only on the condition that Japan be permitted to take control of the region, and thereby increase its power and influence in China. On 7 November 1914, the German garrison at Tsingtao surrendered to the joint Japanese, British and Indian force that had besieged their base.

In early 1915, the Chinese, still seeking a way to join the ranks of the Allied powers, changed tack and offered to place a Chinese army and a contingent of Chinese labourers under British control, for deployment in Europe. Once again, China's offers of assistance were rebuffed. China's next offer, made in June 1915, was to send to Europe an army of just labourers, men who would fight for China's future interests with spades rather than rifles. Their presence would at least remind the Allied powers of China's place in the world and give a future Chinese delegation some claim to a role in the war at peace talks. This offer of 'Labourers as Soldiers' was taken up by the French, with the first contingent of Chinese leaving China in July 1916 and landing in Marseilles in late August.

The British were still resisting Chinese overtures, partly in response to complaints of the British trades unions, which feared that the arrival of cheap Chinese labour would lower wages in

Britain. But British indifference to the Chinese offers ended abruptly in July 1916, as a result of the sobering statistics generated by the British and French Somme Offensive, launched that month. By the conclusion of the battle in November 1916, British and imperial forces had suffered over 400,000 casualties, almost a quarter of whom had been killed or were listed as missing. The catastrophic scale of the losses shook British confidence. Kitchener's volunteer army had been decimated, though he was not alive to see it.* The new Secretary of State for War, Lloyd George, was overheard saying: 'We are going to lose this war.'[30] After just the first four disastrous weeks on the Somme, the British were faced with not only enormous casualties but also a severe labour shortage. General Haig estimated that the army was in immediate need of 21,000 labourers. On 28 July, the British Army Council finally accepted China's offer of labourers, and recruitment began.

Once again, the same sort of eccentric, racialized thinking that had influenced attitudes towards the British Indian Corps came into play. Convinced that the Chinese population of Canton, near British-administered Hong Kong, were too small of stature and too used to a warm climate to endure conditions in northern France, recruitment was focused on the colder northern Chinese province of Shandong, where it was believed that the local people were both taller and sturdier. At the port of Wei-hai-Wei (modern Weihai) the British established a recruitment depot and an administrative station. It was to here that the agents of the private recruiting firm Forbes and Co. reported. With experience of contracting Chinese indentured labourers for work in the gold mines of South Africa, the agents of Forbes and Co. began to criss-cross the valleys and villages of Shandong, offering young men monthly wages, monthly remittances sent back to their family, a free uniform and a chance to travel. On

* Kitchener was drowned, along with many others, when the ship on which he was travelling on a diplomatic mission to Russia, HMS *Hampshire*, hit a mine off the Orkney Islands on 5 June 1916.

recruitment, each would-be labourer was ordered to strip naked and was then examined by a doctor, who checked him for twenty-one separate, disqualifying medical conditions. If the candidate was approved, he was doused with disinfectant, had his head shaved and his thumb-prints taken by a British police officer, a contingent of which had been specially seconded from Scotland Yard. These records were to be used as a means of later identification. Then, the recruit's serial number and name was stamped onto the metal identification bracelet that was fixed around the man's wrist, to be removed only on his return to China.

The first contingent of the Chinese Labour Corps arrived in France in April 1917. They were administered as a unit of the British Army and were subject to British military law. The headquarters of the corps was in Noyelles-sur-Mer, which in 1917 was conveniently near the principal British Army base and depot at Etaples. It was at Noyelles that the main hospital for the Chinese Labour Corps was also established. The Chinese became specialists in digging trenches, and they were regarded as better and faster trench-diggers than white British workers. With the help of Chinese translators – educated students who accompanied the labourers to the war zones – they adapted to innumerable tasks and became among the most capable labourers available to the British. Captain A. McCormick, whose war memoir records his time with the Chinese Labour Corps, among other regiments, regarded them as men 'capable of enduring great physical exertions'.[31] Another British officer, who witnessed the industry and dynamism of the Chinese, concluded prophetically that 'if China were united, if the Chinese had an idea or an ideal to work, or fight for, she could and probably will conquer the world in any sphere. It is an awe-inspiring thought that the riches and material and brains are now lying fallow in that great country.'[32]

By late 1917, the British Directorate of Labour had come to a similar conclusion in its assessment of the skills and capacities of the Chinese. In 1918, a document was issued entitled *Notes on Chinese Labour to All British Officers Working with the Chinese Labour Corps*. It reminded them that Chinese labourers were among the best workers in the world and men capable of skilled, even spe-cialized, work. The army increasingly demanded 'the intelligent distribution of labour' and warned that 'The Chinese are not ignorant. They have brains. Orders and counter orders and unintelligent distribution of labour ... have a demoralising effect ... and induce them to regard our brains as inferior to their own.'[33] The more effective deployment of the Chinese Labour Corps had begun piecemeal, as local commanders noted their capacities and began to catalogue the trade skills that some of the labourers possessed. The increasing technological nature of the war constantly ratcheted up the demand for skilled labour. The British therefore certified 4,725 Chinese labourers as being highly skilled.[34] These skills were put to use by a wide array of army support and supply units. Company 147 of the Chinese Labour Corps worked in Douai, engaged in the highly special-ized task of artillery maintenance. Others worked at the light-railway workshops, maintaining the narrow-gauge engines and rolling stock that transported shells and ammunition up to the front lines. The Motor Transport Central Workshop at Rouen had been assigned Chinese men to work as labourers, and by the start of 1918 they had effectively taken over the running of one truck repair shop, and were also working in the paint shop and the moulding bay of the attached motorcycle workshop. They had come as labourers but had evolved into mechanics.

Three companies of Chinese labourers were assigned to the Central Tank workshop at Erin. This was the great tank hospital, in which the new weapons were maintained, adapted and repaired. Linked to the front lines by rail, it was here that most tanks spent most of their time. After each engagement they were cleaned, stripped and repaired. It was at Erin that the Chinese truly amazed the British authorities. In the frantic build-up to the Battle of Cambrai in November 1917 – the first mass tank offensive in history – the Chinese Labour Corps worked freneti-cally. A total of 476 machines were prepared for the battle. In addition to maintaining and repairing the tanks, Chinese mechanics built 110 tank-towed sledges, which were used to carry equipment into battle. They also scoured the nearby Crécy Forest for brushwood, which they bound together with chains to create 'fascines', enormous one-ton bundles of wood that the tanks carried with them into attacks and used to in-fill trenches that were to be crossed. Chinese engineers even constructed tubular radiators for the tanks.

Despite such highly valued skills, great efforts were made at Erin and elsewhere to keep the Chinese segregated from other men and from local civilians. At Erin, the Chinese were housed in separate huts, away from the British workers. Even Chinese hospitals, like the one constructed at Noyelles-sur-Mer, from which many of the dead of the cemetery came, were sealed zones, surrounded by eight-feet-high barbed-wire fences, which were patrolled and guarded. The security was intended to keep the Chinese in and prevent contact between them and inquisitive civilians, with the Directorate of Labour requiring that 'entry of all strangers to the camps ... should be strictly forbidden'.[35] Nevertheless, among evidence that the separation was not absolute are some vivid and compelling accounts from the pen of Pastor Van Walleghem in Dikkebus. In August 1917, after having spent three years living near the front lines, Van Walleghem suddenly reverted to the same tone of genuine astonishment that had characterized his diary entries of 1914 and early 1915, when he had first encountered British and French colonial soldiers. On 6 August 1917 he wrote:

> *Quite a lot of Chinese have arrived in the area. They are being put to work by the English. Where these men came from, I have no idea. Nor how they got here. Many of them look very young, little older than our boys of 10 or 11 years of age.*

Recovering his composure – as well as finding again his judgemental tone – Van Walleghem went on to record that:

> *Their favourite activity is to stand staring into shop windows, particularly shops with cake, fruit, sweets, etc. If they see something they*

like, they all rush inside en masse, talking nineteen to the dozen. They are always careful to ask the price, but still always suspect that they are going to be cheated. So suspicious! Many of our shopkeepers have had enough of their antics, so that they sometimes make angry gestures for them to leave. You should see them scamper away: like rats up a drainpipe! They are yellow-skinned, with flat noses and slanted eyes. They always wear the same foolish grin on their lips and are continually looking around at anything and everything. It is a miracle that none of them have yet been knocked down on our busy roads.

In another entry he confidently asserted, despite having had only minimal contact with the Chinese, that they 'have little understanding of what the war is really like. If they hear a shell coming, they simply stop and stare – instead of running for cover. And when it explodes, they all begin laughing and clapping. A number of them have already been killed by shellfire in Poperinghe – leaving their comrades doubly dumbfounded.' The same insouciance in the face of gunfire, when exhibited by men of other races in many war memoirs and newspaper reports, was regarded, by contrast, as evidence of fatalistic courage or trench humour.

As Van Walleghem's diary demonstrates, the Chinese Labour Corps near Ypres in the summer of 1917 was not being effectively segregated, as the authorities had hoped, even though, as the pastor noted, 'they are billeted in camps surrounded by barbed wire' and 'an Englishman is attached to every company, to organize their work'. The pastor's observations about the Chinese take up much of his diary, covering several pages across multiple entries that stretch on into 1918 and even 1919. He came to regard them as hard-working, but was alert to what (to his mind) seemed eccentricities or what we would think of today as minor culture clashes:

They are by no means lazy, and work every bit as well as our own people and the English soldiers. But they make a terrible racket all the time. Whenever they pass you in the street the noise is deafening,

all talking together and each one trying to be the loudest. I prefer
listening to them when they are singing; they are really quite good.
They all know a few strange words of English, but most of them have
trouble speaking them properly. I once passed a group of them shortly
before noon, and they all started shouting 'Watch? Watch?' This
was their way of asking the time. I suspect that their stomachs must
have been rumbling, because when I showed them that there were
only five minutes to go before twelve o'clock, they nodded with plea-
sure – and went off to fill up their bellies with their favourite food:
rice. They don't seem interested in anything else; it's rice for break-
fast, rice for lunch and rice for dinner. And always eaten with those
little wooden sticks of theirs. Not so long ago I came across a
Chinaman who was wearing a watch on both wrists. How proud he
was when he saw that I had noticed!'

As is often the case, Van Walleghem's observations shift from
sympathetic curiosity, at times bordering on admiration, to the
comfort of well-worn racial presumptions a few sentences later:
the Chinese, he abruptly reassures himself in one entry, 'are like
big children and that's the way they need to be treated. To keep
them in order, it is more often necessary to use force than argument.' It was for this reason that:

... their sergeants each carry a thin metal rod, which they sometimes
use to 'tickle' the skin of their charges. Not that this causes any
resentment. The offender smiles in that silly Chinese way – and then
does what he is told. They also have other types of punishment. I
recently passed one of their camps and saw one of them with an ox's
yoke around his neck and another with a large block attached to his
neck by a chain. Weighed down in this manner, they were both
forced to dig a ditch along with their comrades.

As well as offering his own characteristically contradictory opinions, Van Walleghem also charted the changing relationship
between the men of the Chinese Labour Corps and the people of
the villages around Ypres. At its core, that relationship

was a commercial one. It might not be the kind of cross-cultural interaction that is often discussed in the context of a war zone, yet trade, barter and commerce have often been the defining relationship between armies and the local people of the nations in which they fight. It was the shopkeepers and innkeepers of the Ypres region who, in Van Walleghem's account, had the most contact with the Chinese, as with all the international labour contingents, and therefore the most to say about them and their habits. Although soldiers and labourers of many nationalities tended to send a proportion of their wages home to families, many did also have money to spend, and those with some freedom of movement found themselves in a society that abounded with new temptations and unfamiliar products. The Chinese and others were consumers in their new environment, as well as being visitors or workers, and it was the café, the *estaminet* and the shop that became the main arenas of cultural exchange. In November 1917, after the Chinese had been in the area around Dikkebus for four months, Van Walleghem came to the conclusion that:

> *The Chinese are child-like but not stupid. They know the value of the goods they are buying and are not easily cheated. They always look for the best and most beautiful things, and will seldom buy cheap rubbish. They are reliable payers, but love to haggle over the price. The most expensive and most attractive shops are the ones that interest them most, and it is usually in these shops that they make their purchases. I don't know how much they earn, but some of them seem to have plenty of money. They buy a lot of pocket watches and rings. Some of the shopkeepers have even learnt a little Chinese, to try and attract their custom. And it works!*[36]

In the same entry, Van Walleghem reported, with some degree of surprise, the news that:

> *An order has been issued to the Chinese forbidding them to enter shops. Civilians are no longer allowed to sell them anything at all. Nobody knows the reason why. Some people say that the Australians*

have been getting the Chinese drunk in the coffee houses, by slipping
rum into their coffee. Others say that they have been giving away too
much to the women and children, making the men-folk jealous.

In early January 1918, Pastor Van Walleghem wrote of an incredible coincidence, in a story set in a local shop, which suggested
the earlier ordinance had been rescinded. It involved a local
Flemish family, the Duriens, and it hinted at the level of global
interconnectedness that existed in the pre-1914 world:

> *A few days ago the Durien family received a letter from their brother*
> *Florent, who is a missionary in China. A Chinaman just happened*
> *to be in their shop at the moment when the letter arrived and saw*
> *the envelope. With a big smile on his face, he rushed off to tell his*
> *compatriots. Half an hour later another Chinaman came into the*
> *shop and claimed that he had lived for a number of weeks in the*
> *village from which the letter was sent, and that he had also seen the*
> *Catholic priest on a number of occasions. He even began to describe*
> *him, and it was indeed an accurate description of Florent. Wanting*
> *to be certain, the Duriens went to fetch photographs of a number of*
> *the missionaries active in China, and in less than a minute the*
> *Chinaman picked out Florent's picture. Unbelievable – but true!*[37]

Despite charming stories such as this, and the wealth of cultural
observations in his diary, the overall picture Van Walleghem
painted of his environment in the latter two years of war was that
of a military frontier – a violent, all-male, drink-sodden zone, in
which the Chinese were merely one of many ethnic 'tribes' who
were often in conflict with one another. Van Walleghem's diaries,
and other wartime memoirs, describe local communities that
were enormously outnumbered by transient military populations, in which regular outbreaks of violence, between groups of
men who were ostensibly allies, were the norm. This violence
could, and did, have fatal consequences. There are graves in war
cemeteries across Flanders of men killed in bar-room fights, or
in disturbances in camps. Thousands of men, many of whom

were psychologically damaged by the experiences of battle, found themselves living in close proximity and sharing facilities. Despite official attempts at segregation, racial antipathies, national rivalries, regimental pride and personal differences fused with a cocktail of testosterone, alcohol and shell-shock (what we today would diagnose as post-traumatic stress disorder) to create a combustible mix. In late November 1917, Pastor Van Walleghem described 'a riot in one of the Chinese camps near Poperinghe', in which 'An English officer was badly manhandled by the Chinese. English soldiers fired into the crowd, killing three of the rioters. Or that, at least, is what they are saying here.' A month later, he wrote that in some of the camps:

> ... the Chinese are starting to get quite rebellious. Yesterday, they stabbed an English officer. Today, there were 30 of them at Busseboom who refused to work. They just lay on the ground, waiting to be hit. Better a few lashes of the sergeant's rod than a broken skull. I passed by the camp at Verhaeghe's and saw three of them tied with arms wide stretched to the wire of the perimeter fence. One of them also had his legs tied. It can't have been pleasant, particularly in this wintry weather. Today it has been freezing hard.[38]

There were other well-documented accounts of fights between the Chinese and Arab labourers. Some of the Chinese, having never left rural China, had been previously unaware of the full range of physical racial differences and struggled to understand why some of their fellow workers had dark skins. They seem to have adopted skin-colour racism easily, taking a particular dislike to the Moroccans. In one incident, three Arabs were killed in a fight with Chinese. On Christmas Day 1917, a serious incident between the Chinese and troops from New Zealand took place in Reninglest, near Dikkebus, under the eye of Pastor Van Walleghem. The pastor's entry for that day reveals that:

> ... it was the New Zealanders who drank, laughed, whirled, twirled, screamed and shouted the day away. When they were drunk, they

*started making trouble with the Chinese. These Orientals are getting
more and more bitter. They split off into small conspiratorial groups,
and later in the afternoon and evening fights broke out at several
places. What wild men they are! We later learnt that thefts had been
reported at various locations throughout the night.*[39]

The conclusion was dramatic and violent. The British sent troops
to 'the Chink camp' to put down what they described as a mutiny.
Nine Chinese men were wounded when the troops opened fire,
and two were killed. Three Chinese men – Zhang Hongan, Wu
Enlu and Zhang Zhide – who were all involved in the incident
were later executed. They are buried in Westouter British War
Cemetery.[40]

THE WESTERN FRONT, DECEMBER 1917. *The Times* of London
has sent one of its correspondents on a tour through the
zones behind the Western Front. Under the headline 'An Army
of Labour, Workers from Distant Shores', he will present an
extended portrait of life behind the lines. 'All the nations seem
to have their encampments among the rustling copses and damp
green pastures of Picardy and Artois,' he begins, continuing:

*It is strange to drive for an hour or two along the winding roads
past the quiet villages – quieter than ever now, for nearly all the
men are away – and the red-roofed farmsteads and to come suddenly upon a scene that carries you half the world away from the
clouded northern skies and the Channel mists. Perhaps it may be a
group of Punjab coolies sitting on their heels round the thin smoke
of a wood fire on which the chapattis are baking; perhaps a squad
of Chinamen in blue or terra-cotta blouses and flat hats, hauling
logs or loading trucks always with that inscrutable smile of the Far
East upon their smooth yellow faces; perhaps a party of sturdy
negroes or Kaffirs, singing and chattering as they march back from
their work for the midday rest and meal: perhaps some squat and*

swarthy Nagas with their long black hair bunched fantastically above their bullet heads, gazing in childlike wonderment at a train of great Army lorries grinding by ... It is like a cinema show for the village children, who will dream of it, one fancies when they are old, and remember how men came from Asia and Africa to work for France in her dire need under the English.[41]

There are also among the encampments and work sites:

... men of various tribes Zulus from Natal and the Transvaal, Cape Kaffirs, Basutos, Swazis, some Mashona, and others ... Many, perhaps most, have worked under white overseers before in the Natal plantations, on Boer-farms, at the mines, or the Durban docks. They have been enlisted in South Africa by arrangement with the Union Government. And they bring with them their own officers, who understand the native and know how to deal with him.

———— • ————

By this time, almost a year after the sinking of the *Mendi*, thousands of South Africans were labouring in France as part of the South African Native Labour Corps. They came from a nation whose leaders resolutely believed that they and they alone truly knew 'how to deal' with black Africans. The partial breakdown of the barriers of race in the military and industrial areas of France and Belgium that was necessitated by the war vexed men in London and Paris; but nowhere was it looked upon with more apprehension and hostility than in white South Africa. When, in August 1914, news had reached South Africa that Britain had ordered the deployment of an Indian Corps to the Western Front, the *East Rand Express* warned:

If Indians are used against the Germans they will return to India disabused of the respect they should bear for the white race. The empire must uphold the principle that a coloured man must not raise his hand against a white man, if there is not to be any law or order in either India, Africa, or any part of the Empire where the white man rules over a large concourse of coloured people. In South Africa it will mean that Natives will secure pictures of whites chased by coloured men, and who knows what harm such pictures may do.[42]

In the racial climate of South Africa, there was no prospect whatsoever that the Union would permit black South Africans to play an active role in the war. The government in Pretoria planned to limit their involvement to working as cheap labour in support of South Africa's all-white army in its campaigns against the German colonies in Africa. When the deadly mining war began on the Western Front, in which both sides dug tunnels beneath the trenches of the enemy to plant explosives and destroy their positions, it was suggested in London that experienced black South Africans might be brought to France from the gold mines of the Transvaal and their specialized skills put to use. That plan was quickly and comprehensively extinguished by the Union government.[43] By the summer of 1916, when the true scale of Britain's labour shortage in France and Belgium had became apparent, and the British had accepted Chinese offers of labour battalions, the Imperial War Council again suggested that black men from South Africa and other parts of British-ruled Africa be recruited as labourers.

White opposition to the creation of a corps of South African labourers coalesced around a fear that if black men were sent to France they might, through some unseen eventuality or emergency, end up being thrown into battle. Even if this worst-case scenario were avoided, there was still the deeply held concern that the 'kaffir' would return home after the war in military uniform as well as with what one member of the South African Parliament had no compunction in describing as 'ideas above his station'.[44] Nevertheless, General Louis Botha, who was at the time both South Africa's prime minister and Minister for Native Affairs, accepted that the exigencies of war made the labour situation critical; by August 1916, General Haig had increased his estimate of the labour shortfall on the Western Front to sixty-thousand. Botha therefore agreed to London's requests, but with several pre-conditions.

Botha's list of conditions was intended to prevent the labourers from gaining any significant access to European society or developing any delusions that their service and sacrifice would lead to any change or improvement in their material conditions or political status at home. Colonel Pritchard, the South African officer appointed to lead the South African Native Labour Corps, was dispatched to Europe to lay out the requirements of the South African government and the Department of Native Affairs. At a conference of 1916, he demanded that black South Africans 'should be employed elsewhere than in the fighting zone'. On no condition were black South Africans to be permitted to take part in the fighting or receive any military training. Next, he wanted to ensure that all 'Natives should be segregated' and that 'they should be administered in accordance with military law under the Army Act by officers appointed by that Government'. By this he meant that the camps in which the black labourers lived were to be subject to the military law of the South African Army. Pritchard also stipulated that the South African labourers were to be placed under the command of white South Africans. The South African government expressed its unease at the thought of black men being commanded by men who did not 'know the native' and many of the officers themselves were former mine compound managers or officials from the Department of Native Affairs.

Above all, the South Africans demanded that the black labourers be strictly segregated from other labour contingents and especially from white civilians in France and Belgium – and particularly that they have no contact with white women. This fear, that their black subjects might come into contact with French civilians who were not as fixed in their racial views as were almost all white South Africans, emerged in the various official discussions. In late 1916 John X. Merriman, Prime Minister of the Cape Colony before it was merged into the Union of South Africa, warned Jan Smuts, then leading South African forces against

Lettow-Vorbeck's *Askari* in East Africa, that 'some of the wisest and most solid friends of the Union government ... regard the introduction of our Natives to the social conditions of Europe with the greatest alarm'.[45] To allay these concerns, Pritchard demanded that the authorities in France ensure, as far as possible, that the black men be prevented from having any significant encounters with 'the social conditions of Europe' and therefore be spared from the 'dangers of contamination'.

While Merriman and much of the Union government looked upon the deployment with 'alarm', the Department of Native Affairs had a somewhat different view, seeing it as a great social experiment in which new methods of segregation could be field-tested. In 1913, South Africa had passed the Natives Land Act, which restricted where black South Africans could live within their own country, and now the white elites were interested in new methods and systems that would prevent black people from having meaningful contact with whites while at the same time harvesting their labour and keeping them passive, divided and unthreatening. At the heart of the Department of Native Affairs' experiment was the use of 'closed compounds' – special encampments, surrounded by barbed wire and guarded to prevent unauthorized access. These compounds were based on systems of segregation then being pioneered in the South African mining industry. They were now to be transplanted to France and fine-tuned under wartime conditions in the hope that the results could be re-exported and adapted, post-war, back in South Africa.[46]

With these pre-conditions agreed, and the systems of segregation and control in place, recruitment got under way. The British had initially requested a contingent of 10,000 men, which was increased to 40,000 in January 1917 after the initial 10,000 figure had been surpassed. Ultimately, 25,000 men were recruited, of whom 21,000 actually left South Africa. Unaware of what their white countrymen had in store for them, there were men who willingly and enthusiastically volunteered. Stimela Jason Jingoes recalled in his memoirs:

When the first World War broke out, I, as a member of the British Commonwealth, felt deeply involved. The picture that the newspapers drew of men doing battle in trenches in the mud and the cold of France, fascinated and horrified me. I followed closely the progress of the war ... and felt growing in me the conviction that I should go and help in some way.[47]

As with thousands of men from societies across the world in which warrior cultures were strong, Jingoes viewed the First World War through the prism of tradition and tribal culture. Looking back into his own family's past, he asked himself: 'I'm a pure coward! What am I waiting here for? My father fought against the Boers; his older brother was also there and, more to the point, so was his younger brother. Why am I putting these things off then! I must have been born a coward.'[48] However, inspired by newspaper accounts and war propaganda, and following the internal battle with his conscience, Jingoes eventually talked himself into volunteering: 'Why should I hesitate? I must go and die for my country and my King!'

Many of Jingoes' compatriots were less enthusiastic. Recruitment in South Africa was slow, and from the authorities' point of view disappointing. It was hampered by a deep inter-generational mistrust of the white authorities by most black communities. Millions of black South Africans did not share Stimela Jason Jingoes' perception of themselves as citizens of 'the British Commonwealth' and felt little patriotic sentiment for a nation in which they had few rights. The Natives Land Act was deeply resented, and it convinced men who might otherwise have considered volunteering that while they were serving abroad the government would take away their land. In an effort to boost recruitment numbers, men were given false and unofficial promises of land and exemption from the Poll Tax and the Pass Laws – none of which were honoured.[49] There were recruitment rallies across the country, in which it was suggested that service was an opportunity for black men to demonstrate their loyalty to the king. When these calls failed, the government began to heavily pressurize young men into enlisting, through the offices of the chiefs. As with men from elsewhere on the African continent, service was forced upon some South Africans. There was even discussion of creating a prison labour corps, as the British had done in India.[50] Some African leaders, ignorant of the plans of their government, hoped that the venture would be an opportunity for black South Africans to receive an education and to see the world, in what one of them called 'a university of experience'.

The first units of the South African Native Labour Corps arrived in France on 19 February 1917, just two days before the disaster of the *Mendi*. In March 1917, Colonel Pritchard issued all white officers commanding black South Africans with the document *Appendix to Notes for Officers of Labour Companies (South African Native Labour)*. It stated that the compounds housing the South Africans 'should be surrounded by an unclimbable fence or wall, in which all openings are guarded'. The fences around them were to be six feet high – oddly, two feet lower than the fences erected around the camps of the diminutive Chinese labourers. The fences were to be topped with barbed wire 'to prevent the natives climbing over'. It was left to the discretion of officers overseeing camps in areas with large civilian populations as to whether corrugated iron screens should be erected to conceal the Africans from the local people (and vice versa). Once in the closed compounds, the South Africans were not to be allowed beyond the enclosing fence unless they were accompanied by a European officer. And when outside the camps they were prohibited from 'entering or being served with wine, beer, or spirits in any *estaminet* or place where liquor is sold, and prohibited also from entering shops or business premises unless under European escort'. Under 'General Remarks, Section 7', the notes demanded that:

> *Care should be taken to prevent unauthorized persons from entering the Camp or conversing with Natives and especially to prevent all familiarity between Europeans and Natives, as this is subversive to discipline and calculated to impair their efficiency as working units.*

It went on:

> *Under the conditions under which they are living in France, they*
> *(the Natives) are not to be trusted with white women, and any*
> *Native found wandering about without a pass and not under the*
> *escort of a white N.C.O. should be returned to his unit under guard,*
> *or failing this, handed over to the Military Police.*[51]

Lieutenant Colonel Godfrey Godley, who was the second-in-command of the Labour Corps, considered the security arrangements so severe that he thought the camps 'identical in every respect' to those housing German PoWs 'except that as regards locality those occupied by the prisoners are in the majority of cases more favorably situated'.[52] The conditions under which the Labour Corps lived and worked was ultimately not a form of military service but something closer to penal servitude, which even risked seriously undermining their value as war workers. Whenever they were required to move to a new area, there was a delay before they could be deployed while the closed compounds were constructed to receive them, almost as if they were a group of men contaminated with some communicable disease.

A British charity, the Aboriginal Protection Society, which had been born out of the Abolition movement of the eighteenth and nineteenth centuries, did its best to supply the black South Africans with some small comforts; but they did so while accepting that the compound system was necessary.[53] The Germans, for their part, made the camps military targets. Aware that deaths of South Africans would further limit recruitment at home, air raids against them were launched. Stimela Jason Jingoes, who experienced a raid on the camp at Dieppe in 1917, reported that in addition to bombs the Germans had dropped leaflets, the text of which (purportedly by the Kaiser) read: 'in this war I hate black people the most. I do not know what they want in this European war. Where I find them, I will smash them.'[54] The violence came not just from the air, and not just from the Germans; in July 1917 four members of the South African Native Labour Corps were shot dead and eleven others wounded when British troops opened fire during the South Africans' attempt to free a comrade who had been arrested.

Even when at work in the docks or warehouses, other, more subtle methods were used by the South African authorities to devalue and diminish the black men they had transported to France. The offer of a free uniform had been one of the supposed attractions to lure men into service.[55] But the uniforms issued to the Labour Corps were deliberately of the very lowest quality. A dull brown in colour and made from shoddy materials, they had been designed to distinguish the South Africans from other labour units and mark them out as men of low status and limited worth. There were no marks or regimental insignia, and rather than a peaked cap the men were given a floppy bush hat. There was nothing about their uniform that could induce in a man much of a sense of pride in his unit or make him believe that his service was valued. The white overseers, by contrast, were given standard South African Army uniforms; the inferior kit was issued exclusively to black men.

If they had happened to have read 'An Army of Labour, Workers from Distant Shores' in *The Times* in December 1917, Botha, Merriman, Smuts and their colleagues would have been extremely satisfied by the account. The black South Africans were being put to good work and were commanded by a white officer who believed he 'knew the native' and was the very embodiment of South African racial attitudes in the early twentieth century. As the reporter explained, the camp commandant:

> ... *himself is an Afrikaner, a landowner and politician, who has strong views on many subjects and expresses them with energy. I ask him whether the South African native can be relied upon for steady labour. He repels the implied suggestion with warmth. 'I come from a country where we know what work means,' he tells me. 'There is no slacking or shirking with us. The South African native has great physical strength, and he does not spare it when he is labouring. Send some of your trades union delegates here: it will open their eyes and do them good.'*[56]

Although there were breakdowns in South Africa's programme of racial containment – much to the frustration of the South African authorities – the men of the South African Native Labour Corps were largely prevented from taking part in the enormous mixing of peoples that took place on the Western Front. Lieutenant Colonel Godley had to accept that the South Africans under his command were being forced to live indefinitely under conditions 'which are unique, as all other units in France, both white and black, are free to move about'. The freedoms available to other groups of soldiers and labourers – the right to enter shops, buy local goods, taste new foods, meet the children, learn smatterings of French and Flemish-Dutch, take part in celebrations – were denied the South Africans. They were the second-class citizens of a racial state that, after the First World War, was to perfect even more efficient systems of exploitation and separation, and expand these systems into new territory in Africa seized from the defeated Germans.

If the Western Front was – looked at in one way – a great experiment in multi-ethnic, multiracial and multinational cohabitation, it was also a testbed of human segregation too.

CHAPTER 8

'WHAT ARE YOU DOING OVER HERE?

Siam, segregation and the Harlem Hellfighters

BANGKOK, 22 JULY 1917. In the dark, early hours of the day units of the police, along with men from the army and navy of the Kingdom of Siam, fan out across the capital Bangkok. They make for pre-arranged rendezvous points and specific addresses. At the city's docks, navy launches head out across the water and disappear into the gloom. Around the newly built railway line leading to the north, soldiers assemble and prepare for action. Each unit follows a detailed plan of operations, the product of eight weeks of preparation, during which time many of the key targets have been kept under constant observation, their movements monitored and recorded. The first mission of the day is undertaken not by soldiers or sailors but by diplomats, who arrive at two foreign legations and hand over documents that contain declarations of war by the Kingdom of Siam against the governments of Germany and Austria-Hungary. Then police and army units begin arresting German and Austrian nationals living in the country, while at the Ministry of Local Government Siam's officials stand by telephones awaiting news of the operations.[1] In the docks, the navy launches appear out of the darkness and slip silently alongside German-owned merchant ships. Siamese sailors use specially built boarding ladders to clamber onto the decks of the German ships, where they seize control of the vessels and arrest their crews. The crews of three German ships have time to damage their vessels, setting small fires – but those are quickly extinguished and the crews taken into custody. On the German-built railway at Koon Tan there are more arrests. Overwhelmed by the Siamese officials, none of the German administrators or engineers has the opportunity to sabotage the lines or the engines, or a vulnerable railway tunnel. The *Straits Times* of Singapore, published a few days later, refers to 'a considerable body of troops' sent north to protect the rail line.[2] The magazine *The Far East*, published in Tokyo, will compliment the Siamese on the 'business-like efficiency' with which they have undertaken a task that other nations have bungled. Everything, it states, has been 'accomplished without causing the least trouble or inconvenience to the general public, who simply woke up from their sleep and saw victory already attained'.[3]

At 7am that same morning, as the round-up of enemy nationals takes place and the German ships are seized, just a few miles away Siam's King Vajiravudh, known also as Rama VI, stands within the white walls of the royal palace wearing the ceremonial red 'victory dress'. In anticipation of the special ceremonies about to take place on this auspicious day, the king carries the sword of King Naresuan, Siam's fearsome sixteenth-century warrior king, and in the early-morning light he and his entourage enter Wat Phra Kaew, the Temple of the Emerald Buddha. Candles are lit and offerings are made to the ancient and exquisite jade figurine, who sits serenely under his ornate pagoda within Wat Phra Kaew. After these offerings, the king proceeds to the royal plaza. There he approaches a tree, specially planted for the day's events and intended to represent Germany – Siam's new enemy. First, the tree is ceremoniously 'disgraced'. This is achieved by dousing it in water, in which the king's feet have recently been washed. With the tree now suitably admonished, King Rama then orders it to be felled, its demise symbolizing the impending fall of Germany.

Siam in 1917 was not a colonial territory of any European power but rather an independent Asian kingdom. Its king – educated at Oxford and Sandhurst – was ambitious, forward-thinking and, when necessary, Machiavellian. He alone had the right to declare war, and he chose which side in the war Siam would take; he also drafted the declaration that was delivered to the German and Austrian governments. Having made the decision to join the Allied powers, Rama VI had used his enormous popularity to convince his people of the wisdom of abandoning neutrality. In newspaper articles the revered monarch had informed the Siamese that their nation had no choice but to turn against Germany, a nation the king assured his people was 'the enemy of the world' and a 'ferocious giant' that was inflicting 'injuries and atrocities' upon all civilized nations.[4] The British and French gladly welcomed Siam, a country on which they had, in the past, foisted much-resented extra-territorial treaties. *The Spectator* in London approved of Britain's new ally, warning that German involvement in the country meant that 'Siam would have become the most convenient of bases for intrigue in South-Eastern Asia, and for the dissemination of discontent and sedition in the British and French Colonies.'[5]

King Rama's denouncement of Germany was so emphatic, and his decision to enter the war so popular, that when the call went out for volunteers to serve in a Siamese Expeditionary Force the rush of applicants outnumbered the places available. The Expeditionary Force was intended to 'make a bit of a show' on the Western Front. With only limited resources, the king and his advisers calculated that the best way to maximize the diplomatic and political impact of their forces was to dispatch highly trained specialists rather than an army of peasant labourers as China had been forced to do. The small but select Siamese Expeditionary Force therefore consisted of 950 qualified pilots, engineers, ambulance drivers and other medical personnel, including surgeons. Led by a Siamese general, they were sent to France under great fanfare in 1918, arriving in June. They were the subject of constantly positive reports in the French press regarding their discipline and behaviour; two Siamese officers were even recommended for the *Croix de Guerre*. Nineteen of their number were killed in the war.

Unlike weak and foreign-dominated China, independent Siam had largely avoided foreign incursions in its history. Although the target of a series of unfair treaties, Siam had escaped the indignities that had been piled upon its giant neighbour to the north. Throughout their short involvement in the First World War, the Siamese made every effort to guarantee that their army of specialists was not confused with the mere colonial conscripts of French Indochina or the contract labourers sent by China. In France, Siamese officials were on hand to ensure that the Expeditionary Force was accorded all rights and respect due to the soldiers of a sovereign allied nation. The Siamese were alert to the subtleties of procedure and diplomacy and were determined to be treated as an equal partner within the Entente. By 1917, both Siam's king and the country's increasingly Westernized political class had come to the same realization as had been reached in 1914 by the leaders of Republican China: that the post-war world would be shaped only by those nations able to win a place at any peace conference. Rama VI and his government set out to use the contribution of the Siamese Expeditionary Force as a means of guaranteeing that place. To this end, Rama VI's government even redesigned the national flag. The old *Thong Chang Puak,* the 'Elephant Banner' consisting of a white elephant on a red background – a depiction of the sacred albino elephants kept for centuries by the kings of Siam within their royal palaces in Bangkok – was, in 1917, replaced with the *Thong Trairong,* Siamese for 'Tricolour'.* This new red, white and blue flag, which remains the banner of modern Thailand, is said to have been specifically

---

* The elephants were (and are) traditional symbols of the kings' wealth and power, and it is from the extremely rare, costly and burdensome animals that the term 'white elephant' evolved. The current King of Thailand, King Bhumibol Adulyadej, has eleven of them. The most 'eminent' is a bull named Phra Sawet Adulyadej Phahnon, who resides at the Klai Kangwon Palace.

designed to sit well alongside the red, white and blue of the French *Tricouleur*, the British Union flag and the US Stars and Stripes, as if its designers could already envisage it fluttering outside the Palace of Versailles.

In 1917 Siam was not the only nation whose leaders made the calculation that it was in their interests to join the war and set themselves alongside the Allies. In the months before the collapse of Russia, the First World War spread to its maximum extent in respect of the number of nations involved. In April, both Cuba and Panama declared war on Germany, followed in August by Liberia, one of the only two non-colonized nations in Africa. In October 1917, Uruguay and Peru broke off diplomatic relations with Germany, and Brazil declared war. The Brazilians, outraged at the sinking of their merchant ships by German U-boats, sent a military mission to France to pave the way for a Brazilian Expeditionary Force, though the end of hostilities meant that only a handful of Brazilians actually saw action on the Western Front. In August 1917 China finally abandoned its neutrality and joined the Allies, a move that gave the British and French an excuse to deploy the Chinese Labour Corps in more dangerous zones that when they were merely the labourers of a neutral nation. Far more significant than all these declarations of war, however, was the one that set the trend on 6 April 1917 and which would transform the balance of power decisively in the Allies' favour: the US declaration of war.

Those in Berlin who quaked at the news of America's entry into the war did so not out of immediate fear of the US Army – diminutive as it was in April 1917 – but in the knowledge of the awesome potential that was contained within that most dynamic and industrious of nations. War against the United States was war against a country built on a continental scale, a land of 100 million people (greater in population than France and Britain combined) and already a superpower in industrial, if not yet military, terms. The bulk of America's people – from the old established East Coast families to the recent immigrants clustered in the great cities of the Midwest – had been drawn from all over Europe, in addition to which there were 9 million African Americans, most of them still in the South, and the remnants of the long-abused indigenous Native American 'Indians'. The mobilization of these varied peoples would involve the transplantation onto French (and ultimately German) soil of these human and material manifestations of American power.

But US mobilization would bring something else, too, in the shape of the complex, sophisticated, hypocritical and violent institution that was American racism. Although fighting in a global, multiracial war, the United States was to remain at all times committed to the principle that its own multiracial army would serve and fight in firm accordance with the prevailing racial attitudes at home. At the core of this was white America's determination that its African-American citizens would not be permitted to gain from their experiences of war and military service any new skills, status or achievements that would alter their lowly status at home. There is perhaps no aspect of the First World War that more clearly demonstrates the gulfs that existed between the Allies when it came to race and the treatment of their non-white citizens and subjects.

★

In the years 1917 and 1918, African Americans were approaching the deepest point in the dark valley of betrayal, terror and oppression that characterized the century between the Civil War of the 1860s and the Civil Rights Movement of the 1960s. By coming to the aid of Britain and France, the United States brought to Europe its own 'huddled masses', the 200,000 African Americans who served in the ranks of the quickly expanded army and who were 'yearning to breathe free' every bit as much as the white Europeans who had abandoned the old continent in previous decades. For these black soldiers it was, though, the Old World – the continent from which America's white immigrants had fled – that offered them the liberty, brotherhood and equality that was denied to them at home. After the war, the black writer and philosopher W.E.B. Du Bois claimed that for the African-American soldiers that 'taste of real democracy and old-world culture, was revolu-tionizing'.[6] Yet what is perhaps most striking about the US Army during the First World War is how effective it was at ensuring that most African Americans were not given access to the revolution-izing freedoms on offer in Europe. Despite their courageous service and endless labour, they ended the war as firmly in the grip of American racism and segregation as they had been in 1914. In some respects, the war even made the position of African Americans *more* precarious and exposed them to even greater violence and abuse.

When President Woodrow Wilson addressed a joint session of Congress on 2 April 1917, calling for the declaration of war, he proclaimed that the United States was not pursuing any self-interest but rather ensuring that the world 'be made safe for democracy'. It was a phrase that chimed with the aspirations and ideals of the peoples of Britain and France, but which largely rang hollow in the black quarters of the Northern US cities and in the farmsteads and shacks of the Deep South. The ultimate status of African Americans in the pre-war nation was summed up in the pithy condemnatory assessment of Archibald Grimke, a black activist and minister at a Presbyterian church in Washington, DC. In the United States, he bemoaned:

Men of darker hue have no rights which white men are bound to respect. And it is this narrow, contracted, contemptible un-democratic idea of democracy that we have been fighting to make the world safe for, if we have been fighting to make it safe for democracy at all.[7]

The editors of *The Messenger*, which was the publication of the civil-rights campaigner A. Philip Randolph, argued that African Americans 'would rather fight to make Georgia safe for the Negro' than follow the injunctions of the white and black elites that they should spill their blood in order to make the world safe for democracy.[8] Even the *New York Times*, in July 1917, made a similar point, warning that America's politicians 'are saying a great deal about democracy in Washington now, but while they are talking about fighting for freedom and the Stars and Stripes, here at home the whites apply the torch to the black man's homes, and bullets, clubs, and stones to their bodies'.[9]

For African Americans, the United States of 1917 was two nations: North and South. By almost every indicator and measurable statistic, African Americans were better off in the North than in the South – better educated, better nourished, better employed and better treated. In the North there was a black, professional middle class. To fight against their oppression, African Americans in the North had formed civil-rights organizations such as the National Association for the Advancement of Colored People and the Universal Negro Improvement Association. There was a black press and a black publishing infrastructure, run by a journalistic elite dedicated to fight for progress and against racism. The cautionary refrain of much of the African-American middle class and some of journalistic elite was 'patience'. Gauging the depth and shocking ferocity of white racism, campaigners – both black and white – concluded that if change were ever to come about, it would take generations, perhaps centuries, and it would only ever be granted, it could never demanded or seized. Even among many of the white liberals who supported black calls for enhanced civil rights, the doctrine of black inferiority was largely accepted. The supposed racial characteristics of African Americans, which had been loaded on to the shoulders of black people by centuries of slavery and racial theory, asserted that they were a people of low intelligence, perhaps irredeemably so. African-American men and women were supposedly innately lazy and lacking in moral courage. According to such views, both sexes harboured a predilection towards crime, and the men in particular were overly sexual and uncontrollably desirous of white women. The modish Social Darwinian pseudo-sciences of racial eugenics, racial anthropology, phrenology and craniology all jostled to add their own patina of scientific legitimacy to long-standing racial theories (and assumptions).

The visceral expression of American racism was lynching, the nation's blood ritual. It was as barbaric as anything that ever took place in Rome's Colosseum. Neither the Democratic nor Republican party, nor President Wilson (who depended upon the votes of racist Southern Democrats), had the political will to control the lynch mobs. The practice was even given a boost by the burgeoning film industry in 1915, when D.W. Griffiths' *Birth of a Nation* was released, a distorted and toxic retelling of the Civil War and the Reconstruction era that followed.[*] In 1916, fifty-four African Americans were lynched. In 1917, the year in which the United States began to conscript black men into the army, seventy African Americans were killed – mostly men, but some women too. The induction of African Americans into the army seemed to have the effect of fanning the flames of racial violence. The killings became more frequent, even in the North, but also more sadistic, even ritualized. African Americans in 1917 were lynched for talking to white women, for walking along the sidewalk, or for attempting to save other men from the mobs; black men were killed on the streets of St Louis, Chicago and New York. The events in St Louis escalated into a widespread and horrific killing spree. In photographs taken of those frenzied killings, the euphoria on the faces of the murderers and onlookers is as horrifying as the mutilated and burned black bodies around which the crowds huddle. Some photographs were even transformed into an ugly but booming trade in postcards – until they were eventually banned by the Post Master General.[10]

From the depths of their dark valley, African Americans had little interest in the war in Europe. Among Northern black communities, who had had access to education and a free press,

---

[*] *Birth of a Nation* portrayed the South's brief period of attempted racial integration as an abomination and depicted a white population saved from black barbarism by the Ku Klux Klan. The film inspired a great upsurge in Klan membership, which in turn led to a spike in the numbers of African Americans assaulted. In some towns where the film was shown, white men formed impromptu gangs and prowled the streets looking for black victims.

there was a natural wave of sympathy for France, a nation known to be significantly more racially tolerant than the United States. Yet that sympathy was not potent enough to induce within African Americans a feeling that the war, or the plight of France, was their affair – any more than white Americans felt any great compulsion to rush *en masse* to the defence of Britain. There was stronger support for the view that if the United States were to enter the war, then African Americans should show themselves willing to take part in the conflict and be permitted to take part by the white authorities on equal terms with white men. If America were to go to war, black men wanted the chance to fight, as their fathers and grandfathers had done in the last years of the Civil War. This was understood to be in the interests of 'the race' as much as in interests of the nation.

During the Civil War the abolitionist and former slave Frederick Douglass had prophesied: 'Once let the black man get upon his person the brass letter, U.S., let him get an eagle on his button, and a musket on his shoulder and bullets in his pocket, there is no power on earth that can deny that he has earned the right to citizenship.'[11] Half a century later, Douglass had been proved tragically over-optimistic. African Americans were supposedly full citizens of the United States, yet they found themselves in the same quandary as colonial subjects in the empires of Britain and France. In 1917 the leaders and opinion-formers of black America made the same calculation that had been agreed by the political elites of the British Raj in 1914: that service in war could be used as a lever with which to prise some concessions and liberties out of their white rulers' hands, after victory had been achieved. Loyalty now would earn sympathy later. As with the Indian political class of 1914 and Frederick Douglass in the 1860s, the black political class of Wilsonian America disastrously under-estimated the determination of a white elite to maintain racial order and keep dark-skinned peoples in their place. If there is a significant difference between the position of Indian soldiers in the British Army and African Americans in the US Army during the First World War it is that while the British were compelled, for reasons of propaganda and military expediency, to temporarily lower some of the barriers of race within which their empire was run, the Americans chose instead to attempt to export to Europe, virtually wholesale, their racial laws and the apparatus and institutions that enforced them.

★

After US entry into the war, it was clear that if Germany were to win the conflict, the final opportunity to do so would be in 1918. By 1919, the balance of military power on the Western Front, combined with the metastasizing German cancers of hunger and defeatism, would threaten to overwhelm both the German people and their army. In the first weeks of 1918, the German High Command under General Ludendorff, the conqueror of Russia, finalized plans for a last great attack against the British and French in the west. The preparations for the German Spring Offensive of 1918 represented the final stages of a race, a sprint to the finish-line with Germany scrambling to defeat the British and the French before America could arm and train a vast conscript army and deploy it on the battlefields. There was a window of opportunity, because in its own race to deploy an American Expeditionary Force large enough to shift the balance of power, the United States had to begin from virtually a standing start.

The US Army of 1917 was small and technologically backward. At around 100,000 men, it ranked seventeenth in the world. In terms of equipment it was in some respects a generation behind the armies of Europe. It had a modern and effective service weapon in the shape of the Springfield rifle, and the early American adoption of light machine guns counted as a blessing; but the army's artillery consisted largely of museum pieces. America had around 200 mainly obsolete aircraft, and no American tank was to appear on the battlefield – or even on the drawing board until after the war. The United States had not known a mass conscript army since the demobilization of the Union Army in 1865, and beyond the nation's tiny army and the National Guard the only military formations were the various state militias. The transformation of this army of 1917 into the force that was 2 million-strong and which would march across the frontiers of Germany in the last weeks of 1918 was an enormous and astonishing undertaking.

The Selective Service Act, America's draft law, was passed in May 1917. It required the registration of all US males aged between 21 and 30, of all races. During the Civil War, 180,000 free African Americans, most of them recently emancipated slaves, had followed Frederick Douglass's injunction and served in the blue uniforms of the Union Army. There had even been a small number of black men who had fought with the Confederacy. As recently as 1898, African-American troops had fought in the Cuban War (against Spanish colonial control). In the first years of the twentieth century, they had performed a role not dissimilar to that of the sepoys of British India and the *Tirailleurs Sénégalais* of French Africa. Two African-American regiments had, for example, been sent to the Philippines in 1900 to put down a revolt against US rule. During that war against the Philippine *Insurectos*, the US Army had concluded that African-American troops were especially suited to the tropical conditions of the Philippines and would be immune to the tropical diseases of the region.* In 1917, despite having received little in return, African Americans could point to their long history of military service as a glorious chapter of the black experience, a source of pride and a record cited in the continuing demands for full citizenship.

Despite the long history of black service, the army authorities of 1917 had concluded that all but a very small proportion of African-American men lacked not just the raw intellect needed to make them effective combat troops, but also the moral qualities of stamina, courage, industry and fortitude that were required of men at war. This reflected a general belief in white America that African Americans were lacking in intelligence, which became a

* The *Insurectos* produced propaganda leaflets and posters that reminded the African Americans who were fighting of the oppression they faced at home, and which encouraged them to reject the orders of the 'white masters' who had instructed them to oppress another 'people of colour'.

justification for providing them with a low standard of education. The predictable result was that white children far outperformed black children in educational achievement, a fact that was, in turn, cited as evidence of African Americans' lower intelligence. It was a self-fulfilling prophecy. In 1917 the US Army entered the war in the belief that modern warfare had become so technological as to be beyond the capacity of most African Americans.

In May 1918, Colonel E.D. Anderson, Chairman of the Operations Branch of the US General Staff, wrote a plan for the deployment of 'colored' men who had been, and who would later be, inducted into the army. While Anderson was confident that 'those colored men of the best physical stamina, highest education and mental development, the cream of the colored draft, will make first class fighting troops', he devoted the bulk of his attention to those who would be left behind, 'after this cream has been skinned off'.[12] Confident that it was appropriate for black men to be drafted into the US Army on similar terms to whites, he warned that:

> ... *a large percentage of colored men [are] of the ignorant illiterate day laborer class. These men have not, in a large percent of cases, the physical stamina to withstand the hardships and the exposure of hard field service, especially the damp cold winters of France. The poorer class of backwoods negro has not the mental stamina and the moral sturdiness to put him in the line against opposing German troops who consist of men of high average education and thoroughly trained. The enemy is constantly looking for a weak place in the line and if he can find a part of the line held by troops composed of culls of the colored race, all he has to do is concentrate on that, break through and then he will be in the rear... .*[13]

In order to substantiate his conclusions, Anderson cited examples of other non-white soldiers serving in Allied armies. Distorting recent history and ignoring all evidence to the contrary, he looked at the record of the British Indian Corps in 1914 and 1915. Despite the fact that these men had helped halt the

German advance at the First Battle of Ypres, faced the newly invented horrors of gas warfare at the Second Battle of Ypres, and participated in the highly complex, well coordinated and (to begin with) successful Battle of Neuve Chapelle, US military authorities concluded that they had failed, because 'colored troops could not stand the nervous strain of trench warfare'. Since American racism (like British racism) regarded Indians as being a people who occupied a higher position on the hierarchy of the races than men of African decent, their presumed failures bode ill for African Americans. If Indians had supposedly struggled on the Western Front, African Americans would – the logic went – fare even worse. Offering a similarly un-nuanced and cursory assessment of the performance of the *Tirailleurs Sénégalais*, Anderson claimed – wrongly – that 'The French had to remove their colored Senegalese troops.' Arguing that non-white troops had broken under pressure, Anderson also claimed that black officers in the French Army were not trusted by the French authorities. While there was a great deal of racism in the French Army, and significant resistance in some quarters to the appointment of black officers, by 1918 there were innumerable examples of black men and officers who had amply demonstrated their abilities and won decorations for their service.*

★

Throughout his long document, Colonel Anderson never argued that black men should be kept out of the army; rather, that once drafted they should be found roles that suited their supposedly limited intellects and in which their purported moral failings would not be an issue. However, almost immediately the reality

* Emmett Scott, the African-American civil-rights campaigner and educator, claimed in his history of the war that French officers fighting with African Americans regarded them as 'entirely different from their own African troops and the Indian troops of the British, who are so excitable under shell fire. Of course, I have explained that my boys are public school boys ... accustomed to the terrible noises of the subway, elevated and street traffic of New York City (which would drive any desert man or Himalaya mountaineer mad) and [they] are all Christians.'

of hundreds of thousands of African Americans being drawn into the army aroused deep hostility in sections of the white American press and public, especially in the South where the idea of black men being trained in the use of firearms, and perhaps made more confident and assertive by the experience of having served their nation, clashed with Southern ambitions to keep them subservient.

It was decided by the army authorities that black and white recruits were to be trained at the same camps. This was not because the army sought to break down the barriers between the races but because its proposals for two black-only training bases in the South were rejected, as it was felt by some that large numbers of militarily trained African Americans concentrated in two camps would constitute a national-security risk. To mollify such fears, it was felt that a preponderance of white troops at every base – at least two white recruits to every black recruit – would reassure concerned white civilians. Nevertheless, when black recruits were housed in army bases near centres of white population there was often uproar, despite the presence of larger numbers of white recruits on the same bases. In various states, such bases led to a tightening of segregation and sporadic out-bursts of exemplary violence and persecution. There was especial hostility to the idea of African Americans from the North being brought to the South for training, as this risked introducing into the Southern states black men who were less cowed and terror-ized by white violence. The fear that these Northern men would contaminate their Southern brothers with progressive, big-city ideas inspired local campaigns to have black regiments relo-cated; on occasion these campaigns were successful. The infamous Mississippi Senator James K. Vardaman, one of the most vocal defenders of lynching, called for all African-American troops to be trained only in the North, despite the fact that most of the recruits actually came from the South. Secretary of War Newton D. Baker rejected Vardaman's demands.

Although black and white were housed on the same bases, they were formed into separate regiments and allotted segregated facilities. Even the trains carrying men to their bases were segregated. While facilities were separate, they were almost never equal. Many African-American recruits lived under appalling conditions; some were housed under canvas and lived without even the most basic equipment, much of which had been prioritized for white recruits. In some camps in the South, African-American recruits became little more than conscripted work gangs, used to perform manual labour and receiving little actual training. There were even incidents in which African Americans were leased by the army to Southern landowners as cheap labour. All that distinguished these unfortunate soldiers from convicts was the absence of chains. But the other symbol of the chain gang – the whip – was a different matter. There were reports of white non-commissioned officers carrying whips and other weapons. Some NCOs had replied to army advertisements looking for white men to take charge of black labour units and who were explicitly 'Experienced in the Handling of Colored Men'.[14] There is further evidence that some NCOs brought the wider, brutal culture of the chain gang into their methods of supervision, including two reports of deaths at their hands and numerous accounts of violence and threats being used to compel black soldiers to work. The African-American recruits themselves were quick to recognize their plight as being little different from that of convict labour gangs on the infamous state farms.

The assignment of African-American recruits to labour duties in the training camps was an early indication of what the army had in mind for most – if not all – of them. Colonel Anderson, in his report of May 1918, was able to reassure nervous white civilians that the recruits were, after all, without black officers and were ultimately, in Anderson's words, 'little more than labourers in uniform'.[15] By attaching an African-American labour battalion to each divisional camp, the labour duties that would unavoidably arise could be done by what Anderson described as 'the ignorant and diseased negroes not suited for service overseas'. This would mean that 'the white combatant troops would be released for constant intensive training'. As the army had no intention of allowing most African Americans anywhere near the battlefields, and as it planned that a large proportion of them would not even be sent overseas, the health criteria for those answering the draft were lowered. African Americans who appeared at their draft boards physically frail, or even mentally ill, and who would have been rejected had they been white, were passed fit for service – fit enough to become labourers under the white NCOs. It was Anderson again who best explained the logic behind this decision. 'In these days of conservation,' he wrote:

> ... *when every rag and bone and tin can is saved, human beings cannot be wasted. These colored men have to be inducted into the service by draft in their turn and it is believed that they ought to be put right to work at useful work which will be of real assistance to the United States in prosecuting the war, and will release men available for other service.*

The result was that around 170,000 of the African Americans drafted into the US Army in 1917 and 1918 never left the United States. They remained on labour duties, in camps, ports and depots across the country.

★

It was the policy of the US Army, wrote Colonel Anderson 'to select those colored men of the best physical stamina, highest education and mental development for the combatant troops'. There was, Anderson concluded, 'every reason to believe that these specially selected men, the cream of the colored draft, will make first-class fighting troops'. The training of this small proportion for possible combat duties became, in large part, a case study in the ingenious sophistication of American racism in the early twentieth century. Although treatment varied from base to base, and state to state, many recruits – especially those who had been put forward for training as officers – received selective and inadequate training. Often, the elements of their training that were left out were those that involved instruction in the use of firearms. For African Americans, there was always a crippling lack of equipment too, a failure of supply far more acute than anything affecting white units. Furthermore, the kits they were issued with were often defunct and the weapons of antiquated patterns, different to those used in service. Some men were assigned to roles and specialisms for which they had not been properly prepared. A whole catalogue of administrative failings and procedural lapses undermined the training and deployment of African Americans, and so great were they that they smacked not of instructional inefficacy but, at times, of something closer to deliberate sabotage. And again, prophesies fulfilled themselves. Convinced that African Americans lacked the intellect to perform as artillery officers, for example, the army provided the few recruits put forward for those roles with inadequate training – which produced men insufficiently competent to perform their roles fully, thus satisfying the army that its initial assessment had been correct.

The first transport ships taking US forces to Europe landed in June 1917, and on board were African-American troops. These early arrivals, like the 160,000 African Americans who were to come later, were channelled into the Services of Supply (SOS), the labour corps of the US Army. African Americans made up one-third of the SOS, even though they represented less than 10 per cent of all draftees. For these men, many of whom had been animated by a genuine sense of patriotism, being consigned to the Services of Supply was a profound humiliation – as it had been for the men from the British Caribbean islands who had been similarly deployed. Men who had dreamed of fighting for their nation or who had felt inspired by President Wilson's evocation of a world 'safe for democracy' found themselves in a branch of army service that, although of critical importance, was routinely the butt of jokes. A song sung by US troops mocked the men of the SOS and the pretentions of the families of SOS members who had the audacity to fly flags from their homes proclaiming their sons were in military service. The most hurtful line ran: 'O mother, take down your service flag, Your son's in the SOS.'[16]

Just as during their time in the training camps back home, the African Americans of the SOS were assigned the most basic tented accommodation and a motley array of clothing. Among the many things they had in common with the men of the South African Native Labour Corps – in addition to poor accommodation, lack of basic freedoms and respect – was that the uniforms allotted to many of them were poor-quality cast-offs. They wore fatigues, basic overalls, or uniforms not good enough for the combat troops. And the United States was so ill-prepared for war in the summer of 1917 that some of the early African-American units were kitted out in old Union 'Blues' – Civil War-era uniforms, dug out of the stores by an enterprising quartermaster. The men who wore those uniforms, the sons and grandsons of slaves, went off to war in the uniforms of the army that had won their emancipation.

Within the SOS, African Americans worked in engineering parties, building depots and warehouses. They laboured on the railways, felled trees, built and repaired roads and worked as quarrymen. As with the Chinese labourers, they were also assigned the grimmest of all jobs. Those working in 'Graves Registration' were often involved in disinterring putrefying bodies from shallow battlefield graves. They would then record the details and re-inter the bodies. Also in common with the Chinese (who were now working for the Americans, as well as for the British and the French), many African Americans of the SOS worked within enemy artillery range: though reduced to the status of labours, they were not exempt from the dangers of the war. At Camp Romagne, near Verdun, 9,000 African Americans working in Graves Registration found the combination of such harrowing work and the open discrimination they faced too much to bear. Two African-American YMCA workers reported that members of the Knights of Columbus Catholic organization erected a tent at the camp on which they placed:

> ... *a sign to keep colored soldiers away. The colored soldiers, heart-sore because they ... alone be forced to do this terrible task of moving the dead from where they had been temporarily buried to a*

permanent resting place, immediately resented the outrage and
razed the tent to the ground. The officers became frightened lest there
should be mutiny, [and] mounted a machine gun to keep order.[17]

Many thousands of African Americans spent the war in the US
supply ports of Brest, Bordeaux and St Nazaire. There, they worked
around the clock in a never-ending rota of shifts to unload the
armada of ships that arrived daily, as youthful America infused the
old continent with its lifeblood and industrial energy. Hundreds
of tons of war materials and supplies were unloaded each day. On
some days the totals ran into thousands of tons or even tens of
thousands. The men worked sixteen-hour days, in all weathers,
and without even gloves to protect their hands. German PoWs,
who were also made to work in the docks, considered the black
stevedores as 'slaves', and noted that they were made to work when
conditions were deemed too extreme even for the prisoners.[18] The
enormous logistical struggle at St Nazaire – to unload cargoes as
well as to land, process and dispatch vast numbers of men with all
the supplies, weapons and equipment of war – was described by
one American writer as 'the battle of St Nazaire'.

There was, however, another war fought in the docks and
warehouses of St Nazaire. Nine-thousand African-American stevedores of the SOS lived and worked in the port and the network
of encampments that surrounded it. There, they became the
target of a campaign of violence, abuse and even murder by the
port's Military Police. After the war, evidence of what took place
was given to the US Congress. A white soldier, Charles Green,
who had worked at the port with the 20th Engineers, saw the
results of one night's violence. When passing St Nazaire's mortu-
ary, Green noticed two bodies on the slab. A soldier in attendance
told Green that the dead men, both of them African Americans,
had been murdered by the Military Police: 'The nigger killer got
them last night,' Green was told, referring to an infamous white
Military Policeman whose reputation had spawned his nickname.
It seems he had shot one of the men through the eye, while the
other victim had a gunshot wound to his chest. The soldier also

explained to Green: 'Oh every time he goes on guard, we get some up here.'[19] The bodies of the black soldiers, Green informed Congress, were later used in medical research. Things were little better at the other US ports of Brest and Bordeaux.

★

Of the African Americans who served their country in the First World War, 80 per cent were consigned to the SOS. Many in the General Staff of the US Army would have been perfectly happy to see that last figure rise to 100 per cent. There was, however, enormous pressure placed on the army and the political class by the African-American middle class and African-American public opinion to allow them to fight for their nation, as their ancestors had done in previous wars. Because of this pressure, and pressure from the French, two divisions were allowed to fight. Of the approximately 200,000 African Americans who went overseas, 42,000 were therefore in combat regiments – 20 per cent of the African Americans deployed, but only 11 per cent of all African Americans drafted.[20]

The '92nd Division (Colored)' consisted of what Colonel Anderson had regarded as 'the cream of the coloured draft', and most of its men came from the South. The '93rd Division (Colored)' had been assembled from various African-American National Guard units, volunteers and draftees from the more liberal Northern and Northeastern states. The 93rd contained four black regiments, the most famous of which was the 369th Infantry Regiment – formerly the 15th New York National Guard, soon to be known as the 'Harlem Hellfighters'.*

The 93rd was trained and dispatched to France on the firm promise that its men would be allowed to fight. They arrived at St Nazaire on New Year's Day 1918 on board the USS *Pocahontas*. Among the men of the 369th Infantry were the forty-four members of the regimental band, some of Harlem's finest

---

* The other units were the 370th Infantry Regiment, the 371st Infantry Regiment and the 372nd Infantry Regiment.

professional musicians, under the leadership of James Reese
Europe, who was a pioneer of ragtime in New York City and the
leading light of the legendary Clef Club.[21] On the dockside at St
Nazaire, the band brought a little of Harlem to France, playing
their arrangement of the 'Marseillaise'. Some have pointed to
this moment as being the first performance of jazz – or more
accurately its musical precursor, ragtime – in France, an event
that marked the beginning of a century-long love affair between
France and black American music. The moment of history was
somewhat lost on the French soldiers present, however, who were
reportedly slow to stand to attention to their national anthem;
the jazz arrangement was so inventive that it took several bars
before they could recognize it for what it was.

While the band was sent on a goodwill tour of France, the
fighting men of the 369th remained near St Nazaire. They were,
as they soon realized, not being rushed to the front or to receive
further training. They were instead being set to work in the SOS,
breaking all the promises made to them – and to black America
in general – that they would be deployed as a fighting unit. Their
rifles were taken from them, and the 369th was ordered to build
warehouses and lay railway tracks. There was *some* further training, but not enough to make them ready for action or allay their
fears that they would spend the war working as 'laborers in
uniform'. While the 369th languished, working for part of the
time in the dreaded port of St Nazaire itself, General Pershing
debated what to do with them and the other black regiments of
the 92nd and 93rd divisions being deployed to France.

On taking command of the American Expeditionary Force
(AEF), General John J. Pershing had insisted that US soldiers
would serve as unified American divisions, under American
command and in their own sectors of the lines. He refused to
permit them to be used simply to fill gaps in French and British
lines. Yet the two black divisions were a political inconvenience,
against which there existed considerable hostility among white
troops and officers. Pershing was warned that white US troops
would find it 'distasteful' to serve alongside African Americans,

and that the orders of African-American officers were unlikely to be obeyed by them. White soldiers were already refusing to salute African Americans of superior rank. The American plan in early 1918 was for the 'Colored' regiments to languish in the SOS, at least for the moment. However, Pershing and the US Army had been pressured by the French, who requested that US troops be transferred to their sectors and used to help rebuild the nation's decimated army, a force that was short of men and whose commanders were haunted by memories of the mutinies of 1917. Pershing's insistence that Americans fight under American command did not, evidently, extend to African Americans, as French demands for US troops combined with American hostility towards their own black comrades to present the perfect solution. In March 1918 he transferred the 93rd Division's four regiments, of unwanted, inconvenient and potentially disruptive African-American combat troops, to the French Army, thereby ridding himself of a perceived problem. Pershing made a similar proposal to the British, offering them the 92nd Division on the same terms. But the British, who had refused to deploy both African and Caribbean troops from their own empire to the Western Front, had absolutely no intention of absorbing into their ranks America's unwanted black regiments and so refused Pershing's offer.[22]

Within the French Army, the four new regiments were to be integrated into an Allied army that was already multiracial. There, they would be given the full and intensive combat training that the US Army had been patently unwilling to offer them. Pershing would later claim that his transfer of the regiments had been intended as a temporary expedient – but there is no documentary evidence to substantiate his claim.[23] On 10 March 1918, the 369th US Infantry Regiment (Colored) became the *Trois-cent-soixante-neuvième RIUS* of the 16th Division of the French Fourth Army. Major Arthur Little, one of the white officers of the 369th, described the unit's strange experience: 'we are "*les Enfant perdu*" [*sic*], and glad of it. Our great American general simply put the black orphan in a basket and set it on the doorstep of the French, pulled the bell and went away.'[24]

At the French training camp of Connantre, south of Reims, the 93rd were transformed into an international hybrid force – American troops under French officers, fighting in French attacks. Their uniforms became the symbol of their new internationalism. While retaining their American tunics, greatcoats and trousers, they were equipped with French helmets (the famous *casques Adrian*), along with French pouches, ammunition belts and gas masks. Their American Springfield rifles were exchanged for French Lebels with their long sword-like bayonets. The Americans adjusted to French rations and benefitted from French wine rations: two quarts a day of the rough, red table wine known as *pinard*. Now under French instruction, they had to learn to read French military maps, with their numerous codes and unfamiliar symbols. They had to master enough rudimentary French to understand military orders, and they were given additional training in the use of heavy machine guns, grenades, grenade-launchers and trench mortars. This training was administered by highly experienced French officers, who had mastered the details of trench warfare. Just as importantly the instructors knew how to make life bearable – if not exactly comfortable – within the trenches, lessons learnt over three years of war.

★

Despite this heightened level of instruction, the units of the 93rd Division were warned by their officers that their training might not be completed before they were required at the front. The week preceding the transfer of the 369th Infantry to French control, Lenin's new Bolshevik government in Russia had formalized Russia's exit from the war when it acceded to the Treaty of Brest-Litovsk. Under the draconian terms of that agreement, Russia's western border retreated eastwards and Germany took control of a new continental empire that was three times the size of the Second Reich itself. Russia lost almost 90 per cent of its coal reserves, one-third of its agricultural output and over a quarter of its population. Most significantly, victory on the Eastern Front allowed Germany to redeploy forces to the Western

Front, which brought a numerical advantage over the Allies in the spring of 1918. Despite the deployment of soldiers and labourers drawn from the empires of Britain and France, and despite the arrival of the first American units, the fifty new German divisions that now appeared in the West in early 1918 tipped the balance in Germany's favour. Along with these new divisions came thousands of artillery pieces and machine guns. The question was whether Germany would be able to exploit this advantage before the influx of US troops tipped the scales back towards the Allies, for each week thousands of Americans were landing at St Nazaire, Brest and Bordeaux. The German High Command, dominated by Ludendorff and Hindenburg, knew that there would come a time when their window of opportunity would close shut.

The inevitable and long-anticipated German offensive came just eleven days after the men of the 369th Infantry Regiment had begun their training within the French Army. In the early hours of 21 March the Germans launched Operation Michael, the opening attack of what they called the *Kaiserschlacht* – the Kaiser's Battle. It began with an artillery barrage of awesome intensity against the British Fifth Army's positions south of Flesquières, in Picardy. A vast tempest of high-explosive shells devoured the front-line trenches. The explosives were inter-mixed with thousands of gas shells, which released enormous clouds of lachrymatory and poison gases (chlorine and phos-gene). The tear gases acted as an irritant, which caused men to rip off their gas masks, leaving their eyes and lungs exposed to the poisons. In just five hours a million shells were hurled at the British. Then, through the gas, which had combined with the morning mist to form a heavy toxic smog, came seventy-six German divisions, spearheaded by storm-troopers in their gas masks, with their terrifying flame-throwers and new light sub-machine guns, and using 'infiltration' tactics to swarm around enemy positions. Across a front of fifty miles they drove back the Fifth Army, before erupting into open country. The British were pushed back to the abandoned battlefields of the Somme, where Kitchener's volunteer army had suffered so terribly two years earlier.

By the end of the first day, the Germans were seven miles behind the British lines. The advance storm-trooper units had penetrated so far that they were beginning to stumble across ammunition depots, warehouses and rest areas. Exhilarated at the news, the Kaiser declared, somewhat prematurely, Day Three of the attack to be a Victory Holiday. As the Germans pushed westwards, the French capital came within the range of 'Long Max', a special long-range howitzer whose quarter-ton shells began to roar down on Paris even though it still lay seventy-five miles away. Two-hundred-and-fifty-six Parisians were killed in the bombardment, and the confidence of the French nation was noticeably shaken. By Day Seven, the Germans had driven a ten-mile wedge between the British and French forces. Yet, just two weeks after the launch of Operation Michael, and as with all previous attacks since the start of trench warfare in 1914, momentum began to wane. It was as if each attack were halted by some invisible but universal law. But some of the reasons Operation Michael stalled were unique to the circumstances of 1918. Exhausted German troops who came across food depots halted and gorged on luxuries they had not seen for years; some re-equipped themselves with British kit, and all saw for themselves the sheer weight of materials being assembled against them. Their own army struggled to bring up their meagre rations and supplies across the still-devastated landscape.

A second German attack, Operation Georgette (also known as the Battle of the Lys), was launched on 9 April, but it took place further north, between Dixmude in Flanders and La Bassée in France. This attempt to extinguish the Ypres Salient – and if successful, press on to the Channel ports – also ran out of steam by the end of the month, but not without inducing a sense of severe crisis among the Allies. On its first day, the Germans attacked over the old battlefield of Neuve Chapelle, retaking the ruined village that had been won by the Indian Corps in March 1915. The Portuguese, who now held the sector with 20,000 men under the command of the nation's future President General Gomes da Costa, were overwhelmed by 50,000 German attackers. Suffering 7,000 casualties, the men from Portugal were routed and pushed back five miles. They left behind many of the dead whose remains now lie in the Portuguese Cemetery; it stands near the memorial to the Indians killed in the same area in 1915.

After the crises of March and early April, the British and the French managed to reconnect their lines and the tide began to turn against the Germans. In the middle of the month, the African-American troops of the 369th Infantry cut short their training and were moved to a relatively quiet sector near Melzicourt, on the edge of the Argonne Forest in Champagne, where they took control of a stretch of line a little under four miles long. Although they represented only around 1 per cent of the American combat force then in action, the 369th in April 1918 were manning 20 per cent of the proportion of the line held by Americans. It was in this period, while acclimatizing to the realities of trench warfare, that the most famous incident in the story of African-American troops in the war took place.

While many a First World War battle is known by the name of the general who devised it, Henry Johnson of the 369th Infantry is probably the only sergeant whose name is attached to a 'battle'. The 'Battle of Henry Johnson' took place on 14 May 1918 in the Argonne Forest. Sergeant Johnson and Private Needham Roberts were on sentry duty when, at around 2am, they heard the sound of German troops in no-man's land cutting the French barbed-wire defences in preparation for a raid. Johnson and Roberts raised the alarm and began to throw hand-grenades at the Germans. Private Roberts was injured almost immediately by a German grenade. As Germans attacked, Roberts lay prone in the trench and passed grenades up to Johnson, who fended off the oncoming troops. After he ran out of explosives, the Germans attempted to rush Johnson, who turned to his French Lebel rifle; it jammed when he attempted to reload it with incompatible American ammunition. At this point Johnson, a rather diminutive figure just out of his teens, fought off the Germans using his rifle

as a club. Seizing a Bolo knife he repelled his attackers; at one
point he was reduced to fighting with his fists.* As American reinforcements arrived to drive off the Germans, Johnson famously
spared the life of a German attacker who had been left behind.
Enemy casualties in the 'Battle of Henry Johnson' were estimated
to have been in excess of thirty, including four dead. The eponymous hero had received twenty-one wounds: a bullet had grazed
his head, he had been shot through the hand and through the
foot, through his lips, and he had received wounds to his flank too.

Most descriptions of the encounter read like the citation for a
posthumous medal – yet Johnson survived both the 'battle' and
his injuries. He and Roberts were awarded the French *Croix de
Guerre*, and overnight Johnson became an African-American
superstar. The legend of Henry Johnson – 'The Black Death' –
began in *Stars and Stripes,* the US Army's own newspaper. On 24
May 1918 it ran the headline 'Two Black Yanks Smear 24 Huns'
and described Johnson and Roberts as 'two strapping Negroes, a
station porter and an elevator boy'. The *New York World*, which
coined the phrase 'The Battle of Henry Johnson', made Johnson
even more famous, describing in grim detail the slaughter he
had rained down upon the Germans with his Bolo knife.[25] In the
Harlem Home News, Marcus Garvey of the Universal Negro
Improvement Association predicted that it was going to require
'the black man to stop the Kaiser's soldiers' and reflected that
there was 'not a more glorious record in the story of the war than
the record of those two boys from the New York 15th' – the
pre-war designation of the 369th Infantry.[26] The sensational
exploits of Johnson were heralded by African Americans as a
vindication of their demands that black men be permitted to
take part in the war as combatants, on equal terms with white
men. That they had only been permitted to do so, thus far, within
the ranks of a foreign army was – for the moment – put aside.

* The Bolo was a large heavy machete, originating in the Philippines,
which was adopted by some Americans after the American–Philippine War
of 1899–1903.

On 27 May 1918, the Germans mounted their third offensive of the spring, this time at the ridge of the Chemin des Dames, where they had decimated the *Tirailleurs Sénégalais* in 1917.[*] Another whirlwind of shells, this time totalling 2 million, was fired at the French. Outnumbered more than two to one, they were driven back. By the end of the month the Germans were on the River Marne, just fifty-five miles from Paris and close to where the war had pivoted in September 1914. In the Allied counter-attack at Belleau Wood, the US Marines sustained appalling casualties in some of the most brutal hand-to-hand fighting of the whole war. Nearby, but fighting as part of the French Army, the 369th Infantry also attacked. By now they were coming to be recognized by the French as a highly capable elite unit.

In June 1918, after a fourth German offensive between Montdidier and Noyon had been halted, the Allies counter-attacked with a force led by Charles Mangin, 'the Butcher', whose forces were spearheaded with an armada of new French tanks. A fifth and final German offensive, in mid-July, was thrown against the defences in front of the towns of Reims and Epernay in the heart of the Champagne region. But the French had learnt the details of the German plans directly from the mouths of German deserters and prepared tactically sophisticated defences, while massing troops for the counter-attack. On 18 July Mangin, once again in favour with the French High Command, led the attack. It was North African units, fighting under the author of the *Force Noire* theory, who led this critical assault.

Six days later, having suffered 900,000 casualties in the various operations of the Spring Offensive and having failed to break through to Reims or Paris, Ludendorff ordered a retreat. The German Army had fired its only arrow and failed to strike the target; it was an exhausted and spent force. Despite having raided British and French stores, materials were running short. It was now that reports of the Spanish Flu among the German

---

[*] This German offensive, Operation Blücher, is often referred to as the Aisne Offensive.

ranks reached the Allies. As the Germans were literally emaciated after years of privation, they were more prone to the infection than the better-fed British, French or US soldiers. Ludendorff's army was fast approaching the end of its capacity to fight on. The British had suffered heavy losses – 200,000 men in June alone – but by then the Americans were landing 250,000 men in France each month. Germany had no choice but to take up defensive positions.

———— —

A E.F. HEADQUARTERS, CHAUMONT, EARLY AUGUST 1918. Colonel Linard, the French Military Attaché at AEF Headquarters in the Haute-Marne, receives instructions to draft a document that will be entitled *Secret Information Concerning Black American Troops*. It is intended to be distributed among French officers and the French civil authorities alike. As a secret military document, not intended for publication and produced for the attention of a foreign army and civilian authorities, it is a clear statement of official US policy on matters of race.

The document – effectively a series of instructions – reminds those 'French officers who have been called upon to exercise command over black American troops, or to live in close contact with them' of the exact 'position occupied by Negroes in the United States'. While conceding that the 'Negro' is 'a citizen of the United States', the document explains that he:

> ... *is regarded by the white American as an inferior being with whom relations of business or service only are possible. The black is constantly being censured for his want of intelligence and discretion, his lack of civic and professional conscience, and for his tendency toward undue familiarity. The vices of the Negro are a constant menace to the American who has to repress them sternly.*

French officers are to be further informed that:

American opinion is unanimous on the 'color question,' and does not admit of any discussion. The increasing number of Negroes in the United States (about 15,000,000) would create for the white race in the Republic a menace of degeneracy were it not that an impassable gulf has been made between them. As this danger does not exist for the French race, the French public has become accustomed to treating the Negro with familiarity and indulgence. This indulgence and this familiarity are matters of grievous concern to the Americans. They consider them an affront to their national policy. They are afraid that contact with the French will inspire in black Americans aspirations which to them (the whites) appear intolerable. It is of the utmost importance that every effort be made to avoid profoundly estranging American opinion.

With this background clearly set out and explained, French officers are, in conclusion, issued with three instructions:

1. *We must prevent the rise of any pronounced degree of intimacy between French officers and black officers. We may be courteous and amiable with these last, but we cannot deal with them on the same plane as with the white American officers without deeply wounding the latter. We must not eat with them, must not shake hands or seek to talk or meet with them outside of the requirements of military service.*

2. *We must not commend too highly the black American troops, particularly in the presence of (white) Americans. It is all right to recognize their good qualities and their services, but only in moderate terms strictly in keeping with the truth.*

3. *Make a point of keeping the native cantonment population from 'spoiling' the Negroes. (White) Americans become greatly incensed at any public expression of intimacy between white women with black men ... Familiarity on the part of white women with black men is furthermore a source of profound regret to our experienced [white French] colonials who see in it an overweening menace to the prestige of the white race.*

Military authority cannot intervene directly in this question, but it can through the civil authorities exercise some influence on the population.

———— • ————

In the first days of August 1918, the French, British and Americans were assembling on the Western Front the forces with which they now intended to break the German Army. On the old battlefield of the Somme, the British had amassed 400 tanks, and between them the Allies had assembled 10 divisions of attack troops – British, French and American men, along with forces from the British and French empires. The Canadians and Australians were to have key attacking roles. The French had been hoarding men for the coming offensive, and Mangin intended to throw his North African and West African troops at the German lines. In the upper echelons of the American Expeditionary Force, something else was brewing too.

The successes of the 369th Infantry on the battlefield and the exploits of Henry Johnson had demonstrated that the integration of the unwanted '93rd Division (Colored)' into the French Army had been an enormous success. Trained by seasoned French instructors, the 369th in particular had developed into one of the most effective combat units in the French forces. They and the other three combat regiments of the division had ceased to be Pershing's problem when he handed them to the French; but by the summer of 1918 they were once causing alarm in the headquarters of the AEF. African Americans and white Frenchmen had faced the dangers of battle together, endured bombardments, suffered the loss of their comrades and charged enemy positions. Quite naturally, strong martial bonds had developed between officers and men. These sentiments were regarded by the US War Department and the US Army with hostile suspicion. It had come to the attention of the Americans that white French troops were saluting African-American officers, and that comrades in arms were shaking one another's hands, irrespective of race.

Furthermore, the black combat troops, now beyond the everyday control of the US Army, had happily integrated into French wartime society too. Despite the widespread racism within French society and the army, its different emphases – on cultural backwardness rather than biology – meant that the French were considerably more racially tolerant than the Americans. African Americans were culturally American even though racially African, and this duality in some ways short-circuited French racism. Some scholars believe that African Americans received better treatment in France than did the men from France's own African colonies. What disturbed the US Army most was the warmth and ease with which the African-American troops were being received by French civilians, including women, a reality that was looked upon by the American authorities with profound distaste.

The response from AEF headquarters was the *Secret Information Concerning Black American Troops*. A statement of intent, it was the determined policy of the US Army, which, like wider white American society, aimed to keep the African American in his place irrespective of the service he was able to offer in the war. The document was issued to French officers commanding African-American troops and to the civil authorities in areas where they were deployed. While the *Secret Information* tacitly forgave the French for having treated African-American soldiers as equals, and put this lapse in standards down to cultural differences and French ignorance of American culture, the document was designed to bring the era of fraternization, familiarity and respect to an end.

After the contents of the *Secret Information* were revealed, in 1919, in the French National Assembly and the African-American press, there was outrage and condemnation. However, the theory was one thing, and the practice was another. In 1918 French officers took little notice of its demands – and under the circumstances they would have had little opportunity to implement them had they chosen to.

The *Secret Information* was dated 7 August 1918. The following day, at 4.20am, twenty-seven divisions of British, French and

American troops launched an attack that arguably represented
the turning point of the war and the beginning of the end for
Germany. The first blow was struck on the Somme, where the
British, Australians and the Canadian Corps advanced after a
lightning artillery bombardment. The Germans were taken by
surprise. As shells thundered down onto their lines, 400 British
tanks attacked, and those that penetrated the German lines
unleashed mayhem in the rear areas. Through the huge gap that
had been punched into the German front by the initial assault,
the great international army swept forward. Among the Canadians
who raced behind the German lines was the Blood Indian Mike
Mountain Horse. His post-war *War Deeds*, painted on calfskin,
included a panel depicting his part in the capture of German
guns, 500 of which were taken during the battle. The assault,
known as the Battle of Amiens, was so successful that General
Haig was genuinely surprised by the scale of men and material
captured. For Ludendorff, though, 8 August was a catastrophic
blow – one that he called 'the Black Day of the German Army'.
What shocked the German commander most were the mass sur-
renders, 12,000 men in all. Whole units had handed themselves
over without a fight, and on occasions whole platoons had even
surrendered to individual Allied soldiers – something that had
previously been unimaginable. Ludendorff recognized that he
was now in command of an army whose morale and will to fight
had begun to disintegrate. There were reports coming in of
German troops jeering at newly arrived reinforcements, accusing
them of prolonging the war. Many of the German defenders were
men who, between March and June, had advanced deep behind
Allied front lines and there seen the great stockpiles of war materials and ammunition – of which an even greater quantity, they
surmised, must still be in the hands of their enemies. They had
realized, sooner than their commanders, that the sheer weight of
enemy firepower and supplies would make the Allies now invincible. Like the British after the Battle of the Somme in 1916, and
the French Army after the calamitous Neville Offensive of 1917,
the German Army had been promised that one final great effort

would bring victory. When that promise had been shown to be hollow, there were no further promises that could be made – and morale collapsed. As the German High Command could see from the letters of the troops that passed through the offices of the censors, thousands of men were willing to accept peace at almost any cost. They hoped for revolution at home, and had decided to effectively withdraw their labour by shirking any duties other than those that were strictly defensive. They had now reached a similar point of despair to that which overwhelmed much of the French Army the year before.

By the end of August 1918, Allied forces had pushed the Germans back almost to the heavily defended Hindenburg Line, the positions from where they had launched the Spring Offensive four months earlier. The Allied commanders, blind to the impending disintegration of the legendary German Field Army, were busy preparing their plans and designing new weapons for their campaigns not just in 1918 but in the year beyond too. Few believed that this time the war could really be 'over by Christmas'. Yet the Battle of Amiens marked the beginning of a series of coordinated and unrelenting Allied offensives that would stretch right up to the Armistice of 11 November. Known collectively as the Hundred Days Offensive, or sometimes called the Grand Offensive, they marked the resumption of mobile warfare on the Western Front.

Today the battles of the Hundred Days Offensive are remembered as being the most tactically advanced operations of the whole war. New weapons were deployed, according to new tactics. Tanks, both heavy and light, worked together in mass formations; the light and portable Lewis light machine gun, an American import, was carried into battle by British and American troops, increasing their firepower while on the advance; aerial observation and photography reached new heights of sophistication and effectiveness, with Allied airmen dominating the skies, scouting out the enemy, looking for tell-tale flashes of enemy guns, and guiding their own artillery batteries' targeting using radios. Attack-aircraft strafed German positions with machine guns and dropped bombs on their troop concentrations. The 'creeping barrage', a protective screen of carefully placed explosive artillery shells, behind which the attacking armies advanced, reached new heights of sophistication and accuracy, as all the lessons in artillery tactics and battlefield communication learnt over four years of war were applied with enormous professionalism. Perhaps most importantly, all these various components were brought together in what became known as 'combined arms operations'.

If the tactical innovation and pace of the Hundred Days Offensive are justly lauded, a less well remembered feature was the battles' international make-up. Among the French attacking forces, which were repeatedly led by Charles Mangin, were the North Africans and the *Tirailleurs Sénégalais*, alongside the long-suffering French *poilus*, veterans of years of misery and frustration. In repeated attacks, the British Army was spearheaded by its Canadian and Australian components, the latter under the formidable and pugnacious Lieutenant General Sir John Monash.

For the AEF, the key struggle of the Hundred Days was the Meuse–Argonne Offensive, a great rolling wave of attacks that lasted from late September until the Armistice, and which involved both of the African-American Divisions – the 93rd Division under French command and the 92nd Division, still under American orders. Although they never fought together as a unified division, all the regiments of the 93rd took part. The 369th Infantry, the 'Harlem Helfighters', participated in the capture of the town of Sechault, enduring very heavy losses. Today a black granite obelisk, a monument to them, stands in the town centre – and an exact replica stands in a New York park. The 370th Infantry, men from Illinois and Chicago's South Side, took part in attacks on the Oise–Aisne Canal and were later to push on into Belgium.

The 371st Regiment – draftees from the rural Carolinas – led an attack on the German stronghold of 'Côte 188' in the Ardennes where, on 28 September, they were lured into a trap by the German defenders, who pretended to surrender only to open fire on the regiment as they approached over open ground to receive the German prisoners; it was a ruse known as the '*Kamerad* trick'. Among the men caught in this deadly trap was Corporal Freddie Stowers. Typical of his regiment, Stowers had been a Carolina farmhand before the war. With the officers of the 371st either dead or wounded, Stowers led an attack on the German machine-gun positions that had done such damage to his platoon. This proved the critical moment, which turned the tide of battle and led to the capture of Côte 188, but in the process Stowers was mortally wounded.

Freddie Stowers was posthumously recommended for the Medal of Honour. There followed seven decades of official silence until 24 April 1991, when the award was presented to Stowers' two sisters by President George H.W. Bush at a ceremony at the White House.

★

Describing the battles of 1918 in his war memoirs, Erich Ludendorff felt the need to regurgitate the now well-worn German propaganda line that the use of black troops, within the armies of the French and latterly the Americans, was somehow unfair and represented a war crime:

> *Where tanks were lacking, the enemy drove black waves towards us, waves composed of African bodies. Woe to us, when these invaded our lines and murdered or, even worse, tortured the defenceless. Human indignation and accusation must not be directed against the blacks who committed these atrocities, but against those who deployed these hordes on European soil, allegedly fighting for honour, liberty and justice.*[27]

Had Ludendorff been able to tour the areas to the rear of the Allied lines, or pay a visit to the ports of Brest, Boudreaux, St Nazaire or Marseilles, he would have realized that the black soldiers taking part – men from the French colonies and African Americans – represented only a very small proportion of the great multiracial legions of soldiers and labourers that his enemies had drawn into the war from their empires and beyond. One US writer, arriving at Bordeaux in 1918 expecting to see mainly 'colored' American troops, was astonished by the scene that greeted her: 'as we landed at Bordeaux, it seemed every man's home. So crowded and varied was its population ... There were many Colonial troops, Chinese laborers and, more or less maimed French soldiers.'[28]

Bordeaux was one node in an immense and intricate system of supply that stretched back from the front-line trenches to the munitions factories of France, and across the Atlantic Ocean to the training camps and industrial plants of the United States. War materials and supplies were being carried to the war on great convoys of ships under all flags, manned by men of disparate races – West Indians, West Africans, Lascars from India, South Americans, Scandinavians. On landing in the ports of France, these supplies were unloaded by the black stevedores of the US Services of Supply. The war materials then passed through the hands of the various labour corps – North African, Egyptian, Indian, British, French, South African, Portuguese, Chinese and German PoW – as they got closer to front lines. Alongside the mountains of supplies, also arriving at the ports of Brest, Bordeaux and St Nazaire were the US Army, in their hundreds of thousands every passing month. If the Canadian Corps became 'the ram which will break up the last line of resistance of the German Army', as described by the overall Allied commander, Ferdinand Foch, then the engines of their assault were the ports, railways and supply systems that fed the front lines.

★

By August 1918, the US '92nd Division (Colored)' was also in the front line. They were known as the 'Buffalo Soldiers Division', a nickname that had been given to African Americans who had fought against the Native American nations in the so-called Indian Campaigns that began soon after the Civil War and lasted up until the 1890s. Having failed to palm off the 92nd Division onto the British, General Pershing had placed it in the US Second Army, under the ultimate command of General Robert Bullard. A committed racist, unshakably convinced of the racial inferiority of black men, Bullard expected the 92nd Division to fail, and he set out to create the conditions in which they would do so – or at least be seen to do so. Bullard turned a blind eye to the 92nd's successes and, worse, spread misinformation about the conduct and effectiveness of the African Americans. 'Poor negroes! They are hopelessly inferior,' he wrote in his private diary.[29] Bullard also had a deep enmity for Major General Charles Ballou, who commanded the 92nd Division. His desire to undermine his rival's reputation was aided by Colonel Allen J. Greer, Ballou's chief of staff and secretly an ally of Bullard. From the inside, Greer spread slander and attempted to sabotage the reputation of the 92nd, playing down their successes and ensuring that news of any difficulties or reversals were widely disseminated.

The 92nd Division consisted of African-American soldiers and a mixture of white and African-American officers, with the latter regarded as inferior and given no opportunity for advancement. (The US Army ensured that on no occasion was a black officer placed in a position of command over a white officer.) As with most African-American troops, the men of the 92nd had received minimal and sub-standard training in their camps at home. In order to bring them up to combat readiness, they were given further instruction by the French.

In September 1918, the 92nd was rushed 300 miles in three days to be deployed near the Argonne. Three of its four regiments were held in reserve, with only the 368th Infantry Regiment being ordered directly into the lines to take part in the Meuse–Argonne Offensive, where they were to fill an expected gap between French and American units attacking the German-held village of Binarville. The 368th entered the line during the night of the 25 September and prepared to attack the next morning. Although assaulting heavily prepared German positions, they were not equipped with heavy cutters and had no grenade-launchers, flares or even maps, and were expected to attack without artillery support from the

American batteries. Poorly trained, operating against these obstacles on a battlefield about which they knew little, and exhausted from an overnight march, they were unable to break through the heavy wire entanglements. Their communications began to collapse, and a request for French artillery support went unanswered. After five days in the line, and after having suffered 58 men killed and over 200 wounded, they were withdrawn to the rear and officially branded a failure.

The official reaction was extreme: the *entire* 92nd Division was withdrawn, as General Bullard pounced on the 368th's failure in order to prove the ineffectiveness of African-American troops. In the weeks that followed, the 368th's failure was widely disseminated and exaggerated. The fact that the 35th Division, made up of white American troops, had also broken and retreated in the same attack was an inconvenient fact that was overlooked, as were the successes of the 92nd and 93rd divisions. US Army authorities focused their attention on the perceived failings of the 368th, putting them down to the incompetence of black officers and the moral weakness of black soldiers. The truth, as the historian John Morrow has written, is that the 92nd Division performed better in combat and received more medals than many white divisions, about which no complaints were made or aspersions cast.[30]

In August 1918 the 92nd Division also proved itself resilient in the face of a sly German propaganda campaign, which sought to exploit the US Army's constant attempts to belittle and segregate its African-American troops. German propaganda leaflets were dropped over the 92nd Division's line, and the tone of them was quite different to the threatening leaflets dropped on the South African Native Labour Corps in 1917. This time, the message was altogether more sophisticated, appealing to a very real sense of injustice and oppression.* One leaflet, entitled *To the Colored*

* In this respect, the leaflets were more akin to those produced by Max von Oppenheim's Bureau of the East that targeted the sepoys of the Indian Corps with appeals to nationalist sentiment and anti-British feelings.

Soldiers of the US Army, set out to remind African-American troops of the racism and brutality to which they were routinely subjected at home. It got off to a bad start by addressing the black soldiers as 'Boys', but after this initial *faux pas* it raised a series of pertinent questions:

> *... what are you doing over here? Fighting the Germans? Why? Have they ever done you any harm? Of course some white folks and the lying English American papers told you that the Germans ought to be wiped out for the sake of humanity and democracy. What is democracy? Personal Freedom, all citizens enjoying the same rights socially and before the law! Do you enjoy the same rights as the white people do in America, the land of Freedom and Democracy? Or aren't you rather treated over there as second class citizens? Can you go into a restaurant where white people dine, can you get a seat in a theatre where white people sit, can you get a Pullman seat or berth in a railroad car or can you even ride, in the south, in the same street car with white people? How about the law? Is lynching and the most horrible cruelties connected therewith a lawful proceeding in a democratic country?*[31]

However, after posing these difficult questions, and painting a disturbingly accurate picture of how American democracy had failed its black citizens, the leaflet then painted an entirely false picture of racial attitudes in Germany. Fourteen years after German soldiers and bureaucrats had conducted a war of extermination in South West Africa, and in the middle of a war in which there had been numerous reported incidents of racial violence against non-white Allied prisoners, German propagandists still felt able to claim that Germany was a nation 'entirely different' to the United States, 'where they do like colored people, where they treat them as Gentlemen and not as second class citizens.' The leaflet went on:

> *You have been made the tool of the egotistic and rapacious rich in America, and there is nothing in the whole game for you but broken*

bones, horrible wounds, spoiled health, or death. No satisfaction whatever will you get out of this unjust war. You have never seen Germany, so you are fools if you allow people to make you hate us. Come over and see for yourself. Let those do the fighting who make the profit out of this war. Don't allow them to use you as cannon fodder.

Finally, the German propagandists invited the black troops to throw away their guns 'and come over to the German lines,' where it promised that 'You will find friends who help you along.'

That there are no reports of soldiers from the 92nd Division seeking out new 'friends' in the German lines suggests that the leaflet was clearly ineffective. However, the ability of its authors to point to uncomfortable truths about the status of black people in the United States must have been deeply disconcerting. Nothing in the German propaganda leaflet contradicted the official American position on race as outlined in the *Secret Information*.*

★

The African-American campaigner Emmet J. Scott reminded readers of his *Official History of the American Negro in the World War* (1919) that ever since the Civil War it had been demonstrated repeatedly that 'If properly trained and instructed, the colored man makes as good a soldier as the world has ever seen. The history of the Negro in all of our wars, including our Indian campaigns, shows this.'[32] Whatever else that sentiment evokes, it reminds us that African Americans were not the sole non-white minority in the United States – nor in the ranks of the US Army that fought in the First World War. Men against whose forefathers those 'Indian campaigns' had been waged were now fighting on behalf of the US government. As with the Native

---

* That Nazi propagandists were able to make near-identical appeals to the black GIs of another world war, two decades later, pointing out the same injustices and the same racial violence, is a tragic indictment of the lack of progress the United States made between the two world wars with respect to the rights and status of its non-white citizens.

Canadians who had served on the Western Front since 1915, Native Americans brought their traditions and beliefs into a modern industrial war. And they were perceived entirely differently by domestic white society from the sons and daughters of African slaves.

Although a long-persecuted non-European minority, Native American men were welcomed into the US Army in a way that in almost every respect was the inverse of the treatment meted out to African Americans. Native men were not forced into segregated regiments, nor deployed in unglamorous support units like the Services of Supply. While the army obsessively set out to marginalize and dehumanize African-American troops, in the same years and in the same conflict it actively celebrated the service and courage of its Native American troops. The First World War proved, therefore, to be a far more positive experience for Native Americans than for their African-American countrymen. Nevertheless, they too were victims of a form of racism. The belief that Native Americans were members of a noble, warrior race was so firmly established within the cultural imagination of white America that Native men were thrust into the front lines, where they were expected to live up to their stereotypes.

On America's entry into the war there had been an initial, concerted campaign for the creation of segregated 'Indian regiments'. However, the US Army had a binary view of race, recognizing only two categories: black and white. Native Americans were thus classified as 'white', and for the most part they served in regular regiments. As only around two-thirds of all Native Americans had been granted US citizenship by 1917, not all of them had to register for the draft. But, overcoming difficulties of language and distance, around 17,000 Native Americans were registered, and over 6,500 were drafted. A similar number enlisted voluntarily, and in total about 13,000 – around one-third of the eligible Native American male population – served in the military during the war.[33] This was a higher proportion than among the white population, although there was huge variation by tribe. While just 1 per cent of Navajo men enlisted, 39 per cent of eligible Osage men and 54 per cent of the Quapaw (both peoples from Oklahoma) joined up.[34]

Native Americans took part in every major US engagement of the war and served in a wide range of roles in various army branches.[35] However, prevailing racial stereotypes encouraged the army to deploy them in roles where their supposed warrior instincts could best be utilized. In the popular imagination, Native Americans possessed a special connection to the land and to nature. They were, it was believed, able to read the landscape and be at one with it. For these reasons they were regarded as being particularly effective scouts, as it was out in no man's land, on patrol or working as observers or snipers, where it was hoped their supposed gifts for agility and camouflage would emerge. These ideas went deep within American popular culture; they were almost universally accepted and rarely challenged. Newspapers, magazines, popular fiction and textbooks all made casual reference to the martial reputation of the 'Indians'. The magazine *Outlook* noted that they were endowed with 'adroit tactics, sense of strategy, and feats of camouflage', these traits the fruits of their 'ancient training in the science of war'.[36] In an article from August 1918, the *New York Evening World* assured its readers that while the Native Americans serving in the war fought in the uniform of the US Army, they were 'none the less courageous for the absence of feathers and war paint'.[37]

It was held that Native Americans were able to navigate without the use of a compass and could lead units of their white comrades to enemy positions, or back to their own positions, in a way that defied easy explanation. Such a belief that Native Americans had an innate predisposition for navigation gave rise to the suggestion that they should be trained for service within the Aviation Corps. The *Washington Sunday Star* posited other potential attractions of the Aviation Corps. Writing during the Hundred Days Offensive, in August 1918, the newspaper argued that:

The Aviation Corps of the Army makes an appeal to the red-skinned youth as fully as to the pale-face. There is a sharp fascination to youthful imagination in learning to take to the clouds like birds of the air. And then there is a kinship with nature, too, in the religion of the genuine Indian, which makes the ability of human beings to rise and go skyward doubly alluring.[38]

The stereotypes that attached to Native Americans were in numerous ways the opposite of those imposed upon African Americans. Whereas the latter were said to break down and panic under the pressure of bombardments, Native Americans were reported as being casually dismissive of the effects of explosions and detonations, even when the shells were falling around them. Whereas Colonel Anderson regarded the bulk of African Americans in the draft as in some way physically deficient, Native Americans were repeatedly described as having perfect warrior physiques and athletic bodies that were entirely suited to hand-to-hand fighting in the trenches or in no man's land. While African Americans were dismissed as moral cowards, Native Americans were continually portrayed as being naturally blood-thirsty, living for the fight and blind to mortal dangers. For African Americans, service in the US Army was a suffocating, daily reaffirmation of their supposed inferiority, where achievements were dismissed. The opposite was the case for Native Americans, some of whom may have, by contrast, suffered under the burden of pressure to live up to the very high expectations on the battlefield.

Within the US Army, differences were noticed – or perhaps imagined – between the abilities and aptitudes of men from different Native American tribes. What emerged was something strangely redolent of the British martial-races theory. As a Pathan and a Gurkha were understood by British officers to have different skills and capacities, US officers came to believe the same was true of their Native American troops. They concluded that the tribes of the Northern Plains – the Sioux, Cheyenne and Nez Perce – were the most aggressive fighters, whereas men from the tribes of the Southwest, such as the Hopis and Navajos, had greater endurance and were therefore superior trench messengers (a dangerous task in which speed and agility were essential).[39] As with the *Tirailleurs Sénégalais*, selected for duties as assault troops on the basis of the theory that only some Africans belonged to the *races guerrières*, some Native Americans found themselves placed into dangerous positions on the basis of cultural expectation. For the *Tirailleurs Sénégalais* this sort of thinking was grimly reflected in their casualty rates. So too for the Native Americans, of whom about 5 per cent of those serving with the AEF died in action; the figure for the AEF as a whole was around 1 per cent.[40] Death rates among some Native American tribes, particular those from Oklahoma and the Dakotas, were even higher, reaching up to 10 per cent.[41]

As numerous writers have pointed out, the military skills that were reportedly demonstrated by men from tribal societies during the First World War can be convincingly explained by experience rather than race. It is much more likely that, as men from predominantly rural backgrounds, many of whom still hunted, they were more accustomed to handling firearms and more used to the conditions of outdoor life than some of their comrades who had left urban lives in the great cities of America. Similar patterns had been noted during previous conflicts, for example during the American Civil War, where men from the predominantly agrarian South proved more comfortable in the saddle (and at times more effective with the rifle) than men from the cities of the North.[42] Equally, in southern Africa the Boer commandos who took on the sickly recruits drawn from Britain's unhealthy industrial cities during the Anglo-Boer War were, unsurprisingly, more adept at mobile warfare on the African veldt. Lifestyle and experience were the key, not race.

If the underlying reasons, then, were more straightforward, the exploits of Native American soldiers nonetheless offered the American press the same dash of exoticism and glamour that the arrival of the Indian Corps had provided the British newspapers in 1914. Their purported ability to apply ancient warrior tactics to the modern battlefield had an effect of humanizing, as well as glamorizing, the war. Colourful descriptions of their martial skills were extremely appealing to editors and popular with readers. Native Americans' war adventures were reported in depth, and sometimes the men themselves were quoted – but even when the men had college degrees and spoke perfect English, the newspapers were unable to resist changing their words into a broken frontier English familiar from dime novels. Alongside this fake 'Indian speak' came all the old clichés: 'Indians' were said to be taking the scalps of German soldiers, of attacking with traditional tribal weapons, of using their rifles as clubs, and of dying with the romanticized stoicism expected of noble savages. There was a particular interest in traditional Native American war cries. A gleeful report had Charles Rogers, a Standing Rock Sioux man who fought with the 18th Infantry regiment, leaping 'over the parapet swinging his old rifle over his head. He let out a yell he had been saving for years, and it was a genuine war-whoop by one of the people who made war-whooping famous'. The Native Canadian Mike Mountain Horse recalled a moment in the trenches when he felt compelled to 'release my pent up feelings in the rendering of my own particular war song', and was later assured by his comrades that his 'war whoop has stopped the war for at least a few seconds'.[43] For him, a man who felt strongly his society's martial traditions, his war whoops echoed across the Western Front for inner reasons. Others may have felt a greater weight of external expectation.

Along with the evidently irresistible temptation to exoticize their exploits, there was also remarkable enthusiasm and sympathy within the US press towards the nation's 'Indian' soldiers. Their service was seen as representing their full entry into US citizenship and as proof of the moral supremacy of American democracy. That white America's former enemies were now in the ranks of its army, fighting against German barbarism, was the American response to Britain's claims to moral leadership on the basis of the willing service of its Indian Army soldiers. The *New York Evening World* in April 1918 commended Native Americans for their capacity to forget the pains of the past and fight for the American flag 'as valiantly as their hostile fathers ever fought

against it'.[44] The skills and martial individualism of the Native
American were set in contrast to the fighting style of the German
soldiers who, it was claimed – quite wrongly – were only able to
fight 'stolidly in masses'.[45]

Those German soldiers, too, had grown up fascinated with the
American 'Indian', in a nation that was utterly captivated by a
romanticized image of the American frontier and deeply drawn
to a simplistic, yet sympathetic, vision of Native American peoples.
Although the age of the wild frontier had drawn to a close during
the 1890s, the figures of the frontiersmen, the cowboy and the
'Indian' still gripped the cultural imagination of Wilhelmine
Germany. In the last decades of the nineteenth century, Germans
had enjoyed various Wild West touring shows, with their highly
distorted, but deeply enticing, vision of frontier life; Buffalo Bill
Cody's Wild West Show had been seen by the Kaiser himself. And
among the cast of these travelling shows were Native Americans,
encouraged to perform in mock battles and hunts. When the
German impresario Carl Hagenbeck established his Stellingen
Zoological Garden in Hamburg, he included *Völkerschaustellungen*
– 'exhibitions of peoples' – including a party of Sioux Indians, by
1910, under the leadership of Chief Spotted Weasel.[46]

While thousands of German boys encountered Native
Americans in these Wild West shows, millions more met them on
the pages of the hugely popular Western novels written by
German authors. By far the most successful of these writers was
Dr Karl May who, like most of his readers, had never set foot on
the American frontier but who made up for his lack of knowledge by cribbing information from maps and the accounts of
travellers. In May's novels his hero, 'Old Shatterhand', shares his
adventures with the Native American Winnetou, who regards this
Germanic cowboy as his 'white brother'. The two men bond
deeply through their shared experience, and the novels are peppered with quasi-anthropological observations about the military
abilities of Winnetou and his people. May depicts Native
Americans as natural scouts, capable of reading the landscape
and in possession of innate senses almost akin to those of

48. In Charles Gustrine's poster 'True Sons of Freedom' (1918), produced in Chicago, Abraham Lincoln looks approvingly upon 'Colored Men' carrying the fight to the Germans. But many white Americans, in the army and wider society, objected to more African Americans in uniform. In truth, the uniforms many of them fought in were French, while by 1918 the Germans had long abandoned the spiked helmet.

49. D.W. Griffith's *Birth of a Nation* (1915) validated the Ku Klux Klan as defenders of American white supremacy.

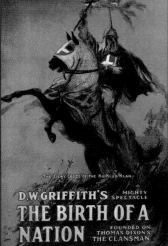

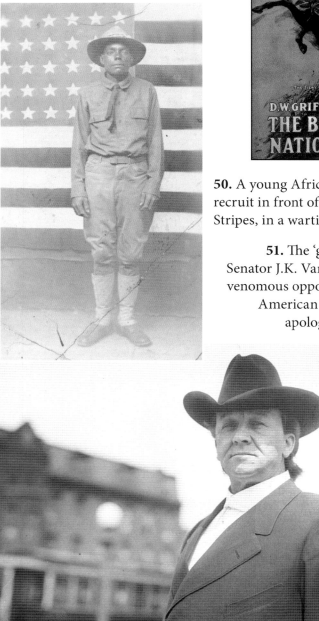

50. A young African-American recruit in front of the Stars and Stripes, in a wartime postcard.

51. The 'great white chief' Senator J.K. Vardaman (*c.* 1915), venomous opponent of African-American recruitment and apologist for lynching.

52. W.E.B. Du Bois (1868–1963) was, as editor of *The Crisis* and a leader of the National Association for the Advancement of Colored People, one of the most powerful advocates of African–American rights in the war era, including those of servicemen.

53. General John Pershing (1860–1948), commander of the American Expeditionary Force, pictured at his HQ at Chaumont (October 1918). His solution to the 'problem' of the African-American army divisions was to offer one (successfully) to the French and the other (unsuccessfully) to the British.

54. Sergeant Henry Johnson of the 369th US Infantry, recipient of the *Croix de Guerre* and the most celebrated African-American soldier of the war. He is pictured aboard ship, returning at war's end.

55. Topping their US Army uniforms with French Adrian helmets, the 369th US Infantry – the 'Harlem Hellfighters' – served with the French Army, acquiring experience, respect and liberties that were unavailable to African Americans still under US command.

56. A still underweight Lettow-Vorbeck (*centre*) recuperates in genteel comfort in Dar es Salaam following his belated surrender.

57. One of Walter von Ruckteschell's terracotta *Askari* reliefs (1938), which glorified Germany's East African campaign in 1914–18 for the Nazi era. Once adorning the Lettow-Vorbeck Barracks, the reliefs now lie in a German park as half-noticed curiosities.

58. 'Protest of German women against the coloured occupation on the Rhine', declares Walter Riemer's propaganda poster (1920). The Rhine runs red, perhaps with blood.

59. Karl Goetz's scabrous anti-occupation medal (1920) focuses its virulent racism on the supposed 'Black Shame' – the accusations of rape levelled at French African soldiers in the Rhineland.

60. War tourism. The US photojournalist Helen Johns Kirtland inspects the remains of a mine swept up on a beach, probably on the Belgian shoreline. Her curiosity was professional, but many women visited the old battle zones to see where their loved ones had perished.

61. Civilians pick their way, after the war, through the obliterated French town of Lens. In the absence of war, the former battle zones became sometimes lawless places of uneasy cohabitation between returning civilians and lingering military personnel, such as the Chinese labourers.

62. Bandleader James Reese Europe (*left,* standing) and his jazz musicians of the Harlem Hellfighters return to New York (February 1919). They were feted on arrival; but demobbed African Americans faced renewed racism.

63. Gurkhas march up the Mall in London, as part of the Victory Parade on 19 July 1919. But not all contingents who had come to the empire's aid were acknowledged, and not all of the dead were remembered.

predatory animals. Among the front-line soldiers on whom May's novels had a deep effect was Adolf Hitler; years later, as *Führer*, he was to shower awards and thanks on May's widow. Another German veteran, the storm-trooper Ernst Jünger, who recorded his war experiences in the celebrated memoir *Stahlgewittern* (*The Storm of Steel*), also remembered May when, during an attack, 'memories of my third grade class and Karl May came back to me, as I was crawling on my stomach through the dew covered and thorny grass, careful not to make the least noise, for, fifty metres in front of us, was the entrance to the English trench'.[47]

It is one of the war's ironies that the white nations of the United States and Germany, in 1918 locked in violent opposition, shared both an animosity towards men of African descent fighting on the battlefield as well as an admiring attachment to the mystique of the 'Indian' brave.

CHAPTER 9

'YOUR SONS WILL REMEMBER YOUR NAME'

Remembering, resenting and forgetting

————— • —————

KASAMA, NORTHERN RHODESIA, 12 NOVEMBER 1918. The sun rises over the equatorial scrub lands at around 5.30 in the morning. On the Western Front, it is not until around 7am that the first tendrils of pale, winter sunlight will stretch out across the frozen battlefields. In France and Belgium, as in Asia and the Americas, today's dawn heralds the first full day of peace, after 1,561 consecutive days of war. But for the German-led forces in Africa, today has no particular significance – it is merely business as usual, the 1,562nd day of a long war. Cut off from the outside world, Paul von Lettow-Vorbeck, still commanding his rag-tag army of sickly German officers, and exhausted and exploited African *Askari* and conscripted carriers, is completely unaware that an armistice has been signed.

Lettow-Vorbeck's brutal safari – always darkly surreal – has become, by now, preposterous. His columns have marched from the town of Kasama to the Chambezi River, while Lettow-Vorbeck, emaciated and half-blind, rides alongside on a rickety bicycle. Despite his own ill-health and the appalling condition of his army, he remains obsessively determined to battle on. Yet the state in whose name he fights has, as of three days previously, ceased to exist. Unbeknownst to him and his army, they are no longer the subjects of the Imperial German Reich but the uncomprehending citizens of a new German republic. The German emperor, to whom Lettow-Vorbeck has remained unswervingly loyal, has been dethroned and Kaiser Wilhelm II is now merely Wilhelm Hohenzollern, a private citizen and a foreign refugee in a Dutch country villa. Oblivious to all this, Lettow-Vorbeck plans his next move. Having recently seized a large stock of quinine, he calculates that he has sufficient supplies of that essential medicine to fight on until June 1919.

Both Lettow-Vorbeck and Heinrich Schnee – technically his superior, being the former Governor of German East Africa – have gleaned enough information from British prisoners and captured dispatches to know that the war has entered a climactic stage. Yet both men remain confident that any peace will be favourably disposed towards Germany's interest, and at the very least guarantee the nation's honour and independence. Although Lettow-Vorbeck is unaware of the pitiful state of his distant fatherland, the appalling condition of his own army is – if he chooses to notice it – painfully evident. In this *ersatz* force, the sergeants are acting as officers, while carriers have been 'promoted' to *Askari*. The most sickly of the remaining German officers are carried through the bush in improvised litters.

Their war has ranged across the region – skirmishes and plunder in Portuguese Mozambique, before crossing back into German East Africa in September 1918, and then on into British-ruled Northern Rhodesia. But in approaching their homelands, *Askari* and carriers have been deserting: for men who have not been paid for two years, the draw of villages, families and children they have not seen for years overwhelms any latent sense of duty. They slip away into the darkness of an African night. The *Schutztruppe* commander complains bitterly that 'The Niggers' love of home is too strong.'[1]

Today, 12 November 1918, Lettow-Vorbeck forces the British into one more engagement, near the abandoned town of Kasama. In the aftermath of the skirmish, there is an important discovery. The German commander learns of the capture of a British motorcycle dispatch-rider, whose documents contain momentous news. They are instructions to the local British forces to locate Lettow-Vorbeck and inform him of the Armistice. Shocked by this news – but still believing that Germany must have secured good terms – on 13 November Lettow-Vorbeck rushes to the Chambezi River to notify another of his commanders of the end of hostilities, and to forestall what might otherwise have been the last battle of the African war. There, on a bridge across the river, a British officer, Hector Croad, walks across the firing lines under a white flag to meet Lettow-Vorbeck, to formally deliver news of the Armistice, and to discuss the German surrender.

In fact, Lettow-Vorbeck's formal capitulation does not come until twelve days later, on 25 November, at Abercorn (later known as the Zambian town of Mbala). The surrendering force consists of only 155 Germans, drastically reduced from the 3,000 at the start of the war. The *Askari* number 1,168, and alongside them there is a strange caravan of 3,000 others – carriers, but also the wives, children and servants of *Askari*. Their presence, more than anything else, explains why so many *Askari* have remained 'loyal' to Lettow-Vorbeck: with their families in train, they are in no position to desert or abandon the cause.

On surrendering, the Germans are permitted to retain their personal arms – swords and pistols – and hurried to Dar es Salaam, where they are treated as civilians rather than as PoWs. The disarmed *Askari* are, by contrast, housed in PoW camps at Tabora, in the centre of the former German colony, and from there slowly sent home; but their dispersal fuels the final catastrophe of the war in Africa, for since the summer of 1918 the men have been struck by outbreaks of Spanish Flu. The disbanded *Askari* become one means by which the pandemic spreads to their families, villages and communities. The number of Africans who will die of this 'disease of the wind' (as the Ethiopians call it) is unknowable, as it pulses across the continent in the coming year.

——— ———

Armistice Day – 11 November 1918, the date that passed Lettow-Vorbeck by – is perhaps the most resonant day of the whole twentieth century. Superficially, it appears to offer a neat end to a messy war. What took place, however, on the 'eleventh hour of the eleventh day of the eleventh month' was a cessation of hostilities rather than a definitive end to war or an agreed peace. Two enormous armies, Allied and German, remained in the field, and among Allied politicians and generals there remained suspicious hostility towards Germany's old generals and the new civilian leaders following in the wake of the Kaiser's abdication. Was this just a ruse to secure Germany a breathing space to regroup and carry on the war? Lloyd George had other concerns, that the exhausted and traumatized men of Britain's volunteer and conscript armies might not be easily persuaded to resume combat operations if the Armistice broke down.[2] He was not alone, as the spectre of revolution weighed on the minds of political leaders and military commanders alike. Germany's leaders feared that their armies might be needed to keep the peace at home in a coming civil war.

In most conflicts the liberation of occupied lands and cities comes as the precursor to final victory; but in 1918 hostilities ceased, and only then did liberation follow. Behind the German front line still lay a great swathe of western France, much of Belgium and all of Luxembourg. Ushering those German troops out of the occupied lands, as the French, British, American and Belgian forces advanced, was the delicate task of the last weeks of 1918. The Allied armies picked their way forward carefully, surveying endless miles of ruins on the way. They first passed across what had been the German rear areas and then through towns, villages and cities that had been occupied for four years. One French civilian recalled, with striking eloquence, the surge of emotions at the moment of liberation, having spent the entire war living under German occupation while the thunder of nearby battle echoed across the landscape. 'For four years,' he wrote, 'we were buried like miners listening to the picks and shovels which we could hear far off, announcing our rescue ... and suddenly the dark pit opened and we saw light.'[3] As Allied forces reached the German border, it was now the turn of German civilians to be subjected to enemy occupation.

On 17 November the first American troops reached the German frontier. They were none other than the African Americans of the 369th Infantry Regiment. As the Allies advanced eastwards, the German Army was crossing the Rhine and – as stipulated under the terms of the Armistice – withdrawing from what had been designated a neutral zone on the right bank of the river. The lands on the Rhine's left bank were then occupied by Allied forces, as were three key bridgeheads at Cologne, Koblenz and Mainz. There were to be no further inroads into Germany, to the horror of Charles Mangin, who had railed against the decision with characteristic fury and uncharacteristic prescience: 'No no no! We must go right into the heart of Germany. The armistice should be signed there. The Germans will not admit that they are beaten. You do not finish wars like this ... It is a fatal error and France will pay for it.'[4]

The make-up of the forces that occupied the Rhineland in late 1918 reflected the international multiracial forces that had defeated the Germany Army on the Western Front. They included not only the 369th Infantry but also the African-American 371st Regiment – as well as some black troops among the British occupation force and the Belgian contingent.[5] The French occupation force at this stage numbered 250,000 men, around 10 per cent of whom were non-white colonial soldiers, including battle-hardened veterans of Mangin's Tenth Army, two regiments of West African troops (5,000 men), a regiment of Madagascans, and North Africans.[6] Despite their small numbers, the sub-Saharan French soldiers would become the focus of a furious German campaign of propaganda and racial hatred.

For Germans, to be 'occupied' by Africans – men considered well down in the hierarchy of races – was a form of humiliation. But that general view of the status of black Africans was held widely in Europe, and beyond. Back in 1858, when a British committee pondered the garrisoning of post-Mutiny India with colonial soldiers, a pamphleteer railed that it was 'out of the question to impose upon India an army of Africans' because it would be 'humiliating and disgusting' for Indians. The author was appalled at the very thought of 'putting in the hands of the most untameable and treacherous beings upon the earth the arms which we dare not trust in the hands of our own Asiatic subjects'.[7] During the First World War, the British government had quietly sought to avoid, wherever possible, placing non-white troops in positions of authority over white enemy civilians. In 1917, the British had even secretly insisted that the German civilians rounded up by the Siamese on their declaration of war be evacuated to white-run camps in British India; the Siamese government was fully awake to the implicit racial slur, but in order to maintain cordial relations with his more powerful ally, Rama VI did not protest, though the move was deeply resented in Bangkok.[8] *

To Germans, the black soldiers who arrived at the end of 1918 represented the first large-scale black presence in German history. Those Germans who had encountered black men before had done so mainly under the very different circumstances of the earlier *Völkerschauen* or had come across isolated members of the nation's tiny pre-1914 black community, made up of temporary visitors, sailors in transit or lone settlers. Few Germans actually made it out to the German colonies in Africa. Some of the initial trepidation and fear now felt among the population of the Rhineland was genuine; but these concerns were to be harnessed, amplified and distorted by a highly effective propaganda campaign that was able – with considerable outside assistance – to transform local unease and opposition into something approaching a contemporary global scandal. It went on to

---

* Closer to our own times, in the early 1990s the British journalist Jason Burke encountered a group of insurgents in occupied Baghdad. Their leader, Abu Mujahed, revealed that for them 'Black American servicemen were a particular target,' because, 'to be occupied by Negroes is a particular humiliation.' Indeed, Burke was told that 'Sometimes we abort a mission because there are no Negroes that we could kill.' See Jason Burke, *On the Road to Kandahar: Travels Through Conflict in the Islamic World* (2007), p. 239.

cause divisions between the wartime Allies, influence relations between France and Germany for a generation, and it flowed directly into the policies, rhetoric and murderous wartime practices of the Third Reich. It also stands out as perhaps the only great success story of Germany's propaganda war. Germany's attempts to portray the deployment of non-white troops had largely failed to gain traction during the war. But now, after other failures – to incite *Jihadi* fervour, to 'turn' African American troops, or to foment revolution in India – at the very end of the conflict and under occupation, Germany's propagandists found their moment. Race presented a fertile cause with which to mobilize whole sections of the population and inspire international sympathy. Germany was, *at last*, a credible 'victim', and Germans were even portrayed as such within the newspapers and debates of their erstwhile enemies.

Within weeks of the arrival of the occupying armies, the German press began to circulate rumours of violent attacks and sexual assaults by black troops on German civilians, and in particular the rape of German women. Although only around 2 per cent of the French occupation forces were black Africans, the campaign focused almost exclusively on them. Hostility against the occupying forces quickly developed. A sign outside one shop read: '*An Franzosen und Neger wird hier nichts verkauft*' – 'Nothing will be sold here to French and Negroes'.[9] But more than that, a concerted and organized campaign dubbed the presence of black troops as '*die schwarze Schande*'– the Black Shame. The propaganda picked up where wartime efforts had left off by claiming that black troops were guilty of violence and mutilation – but particularly rape. It was a campaign that fixated upon the long-standing racist myths of black men as irredeemably savage, being possessed of an irrational propensity for brute violence, and uncontrollably hyper-sexual.

In April 1919, during the Paris Peace Conference, German representations had attempted to gain assurances, to no avail, that 'coloured troops should not be made a part of the army of occupation'. The situation was exacerbated when, amid

Germany's turbulent and violent political struggles, German forces entered the demilitarized region of the Ruhr in 1920 to confront left-wing strikers. The French responded by sending their forces further into Germany on 6 April, and during their seizure of Frankfurt a group of French Moroccan soldiers opened fire on rioters, killing and wounding German civilians. This moment of violence sparked a great surge of propaganda centring on claims of rapes committed by black troops. At the height of it, a special medal was struck by the German artist Karl Goetz, carrying the words '*die Schwarze Schande*' and depicting a white woman chained to a phallus, on the tip of which rested a French Army Adrian helmet. The reverse side showed an African soldier with exaggerated, racialized features and the slogan '*Die Wacht am Rhein*' – 'The Watch on the Rhine', a satirical reference to a German patriotic anthem. At the same time, newspapers condemned African troops as '*vertierte Neger*' – 'animal niggers' – and a poster was produced in which a black soldier, naked except for his Adrian helmet, clutched a white German woman to his chest.[10] A German Socialist in the Reichstag, Frau Rohl, condemned an 'utterly unnatural occupation' while former chancellor Prince Max von Baden appealed to 'the whole civilised world' that 'an end may be put to the occupation of a European country by coloured troops and the unavoidable consequences connected therewith'.[11]

★

Prince Max von Baden's call did not fall on deaf ears, and the figure that was to do so much to propagate German complaints was an Englishman. In the early years of the twentieth century, the journalist E.D. Morel had become world-famous as the hero of the 'Red Rubber Campaign'; more than anyone else, he had exposed the genocidal brutality that was taking place within the Congo when it was still a personal fiefdom of Belgium's King Leopold II. Morel's great moral struggle brought him not only fame but also influence. He was regarded as a 'friend of the African' and viewed as what we today would call a humanitarian.

Opinionated and anti-war (he went to prison for his views in 1917), he was a man of the Left, too, as Secretary of the Union of Democratic Control, and he would go on to become a Labour Party MP. Yet, whatever his views about Africans on their own continent, in an article in the left-wing *Daily Herald* on 10 April 1920 he also revealed himself to believe passionately that African people were racially inferior, morally deficient and had no place on the continent of Europe.

Morel's article was run beneath the headline 'Black Scourge in Europe: Sexual Horror Let Loose by France on the Rhine'. His prose was as lurid as anything produced by German propagandists – and in fact much of it *was* regurgitated German reporting, lacking in dates, times, places and other verifiable details or confirmations. Although, as Morel admitted, 'my information is not yet as complete as I should wish', he justified his haste to publish on the basis that because 'France is thrusting her black savages still further into the heart of Germany … I do not propose to hold my hand any longer.' Despite this, Morel felt confident in reporting that women and girls had gone missing and that the bodies of young women had been found on manure heaps.[12] He listed a long catalogue of 'Horrors', most of them sexual. The cause of all these atrocities, Morel confidently asserted, was the 'barely retrained bestiality of the black troops,' adding that 'for well-known physiological reasons, the raping of a white woman by a negro is nearly always accompanied by serious injury and not infrequently has fatal results'.[13]

Morel expanded his arguments in the pamphlet *The Horror on the Rhine* (1920), which ran to eight editions, the first two selling out within weeks. It was translated into French, Dutch, Spanish, Italian and, inevitably, German. Echoing claims made by the erstwhile German Chief of Staff, Erich Ludendorff, Morel pointed the finger of blame at the French for bringing in men 'from tribes in a primitive state of development'.[14] He explained that for Africans, 'the sexual impulse is a more instinctive impulse, and precisely because it is so, a more spontaneous, fiercer less controllable impulse than among European peoples'.

He reiterated, too, the fear that black soldiers, once deployed in Europe, would not thereafter be easily controlled. 'The militarised African, who has shot and bayoneted white men in Europe,' Morel wrote, 'who has had sexual intercourse with white women in Europe, would lose his belief in white superiority.'[15] This sort of view tapped directly into the fear that had haunted the British and their partners in the dominions since 1914, and which lay behind the British refusal to deploy black men from Africa and the Caribbean in combat duties on the Western Front.

The Horror on the Rhine pamphlet fuelled a self-perpetuating, self-animating scandal. The author of one letter published in *The Spectator* in October 1920 felt that whether Morel's 'facts and figures are or are not true' was an issue that:

> *... scarcely affects the case. It is repugnant to ninety-nine out of a hundred Englishmen to think of black savages from the Congo being forced into any European homes. The consequences of the proximity of the Senegalese, who have been separated from their own women for two years, to white women, and conquered white women, are too obvious to require discussion. It may be said that we too have occupied various lands with coloured troops, but in this case there is surely a difference to be observed. The Indians are unrelated to the full-blooded negro; they have neither his passions nor his ferocity.*[16]

There *were* voices of dissent, and a letter in a following edition of *The Spectator* refuted Morel's claims, the correspondent being 'sure that the Germans have deliberately exaggerated any misdeeds that may have occurred'.[17] But, characteristic of the momentum of *The Horror on the Rhine* was that a number of very similar stories were repeated over and over again. In this respect the campaign echoed Germany's wartime propaganda against the deployment of coloured troops, with its themes of African soldiers collecting human ears and human heads – stories repeated so often that they became, in that apt description by the British journalist Julius M. Price, 'grim yarns'.[18] The great difference was that in 1919–22 Germany's most effective propagandist was a prominent British humanitarian, rather than a faceless intelligence officer in a Berlin back office. James Ellis Barker, a German-born British journalist, thought it 'by no means impossible that the German campaign against the coloured troops of France emanated not so much from the Germans than from Mr. Morel'.[19]

Throughout 1920 and 1921 Morel's work was stocked in great piles in German bookshops, and he became regarded as a hero of the German people. He sent messages to meetings and rallies, and his utterings were reported *ad nauseam*. By framing the debate around sex and rape, Morel had also tapped into a deep German opposition to racial mixing, which had its roots in the German colonial empire. Between 1905 and 1912, a string of debates in the Reichstag had examined the issue, particularly in the four African colonies, and many of the various pseudo-scientific and quasi-legalistic terms that had emerged in the colonies seeped into the language. *Rassenmischung* (race mixing), *Rassenreinheit* (racial purity), *Rassenschande* (racial shame), *Mischlinge* (people of mixed-race) and *die Mischlingefrage* (the mixed-race question) were all, to varying degrees, incorporated into the political discussion. In an age when pseudo-scientific racial theory had begun to mould thinking, notions of purity and contamination became prominent. The magazine *Kolonie und Heimat* believed that at the core of the colonial project was the task of 'keeping our races abroad clean'. This debate had been motivated by the determination of colonial authorities and their supporters to ensure that white German men in the colonies should not have sexual relations or marriages with black women. In 1907 the Colonial Department had redrafted Paragraph 17f of the Colonial Home Rule Act, allowing for the disenfranchisement of German colonists who transgressed in this way.

Yet, the opposition towards racial mixing, and – despite the authorities' attempts – the emergence of a mixed-race population in the colonies, was as nothing compared to the passions and furies unleashed during the Rhineland episode. The taking of black concubines by white settlers was merely a distasteful element of the first stages of colonization, whereas the presence of black soldiers in the Rhineland was portrayed as a threat to the German race itself.[20] However, the most important difference was that the 'vulnerable' genders had been reversed. A toxic brew of fear, defeat, humiliation, racial loathing, hatred for the French victor and sexual mythology gripped the German imagination. Fanned by hysterical but calculated reports in the German and British press, it spread across the world, generating debate and controversy across Europe and in America. As the historian Julia Roos has shown, German women themselves took a leading place in the campaign against the 'Black Shame'. The League of Rhenish Women (*Rheinische Frauenliga*), a semi-official grouping formed with the support of the Reich Ministry of the Interior during June 1920, produced the pamphlet *Farbige Franzosen am Rhein: Ein Notschrei deutscher Frauen* ('Coloured Frenchmen on the Rhine: A Desperate Appeal from German Women'). An appeal for white racial unity, it asked the 'women and men of the white race' to 'Walk with us in spirit on our way of the cross, which is lined with monuments of eternal shame for all of us, the memories of the crimes committed by African savages ... against the white women on the Rhine.'[21] In this febrile atmosphere, German womanhood became the abused symbol of German national honour, and the purported rapes became symbolic of the violation of Germany by France and the Versailles Treaty.[22]

★

The actual evidence as to how the French occupying armies behaved paints a different picture. On the one hand, there *were* police reports confirming cases of both rape and violence that were committed by colonial troops, against both male and female civilians. Also, the German Reich Commissar for the occupied areas collated a list of crimes allegedly committed by French colonial troops between September 1920 and June 1921, and around two-thirds of the recorded cases were of a sexual nature. When black French soldiers were found guilty, they were imprisoned by the French authorities – five of them for sentences of more than five years.[23] However, on 20 February 1921 a report into the alleged crimes, which had been commissioned by Major General Henry T. Allen, the commander of the American troops in Germany, was published in the *New York Times*. It noted that the:

> ... *very violent newspaper campaign attacking the French colonial troops, especially the negro troops, broke out simultaneously throughout Germany, and that the allegations in the German press have been for the most part so indefinite as to time and place and circumstance as to leave it impracticable to verify the alleged facts or disprove them.*[24]

While finding there had been '66 actual known crimes', the investigators concluded that 'the wholesale atrocities by French negro Colonial troops alleged in the German press, such as the alleged abductions, followed by rape, mutilation, murder and concealment of the bodies of the victims are false and intended as political propaganda'. The report also recorded that 'These exaggerated attacks in the German press outside the Rhineland have in several cases been refuted by responsible officials (German) and other citizens of the Rhinelands.' General Allen felt that the prime target of the German propaganda effort was American public opinion.

There is also evidence to suggest that many of the relationships between black French troops and white German women were consensual and in cases some led to marriage. The right-wing journalist Maximilian Harden believed that 'German women were chiefly responsible for the mingling of colored and white blood which has taken place on the Rhine'. An edition of the right-wing newspaper *Der Tag*, from April 1921, complained that alongside the 'Black Shame' there was a 'white disgrace on the Rhine personified by that category of German women of all classes who, driven by greed or perverse sexual desires, throw themselves into the arms of the officers and soldiers' from the French colonial regiments.[25] The American investigation concluded (disapprovingly) that:

The attitude of certain classes of German women toward the colored troops have been such as to incite trouble. On accounts of the very unsettled economic conditions and for other causes growing out of the World War prostitution is abnormally engaged in and many German women of loose character have openly made advances to the colored soldiers as evidenced by numerous love letters and photographs which are now on file in the official records and which have been sent by German women to colored French soldiers. Several cases have occurred of marriages of German women with French negro soldiers.[26]

What motivated the German propaganda barrage was not primarily the safety of the women of the Rhineland but Germany's desire to win sympathy in the court of world public opinion, by appealing to the widely held sentiment that it was innately humiliating for a white population be occupied by non-white soldiers. Despite the US Army investigators calling the 'Black Shame' campaign an 'adroit political move' to counter the wartime hatred of the 'Hun', on 28th February 1921 – just days after the *New York Times* article had appeared – a rally was held in New York's Madison Square Gardens in support of the German demands for the removal of black French troops.[27] Most of the 12,000 attendees were Americans of Irish or German-American descent. At around the same time an organization describing itself as the 'New York Committee Against the Horror on the Rhine' emerged and began to send out invitations for speakers to attend its meetings. President Wilson, in the run-up to that year's presidential elections, had been concerned that the issue would impact on voting patterns among white Southerners.[28] A week after the Madison Square Garden rally, 25,000 people gathered at the same venue to press the opposing view, one of their number denouncing the work of 'these brilliant German propagandists'.[29]

There is uncertainty as to when the French finally withdrew all their colonial troops, and the numbers in Germany at any one time varied enormously. Most of them were withdrawn by 1920, although there were 2,000 stationed in Germany in 1927 and

1,000 as late as 1929.[30] The propaganda campaign portraying them as hyper-sexualized and unrestrained petered out by 1922, and in over a decade of occupation there were hundreds of African troops who had relationships and marriages with white German women and who remained in Germany. Throughout the 1920s and into the 1930s their mixed-race children became the focus of intense hostility. They were called the 'Rhineland Bastards' and regarded as living reminders of Germany's humiliation and defeat. For Adolf Hitler, even this phenomenon was down to the Jews, who had been 'responsible for bringing Negroes into the Rhineland, with the ultimate idea of bastardizing the white race which they hate and thus lowering its cultural and political level so that the Jew might dominate'.[31] To the author of *Mein Kampf*, the French decision to occupy the Rhineland with a force that included black Africans was conclusive evidence of a French-Jewish conspiracy to contaminate German blood, to 'deprive the white race of the foundations for a sovereign existence through infection with lower humanity'.[32]

In April 1933, three months after coming to power, the rapidly Nazifying German state set out to solve the 'Rhineland Bastards problem'. On the orders of Hermann Göring, churches, schools and local authorities were asked to provide the authorities with the names and whereabouts of any mixed-race Rhineland children. A series of 'racial-biological' examinations were then carried out on a small sample of Rhineland children. In the same year, Walther Darre, the Nazi Minister of Agriculture wrote: 'It is essential to exterminate the leftover from the Black Shame on the Rhine ... as a Rhinelander I demand sterilization of all mulattoes with whom we were saddled.' Darre suggested that sterilization take place within two years before the subjects became sexually active. 'Otherwise,' he warned, 'it is too late, with the result that hundreds of years later this racial deterioration will still be felt.'[33] In 1937, with the oldest Rhineland children reaching puberty, Special Commission No. 3 was formed by the Gestapo. Its task was to identify and then forcibly sterilize each of the Rhineland children. Throughout the spring of that year,

Gestapo units arrived at their homes or classrooms and took them directly to a board of race 'scientists'. Once an examination had been carried out to confirm that each child was mixed-race, he or she was sterilized at the nearest hospital. By the end of 1937, almost 400 had been treated in this way.

★

At the vanguard of the US contingent that crossed the German frontier in November 1918 was the 369th Infantry Regiment, the African Americans from New York who were still serving as part of the French Army. Severely reduced after 191 days on the front lines, they were the first American soldiers to enter Germany and the first to reach the Rhine, arriving at the town of Blodelsheim on 20 November, in time to watch the last German units slip back across the river. Of their original complement of 2,000 men, only around 700 remained; the rest were dead or wounded. Another African-American regiment, the 371st, also entered Germany as part of the occupation force, but was hastily recalled to France. There is some evidence that this was motivated by the first rumblings of German opposition to the presence of black soldiers. The 369th remained in Germany until 10 December 1918, and on 17 December the regiment was finally reincorporated back into the US Army. It was at that moment that the shackles of American racism were re-attached too, perhaps even more firmly than they had been in 1917.

In the months immediately after the war, the 369th and the other African-American regiments were kept under tight control as the US Army and War Department increasingly began to monitor them for what it described as 'militancy and foreign influences'. The troops were now assembled together – for the 92nd Division it was the first time they had ever been united as a division. They were then kept as busy as possible, subjected to an intensive period of labour duties, marching and drill. Having avoided labour duties for most of their deployment, the combat units were now reduced almost to the status of 'labourers in uniform'. Some were put to work on the docks, where they coaled ships and patrolled, but the least fortunate were set the detested task of recovering and reburying the remains of the war dead. Keeping the men occupied also reflected the army's determination to end all fraternization with white French civilians (and in particular French women) and to quarantine them from further French cultural influence. Only then could they be fully disabused of any hopes that their service would inspire thanks from their nation or earn them any new rights or respect.

Not all attempts at separation were successful, and in the postwar period racial tensions erupted across the former war zones and in the towns where troops and labourers of various nationalities were billeted. Addie W. Hunton, an African-American YMCA worker, reported how:

> On the first Sunday in April, 1919 St. Nazaire was changed from a quiet port city into a tumult of discord, during which a number of people were killed and wounded. It grew out of the fact that a white French woman and a colored Frenchman entered a restaurant frequented by American officers, in order that they might enjoy their lunch together. An insinuating remark concerning the woman was overheard by her brother, who understood English, and immediately resented it. The restaurant was demolished in a free-for-all fight, which grew in proportions until the French people mounted a machine gun in the middle of the public square, to restore order.[34]

It was during this fractious and uneasy period, while millions of men awaited the ships that would carry them home, that an unknown number of African-American soldiers were killed or went missing. A US Senate investigating committee, which convened in 1923, was presented with the names of sixty-two men, many of them African-American soldiers, who had been executed without having stood trial.[35] In the wave of violence, much of it verging on lynching, at least one French colonial soldier was killed too, mistaken by an American Military Policeman for a US deserter.[36] The evidence presented to the Senate committee included files of testimony from doctors who were present at hangings of black soldiers, including at one where the victim was drugged and sedated on the gallows. Despite the huge amount of evidence laid before the committee, all claims were dismissed. Yet there is no question that there were extra-judicial killings of African-American soldiers in France after November 1918.

———————

DOMFRONT, NORMANDY, SPRING 1919. W.E.B. Du Bois, editor of *The Crisis*, the magazine of the National Association for the Advancement of Colored People, has been in France on a fact-finding mission since January. His movements are being monitored by US Army intelligence, as Du Bois has been under suspicion since 1916, when he began a series of editorials in *The Crisis* that drew comparisons between German war-time atrocities and lynchings in the United States. Now, he arrives in the small town of Domfront, where the American Expeditionary Force has created its own version of segregation. 'Up yonder hill, transported bodily from America,' writes Du Bois, 'sits "Jim-Crow"':

> ... *in a hotel for white officers only; in a Massachusetts Colonel who frankly hates 'niggers' and segregates them at every opportunity; in the General from Georgia who openly and officially stigmatizes his black officers as no gentlemen by ordering them never to speak to French women in public or receive the spontaneously offered social recognition. All this ancient and American race hatred and insult in a purling sea of French sympathy and kindliness, of human uplift and giant endeavor, amid the mightiest crusade humanity ever saw for Justice!*

One day, he accompanies a group of African-American and French soldiers, who gather with the town's mayor and sing the French national anthem. He later describes the scene:

> *The Mayor of Domfront stood in the village inn, high on the hill that hovers green in the blue sky of Normandy; and he sang as we*

sang: 'Allons, enfants de la patrie!' God! How we sang! How the
low, grey-clouded room rang with the strong voice of the little
Frenchman in the corner, swinging his arms in deep emotion; with
the vibrant voices of a score of black American officers who sat
round about. Their hearts were swelling – torn in sunder.

'Never,' Du Bois warns his nation, 'have I seen black folk – and I
have seen many – so bitter and disillusioned at the seemingly
bottomless depths of American color hatred – so uplifted at the
vision of real democracy dawning on them in France.'[37]

Although the war had been over for only two months by the time
Du Bois arrived in France, already the service and the reputation
of African-American soldiers were being called into question by
sections of the white press. Taking a leaf from the playbook of
their former German enemies, reports made unsubstantiated
claims that African Americans had raped and attacked large
numbers of French women. At the same time, the military record
of the African-American combat regiments was being called into
question. Writing to all the departments in which black troops
had been stationed, Du Bois systematically dismantled those
rumours by collating information on any known crimes by
African-American servicemen. It was during his fact-finding tour
that Du Bois obtained a copy of the wartime *Secret Information
Concerning Black American Troops*, published verbatim in the May
1919 edition of *The Crisis*.

What Du Bois also found in France was the profound cultural influence of the African-American troops' transatlantic
deployment. That the strains of the 'Marseillaise' could evoke
such deep emotions in African Americans was testimony to the
significance of their war-time experiences and their encounter
with French culture. Du Bois, who described France as 'the
only real white Democracy', returned to New York and chose
for the cover of the June edition of *The Crisis* a reworked version

of a famous French wartime poster. It depicted a group of African troops – *Tirailleurs* from West and North Africa and a Goumier on a white horse, charging, with the French flag billowing behind them. In the previous edition of the magazine, Du Bois had penned a powerful editorial that was both a summary of the oppression to which African Americans were subject and a rallying cry to fight against it. It ended with a famous statement:

> *This is the country to which we Soldiers of Democracy return. This is the fatherland for which we fought! But it is our fatherland. It was right for us to fight. The faults of our country are our faults. Under similar circumstances, we would fight again. By the God of Heaven, we are cowards and jackasses if now that the war is over, we do not marshal every ounce of our brain and brawn to fight a sterner, longer, more unbending battle against the forces of hell in our land. We return. We return from fighting. We return fighting. Make way for Democracy! We saved it in France, and by the Great Jehovah, we will save it in the United States of America, or know the reason why.*[38]

The 369th Infantry Regiment arrived back in the United States on 12 February 1919. As the ship slipped past the Statue of Liberty, James Reese Europe gathered the regimental band on deck and serenaded the regiment's home city. On 17 February the men marched through Manhattan in a special parade. Lined-up, sixteen abreast – an unfamiliar French formation – they marched up Fifth Avenue, with the regimental band leading the way playing French military marches (to the disappointment of onlookers who had come out in the hope of hearing some jazz). The parade took them through central Manhattan, along streets lined with white Americans, then up into Harlem. As they reached their home neighbourhood, the ranks were opened up so that the family members and friends gathered on the sidewalks could get a clear view of their fathers, sons and brothers. There was huge excitement at the sight of Henry Johnson, the diminutive sergeant who had fought off dozens of Germans using his jammed rifle and a Bolo knife. He was carried through New York City in a convertible, with the Stars and Stripes draped over the back. The man of the hour – the black soldier whom every New Yorker had read about in the newspapers – smiled and waved to the crowds, a huge bouquet of flowers in his right hand. The leader of the Universal Negro Improvement Organization, Marcus Garvey, was said to have wept at the sight of the 369th Infantry parading through the city.

That whites, too, had lined Fifth Avenue was taken by some as a hopeful sign that in the moment of magnanimous victory the United States might be on the verge of a new era of black–white relations. But African Americans returning to their homes in the South quickly understood that far from winning them new respect, their service overseas had cast them in the minds of many whites as dangerous, radicalized black men who needed to be put back in their place. Having seen out one war in Europe, they were coming back to another conflict, in which white mobs would be willing to murder, torture and even incite a general race war in order to maintain the status quo.

On the day of the Armistice, Senator James K. Vardaman of Mississippi, the most implacable enemy of the African American, prophesied that:

> Now that the war is over, we shall soon be face to face with the military negro, and if this country is to be spared much trouble we shall need men in office who can realize the truth that where the negro constitutes any appreciable percentage of the population, he must be kept separated from the white people. Unless that policy shall be pursued, the result will be disastrous for the negro and unfortunate for the white man.[39]

In the spring of 1919, as the numbers of returning African-American soldiers increased, Senator Vardaman called Southern whites to arms. In his own newspaper, Vardaman's Weekly, he proclaimed:

Every community in Mississippi ought to organize and the organi-
zation should be led by the bravest and best white men in the
community. And they should pick out these suspicious characters –
these military, French-women-ruined negro soldiers and let them
understand that they are under surveillance, and that when crimes
similar to this one are committed take care of the individual who
commits the crime.[40]

The institution around which the Southern mobs organized was
the Ku Klux Klan, an organization that had been revived and
reinvigorated during the war years. Even before the first black
troops had arrived home, the Klan and other informal white
mobs had prepared themselves to greet the veterans with a campaign of violence, intimidation and murder. Taking Vardaman's
words to heart in towns in Alabama and Georgia, Klansmen
openly patrolled the night-time streets, intimidating and terrorizing black individuals and communities.

Under Section 125 of the National Defense Act, US soldiers
had the right to wear their army uniforms for three months after
their date of discharge. This military regulation collided with a
deep contempt for the sight of a black man in uniform, which
since the Civil War been capable of rousing sections of the South
to murderous rage. Some Southerners had appealed to the War
Department to prohibit all returning African Americans from
wearing their uniforms. But when that request was refused, some
set out to enforce their demands directly. Ned Cobb, the son of
a slave in rural Alabama, noted in his autobiography (published
under the name Nate Shaw):

What did they do to the niggers after the first world war? Meet em
at these stations where they was getting off, comin back to the United
States, and cut the buttons and armaments off of their clothes, make
em get out of them clothes, make em pull them uniforms off and if
they didn't have another suit of clothes – quite naturally, if they was
colored men they was poor and they might not a had a thread of
clothes in the world but them uniforms – make em walk in their

underwear. I know it was done, I heard too much of it from the ones that come back to this country even.[41]

In April 1919, the *Chicago Defender* explicitly warned returning African-American soldiers that there was a chance that they would be forced out of their uniforms on their return home.[42] Across the South, discharged African Americans in uniform were attacked on the street and forced to flee town.

It was this issue of African Americans in army uniform that was used to bring down black America's great war-time hero. After his return, Henry Johnson had been asked to give a speech at Saint Louis, Missouri. Rather than restrict his address to the dramatic details of his time in the trenches, Johnson unburdened himself of the resentment that he, like all African Americans in the US Army, had developed after years of discrimination and abuse. In a speech that was light on platitudes, Johnson condemned the racism of the US Army. He informed the audience, composed of African Americans and whites, of what every American soldier – black and white – already knew: that white Americans had refused to serve in the same trenches as their black countrymen. While black members of the audience burst into applause, the white reaction was one of injured fury.[43] A warrant was issued for Johnson's arrest for slander. He was charged under Section 125 of the National Defense Act for the crime of wearing his uniform beyond the permitted three months after his discharge. Johnson was silenced and off the lecture circuit. His wounds prevented him from finding other employment and he died destitute in July 1929, forgotten and unrecognized at the age of thirty-two.

It was white fear – of the drafting of African Americans and the fact that on their return they might feel a new sense of empowerment – that lay behind the hostility to uniforms. But the fact was that even before the first African-American veterans landed back in the United States, the country had witnessed a heightening of racial tensions and an increase in lynchings, as if to assert white power over the defenceless as a counterweight to these new perceived threats. Lynching in 1917 and 1918 developed into a protracted theatre of open-air torture, in which large crowds assembled from over great distances to watch the slow deaths of African Americans. The ferocity shocked even those who tacitly tolerated the terrorizing of black Southerners. In May 1918 a white mob lynched the eight-months-pregnant Mary Turner: she was burnt to death, her belly was sliced open and her unborn infant was crushed under the boots of her killers.[44] The newspapers blamed the incident on Mary Turner herself, who was said to have made 'unwise remarks' to the white mob after they had just murdered her husband. Children were not spared. In one incident, two girls and a boy were trussed up and thrown off a bridge; in another, five black children were burnt to death in Texas, and their mother was shot for trying to save them.[45]* It was into this cauldron of race hatred that the African-American veterans returned, their very presence looked on as a threat to the old order, and their uniform, war service and new knowledge and experience of European culture regarded as a provocation. Unsurprisingly, the war had been over less than a month before the first African American soldier was lynched.

Private Charles Lewis from Alabama was honourably discharged from the US Army on 14 December 1918. He was murdered by a white mob in Hickman, Kentucky, later the same day. His mutilated body was left hanging from a rope. He was still wearing his US Army uniform. Three months later, in March 1919, Bud Johnson, another soldier, was burnt to death in Alabama. His skull was broken open with a hatchet and the shards of bone handed out as souvenirs to members of the mob, comprising both men and women. The killings continued. In May 1919, Wilbur Little was beaten to death for wearing his army uniform. Another returning African-American soldier, whose identity remains unknown, was killed along with a black woman in Pickens,

* Neither were the elderly spared. In one incident, Berry Washington, a 72-year-old African American, was lynched in Milan, Georgia, for shooting a white man who was part of a mob attempting to rape two young black girls.

Mississippi, for the crime of 'writing an insulting note' to a white woman.* As in other cases, the soldier was taken from his prison cell by a white gang. As was usually the case, the jailor was strangely absent at the crucial moment and the mob was made up of unidentifiable 'strangers' who were never traced. When the newspapers complained about this double-lynching in May 1919, Senator Vardaman responded with an article entitled 'The Only Remedy is the Rope'. What else, he asked, was a 'decent white man' expected to do when an insulting note had been written to a female member of his family? While claiming to be opposed to mob law, Vardaman stated that he was 'more opposed to negroes writing insulting notes'.[46] He reflected a prevailing atmosphere in which, all too often, contact between black men and white women was reported as rape, attempted rape or 'intent' to rape.

The litany continued. In July 1919, Robert Truett, another soldier, was murdered in Louise, Mississippi. Four more veterans were lynched in August 1919; among them was Clinton Briggs, a decorated soldier, who was chained to a tree and shot between forty and fifty times by a white mob, for refusing to obey a white woman who ordered him off the sidewalk.[47] In September 1919 the body of discharged soldier, L.B. Reed, was found hanged from a Mississippi bridge. Senator Vardaman offered a simple solution to the spate of lynchings and a way to counter 'the evil effects upon the negro's mind of his experience in Europe during the war':

> ... if the negro is content to occupy the position he has occupied since '65, and the place God Almighty intended he should occupy in a white man's country, he will be kindly treated; aye, more, he will be generously treated by his white friends. But when he begins to put on airs, demand social and political equality, right then and there the trouble will begin, and the negro is going to be hanged, shot or otherwise regulated ... The advice I am giving to the white people and the negroes in this instance, is not born of hatred for the negroes

* The contents of the 'insulting note' were never divulged.

*… Just as long as negroes foully murder white men, just as long as
they invade the sacred precincts of the white man's home and perpe-
trate crime against the female members of the white man's family,
just so long will mobs hang negroes. There is no other remedy.*[48]

In all, nineteen African Americans who served their nation in the
First World War were killed by lynch mobs on their return to the
United States. In addition, the nation was rocked in 1919 by a
succession of race riots that spread across twenty-six American
cities. The worst violence took place in Chicago and Washington,
DC, and was motivated primarily by the demands placed on the
labour market by demobilization and the great movements of
labour – both black and white – around the country caused by
the shift away from war production. Distrust of African-American
veterans was deepened by suspicions that among their ranks
were recent converts to Bolshevism, another contagion carried
back from Europe. (President Wilson himself commented that
the black soldier was the most likely means by which Bolshevism
might be transmitted to the United States.) The violence began
in April and was still rumbling on in November, but it reached its
peak in the summer months, leading James Weldon Johnson of
the National Association for the Advancement of Colored People
to dub it the 'Red Summer' of 1919. Despite their underlying
economic causes, events followed a pattern in which white mobs,
often including former servicemen, would attack African
American communities or individuals on the street. Matters
would escalate, with killings on both sides. When asked to justify
their violence in court or in the press, white rioters often complained that the African Americans who had returned from the
war were both militant and over-confident. As in the South, there
was a widespread sense that black soldiers had to be 'put back in
their place'. One of the African-American journals reporting on
events in the capital lamented that:

*The relatives of returned Negro soldiers were beaten and killed on
the streets of Washington, right in front of the White House, under*

the dome of the capitol of the greatest Republic on earth – a Republic
that went to war to beat down injustice, and make the world safe for
democracy. Has the head of this nation uttered one word of condem-
nation of the mob? If so, we have failed to see it.[49]

In 1919, the lynch mobs of the South and the rioters of the Red
Summer accounted for the deaths of perhaps hundreds of
African Americans. It was one of the one of the worst years for
racial violence in American history.

★

What took place in the United States in 1919 was part of a wider
process – official and unofficial, covert and at times open – by
which non-white peoples who had taken part in the war, or who
had offered their support, were put back in their places. African
Americans in the South were pushed back into their allotted roles
as sharecroppers or manual workers, now living under the terror
of the Klan. But many of them rejected this settlement and headed
north, where the 'New Negro' of the wartime generation continued the fight for civil rights and sparked a renaissance in Harlem.

The Caribbean troops, who had fought for Britain, were treated
by their 'motherland' in comparable ways. When the fighting was
over, the men of the British West Indies Regiment were relegated
to menial tasks and denied the pay rises awarded to their white
colleagues. Gathered in December 1918 at a base in Taranto,
Italy, they mutinied – to the shock of the British. One mutineer
was killed by a black NCO, and a bomb was detonated by the
mutineers. Sixty men of the BWIR were put on trial as a result,
and one was sentenced to twenty years in prison while another
was executed by firing squad. The regiment, returning to the
West Indies under guard, was completely disbanded in 1921.

In Taranto, in the American Deep South and elsewhere, it was
evident that barriers between the races that were temporarily
lowered were being hastily raised again. In the eyes of some, it was
happening too late. There had always been those who worried
that the war was expending the energies and power of the 'white

race' in a way that would leave it weakened and permit the colonized peoples of the world to loosen and perhaps even shatter the shackles of colonial rule. Baron Colmar von der Goltz, the Prussian general whom Kaiser Wilhelm had dispatched to Istanbul to help the Ottomans reorganize their army, had predicted in 1916 that 'the hallmark of the twentieth century must be the revolution of the coloured races against colonial imperialism of Europe'.[50] That same year, the American race theorist and eugenicist Madison Grant published *The Passing of the Great Race*, and by March 1919 – just weeks after 369th Infantry had paraded down Fifth Avenue – the bookshops of Manhattan were receiving stocks of the book's third edition. Grant called for a clear separation of the races and for the preservation and purification of the 'Nordic Race' through a programme of eugenics. That year, as African-American veterans were lynched and US cities rioted, the American journalist Lothrop Stoddard was working on his own contribution to the new doctrine of race: *The Rising Tide of Color Against White World-Supremacy*.[51] Stoddard, who discussed his ideas with Grant while drafting his manuscript, intended his book as a clarion call, claiming that the population growth among the 'coloured' races of the world was undermining the ability of the white race to maintain their empires and their dominant position. He predicted the ultimate collapse of the European empires and believed that future historians would come to recognize the First World War as the first step towards the disastrous decline of white global dominance. 'To me,' Stoddard wrote,'the Great War was from the first the White Civil War, which, whatever its outcome, must gravely complicate the course of racial relations.'[52]

Stoddard viewed the various alliances forged during the war between white and non-white nations as disastrous betrayals of 'race-interests', producing an 'unprecedented weakening of white solidarity'. He condemned all sides for having armed and deployed legions of non-white soldiers and believed such policies had dangerously empowered non-white peoples. He harangued Britain for its alliance with Japan, claiming that 'all white men in the Far East, including most emphatically Englishmen themselves,

pronounced it a great disaster'.[53] He attacked Germany for
'plotting even deadlier strikes at white race-comity, not merely by
preparing war against white neighbours in Europe, but also by
ingratiating itself with the Moslem East and by toying with
schemes for building up a black military empire in central Africa'.
Most egregious of all was the reckless behaviour of France, which
during the war 'was actually recruiting black, brown, and yellow
hordes for use on European battle-fields'.[54] In near apocalyptical
terms Stoddard saw the war as 'the first shots of Armageddon',
which had witnessed:

> ... white solidarity literally blown from the muzzles of the guns. An
> explosion of internecine hatred burst forth more intense and general
> than any ever known before. Both sets of combatants proclaimed a
> duel to the death; both sides vowed [to drive] the enemy to something
> near annihilation ... In their savage death-grapple neither side
> hesitated for an instant to grasp at any weapon, whatever the ulti-
> mate consequences to the race. The Allies poured into white Europe
> colored hordes of every pigment under the sun; the Teutonic Powers
> wielded Pan-Islam as a besom of wrath to sweep clean every white
> foothold in Hither Asia and North Africa; while far and wide over
> the Dark Continent black armies fought for their respective masters
> – and learned the hidden weakness of the white man's power ... The
> psychological effect of these colored auxiliaries in deepening the
> hatred of the white combatants was deplorable. Germany's use of
> Turks raised among the Allies wrathful emotions reminiscent of the
> Crusades, while the havoc wrought in the Teutonic ranks by black
> Senegalese and yellow Gurkhas, together with Allied utterances like
> Lord Curzon's wish to see Bengal lancers on the Unter den Linden
> and Gurkhas camping at Sans Souci, so maddened the German
> people that the very suggestion of white solidarity was jeeringly
> scoffed at as the most idiotic sentimentality.[55]

Stoddard and Grant were not lone voices, though others were
less alarmist in their tone. Jan Smuts, the South African general,
was telling guests at a Savoy Hotel dinner in his honour, in 1917,

that 'We have seen, what we had never known before, what enormously valuable military material lay in the Black Continent.' He continued:

We were not aware of the great military value of the natives until this war. This war has been an eye-opener in many new directions. It will be a serious question for the statesmen of the Empire and Europe, whether they are going to allow a state of affairs like that to be possible, and to become a menace not only to Africa, but perhaps to Europe itself. I hope that one of the results of this war will be some arrangement or convention among the nations interested in Central Africa by which the military training of natives in that area will be prevented, as we have prevented it in South Africa. It can well be foreseen that armies may yet be trained there, which under proper leading might prove a danger to civilisation itself. I hope that will be borne in mind when the day for the settlement in Africa comes up for consideration.[56]

★

The rulers of the British Empire were awake to the dangers of a new post-war black consciousness; but there was a greater confidence in an ability to control the forces awoken by the war, added to which there was the perception that victory had proved the power of the British Empire's unity. W.D. Downes of the Royal Sussex Regiment concluded his memoir *With the Nigerians in German East Africa* with the assessment that 'This is the end – Armageddon has been fought and won – the British Empire has made good. It has proved once again in history that it is invincible and can never be broken into from the outside as long as it stands together.'[57] His laudatory prose harked back to what might be called the 'spirit of 1914', that upsurge of pro-empire, pro-British sentiment felt across much – though by no means all – of the British Empire. Rather than ripping apart the fragile assemblage of colonies and dominions, the war had, in some ways, brought the empire together. The four years of struggle were seen by many as the British Empire's finest hour. Among the white dominions and within India a new sense of common purpose was said to have emerged, lubricated in the cases of India and South Africa by the promise of post-war, sub-imperial annexations in Africa. Despite the institutionalized racism that had informed the British deployment of soldiers and labourers, and the large financial burdens placed on Britain's colonial subjects, there was a feeling that war's end was producing a new age in which cooperation and mutual belonging would be the touchstones of empire. Idealists appealed for the preservation in peacetime of a wartime sense of brotherhood. The most optimistic voices – who tended not to hail from the ranks of those who had actually served in the war – hoped that this new sentiment would be powerful enough to overcome, or at least counterbalance, racial and religious tension.* The 1919 edition of the *Wonder Book of Empire*, for children, reassured its young readers that:

> *Our Empire has been welded by blood and tears, by the courage and hopes of many generations, toiling and sacrificing for England's glory. And although we have made serious mistakes, we have no cause on the whole to be ashamed of the way in which we have administered our heritage … We may all be sure that better times are in store for the peoples who have passed under the sway of the British Empire, which, whatever its faults, is founded upon the bedrock principles of justice, humanity and freedom.*[58]

If 1919 was to be the year zero of a new age in which Britain would make amends for 'mistakes' of the past, then the first step might well have been to thank, fully and open-heartedly, all the peoples of the empire for their efforts and to acknowledge their losses. Yet, concurrent with the emergence of a new culture of remembrance ran a parallel process of calculated amnesia. The process of forgetting was partly explained by the appalling

---

* And for the white populations of Canada and Australia, the war had provided founding myths that were critical in the development of national identities that would lead, ultimately, to independence.

magnitude of Britain's own losses – over 750,000 men killed and over 1.5 million injured. But in the post-war years, within the culture of national mourning and in British popular imagination, the war became less global and less multiracial.

One of the first manifestations of this amnesia was the Victory Parade held on the morning of Saturday 19 July 1919 as the main event of the official programme of celebrations one month after the signing of the Treaty of Versailles. Colour photographs taken of the day show the flags of the Allied nations hanging from every building along the route. 'Victory' placards festooned public buildings, and across the broad streets of central London hung yet more flags. The Cenotaph, then a temporary structure of wood and plaster, had been designed for the event by the architect Sir Edwin Lutyens. Piles of flowers had already begun to accumulate at the base of the monument, and as the marching ranks of Allied troops passed, each unit saluted in memory of the dead, as did the Allied commanders Haig, Foch and Pershing, who were all present. Fifteen-thousand soldiers, sailors and airmen took part in the parade – so many that a special camp had to be set up in Kensington Gardens to accommodate them.

In her painting of that day, the Australian artist and suffragette Dora Meeson depicted the Indian contingent marching down Whitehall, passing Horse Guards and moving towards the Mall and Trafalgar Square. The sight of Indian troops marching through the imperial capital was a potent symbol of India's importance; yet the more concrete, political changes that India's middle class and political elite had hoped would be the reward for India's sacrifices did not, for the most part, materialize. And other imperial subjects who had fought for the empire were not even accorded the symbolic recognition of a place in the parade. No troops from the West Indies were present, a final insult to the people of the British Caribbean who had been among the most supportive of the war effort in 1914. Some of those men had sold everything they owned to pay for passage to Britain in order to enlist in the army of the 'mother country', and more generally the impoverished population had poured money they could ill afford into financially supporting the war effort. By 1919 the people of the West Indies, including men like Norman Manley – who had served in the war, seen his brother killed and was later to become Chief Minister of Jamaica – had developed a less idealistic, more clear-eyed understanding of how the empire worked and what their place in it really was. The Nigerian Regiment, which had been sent to East Africa in 1916 to replace white South African troops, was likewise excluded; officials at the Colonial Office had concluded that it would be 'impolitic to bring [to England] coloured detachments to participate in the peace processions'.[59] The public reason given was cost and the lack of available shipping. A letter from Lagos to the newspaper *West Africa* read:

> *In your issue published the week after the Victory march in London, you asserted that Africans could not be in the march because there was no time to get them to England owing to lack of transport. You do not mean to say that Great Britain could not afford to send out two men-of-war to bring them if they had been wanted? …They were fit to assist in breaking the aggression of Germany but they were not fit to be in the Victory march … We live and learn.*[60]

Nigerians would long remember this slight and resent that, while their service had been celebrated in memoirs like those of Captain Downes, there remained no black officers in the West African regiments. It was also noticed that in the neighbouring French colonies there were black men who had risen through the French Officer Corps and even attained the rank of general. For British West Africans, these were signals that their imperial masters were unwilling to imagine the world anew.

Five days before London's Victory Parade, another had been held in Paris. The British Empire was represented – by troops from Britain, New Zealand, Canada and Australia. There was a Serbian contingent, too. A phalanx of troops of the Siamese Expeditionary Force marched past with their nation's new red, white and blue flag, and General Pershing led a large contingent of the American Expeditionary Force. Absent, though, from the US procession were any of the 42,000 African Americans who had served in combat or the multitudes who had worked as labourers. Even the 369th Infantry Regiment, despite having been longer in the line than any other US regiment – black or white – and despite suffering 1,300 casualties and winning the regimental *Croix de Guerre*, was excluded from the parade. The process of erasure had begun. There were other groups, though, that became subject to a still more complete form of amnesia.

★

The 140,000 Chinese men who laboured behind the Western Front were destined, ultimately, to become some of the most forgotten of all of the many participants in the First World War. The inward-looking path taken by China's communist leaders after 1949, combined with growing indifference in European history to the non-military nature of the Chinese contribution, made it possible for the fact that they had ever set foot in the fields of Flanders to evaporate almost completely from memory. However, in 1919 the role of the Chinese remained a subject of current interest, debate and even controversy; with the war over, Chinese still remained in Europe in large numbers. Six months after the Armistice, the British still had 80,000 members of the Chinese Labour Corps at work on the former Western Front, while the French kept on 35,000. Even by the summer of 1919, the British still were employing the services of 50,000 Chinese and the French 25,000.

The Chinese were, in effect, part of the last great army of the war – the army tasked with dismantling and entombing the Western Front itself. That this great scar, which cut across the face of the continent, is today nearly invisible in places is in large part due to the work of the French Emergency Works Service and its British military equivalent: a force of Chinese labourers, military labour corps, civilian contractors and 200,000 German PoWs. Together, they filled in thousands of miles of forward trenches, communication trenches and reserve lines, many hundreds of which had originally been dug by the Chinese in earlier years. In Flanders, the old drainage systems that shed the water from fields into the rivers and tributaries had been shattered by four years of shelling. Now the old channels had to be exhumed and reconnected if the former battlefields were finally to drain. Tanks, too mangled to be repaired even by the skilled hands of the Chinese mechanics, were interred: huge holes were dug and the tanks were simply tipped into them. The work of clearing the battlefields of debris was as dangerous as it was arduous. Around 30 per cent of the approximately 1.5 billion shells fired on the front had failed to detonate, and they included poison-gas shells. Everywhere there were abandoned firearms, grenades and stockpiles of ammunition. It is not known how many Chinese labourers and others died in the clearance operations.

Another task that was allotted to the Chinese was the grim one of collecting the dead and gathering together the broken fragments of human beings that littered old battle zones – the areas the French classified as the 'Zone Rouge'. Intact bodies, identifiable and unidentifiable, were interred in the rough, makeshift cemeteries of the post-war era – fields of simple wooden crosses, temporary and provisional. They were a far cry from the neatly tended war cemeteries that were established later.

In performing these roles, the Chinese became an almost spectral presence in this shattered landscape. Freed, in many cases, from the constant overseeing that had characterized their wartime service, they had greater autonomy than they had ever known. Some became unofficial tour-guides to the battlefields and cemeteries. In the months and years after the Armistice, thousands of civilians – but especially women – travelled to the former Western Front. Widows, mothers, sisters and fiancées came to see where their men had died. They visited graves and walked the battlefields they had read about in newspapers and letters over four years of war. Photographs taken in that period show family groups on their sombre pilgrimages, women in black widows' garb, posing with Chinese men – who stand in the margins, almost cut out of the frame, but who sometimes have been ushered into the centre of the group, portrayed as one of the last curiosities of the war. The Chinese labourers supplemented their incomes by selling 'trench art' – decorated shell-casings of varying quality. The most accomplished of these pieces are stunning and poignant works of art. For a people whose story was destined to be largely forgotten, the act of literally stamping onto brass shell-casings, with hammer and punch, the characters of their language and the mythological creatures of their ancient culture gave physical form to their ephemeral presence.

One photograph shows a man of the Chinese Labour Corps posing for the camera amid the ruins of a graveyard; behind him, and the lines of shrapnel-pocked tombs and obelisks, stands a mound of broken bricks and dust. This image was, at some point after the war, made into a postcard, which allows us to identify the location as the Belgian town of Dikkebus, home to the diarist Pastor Achiel Van Walleghem. The rubble in the backdrop is the eviscerated remains of his parish church. Having plotted the ebb and flow of the war as it appeared to him and his community for four years, he was still in the area to witness the aftermath and to describe the discord and distrust that characterized the immediate post-war period.

At the end of hostilities, the former inhabitants of the war zones rushed back to their homes to reclaim property and salvage any belongings that might have survived the devastation. Some had buried money and valuables in their gardens in the early months of the conflict, and they now returned, spades and shovels in hand, to try and locate their hoards. It was as the civilian population took up residence and began the long process of piecing their lives back together that they encountered the thousands of Chinese labourers. To them, the Chinese were not a curiosity of war but a strange and increasingly unwelcome alien population in their midst. In 1919 the former front lines became a dangerous world of tension and violence.

On a freezing January day in 1919, Pastor Van Walleghem and a friend went for a walk through the ruins of Flanders, from Ypres to Dikkebus, 'to look around the old war zone'. 'Everywhere,' Van Walleghem wrote, 'we saw the same desolation.' With his capacity for off-the-cuff, judgemental remarks (undimmed by four years of contact with non-Europeans), Van Walleghem condemned the Chinese he saw who:

> … *were busy breaking out all the window frames at Alouis Borry's place, for wood to burn … It seems that they do nothing else other than demolish the few things that still remain standing, which they then set on fire. This gives them some kind of barbarian pleasure.…*[61]

In 1915, after the destruction of his church, Van Walleghem had been forced to move to a nearby village, but in May 1919, as he was pleased to note, he 'returned to Dikkebus for good'. There he joined a struggling community of:

> … *about 200 people who were somehow managing to live there. Some of them had been able to make their houses or stables habitable. For the first few days they had to work hard to get out all the earth and wood, where they had been turned into shelters or storehouses during the war years. They were sometimes helped by the Chinese or by German prisoners of war.*[62]

Three months later, the flow of refugees returning to their former homes had increased and, despite the earlier assistance of the Chinese, attitudes towards them had noticeably changed.

> *By July some 350 people had returned. At first they found it hard going, knocking together bits of wood for shelter and levelling the fields. Some of them managed to plant or sow, but in most cases it was too late on in the year, so that the harvest didn't promise much. What's more, the region had been made unsafe by the presence of all different kinds of unsavoury people: the front scavengers and, above all, the Chinese.*

Many of the Chinese had undoubtedly become scavengers to some extent. As British and French control over their day-to-day activities lessened, they scoured the land for wood, most likely to burn: still housed in wooden huts, damaged buildings or under canvas, they struggled to keep warm in the winter of 1919. Others simply made the most of their sudden freedom of movement and explored ruined villages, shifting through the ruins of abandoned homes for anything valuable. In scavenging for wood, the Chinese may well have appeared to the returning refugees to be, in their own small way, continuing the destruction of war. Being unable to communicate with one another, the Chinese and Flemish-speaking locals must have experienced a vast gulf, one widened by mutual suspicions and racial prejudice.

The scope for violence and disorder was just as cavernous. The former front lacked much in the way of a civic infrastructure. The withdrawal of Military Police, who had kept watch on the armies, had not been followed by the return of the civilian authorities. In the vacuum, there was without question a degree of lawlessness. Occupying a zone that was awash with abandoned firearms, some of the returnees armed themselves and believed that the Chinese had done likewise.[63] Unsolved murders and other crimes were attributed to the work of the *Tsjings* – the pejorative Flemish term for the Chinese, which was itself a corruption of the English 'Chinks'. There were some robberies and there may well have been more serious incidents involving the Chinese; nonetheless, these racial strangers provided an easy scapegoat. As the historian Dominiek Dendooven has noted, it seems very likely that 'many of the Chinese horror stories were rumours'.[64] That is not to say that the Chinese were not militant and agitated. Withheld wages, poor conditions, miserable working conditions and the refusal to allow them to return home led to simmering resentment. There were break-ins of civilian homes, stealing, strikes, and at Soissons, in Flanders, an incident that came close to a riot. By May 1919, Van Walleghem concluded that 'the number of English officers was relatively few and they no longer had any control over the Chinamen'. In his account of the events surrounding the infamous murder of Belgian civilian Jules Bailleul, Pastor Van Walleghem reported that Chinese men 'had escaped from their camps and roamed the countryside, armed with rifles and grenades that they easily found on the old battlefields'.[65]

Ultimately, it appears that some men of the Chinese Labour Corps either gave up waiting for a ship home or simply slipped away from the front and entered into French society. Even before the end of the war some had married French women. They, and others, went on to form the nucleus of the first Parisian Chinatown. In following this course, the Chinese were not alone. Members of the Russian Expeditionary Force, who feared returning home to a Russia in the midst of revolution and civil war, made a similar calculation. They stayed on and married French women. African Americans who had experienced in France a world free from racial laws now weighed up conditions in the segregated United States against the difficulties of forging a new life in France – and opted for the latter. Men from North Africa and French Indochina, and men from other European nations who had come to France to fight or labour, also stayed on. In a nation that had lost 1.3 million men, almost 5 per cent of the entire pre-war male population, they were needed.

★

By mid-September 1914, France had endured both the despair of near-defeat and the exultation of salvation. In the Battle of the Frontiers, the nation's beloved armies had been decimated. For France, 22 August 1914 – less than three weeks into the four-year-long war – was the most costly day of the *whole* conflict. On that single day, 27,000 Frenchmen were killed, a death toll greater than that suffered by the British on the first day of Somme on 1 July 1916.[66] But then had come the counter-attacks of the 'Miracle of the Marne'. In the space of six weeks the nation had hovered between calamity and triumph.

It was in the days after victory on the Marne that the French artists Pierre Carrier-Belleuse and Auguste-Francois Gorguet began work on one of the most ambitious artistic projects in all of history. They decided to paint a great panorama of the Allied armies. They began their *grand projet* with no idea how long the war would last or how many nations would be drawn into it; they had no reason to be sure that France would be on the winning side when hostilities ceased, and no way of knowing whether their great painting would be unveiled amid victory celebrations in Paris or hauled back to Berlin as booty of war. Despite all these uncertainties, Carrier-Belleuse and Gorguet, along with nineteen other artists, began work immediately, and on a vast scale. Their evolving project, the *Panthéon de la Guerre* was to become the largest painting every created – 45 feet high and 402 feet long – depicting 6,000 life-size heroes and victims of war.

As the American historian Mark Levitch has revealed in his study of the history of the *Panthéon*, Carrier-Belleuse and Gorguet came to regard the project as their own 'war work', their contribution to France's great national struggle. The painting contained two great symbolic arenas of action: a 'Temple of Glory' and a 'Monument to the Dead'. In front of the Temple of Glory stood a winged statue of the goddess of Victory, and leading up to it was the magnificent 'staircase of heroes'. Throughout the war, the powerful and the celebrated, old warriors and new heroes, came to Carrier-Belleuse's studio at 31 Boulevard Berthier to sit for their place in the *Panthéon*. Those too busy or too important to make the journey were visited by the artists. President Raymond Poincaré was sketched in his office.[67] When foreign politicians and dignitaries passed through Paris, the artists seized the opportunity to sketch them. As the project grew, it garnered semi-official backing and a purpose-built government-funded building to house the painting, displaying it as a cyclorama so that it would completely envelop the viewer. Situated beside the Hôtel des Invalides, it stood at the very heart of French military establishment, near the tomb of Napoleon and close to Place Denis Cochin where the statue of Charles Mangin would later be erected.

The *Panthéon de la Guerre* was completed in 1918, just three weeks before the Armistice was signed, and installed in its new gallery. It rapidly became a popular and critical sensation, seen by 8 million visitors.[68] Yet the tortuous four-year task of completing the painting, and the bizarre future that lay ahead of it, became emblematic of the way in which the international nature of the First World War was lost to popular memory.

There were telling precedents for artists attempting to capture, in oil, the unpredictability of unfolding events. In the Paris of the 1790s, Jacques Louis David, the great painter of the French Revolution, had embarked upon his own epic. The *Serment du jeu de paume* (*Tennis Court Oath*) was intended to capture the moment in 1789 when the representatives of the people had gathered in an indoor tennis court to declare their determination to confront royal power. As the revolution began to devour its own children, David was asked to make changes, to erase the faces of men who had been present but had since fallen out of favour, and to insert the faces of emerging political figures who had not been present. The attempt to paint history as it evolved drove David to near-desperation. Ultimately, the painting was abandoned.

For Carrier-Belleuse and Gorguet, as the war progressed, nations they had never imagined would enter the conflict became allies of France, and space had to be found for them within the *Panthéon*. There was never any question that the French – on whose soil the war was fought – would remain centre-stage, dominating the 'staircase of heroes'; but as other nations threw increasing amounts of their men and more of their treasure into the struggle against Germany, pressure grew for their efforts and sacrifices to be recognized. Their heroes and statesmen earned the right to be added to the growing throng in the crowded canvas. Some nations were never able to make up the ground. Tiny Belgium, a combatant from the very start, was allotted more space than the later entrants Italy and Portugal.[69]

As the war grew in scale and became ever more global, so the painting expanded. The 'staircase of heroes' was widened to make way for new intakes of French men and women who had attained heroic status.[70] The increasingly technological nature of the conflict created another dilemma. Over the four years of fighting, uniforms changed, and weapons were modified or replaced, all of which added to the pressure on the artists to adapt and update. Entirely new weapons, unimaginable in 1914, appeared on the battlefields. While the 75mm field gun – the stalwart with which the armies of France had begun the war – was awarded pride of place in front of the staircase of heroes, the French Renault and Schneider tanks, which had emerged in the later years, were conspicuously absent. To have found space for them would have taken up too much canvas and necessitated a cull among the ranks of the 'heroes'.

While weighing up these competing demands, and caught in the midst of swirling historical events, the artists also had to contend with the issue of how to portray colonial soldiers and the non-European nations. From the start, a genuine effort was made to ensure that the painting *did* capture something of the global nature of the Allied war effort. The most visual and glamorous of the French colonial troops, the North African Goumiers, were depicted in their white robes and on their white Arabian horses, sweeping past a great stone obelisk. However, other colonial troops, along with men of other nations, were lost in the flow of events. The princes and maharajas of India appeared in the large British section, but there was to be no great phalanx of sepoys. Reflecting French support for the African-American regiments, two individuals were represented – they were later identified as those heroes of the 369th Infantry Regiment, Henry Johnson and Needham Roberts. But a whole section of the *Panthéon* that depicted the contribution from Asia, including the French colonies in Indochina, was painted over in 1917 to make way for the Americans.[71] Among those participants lost were the Chinese labourers.[72] China remained represented within the *Panthéon*, but only in the form of a few of its political leaders and its now forgotten Republican flag, fluttering alongside those of the other Allies. The Siamese Expeditionary Force was similarly reduced to merely its dignitaries, rather than the pilots or surgeons who were the real stars of the Siamese contingent.[73]

In 1927 the *Panthéon de la Guerre* was sold and transported to the United States. There it went on display at New York's Madison Square Garden, later being transferred to Chicago where it became one of the exhibits at the World's Fair of 1933–4. By the

1930s, interest in the *Panthéon*, like interest in the war itself, had waned. The once famous painting was put into storage and forgotten. In the 1950s it was eventually donated to the National World War One Museum in Kansas City, where it was cut up, reworked and incorporated into the décor of the building. In its new form, the American section – a late addition to the original – became the centrepiece, with the European nations reduced to supporting parts. The vast majority of the by-now badly damaged painting – around 93 per cent of it – was simply discarded, and in that process still more of the colonial and non-European contingents were lost. The French North Africans, the Japanese, the British Indians all disappeared. For reasons that were to do with parochialism rather than being sinister and Machiavellian, the remarkably inclusive vision of Carrier-Belleuse and Gorguet, like the grand multiracial armies themselves, was lost. In its final, reduced, manifestation, the *Panthéon* became more white, more American and less global. What is left of it in its final resting place is sadly dislocated, diminished in scope and scale, and bears little resemblance to the original.

———————

THE OUTSKIRTS OF HAMBURG, 2014. By the gates of an abandoned army base at Jenfeld, in the Wandsbek district of Hamburg, stands a small, innocuous park. Six miles from the historic city centre, this is not a place that a casual visitor might stumble upon; it is sealed off behind iron railings and a gate that is perpetually locked. Shrouded under the branches of mature trees, and surrounded on two sides by the long back-gardens of neat suburban homes, this pleasant little clearing is known locally as 'Tanzania Park', and within it are monuments to Germany's past so toxic as to warrant their quarantine.

Under the shade of a row of ash trees stand two large terracotta reliefs. Taller than a man and perhaps three metres across, they are memorials to the war in German East Africa. The relief furthest from the gate depicts four *Askari* being led by a white

German officer. The Africans march in symmetrical unison, in profile, rifles slung over their shoulders. They are almost identical, in facial features as well as in arms and uniforms, interchangeable and de-individualized. Beneath their terracotta boots, in Gothic script, are the words 'Deutsche-Ost-Afrika' – a dedication to a colony that, at the time of the monument's creation, had not existed for a quarter of a century. The other relief depicts the carriers of the East African war. Again, four Africans line up, this time led by an Askari. On the slender shoulders of one carrier is a box of ammunition; another carrier strains under the weight of a machine gun, with its broad barrel and folded tripod. In what is perhaps the only concession to realism here, the carriers march barefoot.

Metres away stands another memorial erected in the Nazi era: a brick obelisk, into which are set a series of glazed terracotta plaques listing the campaigns fought by the German Army in Africa during the First World War. The numbers of German soldiers recorded on the plaques as having perished in those campaigns are not greatly divergent from the best estimates of modern historians. The death toll given of the Askari and carriers is utterly fanciful. In this history, re-written in fired-terracotta, only 3,000 Askari and 4,730 carriers died in the four years of fighting in East Africa – as opposed to the third-of-a-million in recent estimates.[74] The plaque commemorating events in German South West Africa best illustrates the gulf between fantasy and grim reality. Below the list of the German dead, and behind the severe hallmark of an Iron Cross, appears a depiction of the port town of Lüderitz and the long, rocky spit known as Shark Island. It was on this bleak promontory that the German Army, in 1905, established a death camp in which it exterminated 3,000 Africans during the war against the Nama and Herero peoples, in which Lettow-Vorbeck fought. High above the ceramic plaques, on a tall brick plinth, sits a Nazi eagle.

'Tanzania Park' is little visited, an inconvenient relic of an unquiet past when the rulers of Germany's Third Reich commissioned memorials in honour of men who died for the

African empire of the Second Reich. The Askari Reliefs were the work of Walter von Ruckteschell, a German officer and artist who had fought alongside Lettow-Vorbeck. His studio was not in Hamburg but in Dachau, the town on the outskirts of Munich that was captured from socialist revolutionaries in 1919 by a unit of the right-wing paramilitary *Freikorps* under the command of Franz Ritter von Epp, another veteran of the German genocide in South West Africa. In among his *Freikorps* ranks were Ernst Röhm, the founder of Hitler's brown-shirted storm-troopers, and Oskar von Niedermayer, the former leader of the German Afghan mission, who, after his adventures in Asia, had embarked upon a scholarly life in Munich. The *Freikorps* unit that took over the streets of Hamburg in the post-war chaos was led by none other than Lettow-Vorbeck himself, the 'Hindenburg of Africa'.[75]

By 1939, when the Askari Reliefs were sent to Hamburg, the town of Dachau was the site of a Nazi concentration camp. Once in Hamburg, Ruckteschell's reliefs were installed not in their present discreet location, but on either side of the main entrance of the Jenfeld Barracks. The unveiling ceremony was timed to mark the fiftieth anniversary of the founding of the *Schutztruppe* of German East Africa and German South West Africa. The barracks – one of the many facilities built by the Nazis as they re-armed and rebuilt the German Army – was renamed the Lettow-Vorbeck Barracks, and each block was dedicated to one of the military heroes of Germany's colonial wars or its First World War struggles in Africa. The men who were housed in those blocks, and who were drilled on the huge parade ground around which they still stand, were trained and readied for another war, a conflict that many Germans hoped would see the return of the African colonies that had been wrested away by the hated Treaty of Versailles.

Only one of the ten figures depicted in the Askari Reliefs is a white German. Their purpose was to give solid form to a powerful post-1918 fantasy: the myth that the *Askari* and the carriers had fought for Germany during the First World War out of loyalty and even affection for their German overlords.[*] Ruckteschell knew better. He had been witness to the routine brutality, coercion and plunder that had characterized the conflict. Yet the figures of the *Askari* and carriers that look out from his reliefs exude calm faithfulness. They are stern but committed. Their symmetry and lack of individualism suggests that they would be mere automatons, were it not for the guidance and leadership of their white officer, who alone stands still, his rifle rested on the ground as he surveys the scene with purposeful confidence. The Askari Reliefs and other forgotten relics, in Hamburg and elsewhere, are features of a post-war process through which Germany sought to make sense of its war in Africa, and to find within it a narrative that could substantiate German grievances and ambitions. It resulted in the confection of an alternative history, in which the mercenary *Askari*, and the carriers, were loyal and willing participants – a fantasy in which Lettow-Vorbeck's self-mythologizing books, *Heia Safari* and *My Reminiscences*, also played a major part.

Tanzania Park and the Lettow-Vorbeck Barracks are today controversial, disputed reminders of a lost Germany and a lost German empire. Like Wünsdorf in Zossen, where the Crescent Camp once stood, the Lettow-Vorbeck Barracks are a place overburdened by the past. The whole space is contaminated by a history that is uncomfortable, and yet not unconformable enough to justify it being completely expunged. The terracotta Swastikas that once adorned the walls of the barrack buildings are conspicuous by their absence, excised by heavy chisel blows: everywhere, stern-faced eagles grip empty wreaths. Yet the relics of the Second Reich remain. Most controversial today is not the bust of Lettow-Vorbeck set into the walls of one of the barracks, nor that the whole complex is named after him, but rather that one block is named *Trotha Haus* and carries a bust of Lothar von Trotha, the general who ordered

---

* In 2005, the Hamburg local authorities working with the Helmut Schmidt University and the Museum of Ethnology added plaques in Tanzania Park that offer an honest, balanced and commendable commentary on the activities of the German *Schutztruppe* in East Africa.

the genocide in South West Africa – a crime that, in the 1930s, remained Germany's only genocide. There are plans to convert the barracks into smart flats for young German professionals. What to do about the names and the terracotta busts of Germany's African 'heroes' is, at the time of writing, yet to be resolved.

In seeking to present an image of itself after 1919 as a just and humane power, beloved by its colonial subjects and wronged at Versailles, Germany found a political reason to celebrate and memorialize the service of Lettow-Vorbeck's black Africans – however inaccurately it was done (and even as Germans were deploring the presence of black Africans on their own soil). In post-war memoirs, novels and histories, Germans painted 'their' Africans sharply and clearly into the official history of the war. It is ironic that at the same moment Britain and the United States were engaged in the inverse process, of airbrushing the service and sacrifices of non-white people out of their national narratives of the war, whether in the histories or in the memorials. It happened in different ways, and to different degrees, and it was not always intentional; its effects were enormously varied and there were those who passionately opposed it. But it is clear from the vantage point of the early twenty-first century that it was largely effective.

Even the question of how, and where, the remains of the dead were laid to rest was not immune from the tendency. That this is so seems to cut across the grain of what we have come to associate with the First World War – a conflict seemingly heavy with the rituals of remembrance and respect for the fallen. It reminds us how forgetting rather than remembering characterized conflicts of an earlier era. Throughout the eighteenth and nineteenth centuries, the idea that the ordinary soldier, killed on the field of battle, should be accorded the honour of an individual and named grave would have been surprising. Men went to 'the wars' and simply did not return. Their bodies were lost and were no more available to their families or honoured by their nations than the bodies of those lost at sea. The only exceptions were the rich or those of high military or aristocratic rank – the two usually went hand in hand – whose remains might be carried from the field of battle and buried with ceremony. The bodies of the common soldiers were, if buried at all, interred in mass graves.[76] When the numbers were overwhelming, bodies were sometimes burnt too, as Sir Walter Scott noted on visiting the field of Waterloo not long after the battle in 1815. The human remains of the Napoleonic Wars even went on to provide economic benefits. In 1822 the *London Observer* was reporting how 'a million of bushels of human and inhuman bones were imported last year' from the old continental battlefields, so that 'Yorkshire bone-grinders' could reduce them 'to a granularly state' for farmers to 'manure their lands'. As the newspaper summed it up wryly, 'a dead soldier is a most valuable article of commerce'.[77] Teeth, too, were wrenched from the skulls of dead soldiers; boiled and sorted, they were then mounted on ivory plates to produce luxury dentures known as 'Waterloo Teeth', supplying the market for decades until the dead of the American Civil War, shipped overseas by the barrel load, offered a new source.[78]

It was also during the American Civil War, however, that the principle of individual interment and remembrance was first established. By 1915 the nations of Europe, starting with France, were concluding that the present sacrifices were so vast, and the suffering so appalling, that each victim should be awarded an identifiable resting place.

The result was that the First World War has become a conflict in which the act of remembrance is intimately connected to the cemetery and the grave and the memorials to the missing. One of the powerful appeals of the beautifully tended cemeteries cared for by the British Commonwealth War Graves Commission (CWGC) – and its French, Belgian, American and German equivalents – is the notion of equality in death, that men of all ranks are remembered equally with the same simple headstones or crosses. (An even greater act of equality and magnanimity can be

seen in the many cemeteries in which *enemy* soldiers are laid to
rest, within the same sacred ground as 'our own'.) In British war
cemeteries in France and Belgium, it is common to see the graves
of Indian soldiers alongside those of their comrades from Britain
and the wider empire. In French cemeteries, the graves of
Tirailleurs Sénégalais, along with those of men from French
Indochina, North Africa, and Madagascar, are clustered together
beneath the French Tricolour with their white comrades. The
Muslim headstones, with their elegant Arabic designs and dedication in Arabic script, stand out from the rows of crosses. At the
vast and humbling Douaumont Cemetery at Verdun, under the
shadow of the austere ossuary in which the bones of the unknown
dead are held, is a whole section of Muslim graves, each headstone orientated towards Mecca.

There is, however, emerging evidence that the great cultural
shift towards individual remembrance was not universally applied
when it came to non-Europeans. They were, at times, treated as
differently in death as they had been in life. First, there is the
question of omission. In the French case, there is a disturbing
discrepancy between the numbers of French colonial soldiers
recorded as killed and the number of graves in the nearby war
cemeteries. The Belgian historian Piet Chielens has raised the
question about a series of clashes in 1914 around the town of
Dixmude. In a desperate encounter on 10 November, two units
of *Tirailleurs Sénégalais* were almost entirely wiped out. The
French commander Pierre Alexis Ronarc'h recorded in his
memoirs that of the 2,000 *Tirailleurs Sénégalais* under his
command, only 600 survived. However, as Chielens points out, in
the nearby cemeteries of the Westhoek district of Belgium, in
which these devastating clashes took place, 'we barely find fourteen Senegalese graves from this period. It is highly unlikely that
they were repatriated.'[79] There is other evidence that when
France did seek to recognize the service of its colonial soldiers,
through memorials as opposed to individual graves, other considerations came into play. It is testimony to French good
intentions that several monuments to the *Tirailleurs Sénégalais*

and other colonial units were erected across the nation after the war, and most still survive despite the destruction of some by the Nazis. Yet, as historian Daniel Sherman has written, the French were concerned that 'Too much recognition of colonial troops as a distinct category ... risked raising uncomfortable questions about their subordinate status within the French empire.'[80]

The British record in this area has been examined by Michèle Barrett, who has sifted through the archives of the Imperial War Graves Commission (IWGC), as the CWGC was originally called. What Professor Barrett has uncovered is a disturbing tale of how, within years of its foundation, the IWGC and British colonial authorities allowed race to become a factor that determined not only how the dead were memorialized, but even which men were remembered and which forgotten. The founder of the IWGC, Fabian Ware, was determined that for those who had fallen in the war there was to 'be no distinction made on account of military or civil rank, race or creed', overturning the earlier practice of memorials only containing officers' names.[81] Officers and men were to be remembered together, with the same simple head-stones and within the same cemeteries. Each British headstone was to be cut from the same Portland stone and engraved with the name and regiment of the fallen soldier, along with other simple details and dedications, and the wealthy were not to be permitted to build grand tombs or obelisks that might over-shadow the graves of men of lesser wealth who had made the same sacrifice. Although these principles were, at the time, regarded as controversial, they were strictly adhered to for almost a century afterwards, across the hundreds of cemeteries that the modern CWGC cares for. Yet tragically, when it came to 'race and creed', the IWGC, influenced and pressured by British colonial authorities, did not always live up to its founding principles.

It was in Africa where the ideals of the Commission collided with prevailing racial attitudes, and where the differential treat-ment of the victims of the war on grounds of race became systemized and routine. In Africa, the general policy was that while the remains of white men killed in the war were to be sought out, exhumed and given proper burials and individual headstones, the remains of 'natives' were not to be searched for. Even where the location of war graves of identified individuals was known and recorded, the remains of those men were not to be transferred to official war cemeteries, nor were the African dead to be given individual headstones or have their field graves designated formally as war graves. When it was proposed that black African victims of the war should be exhumed and identified, these proposals were dismissed as excessive and 'unnecessary' on repeated occasions. It was in 1922 that the British governor of what was by then known as Tanganyika Territory – formerly German East Africa – wrote to officials at the IWGC, stating his opinion that it was 'a waste of Public money' to remember the dead of the Carrier Corps with individual graves, and who is recorded as not caring 'to contemplate the statistics of the native African lives lost in trying to overcome the transportation difficulties' of the East African campaign.[82] The unavoidable implication of his view, that the existing Carrier Corps cemeteries should be 'allowed to revert to nature', was that the dead would eventually – and inevitably – become the missing.

The repeated refrain used by the colonial authorities, on whom the IWGC were dependent, was that things could only be done insofar as 'local circumstances permit'. There were two general justifications offered as to why black Africans were undeserving of individual headstones or even of their names being recorded on war memorials. The first was that as 'pagans', Africans did not understand the significance of graves and would therefore not be able to appreciate them. The second was that Africans were not 'sufficiently civilized to justify the inclusion of their names' on graves or memorials.[83] One other reason also emerged in the correspondence with the IWGC: cost. While it was deemed to be worth expending large sums disinterring the remains of white soldiers, British colonial administrators baulked at the lesser costs of engraving African names into war memorials.

Among the many documents unearthed by Professor Barrett, perhaps the most revealing is the correspondence between Sir

Hugh Clifford, the British Governor of Nigeria, and Arthur Browne – Principal Assistant Secretary of the IWGC. In 1923 Browne wrote:

> *According to our records there are in Nigeria some 37 graves of European and 292 of native soldiers. It is proposed that the graves of European officers and men should be treated on the usual lines as far as local conditions permit. As regards natives, conditions are somewhat different. In Kenya, Tanganyikaland etc. African natives are not being individually commemorated by headstones on their graves, chiefly owing to the fact that no proper records were kept of their places of burial but also because it was realized that the stage of civilization reached by most of the East African tribes was not such as would enable them to appreciate commemoration in this manner. It has therefore been decided to commemorate the native troops and followers in East Africa by central memorials of a general kind with suitable inscriptions.*[84]

As Browne informs the governor, the locations of the graves of the men of the Nigeria Regiment were known to the colonial authorities, and therefore the process of providing them with individual headstones would have been relatively straightforward. The decision from Sir Hugh Clifford in Lagos was that the graves were to be abandoned because 'the erection of individual memorials to African soldiers is unnecessary', and a memorial would suffice.

The previous year, H. Milner, a Clerk of Works at the IWGC, had drafted a report on his work in Kenya, disinterring the remains of men who had died fighting the Germans at Salaita Hill. He wrote:

> *Amongst these remains were one skull with top set of false teeth, one skull with gold stoppings in 3 back teeth of lower jaw, and two skulls had each one gold tooth in the front of the upper jaws, 6 skulls had very low foreheads, apparently of a different race from the remainder but quite unlike African Native skulls. I feel sure that at least 14 of these remains are those of European soldiers.*[85]

From these rough skull measurements – a macabre echo of the craniological measurements undertaken by German anthropologists on their PoWs – Milner decided which races the men belonged to and thus which of them would receive individual graves and which should be interred in mass graves. When drawing the colour line, the British authorities categorized both Africans and Indians as 'natives' but coloured South Africans as white. Indians were accorded more respect, because they followed recognized religions. On occasion, the Christianity of an African soldier was enough to compensate for his status as a 'native' and to earn him a proper grave.

Across British Africa, the hardships and the sacrifices endured by Africans were to be remembered though collective memorials only, not in individual graves. One memorial used to stand in Lagos, not far from where Clifford had his residence. That memorial has now been removed. The most well-known of the First World War memorials in Africa are in the shape of monuments in Dar es Salaam and Nairobi. The former 'Askari Monument' consists of a life-size statue of an African soldier, with rifle and bayonet pressed forward as if charging into a hail of gun fire. The dedication, cast in bronze on a plaque attached to the plinth, was written by Rudyard Kipling, who was employed by the IWGC as a literary adviser. It reads:

> *This is to the memory of the native African troops who fought: to the carriers who were the feet and hands of the army: and to all other men who served and died for their king and country in East Africa in the Great War, 1914–1918. If you fight for your country even if you die your sons will remember your name.*

The same inscription appears on the monument on Kenyatta Avenue in Nairobi. In both cases, Kipling's eloquent words conceal an ugly truth. The monuments do not affirm an official intent to remember the African dead; they are, in reality, the opposite of that: a physical manifestation of the decision to remember Africans only as a mass of indistinguishable humanity rather than as individuals with names and families, hopes and ambitions.

If the individual black African troops and carriers of the First World War in Africa had no one to remember their names other than their sons and their families, it was because the official position, taken by the colonial authorities, and adhered to by the organization established for the purpose of remembering the dead, was to de-individualize Africans – to leave their names off memorials and, worst of all, to abandon known war graves thereby consigning men whose identities were known to the endless ranks of the 'missing'. It is perhaps fitting that it was Kipling, the 'poet of empire' who characterized Africans as 'Half-devil and Half-child', who drafted the prose behind which the final great betrayal of the First World War was so neatly concealed.

★

On Christmas Day 1914, in that bizarre and never to be repeated truce on the Western Front, when German soldiers, singing carols, clambered out of their trenches to share schnapps and cigars with the enemy, they encountered from the British lines men from the Indian subcontinent.[86] In the very first British offensive of the war in March 1915, at Neuve Chapelle, almost half of the attackers were Indians. At Ypres in April 1915, North Africans were some of the first victims of poison gas; they were relieved by British troops, but also by Indian units and a Canadian army that contained Albert Mountain Horse, the Blood Indian from Alberta, whose brother Mike would later come to avenge Albert's death. A million Africans carried and fought for the British in Africa, while hundreds of thousands more were subsumed into Lettow-Vorbeck's deadly and futile war. One-hundred-and-forty-thousand Chinese men travelled across oceans and continents to France and Belgium, to dig trenches and repair the great lumbering tanks, and – although ostensibly working behind the lines – four-thousand of them never returned. These stories have been largely forgotten, along with so many others – the tragedy of the *Mendi*, the Battle of Tanga, the

Ottoman sultan's declaration of *Jihad*, the theories of Charles Mangin, the heroics of the 369th Infantry and Henry Johnson, the experiment of the Crescent Camp, and more. And while, in recent years, the 'forgotten voices' of ordinary Tommies speak louder than they once did, the voices (literally) of men such as Mal Singh, and the strange mirror-image lives of Mir Dast and Mir Mast, are only now re-emerging.

Over a century, the First World War has shrunk; it has contracted and diminished in our imagination, reduced too often to a tragic but monochrome European feud. The struggles in Africa, and in Mesopotamia – where three-quarters-of-a-million Indians served as soldiers and labourers – as well as the battles in Asia and on the Eastern Front have been pushed firmly to the margins. Bitter but narrow debates around the culpability of individual generals, the wisdom of certain tactics or the impact of new weapons have come to dominate discussions of the course of the war, and the powerful poetry of a tiny number of European officers has further narrowed the aperture through which the war has been seen. The sepoys of the Indian Corps get a mention here and there, and from time to time we are reminded of the presence of the *Tirailleurs Sénégalais*; but the thrilling, panoramic, kaleidoscopic span of the war has, like the *Panthéon de la Guerre*, been lost.

To seek to uncover the global nature of the First World War is not to dismiss the fact that the conflict was fought mainly in Europe, and mainly by white Europeans, of whom as many as 16 million died. But, by definition, 'mainly' is not the whole story, and beyond 'mainly' lie the experiences, the sacrifices and the stories of 4 million non-European, non-white peoples, who have remained in the shadows for much too long.

NOTES

Full bibliographical information is given for the first citation of works; authors' or editors' surnames are given for subsequent citations (with dates, if there is more than one work by the author/editor).

Chapter 1: 'Weltkrieg'

1. Brigadier-General Sir James E. Edmonds and Captain G.C. Wynne, *History of the Great War Based on Official Documents by Direction of the Historical Section of the Committee of Imperial Defence. Military Operations. France and Belgium, 1915* [The Official History] (1927), p. 176
2. *Daily Mail* (26 April 1915)
3. Captain Paul Villiers, quoted in George H. Cassar, *Hell in Flanders Fields: Canadians at the Second Battle of Ypres* (2010), p. 108
4. Ibid., p. 107
5. Edmonds and Wynne, pp. 177–8
6. Anonymous, 'The German Gas Attack at Ypres', in Charles F. Horne (ed.), *Records of the Great War III* (1923)
7. Timothy C. Winegard, *Indigenous People of the British Dominions in the First World War* (2012), p. 112
8. James Dempsey, 'Mountain Horse, Albert' in *Dictionary of Canadian Biography* Vol. 14 (2003a); online (accessed 4 April 2014), at www.biographi.ca/en/bio/mountain_horse_albert_14E.html
9. Lieutenant Colonel J.W.B. Merewether and Sir Frederick Smith, *The Indian Corps in France* (1917), p. 304
10. Christian Koller, 'The Recruitment of Colonial Troops in Africa and Asia and Their Deployment in Europe During the First World War', in *Immigrants & Minorities*, Vol. 26, Nos 1/2 (March/July 2008), pp. 111–33
11. 'British Prisoners in Germany', *Hansard* (27 April 1915), Vol. 18, cc. 852–82
12. Adam Hochschild, *To End All Wars: A Story of Loyalty and Rebellion 1914–1918* (2011), p. 141
13. 'British Prisoners in Germany'
14. Dempsey (2003a)

15. Mike Mountain Horse, *My People the Bloods* (1979), p. 140
16. L. James Dempsey, *Blackfoot War Art: Pictographs of the Reservation Period, 1880–2000* (2007), p.168
17. L. James Dempsey, 'A Warrior's Robe', in *Alberta History*, Vol. 51, No. 4 (Autumn 2003b), p. 18
18. Ibid.
19. Benjamin Disraeli, speech of 9 February 1871, in *Parliamentary Debates*, Series III, Vol. CCIV, pp. 81–22; quoted in William Flavelle Moneypenny and George Earle Buckle, *The Life of Benjamin Disraeli, Earl of Beaconsfield*, new revised edition, Vol. 2, *1860-1881* (1929), pp. 473–4
20. A.G. Hopkins and Peter Cain *British Imperialism 1688–2000* (2001), p. 389
21. Bernard Porter, *The Lion's Share: A Short History of British Imperialism 1850–1995*, 3rd edition (1975), p. 239
22. Quoted in Edward Grierson, *The Imperial Dream* (1972), p. 13
23. Anniker Mombauer, *Helmuth von Moltke and the Origins of the First World War* (2005), p. 206
24. Hew Strachan, *The First World War*, Vol. 1, *To Arms* (2001), p. 694
25. Quoted in George Robb, *British Culture and the First World War* (2002), p. 13
26. Edwyn Bevan, *Brothers All: The War and the Race Question* (1914), p. 3
27. Ibid., p. 6
28. Ibid., pp. 7–8
29. 'India and the War' (letter to the editor), in *The Times* (14 September 1914)
30. John Ellis, *The Social History of the Machine Gun* (1975), pp. 92–3
31. Correlli Barnett, *Britain and Her Army: A Military, Political and Social History of the British Army 1509 –1970*, p. 323
32. Quoted in Ellis, p. 103
33. Barnett, p. 324
34. H.G. Wells, *Mr. Britling Sees It Through* (1916), pp. 202–3
35. Jeremy Black, *Introduction to Global Military History: 1775 to the Present Day* (2013), p. 103
36. Ellis, p. 16
37. Sebastian Conrad, *Globalisation and the Nation in Imperial Germany*, translated by Sorcha O'Haren (2010), p. 2
38. Robb, p. 6
39. D.H. Parry, *With Haig on the Somme* (1917), p. 223
40. Sven Hedin, *With the German Armies in the West* translated by H.G. de Walterstorff (1915), p. 163
41. David Reynolds, *The Long Shadow: The Great War and the Twentieth Century* (2013), p. xv
42. Paul Fussell, *The Great War and Modern Memory* (1977), p. 158

43. Santanu Das, 'Introduction' in his (ed.) *Race, Empire and First World War Writing* (2011), p. 4

Chapter 2: 'Across the Black Waters'

1. Merewether and Smith, p. 16
2. Massia Bibikoff, *Our Indians at Marseilles* (1915), p. 12
3. 'The Indian Troops at Marseilles', in *The Times* (2 October 1914)
4. 'Stirring Scenes at Marseilles – Indian and British Troops', in *The Times* (2 October 1914)
5. 'The Indian Troops at Marseilles', in *The Times* (2 October 1914)
6. Merewether and Smith, p. 15
7. 'From King George', in *The Times* (2 October 1914)
8. Jane Tynan, *British Army Uniform and the First World War: Men in Khaki* (2013), p. 131
9. Strachan (2001), p. 1006
10. Minutes of War Councils (PRO CAB.42/1/3)
11. Gordon Corrigan, *Sepoys in the Trenches: The Indian Corps on the Western Front 1914–1915* (1999), p. 35
12. 'India and Her Army', in *The Times* (31 August 1914)
13. Quoted in Sir Ernest Trevelyan, *India and the War* (1914), pp. 8–9
14. Ibid., p. 9
15. *Hansard* (HC Deb 26 November 1914), Vol. 68, cc. 1351–61
16. Santanu Das, 'Indians at Home, Mesopotamia and France 1914–1918: Towards an Intimate History', in Das (ed.) (2011), p. 73
17. *Hansard* (HC Deb 9 September 1914), Vol 66, cc. 574–8
18. Ibid.
19. Bevan, p. 7
20. Killingray, 'The Idea of a British Imperial Army', in *Journal of African History*, Vol. 20, No. 3, p. 421
21. Gavin Rand and Kim A. Wagner, 'Recruiting the "Martial Races": Identities and Military Service in Colonial India', in *Patterns of Prejudice*, Vol. 46, Nos 3–4 (2012), p. 234
22. Bandana Rai, *Gorkhas: The Warrior Race* (2009), p. 246
23. Kaushik Roy, *The Army in British India: From Colonial Warfare to Total War 1857–1947* (2013), p. 80
24. (Major) George MacMunn, *The Armies of India* (1911), p. 129
25. (Sir) George MacMunn., *The Martial Races of India* (1933), p. 2
26. MacMunn (1911), p. 130
27. Merewether and Smith, Appendix 1
28. George Morton Jack, 'The Indian Army on the Western Front, 1914–1915: A Portrait of Collaboration', in *War in History*, Vol. 13, No. 3 (2006), p. 357
29. Quoted in David Omissi, *The Sepoy and the Raj* (1994), p. 102

30. General Sir James Willcocks, *With the Indians in France* (1920), p. 14
31. Corrigan, p. 1
32. Ibid., p. 54
33. Willcocks, p. 29
34. Ibid., p. 83
35. Ibid., p. 44
36. *Hansard* (HC Deb 26 November 1914), Vol. 68, cc. 1351–61
37. Cited in Jack, p. 341
38. Merewether and Smith, p. 49
39. Major Charles Samuel Myers, 'A Contribution to the Study of Shell Shock', in *The Lancet* (13 February 1915), pp. 316–20
40. *Reports of the Censor of Indian Mails in France: Printed reports and abstracts, with related correspondence* (December 1914 to July 1918), British Library Digitised Manuscripts IOR/L/MIL/17347 and IOR/L/MIL/5/828/2; Report of 5–23 January 1915
41. A. Conan Doyle, *The British Campaign in France and Flanders, 1914* (1916), quoted in Jack, pp. 329–33
42. Sir Walter Lawrence to Kitchener (27 December 1915) (PRO WO32/5110), cited in Jack
43. Willcocks, p. 44
44. Howell, printed note (23 February 1915)
45. Willcocks, p. 86
46. Willcocks, p. 311
47. Cited in Jack, p. 333
48. *Reports of the Censor of Indian Mails in France*, Report of 19–30 January 1915
49. Ibid., Report of 5–23 January 1915
50. Cited in Gajendra Singh, *The Testimonies of Indian Soldiers and the Two World Wars: Between Self and Sepoy* (2014), p. 50
51. *Reports of the Censor of Indian* Mails, Report of 30 January 1915, Letter 12
52. Ibid., Report of 17 February 1915
53. Ibid., Report of 3 February 1915, Letter 12
54. Cited in Singh, p. 50
55. Ibid.
56. *Reports of the Censor of Indian Mails*, Report of week ending 27 March 1915
57. Ibid., Report of 17 February 1915
58. Ibid., Report of 10 February 1915
59. Ibid., Report of fortnight ending 23 March 1915, Letter 38
60. Ibid., Letter 58
61. Willcocks, p. 235
62. Edmonds and Wynne, p. 151
63. *Reports of the Censor of Indian Mails*, Report of 9–22 January 1915
64. Ibid., Report of 10–22 January 1915
65. Rozina Visram, *Asians in Britain 400 Years of History* (2002), p. 181

66. Ibid., p. 184
67. *Reports of the Censor of Indian Mails*, Report of 30 January 1915, Letter 20
68. 'Wounded Indians at Brighton', in *The Times* (28 May 1915)
69. *A Short History in English, Gurmukhi & Urdu of the Royal Pavilion Brighton and a Description of It as a Hospital for Indian Soldiers* (1915), p. 9
70. Ibid., p. 5
71. 'The Indian Wounded' (letter to the editor), in *The Times* (5 November 1915)
72. Visram, pp. 171–2
73. *Reports of the Censor of Indian Mails*, Report of week ending 22 January 1915, Letter 21
74. 'Wounded Indians at Brighton'
75. *Reports of the Censor of Indian Mails*, Report of week ending 17 April 1915, Letter 21
76. Ibid., week ending 3 April 1915
77. Ibid., fortnight ending 23 March 1915
78. Ibid., Report of 30 January 1915, Letter 16
79. Macleod to Sir Walter Lawrence, quoted in Visram, p. 182
80. Visram, p. 183
81. *A Short History ...*, p. 13
82. Ibid., p. 15
83. Howell, printed note (23 February 1915)
84. Supplement to the *London Gazette* (10 March 1915), p. 2463
85. Paul Walter's report on the interrogation of the Afridi deserters, Lille, March 6 and 7 1915 (Politisches Archiv des Auswärtigen Amt [PAAA], R21245, f.111), and in Heike Liebau *et al.* (eds), *The World in World Wars: Experiences, Perceptions and Perspectives from Asia and Africa* (2002), p. 162
86. Jack, p. 354
87. John Keegan, *The First World War* (1998) p. 218
88. Merewether and Smith, p. 458
89. Willcocks, p. 255

Chapter 3: 'No longer the agents of culture'

1. John Mosier, *The Myth of the Great War* (2001), p. 63
2. Report of speech by Dernburg in Vienna on 10 December 1915, in *New York Times* (2 January 1916)
3. Helmuth Stoecker (ed.), *German Imperialism in Africa: From the Beginnings until the Second World War* (1986), p. 274
4. Quoted in Byron Farwell, *The Great War in Africa 1914–1918* (1987), p. 105
5. Malcolm Page, *The King's African Rifles: A History* (1998), p. 25
6. Hew Strachan, *The First World War in Africa* (2004), p. 102

7. Strachan (2004), p. 116
8. Geoffrey Hodges, *Kariakor: The Carrier Corps* (1999), p. 23
9. Parliamentary Papers: Africa. No. 7 (HC Deb 14 February 1901), Vol. 89 cc. 67–9
10. Thomas R. Metcalf, *Imperial Connections: India in the Indian Ocean Arena, 1860–1920* (2008), pp. 182–3
11. Cited in Mark Cocker, *Richard Meinertzhagen: Soldier, Scientist and Spy* (1989), p. 76
12. Edward Paice, *Tip and Run: The Untold Tragedy of the Great War in Africa* (2007), p. 40
13. Farwell, p. 163
14. Strachan (2004), p. 108
15. Farwell, p. 171
16. Ibid., p. 170
17. Cited in Cocker, p. 76
18. Farwell, p. 179
19. Leonard Mosley, *Duel for Kilimanjaro: An Account of the East African Campaign 1914–1918* (1963), p. 84
20. Strachan (2004), p. 108
21. Robert Dolbey, quoted in Farwell, p. 256
22. Strachan (2004), p. 143
23. Ibid., p. 149
24. Farwell, p. 295
25. Richard Meinterzhagen, *Army Diary: 1899–1926* (1960), p. 200
26. Strachan (2004), p. 143
27. Quoted in Paice, p. 260
28. Richard Smith, *Jamaican Volunteers in the First World War: Race, Masculinity and the Development of National Consciousness* (2010), p. 90
29. Page, p. 28
30. John Starling and Ivor Lee, *No Labour, No Battle: Military Labour During the First World War,* (2009), pp. 236–7
31. Douglas Hay and Paul Craven (eds), *Masters, Servants, and Magistrates in Britain and the Empire 1562–1955* (2014), p. 505
32. Paice, p. 286
33. Quoted in Paice, p. 394
34. Cited by Michèle Barrett, 'Afterword: Death and the Afterlife: Britain's Colonies and Dominions', in Das (ed.), p. 303
35. Michèle Barrett, 'Subalterns at War: First World War Colonial Forces and the Politics of the Imperial War Graves Commission', in *Interventions: International Journal of Postcolonial Studies*, Vol. 9, No. 3, (2007), pp. 451–74
36. See Wolfgang U. Eckart, 'The Colony as Laboratory: German Sleeping Sickness Campaigns in German East Africa and in Togo 1900–1914', in *History and Philosophy of the Life Sciences*, Vol. 24, No. 1 (2002) pp. 69–89

37. Stoecker (ed.), p. 277
38. Paice, p. 288
39. Strachan (2001), p. 571
40. William Kelleher Storey, *The First World War: A Concise Global History* (2002), p. 163

Chapter 4: 'La Force Noire'

1. Jos Hanou, *Albert Bettanier: The Black Stain* (1887)
2. Richard Tomlinson, 'The "Disappearance" of France, 1896–1940: French Politics and the Birth Rate', *The Historical Journal*, Vol. 28, No. 2 (June 1985), pp. 405–15
3. Richard Tombs, *France 1814–1914* (1996), p. 321
4. Alistair Horne, *The Price of Glory: Verdun 1916* (1962), p. 232
5. René Maunier, *The Sociology of Colonies I: An Introduction to the Study of Race Contact*, translated by E.O. Lorimer (1949; reprinted 1998, 2007), pp. 207–8
6. Edward Berenson, *Heroes of Empire: Five Charismatic Men and the Conquest of Africa* (2012), p. 251
7. Eugène-Melchior de Vogüé, *Les Morts qui parlent* (1899), pp. 225–6
8. C.M. Andrew and A.S. Kanya-Forstner, 'France, Africa, and the First World War', in *World War I and Africa*, special edition of *Journal of African History*, Vol. 19, No. 1 (1978), pp. 11–23
9. Myron Echenberg, *Colonial Conscripts: The Tirailleurs Sénégalais in French West Africa, 1857–1960* (1993), p. 28
10. Joe Lunn, '*Les Races Guerrières*: Racial Preconceptions in the French Military About West African Soldiers during the First World War', in *Journal of Contemporary History*, Vol. 34, No. 4 (1999a), p. 521
11. Charles Mangin, *La Force Noire* (1910), p. 343; quoted in Lunn (1999a), p. 521.
12. Ibid, p. 258; quoted in Lunn (1999a), p. 523.
13. Ruth Ginio, 'French Officers, African Officers, and the Violent Image of African Colonial Soldiers', in *Historical Reflections*, Vol. 36, No. 2 (Summer 2010), p. 63
14. Killingray, p. 422
15. Ginio, p. 63
16. Echenberg, p. 33
17. Joe Lunn, *Memoirs of the Maelstrom: A Senegalese Oral History of the First World War* (1999b), p. 34
18. Cited in Richard Fogarty, *Race and War in France: Colonial Subjects in the French Army 1914–1918* (2008), p. 28
19. Fogarty, p. 29
20. Alice L. Conklin, *A Mission to Civilise: The Republican Idea of Empire in France and West Africa, 1895–1930* (1997), p. 146

21. Fogarty, p. 30
22. Ibid., p.115, and Lunn (1999b), pp. 45–7
23. Lunn (1999b), p. 38
24. Cited in Koller (2008), pp. 116–17, and in Marc Michel, *Les Africains et la Grande Guerre: l'Appel à l'Afrique 1914–1918* (2003), p. 132.
25. See also Roger Chickering and Stig Forster (eds), *Great War, Total War: Combat and Mobilization on the Western Front 1914–1918* (2006), and Hew Strachan, *The First World War* (2003)
26. Manfred Berg and Geoffrey Cocks (eds), *Medicine and Modernity: Public Health and Medical Care in Nineteenth- and Twentieth-Century Germany* (2002), pp. 74–5
27. Erich von Falkenhayn, 'Christmas Memorandum' (December 1915), in *Die oberste Heeresleitung 1915–1916 in ihren wichtigsten Entschliessungen* [The Most Important Resolutions of the Supreme Military Command, 1915–1916] (1920), pp. 176 ff. The original of the Christmas Memorandum has never been found, leading some historians to question its authenticity.
28. Chickering and Forster (eds), pp. 121–3
29. For a very brief overview of Falkenhayn's wider strategy, see Strachan (2003), pp. 182–3
30. Lunn (1999b), p. 137
31. *Le Rire Rouge* (1 January 1917)
32. Phillip Mason, *A Matter of Honour: An Account of the Indian Army, Its Officers and Men* (1986), p. 319; also cited in Killingray, p. 421
33. P.A. Silburn, *The Colonies and Imperial Defence* (1909), p. 174
34. Ibid.
35. Ibid., p. 192
36. Ibid.
37. *Adelaide Advertiser* (9 October 1911)
38. J.A. Hobson, *Imperialism: A Study*, third edition (1902), p. 194
39. Deborah Ann Schmitt, *The Bechuanaland Pioneers and Gunners* (2005), p. 22
40. Major Darnley Stuart-Stephens, 'Our Million Black Army', in *English Review* (October 1916); quoted in Lothrop Stoddard, *The Rising Tide of Color Against White World-Supremacy* (1919), p. 210
41. Ibid.
42. Parliamentary Debates, 5th series, Vol. 82, 2023–5.
43. Koller (2008), p. 119
44. Lunn (1999a), p. 529
45. Alison Fell, 'Beyond the *Bonhomme Banania*: Lucie Cousturier's Encounters with Black African Soldiers During the First World War', made available to author; subsequently published in James E. Kitchen, Alisa Miller and Laura Rowe (eds), *Other Combatants, Other Fronts: Competing Histories of the First World War* (2011)
46. Ibid.

47. Cited in Echenberg, p. 38

48. Several sources refer to German claims of war crimes committed by Gurkhas with the *kukri*.

49. Christian Koller, 'German Perceptions of Enemy Colonial Troops, 1914–1918', in Franziska Roy, Heike Liebau and Ravi Ahuja (eds), *When the War Began We Heard of Several Kings: South Asian Prisoners in World War I Germany* (2011), p. 139

50. Koller (2008), pp. 111–33

51. Dominiek Dendooven and Piet Chielens, *World War I: Five Continents in Flanders* (2008), p. 19, and Koller (2008), p. 123

52. Hedin, p. 250

53. German Foreign Office, *Employment, Contrary to International Law, of Colored Troops upon the European Arena of War by England and France* (30 July 1915)

54. Ibid.

55. Philip Knightley, *The First Casualty: The War Correspondent as Hero, Propagandist and Myth Maker* (1982), p. 67

56. Ibid.

57. Cited in Roy, Liebau and Ahuja (eds), p.21.

58. German Foreign Office

59. Ibid.

60. Ibid., Appendix 1

61. Julius M. Price, *On the Path of Adventure: Illustrated with Jottings from the Author's Sketch Book and a Map* (1919), pp. 57–8

62. Simon Harrison, *Dark Trophies: Hunting and the Enemy Body in Modern War* (2012), p. 121

63. Raffael Scheck, *Hitler's African Victims: The German Army Massacres of Black French Soldiers in 1940* (2006), p. 93

64. Koller (2008), p. 124

65. Harrison, p. 117

66. Echenberg, p. 36

67. Reinhold Eichacker, 'The Blacks Attack'; cited in Sandra Mass, *Weisse Helden, Schwarze Krieger: Zur Geschichte kolonialer Männlichkeit in Deutschland 1918–1964* (2006), p. 172

68. Keegan (1999), p. 329

69. Cited in Lunn (1999b), p. 139

70. Ibid., pp.139–40

71. C.R. Ageron, *Clemenceau et la question coloniale* (1983), p. 80

72. Fogarty, p. 51

73. Ibid, p. 53

74. Koller (2008), pp. 111–33

75. Ibid, p. 64

76. Ibid, p. 65

77. Ibid., p. 64

78. Lunn (1999a), p. 534

79. Lunn, Echenberg, Fogarty, Marc Michel and Charles Balesi have all analysed the casualty figures among the *Tirailleurs Sénégalais*.
80. Lunn (1999a), p. 534
81. Koller (2008), pp. 111–33
82. Scheck, p. 39
83. Ibid., pp. 9–10

Chapter 5: 'Inflame the whole Mohammedan world'

1. Altay Atı, *www.turkeyswar.com*
2. Ibid.
3. For the historical debate on this topic, *see* M. Aksakal, '"Holy War Made in Germany"? Ottoman Origins of the 1914 Jihad', in *War in History* (online journal), Vol. 18, No. 2 (April 2011), pp. 184–199
4. Peter Hopkirk, *On Secret Service East of Constantinople: The Plot to Bring Down the British Empire* (1994), p. 22
5. *Welt am Montag* (21 November 1898), cited in Gottfried Hagen, 'German Heralds of Holy War: Orientalists and Applied Oriental Studies', in *Comparative Studies of South Asia, Africa and the Middle East*, Vol. 24, No. 2 (2004), p. 148
6. Tilman Ludke, *Jihad Made in Germany: Ottoman and German Propaganda and Intelligence Operations in the First World War* (2005), p. 27
7. Black, p. 103
8. Ludke, p.52
9. Charles F. Horne (ed.), *Source Records of the Great War III* (1923)
10. C. Snouck Hurgronje, *The Holy War, Made in Germany* (1915), p. 49
11. Ibid.
12. Lionel Gossman, *The Passion of Max von Oppenheim: Archaeology and Intrigue in the Middle East, from Wilhelm II to Hitler* (2013), p. 87
13. Gerhard Höpp, *Muslime in der Mark: Als Kriegsgefangene und Internierte in Wünsdorf und Zossen* (1997)
14. Anna Grosser-Rilke, *Nieverwehte Klänge* (1937), p. 23; quoted in Hagen
15. Hurgronje, p. 50
16. Sean McMeekin, *The Berlin–Baghdad Express: The Ottoman Empire and Germany's Bid for World Power 1898–1918* (2010), p. 126
17. Ibid., p. 127
18. Henry Morgenthau Sr, *Secrets of the Bosphorous* (1918a), p. 111
19. Henry Morgenthau Sr, *Ambassador Morgenthau's Story* (1918b), pp. 101–4
20. Ludke, p. 53
21. Morgenthau Sr (1918b), p. 112
22. McMeekin, p. 124
23. Cited in Gossman, p. 41n

24. BBC interview with Sean McMeekin

25. '*Unsere Feinde*', in *Berliner Tageblatt* (2 November 1914); quoted in John Frank William, *Corporal Hitler and the Great War 1914–1918: The List Regiment* (2005), pp. 77–9

26. Oppenheim, cited in Gossman, p. 84

27. Strachan (2001), p. 696

28. McMeekin, p. 91

29. Cited in Ludke, p. 88

30. E.E. Evans-Pritchard, *The Sanusi of Cyrenaica* (1954), p. 127

31. I.W.T. Massey, *The Desert Campaigns* (1918), p. 150

32. McMeekin, p. 212

33. John Buchan, *Greenmantle* (1916), p. 6

34. Ibid., p. 7

35. David Harvey, *Monuments to Courage: Victoria Cross Headstones and Memorials*, Vol. 1 (1999), p. 324

36. Das (ed.), p. 1

37. Hurgronje, p. 69

38. Strachan (2004), p. i.

Chapter 6: 'Our Enemies'

1. Max von Oppenheim, cited in Britta Lange, 'South Asian Soldiers and German Academics: Anthropological, Linguistics and Musicological Field Studies in Prison Camps', in Roy, Liebau and Ahuja (eds), p. 152

2. Heather Jones, 'Colonial Prisoners in Germany and the Ottoman Empire', in Das (ed.), p. 176

3. Dietrich Schindler and Jiří Toman, *The Laws of Armed Conflicts: A Collection of Conventions, Resolutions and Other Documents*, third edition (1988), p. 70

4. Jones, p. 179

5. Timothy L. Schroer, 'The Emergence and Early Demise of Codified Racial Segregation of Prisoners of War under the Geneva Conventions of 1929 and 1949', in *Journal of the History of International Law* (online journal), Vol. 15, No. 1 (January 2013), p. 58

6. Hedin, p. 39

7. Schroer, p. 59

8. Rudolf Martin, 'Anthropologische Untersuchungen an Kriegsgefangenen', in *Die Umschau*, Vol. 19 (1915), p. 1017; cited by Britta Lange in Dendooven and Chielens (eds), p. 153

9. Graf von Schweinitz *et al.*, *Deutschland und seine Kolonien im Jahre 1896: Amtlicher Bericht über die erste deutsche Kolonial-Ausstellung* (1897); G. Meinerke (ed.). *Deutsche Kolonialzeitung: Organ der Deutschen Kollonialgesellschaft* (Compendium Vol. 9) (1896); Felix von Luschan,

Beiträge zur Völkerkunde der deutschen Schutzgebiete: Erweiterte Sonderausgabe aus dem 'Amtlichen Bericht über die erste deutsche Kolonial-Ausstellung' in Treptow 1896 (1897); J. Zeller, 'Friedrich Maharero: Ein Herero in Berlin', in U. van der Heyde and J. Zeller (eds) *Kolonialmetropole Berlin: Eine Spurensuche* (2002), pp. 206–11

10. *Berliner Lokalanzeiger* (1 May 1915), citied in Roy, Liebau and Ahuja (eds), p. 32.
11. Andrew D. Evans, *Anthropology at War: World War 1 and the Science of Race in Germany* (2010), p. 1
12. Ibid, p. 99
13. 'Die farbige Hilfsvölker unserer Feinde', in *Deutsche Kriegnachrichten* (4 September 1918); cited in ibid., p. 99
14. Ibid., p. 136
15. Lange, in Dendooven and Chielens (eds), p. 154
16. Roy, Liebau and Ahuja (eds), p. 190

Chapter 7: 'Bablyon of races'

1. Albert Grundlingh, 'Mutating Memories and the Making of a Myth: Remembering the SS *Mendi* Disaster 1917–2007', in *South African Historical Journal*, Vol. 63, Issue 1 (2011)
2. Nigel Thomas, *The German Army of World War I*, Vol. 1, *1914–15* (2003), p. 5
3. Aviel Roshwalh, *Ethnic Nationalism and the Fall of Empires: Central Europe, the Middle East and Russia, 1914–23* (2002), pp. 91–2
4. Adolf Hitler, *Mein Kampf*, Chapter IV 'Munich' (37th Jaico edition, 2007), p. 80
5. *See* David French, *Raising Churchill's Army: The British Army and the War against Germany 1919–1945* (2000), p. 64. At its maximum size in the summer of 1945, the British Army remained slightly under 3 million.
6. Quoted in John Starling and Ivor Lee, *No Labour, No Battle: Military Labour During the First World War* (2009), p. 264
7. Ibid., pp. 264–5
8. Marcus Franke, *War and Nationalism in South Asia: The Indian State and the Nagas* (2009), p. 59
9. Radhika Singha, 'Finding Labor from India for the War in Iraq: The Jail Porter and Labor Corps 1916–1920', in *Comparative Studies in Society and History*, Vol. 49, No. 2 (April 2007), pp. 412–45
10. Tyler Stovall, 'The Color Line Behind the Lines: Racial Violence in France During the Great War', in *American Historical Review*, Vol. 103, No. 3 (June 1998), pp. 737–69
11. Ibid.
12. Ibid., p. 747
13. Dominiek Dendooven, 'Living Apart Together: Belgian Civilians and

Non-white Troops and Workers in Wartime Flanders', in Das (ed.), p. 148

14. The Diary of Pastor Van Walleghem, translations kindly provided by Dominiek Dendooven; entry for Monday 28 August 1916
15. Ibid., entry for Wednesday 9 December 1914
16. Ibid., entry for Sunday 6 June 1916
17. Jozef Ghesquiere, *Veurne tijdens de wereldoorlog 1914–1918*; quoted in Dendooven and Chielens (eds), p. 179
18. Quoted in ibid., p. 178
19. Dendooven, in Das (ed.), p. 146
20. Private papers of Brigadier General L. Maxwell (private letter No. 29, extract from Indian soldier's letter, early 1915), National Army Museum, London, 7402–30; quoted in Jack, p. 360
21. Richard Smith, *Jamaican Volunteers in the First World War: Race, Masculinity and the Development of a National Consciousness* (2004), p. 42
22. Guy Grannum, *Tracing Your Caribbean Ancestors: A National Archives Guide* (2012), p. 76
23. Van Walleghem, entry for Saturday 26 May 1917
24. Ibid., entry for Thursday 29 November 1917
25. Ibid., entry for Sunday 27 May 1917
26. Phil Vasili, *Walter Tull (1888–1918), Officer, Footballer: 'All the Guns in France Couldn't Wake Me'* (2009), p. 139
27. *Short Guide to Obtaining a Commission in the Special Reserve of Officers* (1912), p. 8
28. Quoted in Vasili, p. 139
29. Xu Guoqi, *China and the Great War: China's Pursuit of a New National Identity and Internationalization* (2005), p. 91
30. Wilson, Trevor, *The Political Diaries of C.P. Scott, 1911–1928* (1970)
31. IWM Documents, 11906; quoted in Xu Guoqi, *Strangers on the Western Front* (2011), p. 89
32. Quoted in Xu (2011), pp. 89–90
33. 'Notes on Chinese Labour, August, 1918, Labour Report': PRO /WO 107/37 (The National Archives, Kew)
34. Xu (2011), p. 89
35. 'Labour Report, Appendix to Notes for Officers of Labour Companies; Chinese Labour', Directorate of Labour (1917)': PRO WO 107/37 (The National Archives, Kew)
36. Van Walleghem, entry for Monday 5 November 1917
37. Ibid., entry for Sunday 6 January 1918
38. Ibid., entry for Monday 3 December 1917
39. Ibid., entry for 25 December 1917
40. Xu (2011), p. 142
41. *The Times* (27 December 1917)
42. Quoted in Sol T. Plaatje, *Native Life in South Africa: Before and Since the European War and the Boer Rebellion* (1991), p. 282, and Timothy C.

Winegard, *Indigenous Peoples of the British Dominions and the First World War* (2011), p. 1

43. Killingray, p. 421
44. J.G. Keyter, quoted in Winegard (2011), p. 138
45. Merriman to Smuts (22 November 1916); quoted in B.P. Willan, 'The South African Native Labour Contingent 1916–1918', in *Journal of African History*, Vol. 19, No. 1, special edition on 'World War I and Africa' (1978), pp. 61–86
46. Ibid. (Willan)
47. Stimela Jason Jingoes, *A Chief is a Chief by the People* (1975), p. 72
48. Ibid., p. 73
49. Winegard (2011), p. 168
50. Quoted in Willan, p. 68
51. Ibid, p. 72
52. Albert Grundlingh, *Fighting Their Own War: South African Blacks and the First World War* (1987), p. ix
53. Winegard (2011), p. 176
54. Jingoes, p. 89
55. Winegard (2011), p. 178
56. *The Times* (27 December 1917)

Chapter 8: 'What are you doing over here?'

1. 'Siam an Ally: Why She Declared War on Germany. Neutrality Impossible', in *Straits Times* (30 July 1917), p. 10
2. Ibid.
3. Quoted in Walter F. Vella, with Dorothy B. Vella, *Chaiyo King Vajiravudh and the Development of Thai Nationalism* (1979), p. 112
4. Ibid., p. 111
5. *The Spectactor* (31 August 1917), p. 15
6. Julius Lester (ed.), *The Seventh Son: The Thought and Writings of W.E.B. Du Bois* (1971), p. 130
7. Peter Nelson, *A More Unbending Battle: The Harlem Hellfighters' Struggle for Freedom in WWI and Equality at Home* (2009), p. 20
8. Arthur E. Barbeau and Florette Henri, *The Unknown Soldiers: African-American Troops in World War I* (1996), p. 11
9. *New York Times* (15 July 1917)
10. Richard Lacayo, 'Blood at the Root', in *Time* (2 April 2000)
11. Paul Boyer, Clifford E. Clark Jr, Joseph F. Kett, Neal Salisbury and Harvard Sitkoff, *The Enduring Vision: A History of the American People*, sixth edition (2007), p. 443
12. Colonel E.D. Anderson, 'Disposal of the Colored Drafted Men, 16th May 1918' (US National Archives R.G.165, item 8142–50); cited in Barbeau and Henri, Appendix p. 191

13. Ibid.
14. Quoted in Chad L. Williams, *Torchbearers of Democracy: African American Soldiers in the World War I Era* (2010), p. 109
15. Ibid.
16. Walter L. Haight, *Racine County in the World War* (1920), p. 292; cited in Barbeau and Florette, Appendix p. 191
17. Addie W. Hunton and Kathryn M. Johnson, *Two Colored Women with the American Expeditionary Forces* (1920), p. 31
18. Adriane Lentz-Smith, *Freedom Struggles: African Americans and World War I* (2009), p. 124
19. Quoted in Williams, p. 113
20. Lentz-Smith, p. 111
21. William H. Kenney III, '*Le Hot*: The Assimilation of American Jazz in France 1917–1940', in *American Studies* (1984), pp. 5–24
22. John H. Morrow, Jr, *The Great War: An Imperial History* (2004), p. 244
23. Barbeau and Henri, p. 112
24. Quoted, ibid.
25. Quoted in Colin Grant, *Negro with a Hat: The Rise and Fall of Marcus Garvey and His Dream of Mother Africa* (2008), p. 112
26. Ibid, p. 113
27. Erich Ludendorff, *Meine Kriegserinnerungen 1914–1918* (1919), p. 206; cited in Christian Koller, *Representing Otherness: African, Indian, and European Soldiers' Letters and Memoirs* (2011), p. 130
28. Hunton and Johnson, p. 14
29. Cited in Ulysses Lee, *The Employment of Negro Troops* (1990), p. 15
30. Morrow Jr, p. 253
31. *To the Colored Soldiers of the US Army* (1917)
32. Emmett J. Scott, *Scott's Official History of the American Negro in the World War* (1919)
33. Dendooven and Chielens (eds), p. 135
34. Russel Lawrence Barsh, 'American Indians in the Great War', in *Ethnohistory*, Vol. 38, No. 3 (Summer 1991), pp. 276–303
35. Thomas A. Britten, *Amerians Indians in World War I: At Home and at War* (1997), p. 75
36. Cited, ibid., p. 99
37. Cited in Barsh, p. 277
38. *Washington Sunday Star* (25 August 1918); cited in Barsh, p. 280
39. Britten, p. 105
40. Ibid., p. 82
41. Barsh, p. 278
42. Citied in Britten, p. 105
43. Cited in Timothy Charles Winegard, *For King and Kanata: Canadian Indians and the First World War* (2012), p. 196
44. Barsh, p. 287
45. *Brockton Times* (14 September 1918), cited in Barsh, p. 291

46. Robert W. Rydell and Rob Kroes, *Buffalo Bill in Bologna* (2005), p. 115
47. Quoted in Winegard (2012), p. 111

Chapter 9: 'Your sons will remember your name'

1. Cited in Farwell, p. 350
2. David G. Williamson, *The British in Germany 1918–1930: The Reluctant Occupiers* (1991), p. 11
3. Quoted in Helen McPhail, *Long Silence: Civilian Life under the German Occupation of Northern France* (1999), p. 193
4. G.J. Meyer, *A World Undone* (2006), p. 608
5. Clarence Lusane, *Hitler's Black Victims: The Historical Experiences of Afro-Germans, European Blacks, Africans and African Americans in the Nazi Era* (2003), p. 72
6. Bill Schwarz, *West Indian Intellectuals in Britain* (2003), p. 80
7. Cited in Philip Mason, *A Matter of Honour: An Account of the Indian Army, Its Officers and Men* (1986), p. 319
8. Vella and Vella, p. 112
9. Cited in Lusane, p. 69
10. Dendooven and Chielens (eds), p. 81
11. E.D. Morel, *The Horror on the Rhine*, eighth edition (April 1921)
12. Cited in Peter Fryer, *Staying Power: The History of Black People in Britain* (1984), p. 317
13. Cited in Schwarz, p. 81
14. Ibid., p. 80
15. Dendooven and Chielens (eds), p. 81
16. 'The Horror on the Rhine', in *The Spectator* (1 October 1920), p. 12
17. *The Spectator* (22 October 1920), p. 13
18. Price, pp. 57–8
19. Cited in Lusane, p. 74
20. See Julia Roos, 'Women's Rights, Nationalist Anxiety and the "Moral" Agenda in the Early Weimar Republic: Revisiting the "Black Horror" Campaign against France's African Occupation Troops', in *Central European History*, Vol. 42 (2009), pp. 473–508
21. Cited in Roos, p. 480
22. *See* Roos for an extremely insightful exploration of the interplay between racism, defeat and German paternalism in the Rhineland debates.
23. Lusane, p. 74
24. 'Finds Negro Troops Orderly on Rhine; General Allen Reports Charges Are German Propaganda, Especially for America – Commissioner Dreisel's Cablegram to the State Department', in *New York Times* (20 February 1921)
25. Cited in Roos, p. 485

26. 'Finds Negro Troops …'
27. Erika Kuhlman, 'The Rhineland Horror Campaign and the Aftermath of War', in Ingrid Sharp and Matthew Stibbe (eds), *Aftermaths of War: Women's Movements and Female Activists 1918–1923* (2011), p. 101
28. Lusane, pp. 75–6
29. *New York Times* (19 March 1921)
30. Tina Marie Campt, *Other Germans: Black Germans and the Politics of Race, Gender, and Memory in the Third Reich* (2009), p. 36
31. Hitler, pp. 253–4
32. Ibid., p. 624
33. Jayne O. Ifekwunigwe (ed.), *Mixed Race Studies: A Reader* (2004), p. 84
34. Hunton and Johnson, p. 191
35. *See* US Senate, *Alleged Executions Without Trial In France: Hearings Before a Special Committee on Alleged Executions Without Trial in France, United States Senate, 67th Congress, Relative to Charges That Members of the American Expeditionary Forces Abroad Were Executed Without Trial or Court-Martial* (1923)
36. Hunton and Johnson, p. 191
37. W.E.B. Du Bois, 'An Essay Towards a History of the Black Man in the Great War', in *The Crisis* (June 1919), p. 63
38. W.E.B. Du Bois, 'Returning Soldier', in *The Crisis* (May 1919), p. 1
39. James K. Vardaman, in *The Issue* (14 November 1918); cited in Vincent P. Mikkelsen, *Coming from Battle to Face a War: The Lynching of Black Soldiers in the World War I Era* (2007), p. 59
40. *Vardaman's Weekly* (15 May 1919); cited in Lentz-Smith, p. 83
41. 'Nate Shaw' (i.e. Nedd Cobb), as told to Thomas Rosengarten, *All God's Dangers: The Life of Nate Shaw* (1975), p. 161
42. *Chicago Defender* (5 April 1919)
43. Grant, p. 113
44. Herbert Shapiro, *White Violence and Black Response: From Reconstruction to Montgomery* (1988), p. 146
45. Barbeau and Henri, p. 176
46. *Vardaman's Weekly* (8 May 1919); cited in Mikkelsen, p. 123
47. Barbeau and Henri, p. 178
48. *Vardaman's Weekly* (8 May 1919); cited in Mikkelsen, p. 95
49. *Charleston Messenger*, cited in Barbeau and Henri, p. 185.
50. Colmar Freiherr von der Goltz, *Denkwürdigkeiten*; cited in Strachan (2003), p. 123
51. Published April 1920; Preface dated 'February 28, 1920'
52. Lothrop Stoddard, *The Rising Tide of Color Against White World-Supremacy* (1920), Preface, p. vi
53. Ibid., p. 204
54. Ibid.
55. Ibid., p. 209

56. J.C. Smuts, *Compilation of Public Utterances in Great Britain By Lieut.-Gen. the Rt Hon. J.C. Smuts, P.C., K.C., MX.A. In Connection with the Session of the Imperial War Cabinet and Imperial War Conference* (1917)

57. Captain W.D. Downes, *With the Nigerians in German East Africa* (1919), p. 298

58. Harry Golding, *Wonder Book of Empire* (1919), p. 219

59. James K. Matthews, 'World War I and the Rise of African Nationalism: Nigerian Veterans as Catalysts of Change', in *Journal of Modern African Studies*, Vol. 20, No. 3 (September 1982), pp. 493–502

60. Victor Allen, in *West Africa* (11 October 1919); cited Matthews, p. 502

61. Van Walleghem, entry for Saturday 11 January 1919

62. Ibid., entry for Wednesday 17 May 1919

63. Das (ed.), p. 151

64. Ibid., p. 152

65. Van Walleghem, entry for July 1919

66. Reynolds, p. xix

67. Mark Levitch, *Panthéon de la Guerre: Reconfiguring a Panorama of the Great War* (2006)

68. *Official Guide: Chicago Book of the Fair* (1933)

69. Levitch, p. 50.

70. Ibid., p .50

71. Ibid., p. 64

72. Xu (2011), p. 8

73. Levitch, p. 65

74. Paice, p. 398

75. Ibid., p. 390

76. George L. Mosse, *Fallen Soldiers Reshaping the Memory of the World War* (1990), p. 45

77. *London Observer* (18 November 1822); cited in David Simpson, *9/11: The Culture of Commemoration* (2006) pp. 26–7; also in Christopher Coker, *The Future of War: The Re-Enchantment of War in the Twenty-First Century* (2004), p. 15, and Samuel Lynn Hynes, *The Soldiers' Tale: Bearing Witness to a Modern War* (1998), p. 17

78. British Dental Association, 'Waterloo Teeth', online at: www.bda./org/museum/collections/teeth-and-dentures/waterloo-teeth.aspx

79. Dendooven and Chielens (eds), p. 79

80. Daniel Sherman, *The Construction of Memory i   n Interwar France* (2001), p. 101

81. CWGC website: www.cwgc.org/about-us/our-organisation.aspx

82. Barrett, in Das (ed.), p. 303

83. Cited in Barrett (2007), p. 470

84. Ibid., p. 468

85. Ibid., p. 467

86. Corrigan, p. 126

FURTHER READING

The following selection, while by no means comprehensive, is intended to be useful and accessible to non-specialist readers, and it embraces many of the books that informed *The World's War*. It includes a number of publications from the era of 1914–18, quite a number of which are nowadays available online, as well as core works in the historical literature and some of the most striking and relevant recent assessments.

Barbeau, Arthur E. and Florette Henri, *The Unknown Soldiers: African-American Troops in World War I* (1996)

Black, Jeremy, *Introduction to Global Military History: 1775 to the Present Day* (2013)

Cocker, Mark, *Richard Meinertzhagen: Soldier, Scientist and Spy* (1989)

Corrigan, Gordon, *Sepoys in the Trenches: The Indian Corps on the Western Front 1914–1915* (1999)

Das, Santanu (ed.), *Race, Empire and First World War Writing* (2011)

Dendooven, Dominiek and Piet Chielens (eds), *World War I: Five Continents in Flanders* (2008)

Echenberg, Myron, *Colonial Conscripts: The Tirailleurs Sénégalais in French West Africa, 1857–1960* (1993)

Ellis, John, *The Social History of the Machine Gun* (1975)

Evans, Andrew D., *Anthropology at War: World War I and the Science of Race in Germany* (2010)

Farwell, Byron, *The Great War in Africa 1914–1918* (1987)

Fogarty, Richard, *Race and War in France: Colonial Subjects in the French Army 1914–1918* (2008)

Fussell, Paul, *The Great War and Modern Memory* (1977)

Gossman, Lionel, *The Passion of Max von Oppenheim: Archaeology and Intrigue in the Middle East, from Wilhelm II to Hitler* (2013)

Hedin, Sven, *With the German Armies in the West*, translated by H.G. de Walterstorff (1915)

Hochschild, Adam, *To End All Wars: A Story of Loyalty and Rebellion 1914–1918* (2011)

Hodges, Geoffrey, *Kariakor: The Carrier Corps* (1999)

Hopkirk, Peter, *On Secret Service East of Constantinople: The Plot to Bring Down the British Empire* (1994)

Keegan, John, *The First World War* (1998)

L. Mosse, George, *Fallen Soldiers Reshaping the Memory of the World War* (1990)

Lentz-Smith, Adriane, *Freedom Struggles: African Americans and World War I* (2009)

Levitch, Mark, *Panthéon de la Guerre: Reconfiguring a Panorama of the Great War* (2006)

Ludke, Tilman, *Jihad Made in Germany: Ottoman and German Propaganda and Intelligence Operations in the First World War* (2005)

Lunn, Joe, *Memoirs of the Maelstrom: A Senegalese Oral History of the First World War* (1999)

Lusane, Clarence, *Hitler's Black Victims: The Historical Experiences of Afro-Germans, European Blacks, Africans and African Americans in the Nazi Era* (2003)

McMeekin, Sean, *The Berlin–Baghdad Express: The Ottoman Empire and Germany's Bid for World Power 1898–1918* (2010)

MacMunn, Major George, *The Armies of India* (1911)

Merewether, Lieutenant Colonel J.W.B. and Sir Frederick Smith, *The Indian Corps in France* (1917)

Morrow, Jr, John H., *The Great War: An Imperial History* (2004)

Mosier, John, *The Myth of the Great War* (2001)

Mountain Horse, Mike, *My People the Bloods* (1979)

Nelson, Peter, *A More Unbending Battle: The Harlem Hellfighters' Struggle for Freedom in WWI and Equality at Home* (2009)

Page, Malcolm, *The King's African Rifles: A History* (1998)

Paice, Edward, *Tip and Run: The Untold Tragedy of the Great War in Africa* (2007)

Reynolds, David, *The Long Shadow: The Great War and the Twentieth Century* (2013)

Robb, George, *British Culture and the First World War* (2002)

Scheck, Raffael, *Hitler's African Victims: The German Army Massacres of Black French Soldiers in 1940* (2006)

Smith, Richard, *Jamaican Volunteers in the First World War: Race, Masculinity and the Development of a National Consciousness* (2004)

Starling, John and Ivor Lee, *No Labour, No Battle: Military Labour During the First World War* (2009)

Stoddard, Lothrop, *The Rising Tide of Color Against White World-Supremacy* (1920)

Strachan, Hew, *The First World War*, Vol. 1, *To Arms* (2001)

Vasili, Phil, *Walter Tull (1888–1918), Officer, Footballer: 'All the Guns in France Couldn't Wake Me* (2009)

Vella, Walter F. with Dorothy B. Vella, *Chaiyo King Vajiravudh and the Development of Thai Nationalism* (1979)

Visram, Rozina, *Asians in Britain 400 Years of History* (2002)

Wells, H.G., *Mr. Britling Sees It Through* (1916)

Williams, Chad L., *Torchbearers of Democracy: African American Soldiers in the World War I Era* (2010)

Winegard, Timothy C., *Indigenous People of the British Dominions in the First World War* (2012)

Xu Guoqi, *China and the Great War: China's Pursuit of a New National Identity and Internationalization* (2005)

ACKNOWLEDGEMENTS

I would like to thank my partner Susie Painter for her endless support and tolerance. To my mother Mrs Marion Olusoga, who taught me to read when my schools failed and now continues to teach me grammar, I am, as ever, grateful, for her vital assistance with the early drafts of this book and for work on translations. Thanks also to my agent, Charles Walker, at United Agents, to Richard Milbank at Head of Zeus for his patience and enthusiasm, and to Mark Hawkins-Dady, without whose assistance, knowledge and insight this book would not have been possible.

At the BBC I would like to thank Martin Davidson, Commissioner for History, and Janice Hadlow, Controller Seasons and Special Projects, for taking the risk of bringing to the television screen the stories of men and women whose contributions to the First World War are so often marginalized.

It was through the making of that television series that I crystalized my views on this history, and as with all television projects it was a team effort. I am thus greatly indebted to the hard work and endless enthusiasm of our brilliant Series Producer, Tim Kirby, and our equally insightful Executive Producer, Chris Granlund. Thanks to Ben Crichton for his dedication and camera work and to Alexandra Shaw for her enthusiasm, excellent research and linguistic abilities. Just as critical were the contributions of Wendy Clarke, Monika Kupper, Amanda Robinson, Jane Taylor, Declan Smith, Ian Salvage, Tony Burke, Steve Scales and Michael Duly. I would also like to give thanks to Francesca Kasteliz for helping me to find my voice.

The television series was produced with the invaluable assistance of Dr Santanu Das of King's College London, who acted as its historical consultant. He is one of the scholars whose work is giving voice and form to the millions of non-Europeans who fought and laboured in the First World War, and his passion and network of contacts were invaluable. Thanks also goes to the historians who have been so generous with their knowledge and their time: Alison Fell, Sean McMeekin, Geoff Bridger, Heike Liebau, Edward Paice, Paul Van Damme and Philippe Gorczyinski. Particular thanks go to Dominiek Dendooven, curator of the In Flanders Field Museum in Ypres, arguably the most advanced and immersive museum dedicated to the First World War. Dominiek's generosity, encyclopedic knowledge and his translation of the diary of Pastor Achiel Van Walleghem have been enormously important to both the television series and this book.

The visits to many of the locations that are described in this book were made possible through the help of many communities and organizations. I would therefore like to thank: the Azania Front Lutheran Church Dar-es-Salaam; The Commonwealth War Graves Commission; In Flanders Fields Museum; Garrison Museum, Zossen; the German Consulate in Istanbul; The British Library; the *Lautarchiv* at The Humboldt University, Berlin; the villagers of Komkonga, Tanzania; the Sint-Jan-Baptistkerk in Dikkebus; the Tank of Flesquières Association; The Menin Gate and The Last Post Association at Ypres. The journeys to reach many of these locations were undertaken with the assistance of local fixers: Munir Akdogan, Berk Altunay, Martin Zilger, Evarist Komba and Claire Powell.

David Olusoga

INDEX

WAR OF THE RACES—MEN IN THE GREAT

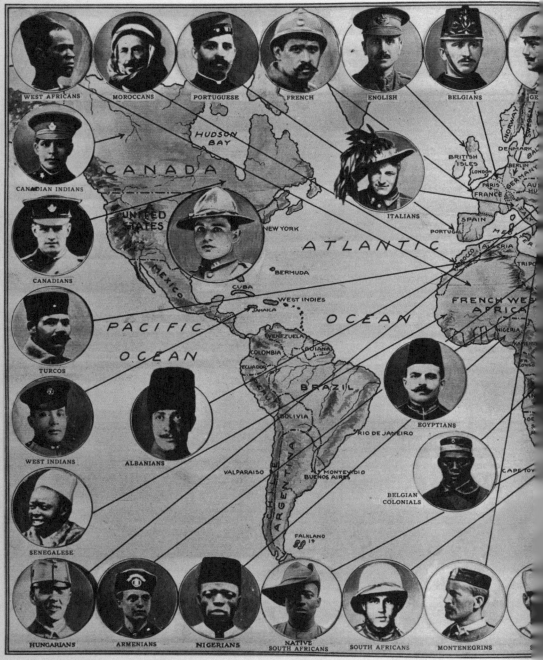

WEST AFRICANS • MOROCCANS • PORTUGUESE • FRENCH • ENGLISH • BELGIANS • GE

CANADIAN INDIANS

CANADIANS

TURCOS

WEST INDIES

ALBANIANS

SENEGALESE

HUNGARIANS • ARMENIANS • NIGERIANS • NATIVE SOUTH AFRICANS • SOUTH AFRICANS • MONTENEGRINS • S

ITALIANS

EGYPTIANS

BELGIAN COLONIALS

HUDSON BAY

CANADA

UNITED STATES

NEW YORK

BERMUDA

CUBA

WEST INDIES

JAMAICA

ATLANTIC

OCEAN

PACIFIC

OCEAN

MEXICO

VENEZUELA

COLOMBIA

GUIANA

ECUADOR

BRAZIL

BOLIVIA

RIO DE JANEIRO

VALPARAISO

MONTEVIDEO

BUENOS AIRES

ARGENTINA

FALKLAND IS

NORWAY • SWEDEN • DENMARK • BAL

BRITISH ISLES • LONDON • BERLIN • GERMANY • AU

PARIS • FRANCE • HU

SPAIN • MED

PORTUGAL • MOROCCO • ALGERIA • TRIPO

FRENCH WEST AFRICA

NIGERIA • KAMERUN • CONGO

CAPE TOWN

IT IS BEYOND DISPUTE THAT IN NO WAR IN THE HISTORY OF THE WORLD HAVE SO MANY RACES AND PEOPLES BEEN
AND THE QUARTERS OF T